SOFT
POWER
SUPERPOWERS

SOFT POWER SUPERPOWERS

CULTURAL AND NATIONAL ASSETS OF JAPAN AND THE UNITED STATES

WATANABE YASUSHI AND DAVID L. McCONNELL, EDITORS
WITH A FOREWORD BY JOSEPH S. NYE, JR.

An East Gate Book

M.E.Sharpe
Armonk, New York
London, England

An East Gate Book

Library of Congress Cataloging-in-Publication Data

Soft power superpowers : cultural and national assets of Japan and the United States / edited by
Yasushi Watanabe and David L. McConnell.
    p. cm.
  Includes bibliographical references and index.
  ISBN 978-0-7656-2248-8 (cloth : alk. paper) — ISBN 978-0-7656-2249-5
  1. United States--Relations--Japan. 2. Japan--Relations--United States. 3. Cultural relations--
Case studies. 4. Intercultural communication--Case studies. 5. Arts, American--Foreign countries.
6. Arts, Japanese--Foreign countries. 7. Popular culture--United States. 8. Popular culture--Ja-
pan. I. Watanabe, Yasushi, 1967- II. McConnell, David L., 1959-

E183.8.J3S65 2008
327.73052--dc22
                                                                2007045034

Printed in the United States of America

The paper used in this publication meets the minimum requirements of
American National Standard for Information Sciences
Permanence of Paper for Printed Library Materials,
ANSI Z 39.48-1984.

BM (c) 10   9   8   7   6   5   4   3   2   1
BM (p) 10   9   8   7   6   5   4   3   2   1

Contents

List of Tables and Figures

Tables

Figures

Foreword

Joseph S. Nye, Jr.

I developed the concept of soft power in 1989 when I was writing a book rebutting the then-conventional wisdom about the decline of American power. After examining American economic and military power, I found that something was still missing—the ability of the United States to attract others and thus increase the probability of obtaining the outcomes it wanted. It has been interesting to see an academic concept migrate to the front pages of newspapers, and to see it used by leaders in China, Europe, and elsewhere over the past two decades. But wide usage has sometimes meant misuse of the concept as a synonym for anything other than military force.

Now Watanabe Yasushi and David McConnell have assembled an excellent set of essays that carefully examine the strengths and limits of the soft power of the United States and Japan. Not only are these countries two of what they call the world's "soft power superpowers," but several essays show how the U.S.-Japanese relationship has been transformed over the years by the interplay of soft power resources ranging from baseball to higher education. And if one believes, as I do, that a good U.S.-Japanese relationship is crucial to the stability and prosperity of East Asia, soft power will continue to play a very important role in the future. Yet as Watanabe shows in Chapter 1, with generational change in Japan and the United States, soft power cannot be taken for granted. That is why the deeper understanding represented by these essays is so important.

Though the concept of soft power is recent, the behavior it denotes is as old as human history. It is implicit in Lao-tzu's comment that a leader is best not when people obey his commands, but when they barely know he exists. In eighteenth-century Europe, the spread of French language and culture enhanced French power. As McConnell points out in Chapter 2, within a decade of the Meiji Restoration, Japan imported some 3,000 hired foreigners and, in 1873, spent a full 1 percent of its national budget on exhibitions of Japanese culture at the World Expo in Vienna. While I developed the concept of soft power in the context of a debate over American power at the end of the twentieth century, there is nothing new or uniquely American about soft power. Likewise, although I introduced the concept in the field of international relations, which tends to focus on states in an anarchic international structure, soft power is not restricted to states or to international relations. Leaders in democratic societies are constantly relying on their soft power of attraction to get elected, and university presidents often find that their soft power is far greater than their hard power. While I focused on governments and diplomacy because of the context in which I first invented the term, it obviously applies to a much wider range of actors and contexts.

For my purposes, I chose an agent-focused definition of power that is quite close to the common usage implied by the dictionary—the ability to influence others to obtain the outcomes one wants. Of the three ways to affect others' behavior—coercion, inducement, and attraction—I used the term "soft power" for the third. But as several chapters in this volume demonstrate, we need to look more closely at the different ways that soft power can co-opt, attract, and entice. What makes people susceptible to attraction? To what extent are perceptions of interests shaped by myths and to what extent by free reasoning? How do agents win the hearts and minds of subjects? Soft power is attraction, but agents can control agendas and structure subjects' preferences so that some things appear attractive that might otherwise not be so. With soft power, the subjects matter as much as the agents. As Watanabe and McConnell point out, "'attraction' is codetermined and persuasion is socially constructed."

Some critics think that I believe that the American way of life is so attractive that others are predisposed to follow Washington's lead, and that I treat interests and identities as "uncontroversial and given."[1] On the contrary, much of my writing has been to warn American policy makers that they cannot take American attraction as given, and that they are in danger of squandering soft power. I point out that there are areas and groups that are repelled rather than attracted by American culture, values, and policies, and that polls show their numbers to be increasing. I also point out that such opponents as Osama bin Laden have impressive soft power among their followers and are struggling by word and deed to increase it and diminish the soft power of the United States (and the rest of the West). Where I do agree with my critics is that the concept of attraction is ripe for further research, and that is why the carefully documented essays in this volume are so valuable.

Culture and Attraction

Drinking Coke or the Boston Red Sox hiring a Japanese pitcher does not necessarily convey power. It is important not to confuse the resources that may produce behavior with the behavior itself. Whether the possession of power resources actually produces favorable outcomes depends on the context and the skills of the agent in converting the resources into behavioral outcomes. This is not unique to soft power resources. Having a larger tank army may produce victory if a battle is fought in the desert, but not if it is fought in a swamp. As David Baldwin has pointed out, whether power resources produce power behavior depends on the context.[2]

I have argued that the soft power of a country "rests primarily on three resources: its culture (in places where it is attractive to others), its political values (when it lives up to them at home and abroad), and its foreign policies (when they are seen as legitimate and having moral authority)." The parenthetical conditions are the key to determining whether soft power resources translate into the behavior of attraction that can influence others toward favorable outcomes. But more research needs to be done on the connection between culture and power behavior. For example, can cultural attraction reduce current extremist appeals in Muslim cultures? Some see an unbridgeable cultural divide. But consider the Islamic state of Iran. Western music and videos are anathema to the ruling mullahs, but attractive to many of the younger generation. In China, many American and Japanese cultural ideas are proving more attractive when they arrive via South Korea. As a university student put it in discussing television shows, "American dramas also show the same kind of lifestyle. We know that South Korea and America have similar political systems and economies. But it is easier to accept the lifestyle from South Koreans because they are culturally closer to us. We feel we can live like them in a few years."[3] As Nakano Yoshiko argues in Chapter 7, Chinese reception of Japanese drama and animation is seen less in terms of nationality than in terms of modernity. Thus, the amount of direct soft power it produces for Japan may be limited. Anne Allison makes a similar point that J-pop may not map closely with Japanese government soft power in America.

Economic Resources: Inducement and Attraction

Economic resources can produce both hard and soft power behavior. They can be used to coerce as well as attract. As Walter Mead has argued, "economic power is sticky power; it seduces as much as it compels. . . . A set of economic institutions and policies . . . attracts others into our system and makes it hard for them to leave."[4] A successful economy is an important source of attraction, as Japan has discovered. At the same time, it can provide resources that can be used as hard power inducements in the form of aid as well as coercive sanctions. Some analysts believe that there is little economic power where there are consensual market conditions. Buyers and sellers consent to a price that clears a market. But as Robert Keohane and I argued some years ago, where there is an asymmetry between buyers' and sellers' dependence on a consensual market relationship, the more dependent party is more vulnerable to the disruption of the market relationship, and that vulnerability can be used as a source of coercive power by the less dependent party.[5]

Sometimes in real-world situations, it is difficult to distinguish what part of an economic relationship is comprised of hard and soft power. European leaders describe the desire by other countries to accede to the European Union as a sign of Europe's soft power.[6] It is impressive, for example, that former Communist countries in central Europe oriented their expectations and revised their laws to comply with Brussels' framework. Turkey today is making changes in its human rights policies and laws on similar grounds. But how much are the changes the result of the economic inducement of market access and how much are they the result of attraction to Europe's successful economic and political system? The situation is one of mixed motives, and different actors in one country may see the mix in different ways.

A number of observers see China's soft power increasing in Asia and other parts of the developing world.[7] The so-called Beijing consensus on authoritarian government plus a successful market economy has become more popular than the previously dominant Washington consensus of liberal market economics with democratic government. But to what extent are Venezuelans and Zimbabweans attracted to the Beijing consensus, to what extent do they admire China's tripling of its gross domestic product over three decades, and to what extent are they induced by the prospect of access to a large and growing market? And even if the authoritarian growth model produces soft power for China in authoritarian countries, it does not produce attraction in democratic countries.

Military Resources and Soft Power

Military force appears to be a defining resource for hard power, but the same resource can sometimes contribute to soft power. Dictators such as Hitler and Stalin cultivated myths of invincibility and inevitability to structure expectations and attract others to jump on their bandwagons. The term "Stockholm syndrome" was developed to describe hostages who were initially coerced by their captors but in the constrained circumstances of stress and fear came to identify with their captors. And some people are generally attracted to strength. As Osama bin Laden has said, people are attracted to a strong horse rather than a weak horse. A well-run military can be a source of attraction, and military-to-military cooperation and training programs, for example, can establish transnational networks that enhance a country's soft power. As Watanabe and McConnell point out, Japan's Self-Defense Forces have produced soft as well as hard power.

Of course, misuse of military resources can also undercut soft power. Indifference to just war principles of discrimination and proportionality can destroy legitimacy. The efficiency of the initial American military invasion of Iraq in 2003 may have created admiration in the eyes of some Iraqis and others, but that soft power was undercut by the subsequent inefficiency of the occupation and the scenes of mistreatment of prisoners at Abu Ghraib. On the other hand, polls show that the use of American military resources for tsunami relief in Indonesia helped to restore some portion of the attraction that had been destroyed by the invasion of Iraq.

Normative Implications

I developed soft power as a descriptive rather than a normative concept. Like any form of power, it can be wielded for good or bad purposes. Hitler, Stalin, and Mao all possessed a great deal of soft power in their heydays, but that did not make it good. It is not necessarily better to twist minds than to twist arms. If I want to steal your money, I can threaten you with a gun, or I can swindle you with a get-rich scheme in which you invest. I can also persuade you that I am a guru to whom you should hand over your estate and that I will save the world. The third means depends on attraction or soft power, but the result remains theft.

We often judge ethics in the three dimensions of intentions, means, and consequences. While soft power can be used with bad intentions and wreak horrible consequences, it does differ in terms of means. Power defined in behavioral terms is a relationship, and soft power depends more on the subject's role in that relationship than does hard power. Attraction depends on what is happening in the mind of the subject. While there may be instances of coercive verbal manipulation, there are more degrees of freedom for the subject when the means involve soft power. I may have few degrees of freedom if the person with the gun demands my money or my life. I have even fewer degrees of freedom if he kills me and simply takes my wallet from my pocket. But to persuade me that he is a guru to whom I should leave my estate leaves open a number of degrees of freedom as well as the possibility of other outside influences arising and influencing the power relationship. After all, minds can change over time, whereas the dead cannot be revived. It is in the dimension of means that one might construct a normative preference for greater use of soft power, even if international relations cannot be based solely on reasoned persuasion.

Realism, Strategy, and Soft Power

Some authors portray the difference between hard and soft power as realism versus idealism, but that is a mistake. Traditional realists were not indifferent to the importance of ideas. In fact, in 1939 E.H. Carr described international power in three categories: military, economic, and power over opinion. Much of this subtlety was lost by the neorealists in their desire to make power measurable for their structural judgments.[8] They committed what might be called "the concrete fallacy."[9] Power was reduced to measurable, tangible resources. It was something that could be dropped on your foot or on cities, rather than something that might change your mind about wanting to drop anything in the first place.

As Machiavelli, the ultimate realist, described five centuries ago, it may be better for a prince to be feared than to be loved, but the prince is in greatest danger when he is hated. There is no contradiction between realism and soft power. Soft power is not a form of idealism or liberalism. It is simply a form of power—one way of getting desired outcomes. Legitimacy is a power reality. Competitive struggles over legitimacy are part of enhancing or depriving actors of soft power. And not just states are involved. Corporations, institutions, nongovernmental organizations, and transnational terrorist networks often have soft power of their own. When I was practicing international politics, I often turned to realism as a first approximation of reality, but I did not stop there.[10] And that is why I believe it is important to combine hard and soft power in strategies that I have termed "smart power."

Incorporating soft power into a government strategy is more difficult than may first appear. For one thing, as mentioned above, success in terms of outcomes is more in the control of the subject than is often the case with hard power. A second problem is that the results often take a long time, and most politicians and publics are impatient to see a prompt return on their investments. Third, the instruments of soft power are not fully under the control of governments. While governments control policy, culture and values are embedded in civil societies. Moreover, soft power depends on credibility, and when governments are seen as manipulative and information is perceived as propaganda, credibility is destroyed. Finally, there are some situations in which soft power provides very little leverage. It is difficult, for example, to see how soft power would solve the current dispute over North Korea's nuclear weapons. However, when a government is concerned about what Arnold Wolfers described as milieu goals, or general value objectives, such as promotion of democracy, human rights, and freedom, it may often be the case that soft power turns out to be superior to hard power.[11] We need more research on particular cases that illuminate the interplay of hard and soft power in successful strategies, and success can be judged in terms of both effectiveness and ethical values. Clearly we need to understand more about how soft power works, not just in U.S.-Japanese relations, but in politics more broadly. These fine essays are an important step in that direction.

Notes

1. Richard Ned Lebow, "Power, Persuasion and Justice," *Millennium* 33, 3 (2005): 552.

2. David Baldwin, "Power Analysis and World Politics: New Trends Versus Old Tendencies," *World Politics* 31, 2 (January 1979): 161–94.

3. Onishi Norimitsu, "For China's Youth, Culture Made in South Korea," *New York Times,* January 2, 2006.

4. Walter Russell Mead, *Power, Terror, Peace and War: America's Grand Strategy in a World at Risk* (New York: Knopf, 2004), p. 25.

5. Robert O. Keohane and Joseph S. Nye, *Power and Interdependence* (Boston: Little, Brown, 1977).

6. Martin Wolf, "Soft Power: The EU's Greatest Gift," *Financial Times,* February 2, 2005, p. 17.

7. Bates Gill and Yanzhong Huang, "The Dragon's Underbelly: Assessing China's Soft Power" (unpublished paper, Center for Strategic and International Studies, Washington, DC, 2005).

8. Kenneth Waltz, *Theory of International Politics* (Reading, MA: Addison Wesley, 1979).

9. The term comes from Steven Lukes, *Power: A Radical View. The Original Text with Two Major New Chapters* (Basingstoke, England: Palgrave, McMillan, 2005).

10. See "Hard and Soft Power," in Joseph S. Nye, Jr., *Power in the Global Information Age: From Realism to Globalization* (London: Routledge, 2004), pp. 1–9. See also Yoichi Funibashi, *Alliance Adrift* (New York: Council on Foreign Relations Press, 1999).

11. Arnold Wolfers, *Discord and Collaboration* (Baltimore: Johns Hopkins University Press, 1962).

Acknowledgments

This volume took shape over the course of two very productive workshops, the first in March 2005 at the International House of Japan in Tokyo, and the second at the Edwin O. Reischauer Institute of Japanese Studies at Harvard University. These stimulating seminars would not have been possible without a generous grant from the Abe Fellowship Program administered by the Social Science Research Council (SSRC) and the American Council of Learned Societies in cooperation with and with funds provided by the Japan Foundation Center for Global Partnership (CGP).

Many individuals assisted us as the manuscript moved from the germ of an idea to a completed product. We would like to thank Frank Baldwin and Takuya Toda-Ozaki of the SSRC, and Chano Junichi, Peter Chapin, Inada Mitsuhiro, Ito Masao, Tadashi Ogawa, and Masako Umeeda of the CGP for their work in developing our initial proposal and setting up the two workshops in Tokyo and Cambridge. Peter Chapin and Michael Fisch kindly served as proficient rapporteurs for the workshops. Margot Chamberlain and Theodore J. Gilman of Harvard University's Reischauer Institute worked hard to organize the second workshop and a public symposium in Cambridge.

Our appreciation extends to the distinguished scholars and practitioners who generously spared their precious time to attend either workshop and offer their perceptive comments. They are Aoki Tamotsu, Michael Auslin, Thomas Berger, Mark J. Davidson, Andrew Gordon, William M. Morgan, and Susan J. Pharr. We would like to offer a special thanks to Joe Nye for providing the intellectual spark for the book and for taking a personal interest in the project.

Patricia Kolb and Makiko Parsons at M.E. Sharpe were extremely generous and helpful in guiding us through the editorial process to achieve this finished product.

It was a real privilege for us to work on this project, largely because of the thought-provoking contributions of our authors. We very much appreciate their hard work, good humor, and creative insights into the dynamics of soft power in the context of U.S.-Japanese relations.

Introduction

Watanabe Yasushi and David L. McConnell

The Significance of Soft Power

Professor Joseph S. Nye, Jr., of Harvard University, first coined the term "soft power" to define a country's ability to achieve its goals by attracting rather than coercing others. According to Nye, an important way to gain international support is to have cultural and political values and foreign policies that other countries see as legitimate and having moral authority. Instead of a reliance on carrots and sticks to exercise influence, a nation's capacity to win hearts and minds is of crucial importance in a global information age (Nye 1990, 2004).

Though the concept that "it is best to win without fighting" is not new—the philosophy of the ancient Chinese strategist Sunzi rested on precisely this idea—Nye's contemporary articulation of soft power has struck a deep chord. Like Robert Putnam's (2001) concept of "social capital," Nye's work constructed a platform for debate for both policy makers and scholars from diverse disciplines. As a result, his notion of cultural power as an alternative to military and economic might has achieved wide currency since its introduction into our diplomatic and political vocabulary.

Since the publication of Nye's 2004 book, *Soft Power: The Means to Success in World Politics,* there has been an explosion in the number of publications devoted to the subject. As just one measure, a Google search for "soft power" in December 2006 yielded 67 million English-language hits, compared to only 60,000 in August 2005.[1] The popular media has been abuzz with articles applying the lens of soft power to topics ranging from the psychology of suicide bombing to China's Africa policy. Academics have begun to weigh in with books and special issues of journals devoted to analyzing soft power.

In our estimation, however, this newfound fascination with soft power has generated more confusion than clarity. Many of Nye's interlocutors have not taken the time to read his work carefully or have responded based on their own agendas. Though there have been some thoughtful responses to Nye's work, to date there has been no serious social-scientific treatment by scholars and practitioners in diverse fields of the strengths and limitations of soft power. Nor has the concept of soft power been systematically applied to the U.S.-Japanese relationship.

Our book attempts to fill these gaps by taking a hard look at soft power through an in-depth analysis of two of the world's "soft power superpowers." Most of the writing on soft power has focused on strategic competitors and rivals of the United States rather than on strategic partners. We believe that the U.S.-Japanese alliance, with its rich history of cultural, diplomatic, economic, and military exchanges, provides an ideal lens through which to assess soft power.

Thanks to generous funding from the Social Science Research Council and the Japan Foundation's Center for Global Partnership, we were able to bring together leading scholars and practitioners from the United States and Japan for two lively seminars on soft power in 2005 and 2006. Joseph Nye, whose commentary opens this book, joined us for the Cambridge conference, along with others from the Reischauer Institute of Japanese Studies at Harvard University. The opportunity for anthropologists, political scientists, historians, economists, diplomats, and practitioners to exchange thoughts across the table has sharpened our collective thinking immeasurably. By focusing our respective methodologies, disciplinary lenses, and real-world experiences on a single topic, this volume allows for a multifaceted and nuanced analysis of soft power.

In this introductory essay, we analyze soft power in relation to an ongoing set of intellectual debates about the nature of power and influence in world affairs. We begin by assessing key issues raised by Nye's book and by his interlocutors, noting, where appropriate, how these issues are addressed by the contributors to this volume. We then briefly describe why the U.S.-Japanese relationship is such a fertile ground for exploring soft power and conclude with a brief description of the organization of the book.

Situating Soft Power: The Intellectual Context

Unlike Samuel Huntington's "clash of civilizations," which was greeted by a storm of controversy, "soft power" has occasioned relatively modest critiques in scholarly and policy-making circles. Many practitioners have found the term useful in conceptualizing their own work, but there has also been confusion that stems from misunderstanding, imprecision, distortion, misuse, and in extreme cases, abuse of the concept. For example, journalists have been quick to pick up on Nye's work, but they often confuse cultural attractiveness with soft power, and resources with behavior. Whether cultural attractiveness can *become* soft power, however, depends on the policy objective itself and on the context and methods of implementation. As Nye himself has noted, just because some foreigners drink Coca-Cola or wear Michael Jordan T-shirts, that does not mean that the United States has power over them. Our volume shows the dangers of conflating source and soft power.

In engaging with the scholarly literature on soft power, we single out four key issues for further elaboration: the relation between hard and soft power, the role of nonstate actors in wielding soft power, the meaning of structural power in multicultural states, and the unilateralist tendencies in Nye's conception of soft power.

Relation Between Hard and Soft Power

Several of Nye's critics have asserted that for all the talk of soft power, in the end the United States relies on hard power; therefore, soft power merely camouflages the intent of great powers to make use of hard power. The most vocal of these critics has been Ferguson (2003), who argued that because countries always try to cloak their power in altruism, soft power is like a velvet glove covering an iron fist. Because soft power is really just a halo of hard power, Ferguson believes that Nye's concept of soft power is simply "too soft."

Nye has responded that "soft power does not depend on hard power" (2004, p. 9), and he points to the Soviet Union as an example of a country that once had a good deal of soft power but lost it after the invasions of Hungary and Czechoslovakia. "Soviet soft power declined even as its hard economic and military resources continued to grow. Because of its brutal policies, the Soviet Union's hard power actually undercut its soft power" (2004, p. 2). He also pointed to Norway and Canada as countries whose soft power is greater than their military and economic standing would suggest—Norway for its conflict mediation and Canada for its stance on international cooperation, which distances it from the United States. Nye's point is that soft power is not merely window dressing; rather, it lowers the costs of accomplishing policy objectives.

At the same time, Nye has never argued that soft power can be a complete substitute for hard power. For him, they are two sides of one coin and "sometimes reinforce and sometimes interfere with each other" (2004, p. 25). Nye was candid in his assessment that some goals can be achieved only by hard power. "North Korean dictator Kim Jong Il's penchant for Hollywood movies is unlikely to affect his decision on developing nuclear weapons" (2006b). Recently, Nye has elaborated on this notion by describing the ability to combine both hard and soft power into a winning strategy as "smart power."[2]

Others have claimed that Nye's distinction between hard and soft power is too rigid. Noya (2006), for instance, critiqued the "dualistic view" of soft power inherent in Nye's framework. Yet as early as 1990, Nye wrote that "the distinction between hard and soft power resources is one of degree, both in the nature of the behavior and in the tangibility of the resources" (1990, p. 181). The case of economic power provides a good example of Nye's thinking. Some scholars and journalists have equated economic strength with soft power, and references in the popular media to "soft power options such as economic sanctions" are not uncommon.[3] As Nye pointed out, however, "there is nothing soft about economic sanctions if you are on the receiving end" (2006a, p. 1). Moreover, an economic embargo is a far cry from economic incentives. For Nye, the crucial distinction is coercion with sanctions versus wooing with wealth. Nevertheless, the line between coercion and free will can be razor thin and difficult to determine.

This volume moves beyond an either-or interpretation in favor of a more dynamic and contextual interpretation of the relationship between hard and soft power. When Japanese hear the term "Self-Defense Forces" (SDF), for example, they immediately associate it with hard power. But depending on how and why the SDF are mobilized, and in what context, they can also be a source of soft power. Agawa Naoyuki (Chapter 13) extends this line of reasoning, suggesting that Japan's hard economic power hurt its image in the 1980s but that its use of hard military power in Iraq was viewed positively. Nor does soft power in image currency necessarily translate into positive economic currency for the nation. Sugiura Tsutomu (Chapter 8) notes that the pirating of Japanese movies and music in China promotes Japanese culture at the same time that it does economic harm to Japan. As Kondo Seiichi (Chapter 11) concludes, the exercise of soft power differs from that of hard power in that the subjectivity of recipients and the methods of transmission greatly influence the final result.

The Role of Nonstate Actors in Wielding Soft Power

Another criticism that has been leveled at Nye's theory is that it is overly "state-centered." For example, in an article with the subtitle "Reflection on the Shallow Concept of Soft Power," Bohas (2006) argued that Nye's notion of soft power does not stress the shaping of foreign societies by nonstate actors and thus their important role in American predominance. Other critics have described Nye's work as preoccupied with government efforts to control forces that are largely outside its reach.

A closer reading of Nye's work shows that he is well aware of the strong influence of nonstate actors such as nongovernmental organizations (NGOs), businesses, universities, religious organizations, ethnic groups, and international organizations (2004, pp. 90–97). Nye also recognizes that governments cannot manage soft power to the same extent as hard power. At the same time, it cannot be denied that Nye's analysis ultimately comes back to the state. He goes to some length, for instance, to describe the perils awaiting governments that ignore soft power.

But should governments be involved in promoting culture industries at all? Our volume is distinctive in the number of chapters that take up this practical policy issue, with contributors offering a range of viewpoints. Former diplomats such as Crowell and Agawa suggest that the state (through its embassies) can and should play a very important and direct role in cultivating soft power, and Matthew Fraser (Chapter 10) reminds us that the American government has long been in the business of using movies and broadcasting to promote its interests abroad. Sugiura and Kondo concur but see the government's role as facilitator in the creation of an environment conducive to the creation of soft power (for example, by encouraging private-sector culture exports or establishing educational exchange programs).

Other authors are more skeptical of the intentions and outcomes behind state-orchestrated programs to produce soft power. Lawrence Repeta's chapter (Chapter 14) on the global spread of freedom of information laws argues that soft power implies a reallocation of influence away from military and economic elites. In his mind, "transnational civil society actors" can play a prominent role in pushing states to enact policies that put knowledge in the hands of ordinary citizens. Imata Katsuji and Kuroda Kaori's analysis of NGOs in the United States, the United Kingdom, and Japan strikes a similar chord (Chapter 15). Though the humanitarian aims of NGOs and a government's foreign policy may sometimes be compatible or even complementary, NGOs are usually not accountable to states and may in fact oppose government actions. These authors concur with Ogoura (2006) that scholarship and culture should be independent of political power and, in fact, are often a means of resisting authority.[4]

Culture, the State, and Structural Power

One of the hallmarks of Nye's treatise on soft power is his clear prose and ability to convey complex ideas without resorting to academic jargon.[5] At the same time, we would like to point out two areas in which Nye's formulation of culture, the state, and structural power diverges somewhat from the ways in which some scholars in anthropology, cultural studies, and related fields have framed these relationships.

First is the tendency in Nye's formulation of soft power to assume a general correspondence between "nation-state" and "culture." As a shorthand, Nye's definition of culture as "the set of values and practices that create meaning for a society" (2004, p. 11) is relatively unproblematic. Easily missed in this definition, however, is the recent rethinking of the assumption that culture is a "localized community" exhibiting an isomorphism between place and ethos. Scholars of globalization today are more likely to talk about the "deterritorialization of culture" (Inda and Rosaldo 2002, p. 10), disjuncture and fragmentation within a culture (Appadurai 1996), and the existence of multiple cultural spaces and frameworks within any given "society" or "nation." Similarly, Nye's discussion of the "state" sometimes gives the impression that governments are singular entities rather than complex sites of competing interest groups and that determining "the national interest" is a relatively simple exercise.

Nye is certainly not unaware of cultural and bureaucratic complexity, as his discussion of diaspora communities (2004, pp. 92–93) indicates. But because cultural power, for Nye, is ultimately redeemed in the form of diplomatic persuasion, his theory requires a linking of state and culture in ways that are easily oversimplified. Several papers in this volume suggest the need for complicating Nye's relatively straightforward mapping of "culture" onto "nation." As but one example, Anne Allison (Chapter 6) suggests that Nye's concept of soft power needs to take into account lines of power that are transnational and cartographies of place that are virtual and constructed. She argues that the early success of Japanese popular culture in the United States was partly due to its "cultural deodorization"—its attraction was less as a product that revealed the essence of "Japaneseness" and more as a signifier of an experience or an effect. Thus, the globalization of Japanese pop culture does not always equate with Japanese soft power, because it may fail to become anchored in something in the country or culture itself and fail to yield a yearning for the "real" Japan.

Our second concern involves Nye's conceptualization of the "structural" face of power, which he describes as "the ability to get the outcomes you want without having to force people to change the behavior through threats or payments" (2004, p. 15). In focusing on "structure" as opposed to "agency," Nye joins a distinguished list of scholars who have called our attention to the "unified schemes or configurations developed to underwrite or manifest power" (Wolf 1999, p. 4). In fact, in his earlier work, Nye referenced Gramsci's argument that the most critical feature for a dominant country is the ability to obtain "a broad measure of consent on general principles that ensure the supremacy of the leading state and the dominant social classes while also offering some prospect of satisfaction to the less powerful" (1990, p. 182).

What interests us here is that most scholarly treatments of structural power are "cautionary tales" about the misuse of power by the state and elites. For example, Althusser's (1971) concept of the "ideological state apparatus" rests on the assumption that the exercise of power in capitalist societies can be subtle, disguised, and insidious. Even in the scholarly analysis of Japan, there is a long history of frameworks (Sugimoto Yoshio's "friendly authoritarianism" and Karel van Wolferen's "enigma of power" are but two examples) that advocate replacing "cultural explanations" of Japanese society (seen as overly essentialist) with analyses of how power holders use institutions and everyday social practices to "indoctrinate" people into seeing the world in a certain way. By contrast, Nye's formulation of soft power is distinctive in its generally positive view of the exercise of power and in the way *structural* power is linked with the *agency* of states. Extending the Althusserian line of thinking, however, several analysts have argued that Nye's formulation of soft power implicates him in the Bush doctrine because "soft power" legitimizes neoliberalism, free markets, and the very values on which military action in Iraq was based ("democracy" and "civilization").[6]

To be sure, Nye did note that "soft power can also adhere to malevolent organizations and networks" (*Soft Power*, 2004, p. 95), and he mentioned Hitler and al-Qaeda as examples of soft power used for sinister means. He has also excoriated secret propaganda missions that undermine American credibility in favor of public diplomacy that is evenhanded, open, and informative.[7] He clearly recognizes the difference between a state engaging in outright indoctrination and a state promoting an ideological environment within which individuals retain some freedom of choice.

Our volume extends Nye's concept of structural power by showing the ambiguity that lies between the extremes. For example, soft power can be deployed by a government for exclusive and nationalistic goals in one context and for multilateralism in another. The exercise of public diplomacy is also fraught with ethical decisions in which the criteria for evaluating policy goals are not always clear. Kondo (Chapter 11) notes, for instance, that in regions such as the Middle East where people still hold deep resentment against colonialism or have firm convictions that do not comply with Western values, even the projection of American ideals is perceived as coercion. Fraser (Chapter 10) concurs that the co-optive power of American pop culture seems far less seductive in regimes based on religious authority as opposed to rival ideologies. He raises the important question of how public diplomacy should be exercised when American values themselves become strongly associated with imposition. Crowell's (Chapter 12) reconstruction of the ingredients that helped the U.S.-Japanese relationship move away from mutual suspicion toward greater trust is instructive in this regard. The overall implication for public diplomacy is that policy makers need to be concerned not only with "nation branding" but also with finding ways to take into account the civil society of other countries, asking how policies are represented and are received by diverse domestic constituents, to an extent never before seen (Melissen 2005).

Is Nye's Concept of Soft Power Too Unilateralist?

Nye has also been criticized for his preoccupation with American influence in the world and with making American foreign policy goals more attractive. There is no question that behind Nye's passionate advocacy of soft power lies concern over the consequences of the Bush administration's foreign policy after 9/11, especially the neoconservative tendency to rely on hard power alone. By concluding *Soft Power* with the exhortation "We have done it before, we can do it again" (2004, p. 147), Nye signaled that a key goal of his book is a "wake-up call" to Americans.

But is Nye's formulation of soft power itself too "American centered"? One of the most trenchant critiques of Nye's work has come from Womack (2005), whose article "Dancing Alone" describes Nye as a unilateralist who sees soft power primarily in terms of making American goals more attractive. Womack charged that Nye "does not see American policy and goals as interactive with the rest of the world" (2005, p. 1). He noted that Nye's emphasis on agenda setting through international institutions, which featured prominently in his 1995 book, *Bound to Lead,* has now faded into the background, replaced with a concern over the "marketing of American preferences." Womack concluded that Nye is thus an outstanding example of "the mistake of trying to understand the world without leaving home" (2005, p. 4).

At first glance, this critique would seem to be ill founded. Nye has long been a promoter of what he calls "complex interdependence," and in *Soft Power* he not only cautions against unilateralism but also embraces multilateralism for solving thorny transnational issues, such as climate change, the spread of infectious disease, and international terrorism (pp. 136–37). Nye has also declared that soft power is not a zero-sum game. Through cooperation, countries can together enhance their soft power. A warning against the "power-game" view of national interest predicated on war, Nye's point is extremely important in a world where national interest exists in a context of various "public interests," including relations not only between states but also among regional alliances and other international actors.

In another sense, too, Nye's notion of "national interest" is far from narrow. At a public symposium held at Harvard University in March 2006, Nye used the term "meta-soft power" to describe the state's willingness to criticize itself. For Nye, such capacity for introspection fundamentally enhances a nation's attractiveness, legitimacy, and reliability. If we take this viewpoint, then regular censorship of opinions and viewpoints that are critical of government policies can run the risk of "consuming" rather than "producing" soft power. Especially in today's information-rich and highly networked global society, such narrow-minded and self-protective behavior will be readily apparent.

Yet Womack's claim that Nye "fails to acknowledge the essentially interactive character of persuasion" (2005, p. 1) has been echoed by others, including Ogoura, who argued that Nye "views things from the perspective of the party exercising power" (2006, p. 2).[8] At times it does seem that Nye oversimplifies the complexity of soft power in spite of his acknowledgment that "the effects of globalization depend on the receiver as well as the sender" (2004, p. 111) because "all information goes through cultural filters" (2004, p. 41). What is needed, we believe, is a sustained concern with the "indigenization of soft power," such that any analysis stresses the ways in which "attraction" is codetermined and persuasion is socially constructed.[9] Importantly, the perspectives of consumers of soft power must be gauged not only through the blunt instrument of public opinion polls but also through in-depth fieldwork that can truly grasp the pulse of local sentiments and the complex ways in which positive impressions of a culture or a policy can coexist with deeply critical elements.

This volume takes a relational-contextual approach to soft power, in which the interaction of policy goals with local contexts and interests is highlighted. Watanabe Yasushi's essay (Chapter 1) on anti-Americanism in Japan stands out in this regard for its conclusion that assessing reactions to a country is a complex business because they come in all shades; to conceive of soft power in one-dimensional terms (along one axis of pro versus con) is too simplistic. David McConnell (Chapter 2) shows that in spite of considerable goodwill toward Japan among alumni of the JET Program, its soft power potential has been somewhat muted by the reinterpretation of program goals in prefectural offices and local schools. Understanding the cultural context of policy implementation is even more important than grasping policy goals. In Chapter 7, Nakano Yoshiko investigates consumer motivations and describes the Chinese reception of Japanese drama and animation in terms of "approachable modernity": Chinese receptivity of J-pop is less a vehicle for cultivating favorable attitudes toward the Japanese state than it is a function of the desire for "how-to" guides for middle-class life.

Soft Power and U.S.-Japanese Relations

Nye has noted that Asia is likely to become the most important arena of soft power in the future, regaining the central place that it occupied as a supplier of world products in the early 1800s. Unfortunately, most of the recent writing on soft power in Asia has focused on the rise of China and, to a lesser extent, India as rivals of the United States. Lost in this obsession with potential economic and military competitors of the United States are the lessons to be learned from one of the most successful bilateral relationships in the twentieth century. In just over fifty years, the U.S.-Japanese relationship has shifted from one marked by tremendous asymmetry in power relations, including propaganda machines that demonized each other's peoples, to an alliance based on reciprocity and mutuality. It behooves us to ask how soft power contributed to an unlikely marriage coming so far in such a short time.

Certainly, a crucial part of the story is the shared security arrangement and the close, if sometimes controversial, economic ties between the two countries in the postwar period. At the same time, the impact of mutual cultural fascination and exchange should not be underestimated. As Miyoshi (1991) reminded us, the lion's share of Japan's relationship with the world since the Meiji period has involved an elliptical affair with the United States, in spite of (or perhaps because of) the very different cultural and historical trajectories in the two countries. In Chapter 9, Sayuri Guthrie-Shimizu charts the course of this relationship through a historical analysis of baseball as soft power, illuminating the process by which baseball was introduced to and received in Japan in the pre–World War II era, reinvented during the U.S. occupation, and further developed in the postwar era. Her analysis reveals a complex trajectory of Japan's acceptance of the United States, which rejects an easy characterization of "Americanization." Nevertheless, as a highly popular sport and successful commercial enterprise on both sides of the Pacific, baseball highlights soft power's long-term potential for drawing two adversaries closer in vision and in practice.

To be sure, the path has been rocky, and the close ties enjoyed today were by no means a foregone conclusion. The ongoing presence of sizable American military forces in Japan, for example, creates the potential for incidents that can significantly damage the American image and its soft power. This is especially true in Okinawa. The 1995 rape of a twelve-year-old Okinawan girl by three American servicemen incited massive demonstrations in Okinawa and led to a formal agreement between the two countries to shut down the Marine Air Station at Futenma and return the land to local control. Yet over time, the evolution of cultural relations from sporadic, loosely regulated encounters to highly organized networks of cultural and educational exchange has partially mitigated the effects both of isolated events and of pervasive structural conflicts that "consume" soft power. In Chapter 12, Crowell tells us exactly how this relationship evolved. He argues that in spite of numerous challenges such as the language barrier, the U.S. military presence, and Japan's closed reporters' clubs, the unlikely development of a positive bilateral relationship is due to factors on both the Japanese and the American sides. In Japan, these include a strong interest in the United States, a well-educated public, and American access to Japanese opinion leaders; on the American side, the process has been assisted by generous resources, an openness to presenting diverse viewpoints, and, importantly, the appointment of highly respected elder statesmen (such as Mike Mansfield, Walter Mondale, and Howard Baker) to the key role of ambassador. In Chapter 13, drawing on his firsthand experience in the Japanese embassy in Washington, DC, Agawa completes the story, revealing the specific institutional structures, budgets, and programs that helped create this atmosphere of trust.

It is fashionable now to see Japan as collapsing underneath its political and economic misfortunes, while China displaces Japan as Asia's leader. As Mulgan (2005) reminded us, though, Japan is an emerging, not a retreating power: Its economic power is almost unmatched, it is a "virtual nuclear weapons state," and, its inability to obtain a seat on the United Nations Security Council notwithstanding, it is playing a more visible role on the world stage than before. Moreover, Japan's "gross national cool"—the term coined by McGray (2002) to describe Japan's growing cultural influence, from pop music, architecture, and fashion to consumer electronics, cuisine, and animation—is way up. Japanese-language study is on the increase around the world, and in 2006 Japanese passed French for the number two position among languages that attract foreign test takers.[10] Though it is likely that Japan's influence in Asia is primarily a product of its economic strength as opposed to its cultural power (Pempel 1997, p. 75), it is misguided to view Japan as anything but a key player in the future of soft power in Asia.

Yet many challenges remain. During the Cold War, the U.S.-Japanese alliance was the cornerstone of American power in the Asia-Pacific region. Many observers were concerned that the alliance would become anachronistic after the end of the Cold War (Green and Cronin 1997). Such has not been the case, but in fashioning a revitalized U.S.-Japanese relationship, soft power has proven to be more important than ever before. In this respect, our volume takes a close look at the challenges facing international higher education as a key vehicle of soft power on both sides of the Pacific. Philip Altbach and Patti McGill Peterson (Chapter 3) analyze the conditions (differentiation, transparency, organization, academic freedom, and openness to debate) that have enabled American higher education to be regarded as the gold standard of academic structure, curriculum, and research worldwide. They also note that serious challenges face American higher education, including the chilling effect of 9/11 on access by foreign students and scholars, coupled with the increasing success of other countries (especially India and China) in developing knowledge-based economies. By contrast, appraisals of the soft power of Japanese universities by Yonezawa Akiyoshi (Chapter 4) and by Ellen Mashiko and Horie Mikie (Chapter 5) provide a bleak assessment. Yonezawa profiles five Japanese universities that are offering innovative programs, and Mashiko and Horie point out the growth in university-based initiatives to build lasting relationships through educational exchange programs. Overall, however, these authors concur that the potential role of Japanese higher education in building and sustaining soft power is largely unfulfilled.

The Organization of the Book

After introductory articles on the fundamental theme of perception and soft power, the essays in this book move across four arenas in which soft power is deployed: international higher education, popular culture, public diplomacy, and civil society. As a group, they try to avoid the conceptual pitfalls often associated with soft power by paying close attention to the historical conditions under which soft power develops and to the socially contingent qualities of its emergence. Though our contributors use a variety of methodological techniques, they all express dissatisfaction with the notion that soft power is unimportant because its efficacy is difficult to measure and evaluate. In fact, as with the concept of love, the more rigorously one thinks about power, the harder it is to measure and evaluate. Here, too, sources and power must not be conflated; even if sources can be quantified, it does not necessarily follow that the sum of the sources and the sum of power will be proportionate. Although soft power is difficult to quantify, it is significant precisely because the dynamics of international politics are articulated in terms of power. The criticism that soft power is unimportant because it cannot be precisely measured seems to us to put the cart before the horse. This is not to imply that the issue of measuring soft power is unimportant. If soft power has political meaning, then it must be because it has a behavioral impact. The contributors to this volume offer numerous examples of how attention to cultural diplomacy can shape foreign policy outcomes.

Perception

The two essays in Part I set the tone for the book by pointing out the importance of analyzing soft power in light of the multiple cultural and political contexts in which a country's attractiveness can play out. If beauty is in the eye of the beholder, then we must take the social embeddedness of perceptions seriously. In this vein, Watanabe analyzes the formation of anti-American sentiments and discourse in Japan since the late 1990s. Even though most Japanese maintain highly favorable attitudes toward the United States, anti-Americanism "lite" is on the rise. Watanabe reveals the new and subtle forms anti-Americanism is taking and analyzes the underlying causes. Similarly, McConnell's analysis of a major Japanese program to "import diversity" in the form of "assistant language teachers" from the United States and other countries shows how the capacity to produce soft power for Japan is contingent on the nature of the social environments operating "downstream" in the policy system and the broader cultural tendency to view internationalization as "situational accommodation." He also demonstrates the complex, if generally positive, reactions of JET Program alumni to their Japan experience and the varied ways in which they maintain connections with Japan upon returning home.

International Higher Education

The three chapters in Part II elaborate on Nye's argument that education systems and educational exchange programs can be formidable sources of soft power. Altbach and Peterson, for example, argue that American higher education is the gold standard worldwide in part because of the decentralized system, which allows for transparency, differentiation, and openness. Conversely, Yonezawa argues that Japanese higher education is in crisis in part because its inflexibility has led to a slow response to the challenges of globalization. Mashiko and Horie show the long-term potential of both university-based and government-sponsored exchange programs to close the perception gap and foster better bilateral relations. Overall, these papers reinforce Nye's important insight that soft power doesn't mean just better advertising; it means making serious efforts to understand the perspectives, languages, and histories of other countries and to forge institutional and personal linkages among them.

Popular Culture

The five chapters in Part III share a focus on consumers' perspectives of soft power to understand why others are attracted (or not attracted) to American and Japanese culture. Allison's chapter examines the reception of Japanese popular culture products (video games, Pokémon, comic books, trading cards, Hello Kitty trinkets, and so forth) by American children and parents. Early attempts to market J-pop in the United States were noteworthy for the attempts to erase signs of Japanese culture, but more recently, J-pop has become more deterritorialized. There are more joint mixed productions that juxtapose cultural codes, both American and Japanese, and recent attitudes of American youth who adopt J-cool suggest a willingness to go beyond the cultural orbit of "Americanness" and the hegemony of the global imagination it once held. Nakano's chapter notes that although Japanese drama has softened the edges of Chinese views of Japan as a military aggressor (by providing alternative images of a kinder, gentler Japan), it is a mistake to put the nation-state at the center of an analysis of soft power. The Japanese government has not participated in the diffusion of J-pop to China, and the recipients usually judge pirated goods by their quality and their particular interest rather than by country of origin.

The final three chapters in the section on popular culture analyze businesses, baseball, and movies and broadcasting, respectively, through the lens of soft power. Sugiura extends Nye's concept of soft power to the business world by drawing an analogy between the soft power of nations and the soft power of companies. Sugiura argues that companies with soft power can sell products by reputation alone, without lowering prices. As an economist, he also tries to quantify McGray's concept of "gross national cool," showing that Japanese culture-related exports grew significantly over the past decade. Shimizu's historical analysis of baseball demonstrates the importance of a fine-grained account of soft power as it develops over time. U.S.-Japanese relations on the baseball diamond not only reflected macrolevel developments, but also mediated the political and economic conflicts that arose in the bilateral relationship. Fraser concludes this section by showing how the American movie and broadcasting industries provoke contradictory reactions in different regions of the world depending on the specific conditions and contexts. Along with many of the contributors to this section, he argues that even though pop culture can be seen as trivializing serious discussions of soft power, its symbolic potency gives it a powerful, if unquantifiable, role in shaping foreign policy.

Public Diplomacy

The authors of the three chapters in Part IV, on public diplomacy, have decades of experience in the diplomatic corps and bring their considerable expertise to bear on the practical and ethical issues in wielding soft power. Moving across cases as diverse as Japan's economic rise, war apologies, exchange programs, and terrorism, Kondo shows how Japan's "reserved presentation" and the "aggressive projection" of American soft power can have both positive and negative effects. Kondo also analyzes the cooperative interaction that makes soft power a plus-sum game and distinguishes it from propaganda. Finally, Kondo outlines his vision of the government as a "network hub" and facilitator of private-sector creations; it should focus on low-visibility efforts to create a fertile environment for actors connected to one another horizontally.

Crowell draws on his experience as a practitioner to illustrate the specific ways that the U.S. embassy fosters daily and strategic communication with Japanese, as well as the formation of lasting relationships. Since 9/11, he argues, the American tendency to subordinate cultural and educational activities to policy advocacy has intensified and public diplomacy has acquired a propagandistic cast. Agawa's main argument is that the close bilateral ties between Japan and the United States are in part a result of the effective use of soft power by the Japanese government. He provides fascinating details of how public diplomacy actually operates in Japan and is upbeat in his assessment of the successes of Japan's public diplomacy.

Civil Society

The final two chapters of the book, in Part V, address the considerable role of nonstate actors in wielding soft power. Repeta's chapter explores the spread of freedom of information laws in the United States and Japan as a form of soft power. He shows that the United States had been a leader in promoting the idea that the right to know is inherent in representative democracies, where sovereignty resides not with a king but with the people. Beginning with the United States in 1966, the number of countries adopting freedom of information laws has risen to more than sixty today. He cautions, however, that implementation systems of freedom of information acts vary widely, and that even the United States has backtracked in recent years. Though a small group of proponents who were inspired by the U.S. freedom of information laws has existed in Japan for thirty years, it was only in 1995 under Socialist prime minister Murayama that a committee was appointed to seriously propose a national freedom of information law for Japan. The Diet passed a law based on the resulting proposal in 1999, but, curiously, the Japanese government today seems not to recognize this as a source of soft power. Imata and Kuroda's chapter not only analyzes NGOs that exhibit a basic compatibility between humanitarian aims and foreign policy, but also assesses those that oppose government actions, as well as "transnational civil society actors," which are even less accountable to governments. Moreover, their chapter offers an insider's account of Japan's small but growing NGO movement, including their studies of the Japan Platform and the Global Call to Action Against Poverty.

Conclusion

The discourse on soft power cannot be separated from the historical moments that condition its possibilities. In this sense, it is worth asking why "soft power" has become something of a buzzword in both Japan and the United States in the first decade of the new millennium. On the American side, its popularity is in part a reaction to the overreliance on military power in the Bush administration and the ways in which neoconservatives have ignored Teddy Roosevelt's advice: now that the United States has a big stick, it should learn to speak softly.[11] In Japan, the impulse is the mirror opposite. As Agawa notes, history (namely, the renouncing of force in its constitution) has put Japan in a position where it must rely on soft power more than other countries do. Because Japan came off a long recession in the 1990s and has been constrained by what Berger has called its "peculiar culture of anti-militarism" (1997, p. 191), casting foreign policy in terms of soft power appeals greatly to policy makers eager to raise Japan's status in world affairs.

At a time when the United States and Japan are increasingly turning to hard power to deal with threats in the Middle East and North Korea, this book demonstrates the crucial importance of public diplomacy through long-term cultural and educational engagement. A "cool Japan" burdened with a weird sort of nationalism or a narrowly defined national interest will simply turn people off around the world. So, too, will the United States as a "principal power" if it does not demonstrate respect for the cultural worlds of people who may not share its values. Collectively, then, these chapters offer a strong corrective to American solipsism and Japanese exceptionalism at this important historical juncture.

Notes

1. Because Google tweaks its algorithm from time to time, the comparison is somewhat imprecise, but the dramatic increase is nonetheless quite clear. A Japanese-language search revealed 130,000 hits as of August 2006, compared to a mere 3,000 hits a year earlier.

2. Etzioni (2006) concurred that mixed power is best. "Just as hard power does best when accompanied by soft power, so the other way around: soft power works much better when it is known that if all else fails, hard power might well follow."

3. See Drifte's (1996) analysis of Japan's foreign policy in the 1990s as one example of this tendency.

4. For a thorough investigation of a wide spectrum of issues concerning Japanese NGOs, see Schwartz and Pharr (2003).

5. Reflecting on his stint as assistant secretary of defense in the Clinton administration, Nye noted that he was "struck by the irrelevance of my former colleagues to my policy-making contemporaries. The academic language was often impenetrable, but more important, the cacophony of contradictory ideas rarely provided much leverage on the world" (Nye 1998, p. 166).

6. See, for example, Coronado (2005, p. 7). A similar argument is made by Steger (2005).

7. See Nye (2003).

8. Similarly, Rose (2005) rejected Nye's interpretation of the spread of English as a soft power resource for the United States. He argued that the dominance of English encourages Americans to be introverted, while people who use English as a second language are more likely to have a cosmopolitan understanding of American political interests as well as their own. The global diffusion of English tends to increase the soft power of non-Americans for whom English is *not* their native language and weaken the influence of Americans, who mistakenly assume that because those with whom they communicate are speaking English, they also share the same political values and goals.

9. See Garon and Maclachlan (2006) for a similar approach to a different question: Has the consumer revolution in East Asia converged toward the endpoint of the American model?

10. The number of foreigners who sat for the standard certification test in Japanese proficiency reached a new high of 530,000 persons in 2006 (up from 350,000 two years ago). See Japan Foundation (2006).

11. Nye (2003) makes this point in an article on the differentiation between propaganda and soft power.

References

Althusser, Louis. 1971. *Ideology and Ideological State Apparatuses.* New York: Monthly Review Press.

Appadurai, Arjun. 1996. *Modernity at Large: Cultural Dimensions of Globalization.* Minneapolis: University of Minnesota Press.

Berger, Thomas U. 1999. "Alliance, Politics, and Japan's Postwar Culture of Anti-Militarism." In *The U.S.-Japan Alliance: Past, Present and Future.* Ed. Michael J. Green and Patrick M. Cronin, 189–207. New York: Council on Foreign Relations Press.

Bohas, Alexandre. 2006. "The Paradox of Anti-Americanism: Reflection on the Shallow Concept of Soft Power." *Global Society: Journal of Interdisciplinary International Relations* 20 (4): 395–414.

Coronado, Jaime Preciado. 2005. "Between Soft Power and a Hard Place." *Journal of Developing Societies* 21 (3–4): 7.

Drifte, Reinhard. 1996. *Japan's Foreign Policy in the 1990s: From Economic Superpower to What Power?* New York: St. Martin's Press.

Etzioni, Amitai. 2006. "Outside View: The End of Soft Power." UPI, February 27.

Ferguson, Niall. 2003. "Think Again: Power." *Foreign Policy*: 18–24 (March/April).

Garon, Sheldon, and Maclachlan, Patricia L. 2006. "Introduction." In *The Ambivalent Consumer: Questioning Consumption in East Asia and the West.* Ed. Sheldon Garon and Patricia L. Maclachlan, 1–15. Ithaca, NY: Cornell University Press.

Green, Michael J., and Patrick M. Cronin, eds. 1997. *The U.S.-Japan Alliance: Past, Present and Future.* New York: Council on Foreign Relations Press.

Inda, Jonathan Xavier, and Renato Rosaldo. 2002. "Introduction: A World in Motion." In *The Anthropology of Globalization: A Reader.* Ed. Jonathan Xavier Inda and Renato Rosaldo, 1–36. Oxford: Blackwell Publishing.

Japan Foundation. 2006. "Results of the 2006 Japanese-Language Proficiency Test." http://momo.jpf.go.jp/jlpt/e/result_e.html. (accessed December 15, 2007).

McGray, Douglas. 2002. "Japan's Gross National Cool." *Foreign Policy* 130 (May–June): 44–54.

Melissen, Jan. 2005. *Wielding Soft Power: The New Public Diplomacy.* Clingendael: Netherlands Institute of International Relations.

Miyoshi, Masao. 1991. *Off Center: Power and Cultural Relations Between Japan and the United States.* Cambridge, MA: Harvard University Press.

Mulgan, Aurelia George. 2005. "Why Japan Still Matters." *Asia-Pacific Review* 12 (2): 104–21.

Noya, Javier. 2006. "The New Symbolic Power." *Place Branding* 2 (1): 53–67.

Nye, Joseph S., Jr. 1990. "The Changing Nature of World Power." *Political Science Quarterly* 105 (2): 177–92.

———. 1998. "Keeping Realism Relevant." *Foreign Policy* 111:166–67.

———. 2003. "Propaganda Isn't the Way: Soft Power." *International Herald Tribune,* January 10.

———. 2004. *Soft Power: The Means to Success in World Politics.* New York: Public Affairs.

———. 2006a. "Think Again: Soft Power." *Foreign Policy* (February). http://www.foreignpolicy.com/story/cms.php?story_id=3393.

———. 2006b. "In Mideast, the Goal Is Smart Power." Op-Ed. *Boston Globe,* August 19, p. A15.

Ogoura, Kazuo. 2006. "The Limits of Soft Power." *Japan Echo* 33 (5): 60–65.

Pempel, T.J. 1997. "Transpacific Torii: Japan and the Emerging Asian Regionalism." In *Network Power: Japan and Asia.* Ed. Peter J. Katzenstein and Takashi Shiraishi, 47–82. Ithaca, NY: Cornell University Press.

Putnam, Robert. 2001. *Bowling Alone: The Collapse and Revival of American Community.* New York: Simon and Schuster.

Rose, Richard. 2005. *Language, Soft Power and Asymmetrical Internet Communication.* Research Report No. 7. Oxford Internet Institute.

Schwartz, Frank, and Susan Pharr. 2003. *The State of Civil Society in Japan.* Cambridge, MA: Cambridge University Press.

Steger, Manfred. 2005. "From Market Globalism to Imperial Globalism: Ideology and American Power After 9/11." *Globalizations* 2 (1): 31–46.

Wolf, Eric. 1999. *Envisioning Power: Ideologies of Dominance and Crisis.* Berkeley: University of California Press.

Womack, Brantly. 2005. "Dancing Alone: A Hard Look at Soft Power." *Japan Focus.* http://japanfocus.org/products/details/1975 (accessed January 5, 2006).

I

Perception

1

Anti-Americanism in Japan

Watanabe Yasushi

Anti-Americanism is on the rise across the globe. The world's reaction to the predominance and ubiquity of the United States has exposed the multiplicity and complexity of antipathy toward the nation. It is a mixture of hatred and fascination, repulsion and attraction, present equally on the Right and on the Left, and a matter of legitimate and pressing concern to both industrial and industrializing societies in the age of globalization. Many traits Americans most revere, such as democracy, freedom, and individualism, can be construed in a negative light and encounter substantial expressions of local resistance, even as they become global standards. As various localities around the world struggle, one way or another, to make sense of this historically and culturally unique locus of the United States, the repercussions of anti-Americanism on the construction and practice of local identities bear close scrutiny. Japan, one of the closest allies of the United States, is no exception.

This chapter focuses on Japan's new anti-Americanism since the late 1990s—a new combination of nationalism, resentment against what Japanese perceive to be an isolationist United States that is ignoring Japan, and fear of American domination. I have explored the ways in which "America" is construed in recent popular literature on the United States and how it is propagated, consumed, and appropriated in contemporary Japan. My goals are to locate this phenomenon within a wider sociocultural and historical milieu and investigate its theoretical and policy implications. While Joseph Nye's accounts of Japanese perception of the United States in *Soft Power* (2004) are relatively short and positive, I aim to examine it in more depth in this chapter.

"Anti-Americanism" is used here interchangeably with, and as shorthand for, anti-American sentiment and discourse. Less coherent and tangible than an ideology, it is as vague and heterogeneous as "Orientalism," "racism," and "anti-Semitism." While mere opposition to U.S. policies and attitudes should not in itself be sufficient to constitute anti-Americanism, the term is based on the idea that "something associated with the United States, something at the core of American life, is deeply wrong and threatening to the rest of the world" (Caesar 2003, para. 3). Nye more concisely defines anti-Americanism as a "deeper rejection of American society, values, and culture" (Nye 2004, p. 38) and treats it as undermining American soft power.

Comparative and Transnational Perspectives

According to the most recent Cabinet Office (2006) poll on foreign affairs in Japan, 75.3 percent of the respondents feel "an attachment" to the United States. This figure has changed little in recent years, and the percentage is quite high when compared to that for those who feel an attachment to Russia (15.4 percent), China (34.3 percent), South Korea (48.5 percent), Southeast Asia (45.5 percent), southwest Asia (25.5 percent), Western Europe (60.3 percent), Australia and New Zealand (61.8 percent), and the Middle East (17.5 percent).

The same poll shows that 82.7 percent of the respondents regard Japan's current relationship with the United States as good. This figure has remained more or less the same in recent years, and, again, it is remarkably high when compared to the percentages of those who regard as good Japan's relations with Russia (21.0 percent), China (21.7 percent), South Korea (34.4 percent), Southeast Asia (52.3 percent), southwest Asia (37.1 percent), Western Europe (64.4 percent), Australia and New Zealand (65.8 percent), and the Middle East (25.7 percent).

The Yomiuri-Gallup polls, which have been conducted since 1978, have consistently demonstrated that Japanese respondents select the United States as the "most reliable" other country in the world. These polls indicate that the Japanese public's perception of the United States has been rather positive and stable, and that the United States holds a special status in the public consciousness of the Japanese.

According to a recent report by the Japan National Tourist Organization (2007), the United States was the most popular destination for Japanese overseas travelers until 2001. In 2000, 5 million Japanese visited the United States, while 3.6 million traveled to China (including Hong Kong), 2.5 million to South Korea, 1.2 million to Thailand, and 1 million to France. In 2002, China became the most popular destination, with 4.3 million visitors, followed by the United States (3.6 million), South Korea (2.3 million), and Thailand (1.2 million). In 2006, 3.7 million visited the United States, while 5 million traveled to China, 2.3 million to South Korea, and 1.3 million to Thailand.

According to the most recent report by the New York–based Institute of International Education (2006), the number of Japanese studying in the United States has tripled over the past two decades and stayed around 38,000–40,000 in recent years. Japanese constitute the fourth-largest population of foreign students in the United States.

According to a recent report by Japan's Ministry of Education, Culture, Sports, Science, and Technology (2006), this figure is exceedingly high when compared to the number of students from Japan studying in China (12,765), the United Kingdom (5,729), Australia (3,462), France (2,490), Germany (2,438), Taiwan (1,825), Canada (1,460), and South Korea (938); it represents about 60 percent of Japanese studying overseas.

It is worth noting that the number of students, unlike that of tourists, has remained little changed in spite of economic recession, a decrease in the number of school-age children in Japan, and the whole complex of consequences of the September 11 terrorist attacks in New York and Washington, D.C. These facts are only a few examples that illustrate the special status of the United States in terms of acceptance and permeation in Japan.

At the same time, in spite of (or perhaps because of) this special status, the United States has been a constant reference of new vocabularies in Japan, both positive and negative. In the books and articles consulted for this chapter, I encountered a multitude of words coined to depict Japanese attitudes toward the United States, including such popular terms as the following:

知米 *(chibei:* well-informed about the United States)
親米 *(shinbei:* pro-American)
好米 *(kobei:* favoring the United States)
拝米 *(haibei:* admiring the United States)

反米 *(hanbei:* anti-American)
嫌米 *(kenbei:* hating the United States)
排米 *(haibei:* rejecting the United States)
侮米 *(bubei:* despising the United States)
哀米 *(aibei:* pity for the United States)

飽米 *(hobei:* enough of the United States)
厭米 *(enbei:* weary of the United States)
倦米 *(kenbei:* tired of the United States)

恐米 *(kyobei:* fearful of the United States)
怯米 *(kyobei:* scared of the United States)

脱米 *(datsubei:* leaving the United States)
離米 *(ribei:* distancing from the United States)

従米 *(jubei:* obeying the United States)
追米 *(tsuibei:* blind obedience to the United States)

These rhetorical expressions clearly exemplify the ingenuity and struggle of the Japanese in making sense of the special status of the United States as a preeminent cultural "other." They are also evident in the sheer volume of popular literature—including a whole range of negative and provocative titles—on the United States in recent years. No other country holds such a special status in the literary imagery of the Japanese. Of particular interest to us is the locus and implication of anti-American discourse and sentiment manifested in this literary practice.

The latest survey by the Pew Global Attitudes Project (Pew Research Center for the People and the Press 2007), conducted among 45,200 people in forty-seven countries in spring 2007, reveals that discontent with the United States had grown during the previous six years.

Japan is no exception, with a favorable view dropping from 72 percent to 61 percent. Still, popular approval of the United States remains higher in Japan than in India (59 percent), South Korea (58 percent), Mexico (56 percent), Canada (55 percent), and Great Britain (51 percent), and significantly higher than in Russia (41 percent), France (39 percent), China (34 percent), Germany (30 percent), Indonesia (29 percent), Egypt (21 percent), Pakistan (15 percent), and Turkey (9 percent).

Unlike in South Korea, another longtime U.S. ally in northeast Asia, there was no boycotting of American products in Japan, and protests against U.S. military bases were far less massive and violent than elsewhere. In recent years in Japan, physical attacks against Americans, the U.S. flag, or U.S. government offices have rarely been undertaken as a collective action against the United States. The way in which Japan has expressed its anti-Americanism appears to be more indirect, subdued, and intricate.

To clarify the locus and implication of this distinctive (if not unique) feature, the following section explores the varied contexts and expressions of anti-American discourse and sentiment in contemporary Japan.

Historical Perspectives

Anti-Americanism, as articulated in literary practice in Japan, is by no means new. In 1909, for example, the historian Asakawa Kan-ichi expressed a concern that the Japanese tended to take more pleasure in pointing out U.S. shortcomings as they became more cultivated. Ten years later, the scholar and diplomat Nitobe Inazo related that there was a tendency in Japan, even among top diplomats and military officers, to despise the United States. More recently, Honma Nagayo (1995), a noted expert on U.S.-Japanese relations, in warning about the rise and spread of anti-American discourse and sentiment of late, pointed out that a sense of respect for the United States had been lost among well-educated Japanese by the time of World War I. Kamei Shunsuke (2000), another eminent Americanist, echoed Honma's concern in arguing that the dichotomy and oscillation between "拝米 (haibei: admiring the United States)" and "排米 (haibei: rejecting the United States)" has been conspicuous in the social imagery of the Japanese ever since the Meiji period.

In recent years, however, the tradition of anti-American discourse and sentiment as a mode of thinking has been reinvented in new contexts. In the late 1980s, with the unprecedented prosperity of the Japanese economy and the prolonged downturn of the U.S. economy, the idea that "we have nothing to learn from the United States anymore" flourished in Japan, and the United States was increasingly perceived as declining, decaying, and falling apart. Paralleling this was the rise of a self-congratulatory tone in public discourse, including the popular literary genre of *Nihonjin-ron* (theories of "Japaneseness") (Watanabe 2000). While things that were perceived to be unique to Japan and its people were remembered, invented, and mobilized in making sense of this new development, all that was conjectured as characteristic of the United States was rejected: American policies on crime, diplomatic affairs, the economy, education, energy, the environment, family, finance, human rights, infrastructure, the military, technology, transportation, and welfare were denounced; news reports on crime, drug use, guns, lawsuits, materialism, me-ism, moral corruption, poverty, racial discrimination, and individual bankruptcy were negative in tone. The United States increasingly became the model of how not to be, rather than an example to emulate.

The image of the United States was further damaged by a series of "Japan-bashing" and *gaiatsu* (outside pressure) incidents in the late 1980s and early 1990s. In particular, sharp American criticism of Japan's unwillingness to contribute troops and its "checkbook diplomacy" at the time of the Persian Gulf War intensified anti-American discourse and sentiment and stiffened Japan's national pride as a sovereign state.

It was during this period that the expression "嫌米 (*kenbei:* hating the United States)" was coined to describe the new feelings of the Japanese toward America. The word became so rampant as to appear in *Gendai yogo no kiso chishiki* (The encyclopedia of contemporary words) in 1992. The *New York Times* (October 16, 1991) reported, "Japan has coined a new word to reflect their sentiment toward America: *kenbei.*" The article described the word as meaning a "dislike of the United States. . . . There is a growing feeling that on trade issues, the United States is bullying Japan arrogantly making demands on every trivial matter that does not comply with the American standard of justice. . . . Those on the U.S. side are still leaning heavily on Japan, never reflecting on their own country's shortcomings. . . . And those on the Japanese side are still bowing before the American demands, as if doing so was Japan's fate."

In 1991, then–secretary of state James Baker stated in Tokyo, "I want to leave no doubt that the United States is fully committed to working with Japan and others in the region to shape a new era in world affairs and a new order in Asia. Neither of us can afford the narrow self-indulgence of bashing or *kenbei.* Neither of us will prosper in a world that retreats into protectionism" (Baker 1991).

Mid-1990s to Early 2001

The image of the United States as bashing and pressuring Japan gradually faded as the economic conditions of the two countries began to reverse themselves in the mid-1990s. Instead, the perception of the United States as the sole winner in the new world order of globalization in terms of culture, finance, information, military, politics, science, and technology became the dominant one. The ingenuity of U.S. society and its policies were idealized and held up as examples for Japan to emulate, while at the same time a discourse on its "hidden and dark motivations" was constructed and appropriated to account for Japan's failure—its "lost decade."

It was during this period that such sensational expressions as *dai ni no haisen* (second defeat), *zokkoku* (tributary country), and *gojyu ichibanme no shu* (fifty-first state of the United States) appeared in public discourse to describe what Japan was all about, and that books with such provocative titles as *Nihon kaimetsu* (The destruction of Japan) (Mizuno 1998), *Nihon wa naze senso ni ni-do maketaka* (Why Japan lost the war twice) (Omori 1998), *Nihon sai-haiboku* (The re-defeat of Japan) (Tawara and

Yamada 1998), and "*Nihon-nuki*" *gemu* (Playing the "without Japan" game) (Hamada 1999) crowded bookstore shelves.

The United States was portrayed as the hegemonic super- or hyperpower, which engaged with the world unilaterally, using a double standard. Washington's refusal to release funds for the United Nations and to ratify the Kyoto Protocol, the Comprehensive Test Ban Treaty, the Anti-Ballistic Missile Treaty, the International Criminal Court, and the Landmine Ban Treaty were denounced; "globalization" was apprehended as mere Americanization of money, mass media, and military power. Various national publications began discussing the rise of anti-American discourse and sentiment under such titles as "'Kenbei' sainen" (Revival of "*kenbei*"), "Hanbei-ron ni hi ga tsuita" (Anti-American discourse ignited), and "Kenbei kanjo dehajimeru" (*Kenbei* sentiment has come to the fore).

In January 1998, shortly after his appointment as ambassador to Tokyo, Thomas Foley (1998) remarked:

> While I was preparing to come here, I read a great deal about current attitudes, paying special attention to what the Japanese were writing and saying about the United States. I was, of course, familiar with the term "Japan-bashing." This unpleasant phrase usually surfaced in commentaries and discussions of particularly acrimonious trade disputes. However, the more I read, the more I came across the term "Japan passing." Distinguished commentators and journalists and essayists and editorialists were writing lengthy pieces expressing regret that the United States was abandoning Japan for China. Their argument went something like this: America could see that its future market in Asia was in China and therefore increasingly turned its attention to China at the expense of its relationship with Japan. Nothing could be further from the truth.

Yet when President Clinton did not stop over in Japan on his way back from China in June 1998, a feeling spread that the United States was practicing a policy of "Japan passing" (or "Japan nothing"), failing to pay due respect to the United States' longtime ally in the Asia-Pacific region.

This discourse of crisis, saturated with both self-torture and anti-American sentiment, provided a platform from which anti-American conservatism gained ground in public discourse. Author and politician Ishihara Shintaro, who had earlier coauthored sensational books with Morita Akio (1989), Eto Jun (1991), and Mahathir Mohamad (1994), continued to publish books with such provocative titles as *Sensen fukoku "NO" to ieru Nihon keizai* (Declaration of war—A Japanese economy that can say "NO") in 1998, *"Amerika shinko" o suteyo* (Let's discard "admiration for the United States") in 2000, *Katsu Nihon* (The Japan that wins) with Tawara Soichiro in 2000, and *Eien nare, Nihon* (Forever, Japan) with Nakasone Yasuhiro in 2001. At the same time, conservative intellectuals such as Hasegawa Michiko, Nishibe Susumu, and Saeki Keishi sharpened their critique of the United States by reexamining such notions as "capitalism," "democracy," "equal opportunity," "freedom," "free trade," "human rights," "individualism," and "modernity," as these concepts are interpreted and implemented in contemporary America. During the Cold War, Japanese conservatives, with the exception of Far Right activists, had been mostly pro-American. This was based on their opposition to socialism and communism; anti-Americanism had more to do with liberals in academia, the mass media, labor unions, peace and human rights groups, and activists on the Far Left. Thus, in the 1990s, the rise of anti-American conservatives was a conspicuous development.

Popular conservative monthly magazines such as *Seiron* and *Shokun,* which reach an average of 80,000–100,000 people, have reported a marked increase in the number of younger readers (those in their twenties and thirties) and women. *Sapio,* another conservative monthly magazine, which reaches an average of 120,000 readers, has targeted the younger generation and now reports that two-thirds of its audience are in their twenties and thirties. This success is attributed partly to *Goman-izum sengen* (Declaration of arrogance), an elaborate and chauvinistic eight-page cartoon series authored by Kobayashi Yoshinori, which constantly makes negative references to the United States. The total sales of its collected six volumes reached 2 million by 2001.

As a list of books and magazines from this period indicates, titles became rather sensational, even chauvinistic, and they were often expected to be so in order to appeal to public sentiment and reach out to a wider audience. The cover of the international edition of *Newsweek* for January 31, 2000, for example, had a photo of a fat cowboy in an American flag T-shirt with his belly hanging out, with the headline "Honk If You Hate America," and the subtitle was "Buddy or Bully? Rethinking the Role of the United States." *Newsweek*'s Japanese edition (February 2, 2000) translated the headline as "Amerika ni igi ari" (An objection to the United States!) and the subtitle as "Sekai-ju kara kirawareru goin de migatte na cho-taikoku" (The forcible and selfish superpower hated all around the world). The cover story, "The Superpower They Love to Hate" was translated as "Sekai-ju ni hiroagaru 'kenbei' no uzu" (A storm of "*kenbei*" spreading worldwide).

A 1998 TV commercial for Suntory's canned coffee, whose ads were known for using the word "*gatsun*" to describe situations involving a forceful impact, won immediate popularity. As Todd Holden (2001) described it:

> Salarymen sit in a smoky bar after a long day of work. One man, wiping his hands and face with a moist towelette, rants: "All this talk about globalization, etcetera . . . but Japan is made a fool of by the world. . . . Once and for all we have to speak out gatsun."
> He pushes his glasses atop his head. "*If it were me, I would say it!*" He wipes his face vigorously with the towelette: "*I'd say it, gatsun.*" Superimposed over his image is his personal data in white letters: *Itoh Masayuki, 37 years, corporate man.* The frame fades to black and white, freezes. Action resumes with Itoh throwing his towel down in disgust and declaring: "*Because I'm that type!*"
> Cut to an extreme close-up of the towelette—now lying on someone's knee. As the camera pans back, we find the knee belongs to Bill Clinton—or, at least, an actor of amazing likeness. He is seated opposite Itoh-san in a room that looks very much like the Oval Office. Surrounding the two are translators, advisors and secret service agents. The presidential look-alike flicks the towel off his leg with disdain and says in Clinton's distinctive drawl: "*So! I'd like to hear your honest opinions. . . .*" To the swell of mariachi music Itoh gulps hard, stares vacantly at the President, and tries to muster that suddenly elusive "*gatsun.*"

This TV commercial was initially scheduled to air until the end of 1998. It continued to air for three extra months, however, due to enthusiastic public reception, and it was awarded a gold medal by the All Japan Radio and Television Commercial Confederation in 1999.

Many editors and scholars whom I interviewed shared the observation of Iokibe Makoto (2000), an authority on Japanese diplomatic history, that criticism of the United States became increasingly conspicuous in the 1990s even among the bureaucrats, business leaders, journalists, scholars, and writers who had been known as 知米 (*chibei:* well-informed about the United States).

It was also pointed out that, even if "anti-Americanism" is too strong a word, the locus of public interest has gradually shifted from the United States to elsewhere, especially to Asian countries. My interviews revealed that American studies is no longer a popular major at colleges; that private foundations are more eager to support Asia-related programs than those focused on U.S.-Japanese relations; that television variety programs tend to focus more on Asia and Africa at the expense of the United States; and that emphasis on the alliance with the United States is often taken as a pro forma mannerism. A freer flow of people, goods, money, and information across Asia is believed to be solidifying an imagined community of Asia, whether invented or rediscovered, especially among the younger generation, and, thus, to be contributing to a relative decline of interest in, or preoccupation with, the United States.

September 11, 2001, and After

The results of public opinion polls about the 2003 war in Iraq differed significantly from one survey to another and fluctuated according to the stage of operations. Shortly after the initial strikes at the end of March, however, 59 percent (*Asahi Shinbun,* March 22), 63.6 percent (*Sankei Shinbun,* March 24), and 65 percent (*Mainichi Shinbun,* March 22) of the respondents disapproved of the U.S. attacks. Considering the fact that, in a poll conducted by *Asahi Shinbun,* the rate of disapproval of the war in Afghanistan was 43 percent at the same stage of operations in 2001, it can be inferred that the Iraq war has further eroded the image of the United States in Japan. Antiwar demonstrations, though modest in size and action, took place in local cities across the nation, at the American embassy in Tokyo, and at consulates in other cities.

The discourse on the United States has become more provocative since the war in Afghanistan. Books on the "neoconservatives" in the Bush administration, the imperialist conspiracy of the United States, and the intertwined fate of Japan are plentiful. As international affairs specialist Nishizaki Fumiko (2003) described it, "The derogatory practice of explaining American behavior as analogous to that of cowboys and sheriffs in Western film, once thought to be too banal and simplistic, reemerged in public discourse. Apparently, the temptation to see the United States as a reckless, brash youth was too strong to resist" (p. 64).

The observation of Moises Naim (2003), editor of *Foreign Policy,* about "lite Anti-Americanism" holds true in the Japanese context: "Unfortunately, it has become all too easy for those who disagree with specific U.S. policies to believe and disseminate the worst possible assumptions about the malicious nature, dark motivations, and hidden agendas of the United States—including horrible falsehoods" (p. 96).

Even some highly academic works by respected scholars are accompanied by provocative titles. Mori Koichi's book (2003) on religious fundamentalism in the United States was titled, at the request of its publisher, *"Joji Busshu" no atama no nakami* (The contents of the head of "George Bush"), with a scornful cartoon of the president on the cover. Nojima Hidekatsu's book (2003) examining the nature of American literature is entitled *Han-Amerika-ron* (Anti-American discourse), although it has little to do with anti-Americanism per se. When a Japanese edition of *Courrier International* was founded in the autumn of 2005, its publisher (Kodansha) ran a full-page advertisement in major newspapers with the headline "Amerika dake ga 'sekai' deshohka?" (Is America the only "world"?), declaring that it seeks to feature news from other countries.

Anti-Americanism in this period was closely related to anti-Bush feeling. According to a poll of thirty-five countries conducted by global research company GlobeScan Inc. and the University of Maryland, mainly in summer 2004, 43 percent of Japanese respondents backed John Kerry, compared with just 23 percent for George Bush, for the presidential elections in 2004.

It is worth noting that the Japanese Association for American Studies selected "The Loci of Anti-Americanism" as the theme of a symposium at its annual meeting in 2003, and featured "Images of 'America' in Conflict" in the *Japanese Journal of American Studies* (2003) published by the Japanese Association for American Studies.

Of additional interest in this period is that commentary on the United States has been imported from overseas. Such publications as *Addicted to War* (2002) by Joel Andreas, *9–11* (2001) by Noam Chomsky, *The Eagle's Shadow* (2002) by Mark Hertsgaard, *Stupid White Men* (2002) and *Dude, Where Is My Country?* (2003) by Michael Moore, *Anti-Americanism* (2003) by Jean-Francois Revel, and *Why Do People Hate America?* (2002) by Ziauddin Sardar and Merryl Wyn Davies have been quickly translated. Moore's *Stupid White Men* sold nearly 180,000 copies in the six months after its Japanese translation appeared in October 2002. The film Moore directed, *Bowling for Columbine,* attracted almost 20,000 people across the nation in less than two months. "Lite anti-Americanism" can thus be externally confirmed in the age of globalization.

The confrontation between anti-American conservatives (*hanbei hoshu*) and their pro-American counterparts (*shinbei hoshu*) has become intense over the issue of the direction of Japanese diplomacy. Anti-American conservatives such as Kobayashi Yoshinori, Hasegawa Michiko, Nishibe Susumu, Saeki Keishi, and Soejima Takahiko call for a true restoration of Japanese sovereignty and criticize Japan's blind compliance with U.S. policies. Pro-American conservatives, including Agawa Naoyuki, Okazaki Hisahiko, Takubo Tadae, and Yagi Hidetsugu, warn of the futility of anti-Americanism and see cooperation with the United States to be in Japan's best interests. With anti-American conservatives more grounded in the humanities and their pro-American counterparts in policy, the annual policy publication *Nihon no ronten 2003* (Issues for Japan 2003) listed their debate as one of the major issues in contemporary Japan.

Even the Atarashii Rekishi Kyokasho o Tsukuru Kai (Association for History Textbook Reform), a group of conservative intellectuals aiming at correcting the liberal-leftist or "self-flagellating" biases in history textbooks from an ethno-nationalistic perspective, are reported to be split over the legitimacy of U.S. operations in Iraq. Nishio Kanji, a theoretical pillar of the group and a longtime critic of the United States, has turned more sympathetic to the United States, a stance that his collaborators Kobayashi Yoshinori and Nishibe Susumu view as compromising and self-defeating.

Closely related to this phenomenon is that the discourse of anti-American conservatives resonates with that of liberals on the Left in their antipathy to U.S. hegemony and Japan's blind obedience to it as a client state. While liberals seek a pacifist world based on multilateral or international cooperation and cosmopolitanism, their understanding of the status quo has much in common with that of anti-American conservatives. Shiomi Takaya, who founded the Red Army Faction in August 1969 (and was imprisoned for twenty years), today insists on the restoration of nation and state as the basic units of human existence and defends patriotism as a breakwater against U.S.-led globalization (Shiomi 2001). Although this is not a popular sentiment on the contemporary Left, the patriotic Left is finding common cause with conservatives, especially those in the anti-American wing. It is worth noting, in this regard, that Kimura Mitsuhiro, a Far Right activist, joined a September 11 anniversary press conference in 2002 with such liberal leftists as Oda Makoto and Chibana Shoichi to issue a statement opposing the U.S. strikes against Iraq.

Theoretical Implications

Whether it is applauded or criticized, the United States has long held a special status in the public consciousness of the Japanese. No other country has replaced it as a preeminent cultural "other." Constructing and appropriating "America" as a primary reference, a variety of Japanese individuals and institutions have struggled to make sense of where they came from, what they are, and where they are going. Such soul-searching, whether self-congratulatory, self-critical, or self-awakening, could easily be framed in a "national," if not necessarily "nationalistic," discourse, as is most conspicuous in the popular genre of *Nihonjin-ron* (Watanabe 2000).

In the mid-1990s, however, the role of the United States in the process of globalization became so hegemonic that the conventional dichotomy between the "conservative (pro-American)" and the "liberal (anti-American)" has become increasingly more complex. With the rise of anti-American conservative discourse in the late 1980s and the spread of anti-American discourse in the post-9/11 period, it has become more legitimate to add another axis—pro-American or anti-American—in order to better understand the politico-ideological map of Japan today, and this is especially so for those concerned with U.S.-Japanese relations.

Pulitzer Prize–winning journalist and author Thomas Freidman (1999) proposed two axes—the social-safety-net/let-them-eat-cake axis, and the separatist/integrationist axis—as a way to understand the national politics of the United States in the 1990s. Here the social safety net corresponds to liberals such as Bill Clinton and Dick Gephardt, the let them eat cake to conservatives such as Newt Gingrich and Ross Perot, the separatist to anti-globalists such as Dick Gephardt and Ross Perot, and the integrationist to pro-globalists such as Clinton and Gingrich. In other words, Clinton was closer to Gephardt on issues of welfare and social security, but much closer to Gingrich on those of free trade. As globalization is often identified with Americanization in Japan, we may be able to replace the separatist/integrationist with the anti-American/pro-American axis and cross it with the liberal/conservative axis. In the further scrutiny of Japan from an international and comparative perspective, one of the significant repercussions of Americanization may lie in the reconfiguration of Japan's politico-ideological map or cultural politics on the domestic, national level. This is particularly the case with the conservative, and what it means to be "conservative" has become a focus of intellectual and political reflection in today's public discourse.

With the prevalence of anti-American sentiment and discourse on both sides of the political spectrum, "pro-American" can be easily taken as blind compliance with or obedience to U.S. policies, and such words as "従米" (*jubei:* obeying the United States) and "追米" (*tsuibei:* blind obedience to the United States) have the same negative connotation today as the term "liberal" does in the United States.

At the same time, with the proliferation of "national" discourse (including nationalistic or patriotic stances) on both sides of the political spectrum, it has become more difficult to justify a pacifist prescription based on multilateral or international cooperation and cosmopolitanism. This is especially true today, when Japan could face a series of tensions with China and North and South Korea.

The distinction between the two major parties, the Liberal Democratic Party (LDP) and the Democratic Party of Japan (DPJ), is growing less clear-cut in this regard, when some DPJ politicians (e.g., Maehara Seiji, Nagashima Akihisa, and Noda Yoshihiko) sound far more hawkish than their liberal LDP counterparts in their perceptions of history, security, and defense. The traditional carriers of pacifist and cosmopolitan agendas, the Japanese Communist Party and the Social Democratic Party, have significantly lost their seats in the Diet since the end of the Cold War and the introduction of the small-constituency system in 1996.

Policy Implications

Considering the positive and stable public perception of the United States, shown by the public opinion surveys cited above, we should not overestimate these transfigurations of public discourse, especially those that take place primarily in literary circles. It is even possible to reject them entirely, as some respondents actually did in my interviews, as fictitious constructions of the mass media. Yet we should not underestimate the efficacy of the mass media in the construction of reality in the age of postmodern politics.

This is especially so when populist images and sound bites are used to undermine the existing state of society, and the temptation to oversimplify the complexity of social realities is ever strong. Since the mid-1980s, news programs have become more entertaining and sensational—*News Station, Sunday Projects,* and various "wide shows" or info-variety/infotainment-variety shows in the morning, in the afternoon, in the evening, and at night.

Neither should we forget that the mass media, while shaping public opinion, are also shaped by public opinion and cannot maintain their influence if they become too far detached from the sentiment and disposition of society. Anti-Americanism is a minority view in the polls, yet it is a vocal minority view that has the potential to resonate more widely than its minority status would suggest and thus to inform the policy-making process. As such, those concerned with future U.S.-Japanese relations need to regard it seriously.

Currently, anti-American sentiment and discourse appear to have become less legitimate amid the ongoing tensions with North Korea (e.g., kidnapping, missile and nuclear tests) and with South Korea and China (e.g., territory disputes, history issues, textbooks, war memories). These frictions, while sensitizing Japanese nationalism, have made the Japanese public recognize the indispensability and advantage of the U.S. presence in Japan and East Asia at large.

The heightened nationalism has nurtured a political environment in which the current Japanese prime minister, Abe Shinzo, can proudly declare that he will revise the constitution. The constitutional revision under the leadership of Abe, if ever realized, would lead to Japan's discarding a pillar of its postwar development—self-restraint in military activities—that has helped the nation gain trust and a respected position in the international community, especially in northeast Asia.

On the one hand, the revision is considered to be a welcome change by the United States in order to strengthen the security alliance between the two countries, including the exercise of the right of "collective self-defense" and the implementation of "transformation" of the U.S. military. On the other hand, Abe, calling for a "departure from the postwar regime," does not hide his dislike of the war-renouncing constitution. He views with disdain the core part of the preamble of the constitution, which sets forth Japan's determination to "preserve our security and existence, trusting in the justice and faith of the peace-loving peoples of the world." He calls it a degrading "signed deed of apology (*wabi jomon*)" from Japan to the Allied powers.

Abe has been a strong supporter of former prime minister Koizumi Jun-ichiro's visits to Yasukuni Shrine. (Abe himself paid a secret visit to the shrine in April 2006.) Koizumi's visits triggered a series of protests and anti-Japan demonstrations in China and South Korea (which, in turn, further reinforced and justified Koizumi's strong support for, and reliance on, the United States). The visits also raised concerns in the United States, not only as destabilizing to the East Asia region, in which the United States has a great political stake, but also as jeopardizing the very foundation of U.S.-Japanese relations in the post–World War II period.

Some hawkish Japanese politicians have begun breaking the long-standing taboo against mentioning the nuclear armament of Japan, which could undermine the principle of the U.S. nuclear umbrella and thus upset many American politicians on a bipartisan level. The U.S. House of Representatives, however, began debate on House Resolution 121 in spring 2007, calling on the Japanese government to apologize and provide accurate public education about the wartime abuse of "comfort women."

These developments well demonstrate the difficulty of being a "conservative" in today's Japan, supporting the nation's own sovereignty while maintaining close ties with the United States. A political leader is expected to maneuver within Japanese politics so that independence and dependence do not look mutually exclusive. This process demands a high level of political deliberation in cooperating with the United States in its war against international terrorism and the transformation of its military, and improving relations with China and South Korea, which deteriorated during Koizumi's tenure.

It would be rather perilous and tragic if support for a U.S. policy were automatically dismissed as an act of *jubei* or *tsuibei* and if, in turn, opposition to the United States were intrinsically to have populist appeal. We must remember that the United States has been a campaign issue in elections in Germany, South Korea, Pakistan, and South American countries during the past several years, and that the fundamentalist terrorism of Aum Shinrikyo in Tokyo in 1995 was undertaken as an anti-American crusade.

The diffusion of anti-Americanism could deter the United States from active engagement in East Asia, a result that would be extremely detrimental when U.S. engagement is indispensable and irreplaceable in coping with regional and security issues. "Active U.S. engagement may not always be the best recipe for international problems," as Naim (2003) argued, "but it is often the only one available" (p. 95). The ascendancy of anti-Americanism in the region is a problem for the United States, not only strategically but also economically, since one-third of U.S. trade is conducted in the region.

Naim (2003), echoing Nye's famous thesis on the paradox of American power (2002), cogently spells out the cost of Washington's disdain and carelessness about the negative effects of "lite anti-Americanism" around the world today:

> The United States can invade Iraq without the blessing of the United Nations. But its military needs bases in other countries, its counterterrorist agencies need the help of other intelligence services (even those of France), its financial regulators need to work closely with regulators abroad, and its nation-builders in Afghanistan, and in Iraq, need the help and the money of other countries. . . . The United States will soon discover that it depends on the goodwill of other governments as it does on the lethal efficacy of its military to achieve its international goals. In turn, that goodwill depends heavily on the mood and attitudes of domestic constituencies at home and around the globe. That is why the worldwide ascendancy of lite anti-Americanism is a dangerous trend. And not only for Americans. (p. 95)

According to the most recent Yomiuri-Gallup poll (December 2006), 53 percent of Japanese said the U.S.-Japanese relationship was in good shape. Their optimism was shared on the other side of the Pacific, where 61 percent of Americans said ties were good. However, while 76 percent of Americans said they trusted Japan, only 41 percent of Japanese said they trusted the United States. Forty-seven percent of Japanese said they did not trust the United States, and more Japanese respondents each year have said they do not trust the United States consecutively for the past four years. Only 21 percent of Americans said they did not trust Japan.

The Kyodo-AP poll on U.S.-Japan Attitudes (July 2005) also revealed that 52 percent of Japanese, up by 26 percent since the end of the Gulf War in 1991, did not trust the United States, whereas 59 percent of Americans trusted Japan. For polls focused exclusively on bilateral relations, the overall results remain positive and stable. Yet these polls clearly demonstrate that Japanese respondents are not as positive and affirmative toward the United States as their American counterparts are toward Japan. While tensions and conflicts are often the flip side of a close relationship, we should not overlook this obvious disparity, even when the official, intergovernmental relations between the two countries are boasted to be at their best in history.

Much of the debate in Japan on whether to revise the constitution and how to participate in an "East Asian Community" will depend partly on how Japanese perceive and understand the United States. At the same time, the outcome of the U.S. efforts against international terrorism and for the promotion of freedom and democracy will, to a great extent, depend on how foreign countries, including Japan, view and support the United States. Fouad Ajami (2003), an expert on Middle Eastern issues as well as an outspoken supporter of the Iraq war, argued that "the United States need not worry about hearts and minds in foreign lands" because "in the age of Pax Americana, it is written, and fated . . . that plotters and preachers shall rail against the United States—in whole sentences of good American slang" (p. 61). Reality is not that simple—for Americans or for Japanese.

References

Ajami, Fouad. 2003. "The Falseness of Anti-Americanism." *Foreign Policy*, No. 138, pp. 52–61, September–October 2003. Washington D.C.: Carnegie Endowment for International Peace.

Baker, James. 1991. "The U.S. and Japan: Global Partners in a Pacific Community." Speech given at the Japan Institute for International Affairs, Tokyo. http://dosfan.lib.uic.edu/ERC/briefing/dispatch/1991/html/Dispatchv2n046.html (accessed June 22, 2007).

Cabinet Office. Government of Japan. 2006. *Gaiko ni kansuru yoron chosa* (Public opinion poll on foreign affairs). Tokyo: Cabinet Office, Government of Japan.

Caesar, James. 2003. "A Genealogy of Anti-Americanism." *The Public Interest.* http://www.travelbrochuregraphics.com/extra/a_genealogy_of_antiamericanism.htm (accessed June 22, 2007).

Foley, Thomas. 1998. "Remarks." Speech given at the America-Japan Society, Tokyo. http://tokyo.usembassy.gov/wwwh2662.html (accessed June 22, 2007).

Friedman, Thomas. 1999. *The Lexus and the Olive Tree.* New York: Farrar, Straus, and Giroux.

Gendai yogo no kiso chishiki, 1992 (Encyclopedia of contemporary words, 1992). Tokyo: Jiyu Kokuminsha.

Hamada, Kazuyuki. 1999. *"Nihon-nuki" gemu* (Playing the "without Japan" game). Tokyo: PHP Kenkyujyo.

Holden, Todd. 2001. "Resignification and Cultural Re/Production in Japanese Television Commercials." *Journal of Media and Culture* 4 (2). http://journal.media-culture.org.au/0104/japtele.php (accessed June 22, 2007).

Honma, Nagayo. 1995. "Chishiki-jin ni Miru 'Kenbei' no Keifu" (Genealogy of *"kenbei"* among intellectuals). *Ronza.* Tokyo: Asahi Shinbun.

Iokibe Makoto. 2000. "Omoi o kyoyu suru ryo-kokumin" (Two nations sharing thoughts). In *Yomiuri Shinbun, Yoron chosa ni miru Nichibei kankei* (U.S.-Japan relations as seen through public opinion polls). Tokyo: Yomiuri Shinbun.

Institute of International Education. 2006. *Open Doors 2006: Report on International Educational Exchange.* http://opendoors.iienetwork.org/?p=89251 (accessed June 22, 2007).

Ishihara Shintaro. 1998. *Sensen fukoku "NO" to ieru Nihon keizai* (Declaration of war: The Japanese economy that can say "NO"). Tokyo: Kobunsha.

———. 2000. *"Amerika shinko" o suteyo* (Let's discard "admiration for the United States"). Tokyo: Kobunsha.

Ishihara Shintaro and Eto Jun. 1991. *Danko "NO" to ieru Nihon* (The Japan that firmly can say "NO"). Tokyo: Kobunsha.

Ishihara Shintaro and Mohamad, Mahathir. 1994. *"NO" to ieru Ajia* (The Asia that can say "NO"). Tokyo: Kobunsha.

Ishihara Shintaro, and Morita Akio. 1989. *"NO" to ieru Nihon* (The Japan that can say "NO"). Tokyo: Kobunsha.

Ishihara Shintaro and Nakasone Yasuhiro. 2001. *Eien nare, Nihon* (Forever, Japan). Tokyo: PHP Kenkyujo.

Ishihara Shintaro and Tawara Soichiro. 2000. *Katsu Nihon* (The Japan that wins). Tokyo: Bungei Shunju.

Japanese Association for American Studies. 2003. *The Japanese Journal of American Studies,* No. 14.

Japan National Tourist Organization. 2007. *Visitor Arrivals and Japanese Overseas Travelers.* http://www.jnto.go.jp/jpn/downloads/070412stat.pdf (accessed June 22, 2007).

Kamei Shunsuke. 2000. *Amerika Bunka to Nihon* (American culture and Japan). Tokyo: Iwanami Shoten.

Kyodo-AP poll. *Yomiuri Shimbun.* July 24, 2005. Tokyo: Yomiuri Shimbun.

Ministry of Education, Culture, Sports, Science and Technology. 2006. *Wagakuni no Ryugakusei Seido no Gaiyo* (Summary of the system for students studying abroad in Japan). http://www.mext.go.jp/a_menu/koutou/ryugaku/06082503/001.pdf (accessed June 22, 2007).

Mizuno, Takanori. 1998. *Nihon kaimetsu* (The destruction of Japan). Tokyo: Tokuma shobo.

Mori Koichi. 2003. *"Johji Busshu" no atama no nakami* (The contents of the head of "George Bush"). Tokyo: Kodansha-bunko.

Naim, Moises. 2003. "The Perils of Lite Anti-Americanism." *Foreign Policy,* No. 136, pp. 95–96. May–June 2003. Washington D.C.: Carnegie Endowment for International Peace.

Nihon no ronten 2003 (Issues for Japan 2003). 2003. Tokyo: Bungei Shunju.

Nishizaki Fumiko. 2003. "A Global Superpower or a Model of Democracy?" *Journal of American Studies,* No. 14, pp. 49–68. Tokyo: The Japanese Association of American Studies.

Nojima Hidekatsu. 2003. *Han-Amerika-ron* (Anti-American discourse). Tokyo: Nanundo.

Nye, Joseph. 2002. *The Paradox of American Power.* New York: Oxford University Press.

———. 2004. *Soft Power: The Means to Success in World Politics.* New York: Public Affairs.

Omori Minoru. 1998. *Nihon wa naze senso ni ni-do maketaka* (Why Japan lost the war twice). Tokyo: Chuo-koron-sha.

Pew Research Center for the People and the Press. 2007. "Global Unease with Major World Powers." http://pewglobal.org/reports/display.php?ReportID=256 (accessed June 28, 2007).

Shiomi Takaya. 2001. *Saraba Sekigun-ha watashi no kofuku-ron* (Farewell to the Red Army: My ideas of happiness). Tokyo: Okura Shuppan.

Tawara Soichiro and Yamada Atsushi. 1998. *Nihon sai-haiboku* (The re-defeat of Japan). Tokyo: Bungei-shunju.

Watanabe, Yasushi. 2000. "Japan Through the Looking-Glass: American Influences on the Politics of Cultural Identity in Post-War Japan." *Passages: Journal of Transnational and Transcultural Studies,* pp. 21–36, Vol. 2, No. 1. Leiden: Brill.

Yomiuri-Gallup poll. *Yomiuri Shimbun.* December 16, 2006. Tokyo: Yomiuri Shimbun.

2

Japan's Image Problem and the Soft Power Solution

The JET Program as Cultural Diplomacy

David L. McConnell

Although Japan achieved what is arguably the most dramatic economic turnaround in the twentieth century, its image problem in the world persists. To be sure, the rise of China, coupled with Japan's prolonged recession in the 1990s, has shifted international scrutiny away from Japan's trade practices. Moreover, Japan's constitutional rejection of military aggression, its reputation as a politically stable and safe society, and the recent increase in its popular culture exports constitute an attractive combination of soft power resources. Try as it might, however, Japan has not been able to shake its image as an insular society.

This is the gist of Nye's (2004) argument with respect to Japan. Nye went on to note that even though Japan's soft power has increased since the 1980s, it is limited by residual suspicion that lingers abroad, especially in Asian countries. In addition, Japan faces serious demographic challenges, and its language is not widely spoken. Nye concluded that Japan, having reinvented itself twice—after the Meiji Revolution and after World War II—needs a third cultural makeover; not an impossible task, but a difficult one.

This chapter examines a high-profile effort to achieve that goal: the Japanese government's flagship program to "open up" Japanese society and to change its image abroad. The larger goal of this chapter is to use the Japan Exchange and Teaching (JET) Program as a window on the process by which the state wields soft power and thus to answer a broad set of questions about the role of perception and context in the state's promotion of soft power. Is "the state" best viewed as a monolithic entity or as the site of competing interests? Can government-initiated reforms produce unexpected results outside the framework of the state? What happens when a disconnect exists between public diplomacy and the "product" that is being advertised? Do consumers of soft power differentiate between attraction to culture and attraction to the policies of the state? Finally, can long-term investments in soft power through educational exchange pay dividends, and if so, what kind and for whom?

Origins of the JET Program: The Soft Power Antidote

The proposal for the JET Program grew out of a dilemma faced by Japanese policy makers in the mid-1980s. In spite of its considerable economic accomplishments, Japan continued to suffer from an acute image problem. Japanese officials were under intense pressure from the United States and Europe to reduce the trade surplus and to dismantle the formal and informal barriers to foreign investment in Japan. In the educational sphere, in spite of positive attention from some U.S. academics and policy makers, schools continued to be criticized for their inflexibility. Media reports focused on Ministry of Education officials who promoted nationalistic textbooks, "returnee children" who were forced to give up the cognitive and interactive styles they had acquired abroad, and teachers and students who studied English for six years but could not speak the language. Though some of these reports perpetuated stereotypes, others could not be dismissed so lightly.

At a time, then, when pluralist nations around the world were struggling to integrate their ethnically diverse populations, Japan's government was trying to solve a problem of precisely the opposite order: to "create" diversity and to acquaint its insulated people with foreigners at the level of face-to-face interaction. One solution was to drop thousands of college graduates from primarily Western countries into secondary schools and local government offices all over the nation—a soft power antidote to the friction and misunderstandings created by the projection of Japan's economic power into the global arena.

Conceived during the height of the U.S.-Japanese trade war in the mid-1980s, the proposal for the JET Program was first presented as a "gift" to the American delegation at the "Ron-Yasu" (American president Ronald Reagan and Japanese prime minister Yasuhiro Nakasone) summit in 1986. It was a classic example of what Aurelia George (1991, p. 7) has called "package diplomacy," whereby Japanese negotiators present a plan that may be tangential at best to American demands but nonetheless demonstrates their good intentions. At considerable expense, the Japanese government would invite young college graduates (hereafter, assistant language teachers, or ALTs) from the United States and several other English-speaking countries "to foster international perspectives by promoting international exchange at local levels as well as intensifying foreign language education."[1]

More than two decades later, with an annual budget of approximately a half billion dollars and participants numbering about 5,500 a year from more than forty countries, the JET Program still stands as a key pillar in a top-down effort to create "mass internationalization." Noting that it eclipses in magnitude even such highly regarded programs as the Fulbright Program and the Peace Corps, Japanese officials have proclaimed the JET Program one of the greatest initiatives undertaken since World War II related to the field of human and cultural relations. Indeed, as the chapters by Agawa (Chapter 13) and Kondo (Chapter 11) in this volume demonstrate, current and former Japanese diplomats continue to think quite highly of the JET Program.

At first glance, the JET Program seems to be a noteworthy case of the government going against the grain of a long history of tightly regulating the flow of people across its borders. Yet a closer inspection reveals that Japan's interaction with the outside world can be characterized as a series of pendulum swings, with each era of openness followed by a period of conservative reaction (Goodman 1990). Anxiety about the loss of native culture grew sharply in the period following the wholesale borrowing from Chinese culture in the seventh to ninth centuries, for example. Conversely, the more than two centuries of seclusion during the *sakoku* period (roughly 1600–1868) was followed by a fervor for Western things and a desire to showcase Japan's culture to the world. Within a decade after the Meiji Restoration, Japan imported approximately 3,000 "hired foreigners" (*oyatoi gaikokujin*), a remarkable historical precedent to the JET Program. Moreover, in 1873, a full 1 percent of the national budget was spent on exhibitions of Japanese culture at the World Expo in Vienna. There is nothing new about the state trying to link Japan up with the rest of the world.

What is new, however, is the changed world context, and the JET Program provides a useful lens for examining the possibilities and the pitfalls inherent in a top-down state intervention to shape international perception. In *Importing Diversity* (McConnell 2000), I wrote about the JET Program's effects on English education and on local communities within Japan. In this chapter, by contrast, I analyze the JET Program as a vehicle for cultural diplomacy. After more than twenty years of operation and viewed within the context of U.S.-Japanese relations, what have been the effects of the JET Program in enhancing foreign understanding of Japan?[2]

Disconnect Between Message and Policy: Turf Wars and Competing Priorities at the National and Local Levels

The official launch of the JET Program (over a gourmet dinner served by kimono-clad hostesses at a five-star Tokyo hotel) was a major media event attended by cabinet-level ministers and prefectural governors. Referring to the JET participants as "cultural ambassadors" and "reformers," these policy makers exhorted the foreign youth to play their part in the great experiment of internationalization that was sweeping through Japanese society. A spirit of optimism and goodwill carried the day. It was hard to construe the gala event as anything but a triumph of public diplomacy.

Unfortunately, though, the flowery rhetoric was not matched by program policies to ensure the readiness of Japanese schools and communities to host the foreign teachers. The result was a culture clash of monumental proportions during the first three years of the program. One reason for this was that each of the three ministries in charge of the JET Program (Home Affairs, Education, and Foreign) had its own goals for the program. For example, Home Affairs officials, who controlled most of the program's budget and overall operation, saw the program as a means for getting on the bandwagon of internationalization and tended to see its goals in terms of regional development. For its part, the Education Ministry was charged with overseeing the team-teaching portion of the program, and officials there saw the main goals of the program as promoting conversational English. Officials from the Education Ministry, however, initially opposed the plan for the JET Program because they feared it would lead to widespread resistance among Japanese teachers of English.

Finally, the Foreign Ministry has viewed the program primarily as a diplomatic asset to raise Japan's status abroad. But good foreign policy does not always make good domestic policy. In one incident, Prime Minister Takeshita announced on a trip to Europe in 1988 that French and German participants would join the JET Program the following year. His speech, written by the Foreign Ministry, came as a complete surprise to Education Ministry officials, who were forced to scramble to find teaching positions for the new ALTs in the English-dominated foreign-language environment of Japanese secondary schools.

Another key factor hindering smooth implementation has been the different reactions to the JET Program at the national, prefectural, and local levels. While governors and mayors have been surprisingly enthusiastic about welcoming hundreds of foreigners each year, the curriculum specialists (*shidoo shuji*) and other local officials who work with the JET participants on a daily basis typically see their responsibilities as a heavy burden. But it is at the school level where the symbolic agreement on internationalization, so easy to maintain when kept at a level of generality, begins to break down. The most powerful realities in secondary schools in Japan are preparation for entrance exams and the cultivation of proper character and morality in students. The discrepancy between the mandate of teaching conversational English and the reality of entrance exams has led to an immense contradiction, resulting in the underutilization of many ALTs. Key program goals have thus been reinterpreted by Japanese teachers so that internationalization is conceived of as a situational accommodation to Western demands more than a fundamental cultural change.

To be sure, the Japanese teachers and curriculum specialist are not a homogenous group; some view the ALTs as a virus whose potentially deleterious effects needs to be carefully controlled, while others see them as much-needed medicine for an outdated education system. But the large majority are quite ambivalent about the program. Though they tend to see the JET Program as a "cause" and to do their part to accommodate the ALTs, they also complain bitterly about the extra work and try to shield the effects of the ALTs' presence from the rest of the system. The effectiveness of the program has thus been partly neutralized by the difficulties in integrating the ALTs into local schools. Though team teaching has now become a routine part of the English curriculum throughout Japan's secondary school system, the overall effects have been fairly modest. As Yonezawa notes in Chapter 4, the TOEFL scores of Japanese students are still among the lowest in the world, and the early optimism that the JET Program would serve as a catalyst for major restructuring of the university entrance exams (to emphasize oral over written English) seems somewhat misplaced. Overall, it is hard to avoid the conclusion that the policy lever is simply not strong enough to move the rock of deeply institutionalized practices.

The JET Program: Soft Power in Action?

According to Nye, international educational exchange programs such as JET are the third pillar of public diplomacy that enhances a nation's soft power. The goal of such programs is "the development of lasting relationships with key individuals over many years through scholarships, exchanges, training, seminars, conferences and access to media channels" (2004, p. 109). This dimension of public diplomacy, in his view, helps to "create an attractive image of a country and . . . improve its prospects for obtaining its desired outcomes" (2004, p. 110).

If the effects of the JET Program on English education and on local government have been mixed, what about its goals as a cultural exchange program? Nye references the JET Program as a positive example of Japan's use of cultural diplomacy, noting that large numbers of JET alumni are active in many countries. Certainly, the Foreign Ministry has been wildly enthusiastic about the JET Program precisely because of its potential for enhancing foreign understanding of Japan. On the occasion of the tenth anniversary of the JET Program, for example, Hisaeda Joji, director of the Second Cultural Affairs Division at the Foreign Ministry, bluntly stated:

> From the viewpoint of the Ministry of Foreign Affairs, it is significant as a part of Japan's national security policy that these youths go back to their respective countries in the future and become sympathizers for Japan. In the case of the United States and France, for instance, they often get criticized by many countries for promoting their own independent international policies. All the same, they will carry through these policies because these nations have sufficient national strength. . . . In Japan's case, the nation is far from possessing such strength to carry out policies in defiance of world opinion. Therefore, highly deliberate, even artificial efforts are required to create sympathizers for Japan as part of a national security policy. From this point of view, we consider the JET Programme is an extremely important and at the same time effective policy instrument. (The JET Programme, p.192)

Hisaeda's appraisal is consistent with the thinking behind the recent creation of a Public Diplomacy Department in the Foreign Ministry "to increase understanding of Japan and sympathy for our approach to life through a variety of cultural exchanges" (Kondo 2004, p. 34). Similarly, the report issued to Prime Minister Koizumi on July 11, 2005, by the Council on the Promotion of Public Diplomacy describes the goal of Japan's foreign policy as "Establishing Japan as a Peaceful Nation of Cultural Exchange" (Aoki, Kondo, and Wang 2005, p. 31).

Indeed, the very structure of the JET Program and a wide range of program policies make the most sense when viewed in terms of the goal of building a constituency of pro-Japan youth in participating countries. For example, the three-year limit on participation and the age limit of forty make little sense if Japan's goal is to open up its society to foreigners. But as one Foreign Ministry official confessed, "From the standpoint of having these people as assets to Japan's foreign relations, extending the length of service means more or less slowing down increase in the number of such people through decrease in the number of invitees. Also, with regard to the age limit of thirty-five, it is possible that it was considered better to invite younger people than older ones from the viewpoint of building up diplomatic assets for the future."[3]

In the remainder of this chapter, however, I want to caution against an uncritical view that equates the mere existence of a cultural exchange program with a corresponding increase in "soft power." Before the JET Program is labeled an unqualified success in cultural diplomacy, several questions need to be asked that are consistent with Nye's framework. First, do program policies actually promote an attractive image of the country? Second, how do the JET Program participants translate and interpret their experiences in the JET Program? Based on their experiences in the program, does Japan become more attractive to them, and if so, in what respects? Finally, what have JET alumni actually done with their experiences upon return to their home countries that furthers the understanding of Japan abroad? In posing these four questions, I hope to avoid the "[conflation of] attention, attractiveness and persuasion" (Womack 2005, p. 3) in the analysis of soft power and to move beyond the producer's point of view to consider the views of consumers of Japan's soft power.

Foreign Pressure and the Evolution of JET Program Policies

Nye himself admitted that policies that appear narrowly self-serving can consume rather than produce soft power. Thus, how educational exchange programs are structured can make a big difference in the quality of a participant's experience of another culture. The details matter tremendously in determining whether cultural exchange programs consume or produce soft power.

With respect to the JET Program, the evolution of program policies has been nothing short of dramatic. During the early years of the program, the concept of internationalization began to break down as soon as the reform-minded college graduates were dispatched to secondary schools and local government offices. Many were shocked when their offices sent them out to schools on a "one-shot basis," where they were wheeled out like living globes in classroom after classroom. The realities of entrance exams and students' poor English conversational abilities left most participants feeling underutilized at best and intentionally misled at worst. The informal grapevine was abuzz with the dark view that the government was using the JET Program as mere window dressing.

To compound problems, a number of serious incidents—from suicides of JET participants to drunken-driving accidents to accusations of sexual harassment and racial discrimination—shook program morale in the early years. In reaction to the perceived feebleness of the government's response, more than 90 percent of JET participants joined a "quasi-union" known as the Association of JET (or AJET) to press the relevant ministries for improvements in program policy. In the print media, domestic and foreign critics alike began to second-guess the government's intentions. Almost overnight the JET Program had become a political football for critics of all stripes.

Yet ten years later, when the dust had cleared and expectations had been adjusted, the JET Program was being touted by Japanese government officials as one of the greatest policies in the postwar era. The percentage of JET participants who break their contracts and leave early had declined from a high of 3 percent in the first year of the program to less than 1 percent after 1991. The satisfaction levels of the JET participants had improved markedly as well. Two examples are worth mentioning as illustrations of the process by which the Japanese government has tackled the problems brought to its attention.

First, to counter the complaints about underutilization of ALTs in the teaching dimension of the program, the Council of Local Authorities for International Relations (CLAIR)—the administrative office of the JET Program in the Home Affairs Ministry—required every ALT to have a "base school." For its part, the Ministry of Education hired a full-time foreigner to serve as team-teaching consultant, sponsored team-teaching research and seminars at its laboratory schools, and revised the textbooks and the course of study to upgrade the listening and speaking dimensions of English-language teaching. Through prefectural and local education offices—what Rohlen (2002, p. 180) has called the institutional "middle ground" of Japanese education—they began supporting workshops and materials on "how to team teach." Though the contradictions between the promotion of conversational English and the realities of the entrance exams are still present, it is now rare to find Japanese teachers of English who are unfamiliar with team teaching or with hosting an ALT at their schools.

Second, in terms of program administration, CLAIR and the relevant ministries took a number of steps to address concerns raised by AJET. They hired a number of JET alumni to work as "program coordinators" in the national office; they improved program policy to encourage Japanese-language study; they set up a counseling system for JET participants; they expanded the numbers of participating countries, as well as the racial and ethnic diversity of participants from any given country; and they added fourth- and fifth-year positions as "elementary school ALT" or "specialist prefectural advisor" for JET participants who wanted to stay in the program for more than three years. As each of AJET's programmatic concerns was addressed, the organization began to drop its confrontational stance. Membership fell to around 30 percent, and its activities today focus mostly on providing cultural information and social and recreational outlets for JET participants.

These developments in program policy over the past twenty years would seem to support Hannerz's (1989) argument that the consequences of transnational cultural flow must be understood as they unfold over time. Two points are worth noting. First, changes in program policy have almost always come in reaction to pressure from the JET participants themselves rather than as a product of endogenous evolution. Second, the public justifications for the program have shifted over the course of its implementation. Proclamations about opening up Japan and demonstrating that foreigners can be "part of the group" have gradually given way to fairly direct statements from Foreign Ministry officials about the desire to create a pro-Japan faction in participating countries.

Winning the Hearts and Minds of Foreign Youth?

Cross-cultural exchange does not automatically break down cultural barriers. It can just as easily confirm existing prejudices. Nye himself noted that "the effects of globalization depend on the receiver as well as the sender" (2004, p. 111) because "all information goes through cultural filters" (p. 41). The anthropological literature on Japan, of course, is filled with studies of how imported culture is filtered and recontextualized into the everyday experience of people (see Tobin 1992 as one example). How do JET alumni interpret and filter their Japan experience? My interviews with JET alumni suggest that in answering this question we need to go well beyond simplistic appraisals of whether JET alumni "liked" the JET Program or Japan. In fact, we must begin by noting the considerable diversity in the motivations and styles of engagement with Japanese culture that are represented among JET participants.

Although JET participants represent a fairly privileged group in terms of social class and educational backgrounds, they have a wide range of motivations for entering the program. Some hope for a leg up in the business world, while others have family connections or express an academic interest in Japan. Still others have a deep interest in teaching or in martial arts. The continuum thus runs from those who come with what their Japanese hosts disparagingly refer to as a superficial interest (*karui kimochi*) to others who are deeply interested in and knowledgeable about all aspects of Japan. The majority view the JET Program as a chance to see the world and perhaps take some time off from school before making their career plans, all the while harboring a vague expectation that the experience may be beneficial later down the line. Similarly, the stances taken by JET participants toward engagement with Japanese culture and institutions run the gamut from those who are content to remain outside the social expectations operating in Japanese schools to others who practically reject their own culture in the rush to embrace Japanese language and society.

Recognizing this diversity in motivations and styles of engagement with Japanese culture among JET participants allows for a clearer comprehension of the perceptions of Japan held by JET Program alumni. Internal efforts to evaluate the JET Program have most often taken the form of a questionnaire designed to discover the satisfaction levels of current JET participants and JET alumni. The responses are quite positive. According to the 2004 JET alumni survey conducted by CLAIR, fully 85 percent of respondents said they would "absolutely" recommend the JET Program to a friend, while 12 percent said they "probably" would. In the same survey, 57 percent of respondents said they enjoyed their experiences in the JET Program "very much," and 38 percent said they enjoyed the JET Program "for the most part." In general, the program receives high marks from its participants.

In addition, regardless of their orientation to Japan, all but one of the thirty alumni I interviewed in the summer and fall of 2005 felt that the program had had a significant impact on their lives. Many talked in glowing terms about how the experience had broadened their view of the world. "The JET Program really helps you figure out what your choices are in life," noted one former participant. "I definitely got social capital out of it," claimed another. A third noted, "I am sure my experience in Japan has shaped the person who I have become. The world feels smaller, the foreign news more real, people more connected." Such responses are probably not uncommon in any well-designed cultural exchange program.

Much more interesting, however, are the *perceptions of Japan* on the part of JET

Program alumni. The responses to one question on the 2004 JETAA (JET Alumni Association) Survey about how their perceptions of Japan have changed as a result of the JET Program stand out in this regard. Only 30 percent of respondents answered, "Yes, positively," while 60 percent replied, "Yes, positively and negatively." In short, nearly everyone felt that their perceptions of Japan had changed as a result of the JET experience, but most recognized the complexities and ambiguities involved in their shifting views of Japan. Moreover, there was not always a clear connection linking the quality of the JET experience, one's subsequent view of Japan, and the likelihood of ongoing involvement with Japan.

Some JET alumni who had extremely positive experiences simply disappear into the woodwork upon their return home. For example, when I interviewed Christine, an ALT in Ehime-ken from 1997 to 1999, she embraced the label of Japan sympathizer:

> JET was such a great experience for me. The Japanese teachers I met were eager to learn English, and I developed many friendships with them. I am more deeply sympathetic and aware of Japanese culture, customs and people now. I actually found life kind of dull upon returning to the USA for quite some time. I found people here abrasive, extremely overweight, and appearing unorganized compared to the Japanese. [JET] changed the way I looked at people around me. I really feel like an advocate for the Japanese people and culture now.

Yet in spite of her obvious affinity for Japan, Christine, who has worked at United Way for the past five years, admits that apart from exchanging greeting cards with a few Japanese friends once a year, "I really haven't had much contact with Japanese culture." In fact, Christine, like many JET alumni, has maintained closer ties with other JET alumni than with her Japanese students and coworkers. From the standpoint of Japan's soft power, Christine's potential for influencing U.S.-Japanese relations seems completely untapped, at least for the moment.

Conversely, some JET alumni who had a very difficult time in the JET Program or who hold fairly negative views of the Japanese state have ended up with extensive Japan involvement. Consider the case of Dan, who describes his year in JET as a "very lonely and isolating time in a farming village that didn't want to have a JET but got one anyway." He says he was left "with absolutely no structure" and "never made any Japanese friends." For Dan, JET was "a fascinating experience that I am daily grateful I did, and daily grateful is over." Yet because Dan worked for six years at two major airlines, he has used his travel benefits to return to Japan many times to see non-Japanese JET friends and says he has "used my Japanese language and cultural skills to good effect in my career to date." At the same time, he remains highly critical of the Japanese government.

Some JET alumni were even put off by the insinuation that they might have become more sympathetic to Japan as a result of the JET Program, preferring instead a more layered interpretation of the change in their perception of Japan. The following quotes from alumni I interviewed are illustrative of this more nuanced response:

"Sympathizer" is totally the wrong word. I can celebrate this part and criticize that part. I'm not a U.S. sympathizer either. Most people in the JET Program are critical thinkers who had an experience and understand it. We now have more information to create plans of action, and from a policy perspective, that's better.

I don't think I'm more sympathetic as such. In some ways Japanese people are very fortunate and live fairly comfortable, excessive lives. I just see it now as a place with pros and cons, just like anywhere else.

I can't say that I "understand" Japan, but I can take a good look at things and have an open-minded point of view. More sympathetic? I'm not sure. Fair . . . maybe.

On the whole, I loved Japan. I am immeasurably more sympathetic to Japan than I was before. But some Japanese ways of life I have difficulty empathizing with, for example environmental matters and overpackaging of consumer products. I was appalled by the way immigrants from Korea and China are treated in Japan. Don't get me started on gender equality. . . . I now think of Japan as a delightful place of paradoxes.

On balance, the JET Program has certainly made Japan more attractive to a cohort of young people who return to their home countries with new knowledge and a deeper experiential base from which to judge media portrayals of Japan. But the responses of JET alumni suggest that there is a real danger in talking about soft power as if it were simply a popularity contest among nations. Many shades of affection and distaste toward Japan are represented within the alumni population, and somewhat romanticized notions of Japan often coexist with deeply critical elements.

The Alumni Ripple Effect

The concept of soft power not only involves the attractiveness of a country's values but also implies the ability to translate that attractiveness into policies that benefit the country. As noted earlier, this view of the JET Program as a national asset is very prominent in the Foreign Ministry. However unrealistic it may be to expect that a future president of the United States will be a JET alumnus, Japanese policy makers clearly hope that JET alumni will, over time, find their way into influential positions in their home countries and will maintain their relationships with Japan over the long term.

The establishment of the JET Alumni Association is probably the best example from the program's history of JET participants and Japanese hosts working effectively to promote the understanding of Japan abroad. Though the Ministry of Internal Affairs and Communications and the Ministry of Foreign Affairs have an ongoing turf war over control of JETAA,[4] generous funding is nevertheless available for a quarterly alumni newsletter called *JET Streams,* and each year representatives from regional chapters gather for a JETAA International Conference. An annual essay contest was begun in 1993, and enterprising JET alumni have ensured that the JET Program is well represented in cyberspace. All told, there are more than forty-five JETAA chapters in fifteen countries serving a membership base of approximately 20,000 JET alumni (almost half of the 46,000 former participants).

What do these JETAA chapters actually accomplish? Some of their activities do seem to be of direct benefit to the state. One very tangible benefit of the JET Program has been a steady pool of qualified employees for positions in the Japanese consulates abroad. In fact, I could not find a single consulate in the United States that did not have at least one JET alumnus on its staff, and many now employ several JET alumni. In addition, JET alumni are now an integral part of the recruitment of new JET participants, and they are often invited to gatherings involving Japanese dignitaries.

Another important development that directly benefits the Japanese state is the incentive that the JET Program has created for alumni to join the diplomatic corps in their respective countries. In the specific context of U.S.-Japanese relations, for example, the JET Program now rivals the Peace Corps as a key supplier of young Americans willing to serve their country in the foreign service. As of the summer of 2005, six JET Program alumni were working in the U.S. Embassy in Tokyo; one noted that in his orientation class, JET Program alumni had numbered eleven compared to thirteen Peace Corps alumni. Though these JET alumni will be posted to various countries throughout their careers, their knowledge of Japanese language and culture will no doubt benefit the Japanese government in numerous ways.

Interviews with CLAIR officials and a closer analysis of these JETAA organizations, however, reveal that at least a third of the eighteen JETAA chapters in the United States are relatively inactive, hindered in part by the geographic barriers they face in getting JET alumni together on a regular basis. Another third seem to focus primarily on providing social opportunities for JET alumni, such as *shinnenkai* (New Year's parties) or *hanami* (cherry-blossom-viewing) picnics, or helping them with their career options. Not surprisingly, the JETAA chapters that are most active in terms of outreach to local communities tend to be those in the major metropolitan areas—New York, Washington, D.C., Chicago, Honolulu, and the big cities on the West coast. For example, the Southern California chapter has sponsored a "Japan in a suitcase" outreach program to local elementary schools. In addition, a number of JETAA chapters have become involved in events sponsored by local Japan-America societies, such as the annual Japan Bowl, in which high school students throughout the state compete with one another on their knowledge of Japanese customs, language, literature, and history.

Another way to measure the JET Program's ripple effect is to ask whether the governments of other countries have looked to the JET Program as a model. At least two examples of similar programs exist. South Korea has established a smaller program that is clearly modeled on JET. In 2005 the English Program in Korea (EPIK), sponsored by the South Korean government, hired approximately 190 college graduates from six countries (the United States, the United Kingdom, Canada, Ireland, Australia, and New Zealand) to teach English in public elementary and secondary schools throughout the country. A second example comes from the Fulbright Commission in the United States, which has added a new category of awards for many of their countries that bears a striking resemblance to the work of the ALTs in Japan. These teaching assistantships are now available in twenty-one of the countries to which Fulbright sends its American grantees.

Much of the alumni ripple effect, however, seems to occur in a space that is well outside a governmental framework. First and foremost in this respect are the thousands of JET alumni who have gone on to careers that draw on or further their expertise in Japanese language and culture. Though accurate data on the precise number of alumni who have pursued work or study related to Japan is unavailable, CLAIR does maintain a Web site for JET alumni to log in and update their work histories. In August 2005, of the 3,747 individuals who had voluntarily updated their information on this site, 1,772 (roughly 5 percent of the total alumni population) indicated they had jobs related to Japan. Responses to the 2004 JETAA Survey, though, show a higher level of engagement: 25 percent of respondents said they were keeping up with their Japanese-language ability, and 13 percent said they were pursuing further studies or work related to Japan.

The Japan-related occupations of American JET alumni run the gamut from jobs in the private sector to government to academia to nonprofit work; from non-Japanese companies that do business with Japan to Japanese companies based in Japan; from large multinationals to small firms to self-employment. Thousands of JET alumni have returned home to study Japan-related topics in graduate school and to take up positions in academia. Other JET alumni have gone on to promising careers in journalism—Bruce Feiler, who wrote *Learning to Bow* (1991) about his experiences in the JET Program, is but one example. In some cases, the careers of JET alumni align quite well with the interests of the Japanese government: Roughly 1–2 percent of JET alumni return to teach Japanese language in their home countries, for instance. In other cases, though, these "Japan-related careers" can involve activities that are indirectly or directly critical of Japanese government policies; one alumnus works for a nonprofit that grew out of opposition to the Japanese government's textbook policies.

Other JET alumni invest significant time, outside the framework of their careers, in maintaining the relationships they cultivated in Japan. "I've so far had nine weeks of Japanese visitors here, and two Japanese friends are coming in 2006 to stay with me for a few weeks," commented one alumnus. Another alumnus who worked at the South Carolina Governor's School for Arts and Humanities sponsored a film club and a letter exchange with students from his high school in Yamaguchi-ken. It appears, however, that the activation of these "Japan networks" decreases over time as the emotional immediacy of the JET experience recedes.

For most JET alumni, however, connections with Japan during "life after JET" take place not through Japan-related work or reciprocal visits with Japanese friends, but through the mementos they bring home, contact with Japanese food and popular culture, and a heightened interest in Japan in the news. "I still love Hello Kitty," noted one alumnus. "My apartment is a shrine to my years in Japan," noted another, "and I'm still dedicated to my once-a-week visit to a Japanese restaurant." For these alumni, memories of their "Japan experience" are kept alive through the ongoing consumption of Japanese artifacts, news, and food in ways that are personally meaningful. In one sense, their soft power potential is mostly latent, but they also may exert a subtle yet powerful influence on family, friends, and acquaintances simply by "talking up" Japan.

Conclusion: Perception, Context, and Soft Power

The implications of this chapter for understanding soft power in theory and practice are several. Ultimately, for Nye, soft power is wielded through the state apparatus and redeemed in the form of diplomatic persuasion. In this respect, educational exchanges are probably more crucial in attaining what Nye (2004, pp. 16–17) refers to as "milieu goals" (shaping an environment conducive to peace, democracy, open markets, etc.) rather than "possession goals" (short-term policy outcomes). As we have seen, however, the diffuse outcomes of government-sponsored educational exchange programs are highly contingent on the perceptions and the sociopolitical environment that exist at each level of the policy system.

Of course, Nye did acknowledge the crucial role of both context and perception in shaping the projection and reception of soft power. Because his is a macrolevel theory, however, he sometimes gave the impression that states are singular entities with clearly identifiable objectives. This chapter reminds us that governments are multifaceted sites of diverse and competing interests (Hamada and Sibley 1995) and that policies go through a complex process of reinterpretation as they move downstream (Levinson and Sutton 2001).

The responses of JET Program alumni also suggest that there are dangers in conflating nation-state and culture in conceptualizing soft power. Many alumni were at great pains to separate their love of Japanese culture and people from their views about the Japanese state, and, in their minds, deeply critical views of Japan often coexisted with positive elements. Here again, Nye recognized that cultural attractiveness and the attractiveness of a policy or government are two different things. Nevertheless, his view of culture as "shared values" and his assumption that "culture" can be mapped onto "nation" in a fairly straightforward manner seems somewhat too simplistic to capture either the fractured nature of contemporary cultures or the realities of pluralist nations and transnational culture flows.

To point out these complexities is not at all to suggest that the JET Program is anything but smart foreign policy for Japan. Nye is undoubtedly correct in labeling the JET Program an important component of Japan's soft power. Moreover, the genius of the JET Program is that Japan increases its soft power with respect not only to its foremost ally but also to dozens of countries around the world. That this long-term impact often takes the form of personal relationships and international cooperation in a framework that does not necessarily involve the state is not at all inconsistent with Nye's claims about soft power.

Nye was also correct in reminding us that the most important part of public diplomacy is "the last three feet"—the face-to-face dimension of human exchange. In this respect, the linguistic dimension of soft power cultivated through educational exchange is worth highlighting. The JET Program is not teaching people to *like Japan* so much as it is teaching them to *communicate with Japanese.*[5] The tens of thousands of people who have taught in the JET Program do not always return home with unequivocally positive views of Japan, but their perspectives are more realistic and their comfort level in interacting with Japanese people is higher. In the long run, the JET Program probably serves Japan's interests not through the creation of a pro-Japan faction among JET alumni but through the creation of a cohort of young people who have experienced Japan in all its diversity and can thus add critical insights to public and private conversations about Japan in their home countries. Importantly, the JET Program accomplishes this by pulling people out of their cubicles and inserting them into the world of Japanese schools, unlike many study abroad programs that create foreign ghettos.

Finally, the JET Program raises a much broader question of whether a "top-down approach" to cultural exchange, in which the government takes the lead, is the most productive one. As Ogoura noted, the Japanese government's role in international exchange has been increasing at the expense of the role of private foundations. "The government," he wrote, "is frantically conducting cultural exchange projects under the spell of an odd set of ideas about national interests" (2004, p. 30). In a slightly different vein, Campbell (1993, p. 53) has noted that government programs such as JET that attempt to build cooperative relationships outside areas of binational conflict are not usually successful in stemming the tide of negative information.

However, government-sponsored programs can often mobilize resources to a level that would be inconceivable in the private sector or with nongovernmental organizations. The leveraging of the *koofuzei,* or local allocation tax, to raise the budget for the JET Program is a case in point. And, with innovative thinking, government policies can be designed to transcend organizational sectoralism (Montgomery 1995). While many top-down programs entail a uniformity that comes with government regulation of culture, the JET Program largely avoids this outcome because the government cannot control the spontaneous interactions of thousands of people sent to every far-flung corner of Japan. Because the "last three feet" always entails unscripted interactions, the JET Program avoids the pitfalls of public diplomacy that advertises a party line. As Nye pointed out, such educational exchanges are far more effective than mere broadcasting (2004, p. 111).

The ultimate irony, of course, is that the specific problem of U.S.-Japanese trade conflict in the 1980s that gave rise to this "soft power intervention" has largely disappeared. To their credit, Japanese officials maintained the program throughout the recession of the 1990s, thus quietly laying the groundwork for the human dimension of a policy environment that will benefit Japan for decades to come.

Notes

I am grateful for grants from the Great Lakes College Association's Japan Travel Fund and from the College of Wooster's Faculty Development Fund to support travel to Japan in the summer of 2005 to gather data for this chapter.

1. Job types are divided into three categories. Assistant language teachers (ALTs), who are based in public secondary schools or offices of education and make up roughly 90 percent of participants, are responsible for team teaching English classes with Japanese teachers of English.

Coordinators of international relations (CIRs) are placed in prefectural or municipal offices, where they assist in international activities. Sports exchange advisors (SEAs) assist local schools and communities in teaching and promoting a particular sport at which they excel.

2. I have been gathering data on the JET Program since its inception in 1987. During two years of intensive fieldwork in Japan between 1988 and 1990 and six follow-up trips between 1993 and 2005, I observed many "team taught" classes; conducted numerous interviews with Japanese administrators, teachers, students, and JET participants; and collected many in-house documents. Additional data for this paper was obtained through an analysis of Web-based materials on the JET Program Alumni Association and interviews with a snowball sample of thirty JET Program alumni.

3. The age limit was initially set at thirty-five years but was increased as a result of ongoing complaints from applicants and current JET participants. Similarly, a fourth- and fifth-year option for continuing JET participants was instituted on a limited basis.

4. From a purely practical standpoint, it has been more difficult for CLAIR to support the JETAA chapters because CLAIR has only seven overseas offices—New York, London, Paris, Singapore, Seoul, Sydney, and Beijing—compared to the many dozens of consulates operated by the Ministry of Foreign Affairs.

5. I am indebted to Thomas Berger of Boston University for this important distinction.

References

Aoki Tamotsu, Seiichi Kondo, and Min Wang. 2005. "Cultural Exchange: A National Priority." *Japan Echo* 32 (6): 31–35.

Campbell, John C. 1993. "Japan and the United States: Games That Work." In *Japan's Foreign Policy After the Cold War: Coping with Change.* Ed. Gerald Curtis, 43–61. New York: M.E. Sharpe.

Feiler, Bruce. 1991. *Learning to Bow: Inside the Heart of Japan.* New York: Ticknor and Fields.

George, Aurelia. 1991. "Japan's America Problem: The Japanese Response to U.S. Pressure." *Washington Quarterly* 14 (3): 5–19.

Goodman, Roger. 1990. *Japan's "International Youth": The Emergence of a New Class of Schoolchildren.* Oxford: Oxford University Press.

Hamada Tomoko and Willis E. Sibley, eds. 1995. *Anthropological Perspectives on Organizational Culture.* New York: University Press of America.

Hannerz, Ulf. 1989. "Notes on the Global Ecumene." *Public Culture* 1 (2): 66–75.

The JET Programme: Ten Years and Beyond. Tokyo: Council of Local Authorities for International Relations, 1997.

Kondo, Seiichi. 2004. "A New Direction for Japanese Diplomacy." *Japan Echo* 31 (6): 31–34.

Levinson, Bradley A.U., and Margaret Sutton. 2001. "Policy as/in Practice: A Sociocultural Approach to the Study of Educational Policy." In *Policy as Practice: Towards a Comparative Sociocultural Analysis of Educational Policy.* Ed. Bradley A.U. Levinson and Margaret Sutton, 1–22. Westport, CT: Ablex Publishing.

McConnell, David L. 2000. *Importing Diversity: Inside Japan's JET Program.* Berkeley: University of California Press.

Montgomery, John. 1995. "Beyond Good Policies." In *Great Policies: Strategic Innovations in Asia and the Pacific Basin.* Ed. John Montgomery and Dennis Rondinelli, 1–13. London: Praeger.

Nye, Joseph S., Jr. 2004. *Soft Power: The Means to Success in World Politics.* New York: Public Affairs.

Ogoura, Kazuo. 2004. "Shaping Japan's Cultural Products as 'International Assets.'" *Japan Echo* 31 (6): 27–30.

Rohlen, Thomas P. 2002. "Concluding Observations: Wider Contexts and Future Issues." In *National Standards and School Reform in Japan and the United States.* Ed. Gary DeCoker, 177–205. New York: Teachers College Press.
Tobin, Joseph J., ed. 1992. *Re-Made in Japan: Everyday Life and Consumer Taste in a Changing Society.* New Haven, CT: Yale University Press.
Womack, Brantly. 2005. "Dancing Alone: A Hard Look at Soft Power." *Japan Focus,* November 16. http://www.japanfocus.org.

II

Higher Education

3

Higher Education as a Projection of America's Soft Power

Philip G. Altbach and Patti McGill Peterson

Higher education has always served as an international force, influencing intellectual and scientific development and spreading ideas worldwide. Its sphere of influence encompasses people and institutions. The experience of studying, either in one's own country or abroad, helps to shape one's worldview and attitudes toward society and culture. This chapter focuses on the part that higher education has played in supporting America's ascendant role in international education and in defining America's place in the hierarchy of nations.

Invented and expounded by Joseph S. Nye, Jr., the idea of "soft power" encompasses the nexus of influences in world affairs that relate to culture, science, technology, and other subtle forces. In *Soft Power,* Nye explored the interaction of soft power with hard power in trade treaties such as those created by the World Trade Organization, military alliances, and direct involvement by one country in the affairs of another (Nye 2004). Recent discussions in U.S. government circles about America's public diplomacy around the world refer frequently to the strength and attractiveness of the country's higher education system and the effectiveness of educational exchange as a way to explain American values to the rest of the world—themes emphasized by Joseph Nye throughout *Soft Power.*

With polls indicating rising anti-Americanism worldwide, there has been a commensurate increase in discussions about reinvigorating America's public diplomacy efforts among officials including the secretary of state and members of the Senate Foreign Relations Committee, as well as a significant amount of press coverage. Ultimately, the concept of public diplomacy, which consists of engaging, informing, and influencing citizens of other countries, is the same as Nye's concept of soft power.

What is not clear at this point is how the United States will choose to exercise its soft power. Much advice, whether officially requested or freely offered, focuses on the importance of long-term engagement of foreign populations through educational and cultural exchange as opposed to short-term propaganda campaigns. The American Academy of Diplomacy recommended a multibillion-dollar endowment for America to fulfill a long-term and sustainable commitment to both exchange programs and the improvement of international understanding in the American education system. The purpose of the endowment would be to fund youth exchange programs, underwrite the

Fulbright Program, and make selective grants to educational institutions in the United States to enhance the teaching of international relations, history, and foreign languages (American Academy of Diplomacy 2004). The Public Diplomacy Council, a nonpartisan group of professionals with extensive foreign service experience, called upon the administration and Congress to revitalize public diplomacy efforts, integrating them into all foreign policy deliberations, and supporting their contribution to the security and well-being of the United States. Among its recommendations was an increase in educational exchange programs (Public Diplomacy Council 2005).

The current emphasis on "winning the hearts and minds" of people in the Muslim world has included strategies for bringing more secondary school youth and university students from the region to study in the United States. Many people who are concerned about the way the United States is currently perceived among Muslim populations see international education as an essential part of America's strategy to foster greater mutual understanding (Djerejian 2003; Council on Foreign Relations 2003).

The current discussion about how to structure U.S. soft power has a much larger and longer context. International education and academic exchange have played a role in international relations for a very long time. Understanding that context and appreciating the special strengths of American higher education and the competition it will face will be important in determining how the United States can best exercise its public diplomacy in the future.

Historical Perspective

The relationship between soft power and international education is not a new phenomenon. Students have studied abroad since the origin of the modern university in the Middle Ages and have been influenced by what they learned and experienced. Faculty members and researchers also have crossed borders for millennia, and knowledge has always been international in scope. Indeed, medieval universities were international institutions, bringing together students and faculty from many European countries and operating in a single language, Latin (Haskins 2002). Through its strong emphasis on theology and canon law, the medieval university served as a bastion of power for the Catholic Church. The Jesuit mission of spreading the faith through education was an important aspect of the church's soft power. Historically, the Jesuits recognized education as a powerful force and established schools and universities around the world to spread knowledge and Roman Catholicism (O'Malley, Bailey, Harris, and Kennedy 1999). Missionaries from various other Christian denominations were also actively involved in higher education overseas (Ashby 1966; Lutz 1971).

Colonial administrators often saw higher education as a useful accompaniment to their work. The British were particularly adept at developing institutions on site and at sending promising students from the colonized regions back to England to study at British universities. British-style colleges and universities were established in India as early as 1835, and students educated at these institutions provided the backbone of the colonial administration for a century or more (Basu 1974). Colonial education also led to the rise of nationalist movements. Mohandas Gandhi and Jawarhalal Nehru were, after all, educated in colonial schools in India and then in England.

The United States, during its brief period as a colonial power, used higher education as part of its colonial policy. It established higher education institutions in the Philippines as part of its presence in that country (Gonzalez 2004). However, the United States played a far more active role in spreading its cultural and political ideas during the Cold War.

American higher education played a role in the ideological struggle with the Soviet Union. Academic exchanges, scholarship programs, and research projects were sponsored by the U.S. government, private foundations, and other agencies—with the goal of contributing to a positive American image worldwide as well as of creating links with academics and other sectors internationally. Some analysts criticized governmental links with academe, while others saw these efforts as essential to American foreign policy (Coombs 1964; Altbach 1971; Chomsky 1997).

The U.S. government's response to the Cold War also prompted more federal support for the rise of the American university to an international leadership level. Nationally funded grant programs in the sciences, mathematics, language, and area studies contributed to this rise. In the post–World War II period, American higher education, especially its research universities, achieved world-class preeminence. Attracting students and scholars, the United States became the largest host country for international students. Further, English was established as the principal language of science and scholarship, and U.S. universities came to dominate scholarly and scientific communication as well. Boosted by the battle over ideas of the Cold War, the strength and attractiveness of American higher education became a critical element for the U.S. government in its outreach to other nations.

The Conditions for American Academic Influence

A number of elements of the U.S. academic system account for its worldwide influence. American colleges and universities are often cited as the gold standard in terms of academic structure, curriculum, and research. They are increasingly used as a model for the development of new universities around the world. American research and scholarship are also considered to be world-class. The international reputation of science in the United States is a key element of its soft power (Pew Research Center 2003). The paradigms and results of research are widely influential internationally and also tend to dominate the networks of knowledge dissemination—journals and the Internet (Altbach 2001).

In addition to its dominant role in the academic hierarchy worldwide, the United States has the most highly complex and diversified higher education system in the world; only China enrolls more students, but its higher education system is not as well developed as that of the United States. In addition to the widespread influence of American research universities, a more diverse range of institutions are attracting foreign populations and are becoming models for other countries seeking to expand vocational postsecondary education. In recent years, America's community colleges have increased their efforts to attract foreign students, and they have discovered a very receptive market for the type and cost of the education that they offer. In particular, their business management and computer science programs have been attractive to foreign students. The result is that over the past decade, international student enrollments at U.S. community colleges have risen by almost 60 percent. The fact that there is a differentiated academic system offering study opportunities at many levels is an advantage in the United States. While a high proportion of international students study at the top-tier research universities, significant numbers can be found throughout the academic system.

The organization of the American academic system also appeals to international students. Programs of study are, in general, transparent and tightly organized. The U.S. course-credit system permits students to measure their academic progress and, if necessary, to transfer from one academic institution to another. Credit is given for individual courses, and there is frequent feedback on academic work. It is possible to transfer certain academic course work from one university to another. Graduate programs are designed so that students know the curriculum and can calculate the time it will take to earn a degree. This overview is in contrast to that of many other countries, where graduate study is not as well organized. So attractive are these and other aspects of U.S. higher education that the European Union, through the Bologna initiatives, is adapting many of these practices to meet European needs.

American higher education is also attractive to faculty members and researchers. The academic ranks are well-defined, and U.S. academic institutions have traditionally been willing to appoint foreigners to academic posts (in sharp contrast to many other countries, including Japan, where it has been difficult for noncitizens to obtain professorships). The immigration of highly educated people—some fleeing repression and others coming to improve their working conditions—has been and continues to be an important catalyst for intellectual and scientific life in the United States.

The academic working conditions in the United States are also generally attractive. Academic freedom is an accepted norm, and there are few restrictions on teaching or research. The past several decades have witnessed some deterioration in academic work—for example, an increase in the number of part-time as compared to full-time staff, some cutbacks in appointments, and slow salary growth. But in contrast to higher education institutions in many other countries, American universities and colleges are attractive places to teach and study.

With English the official language of scholarship, the United States benefits from having the largest English-speaking academic system in the world. Not only is English the most widely studied second language worldwide; it is the lingua franca of both science and international business. Countries that offer higher education in English have an inherent advantage in the international marketplace, so much so that many nations—including China, Japan, the Netherlands, and even France—are offering academic programs in English.

American universities, and American culture generally, have traditionally been open to international students. The United States, as a multiethnic and multiracial society, has a long experience with immigrants and is viewed as tolerant of people of various backgrounds. Despite a documented history of racial discrimination, the United States is seen abroad as an open society in comparison to many other countries. American universities have faculties that include people from many nationalities and backgrounds. This openness is an attractive feature for international students and scholars.

For these and other reasons, American higher education has drawn students, faculty members, and researchers from many countries. They have come to the United States to study and in some instances have returned home after obtaining their academic degrees or after a period of employment in the United States. Others stay and make their careers in the United States. Still others study for shorter periods of time, experiencing American culture and academe, but obtain their degrees at home. Visiting scholars and researchers (97,000 in 2005) come to the United States for periods of research or study. The myriad ways in which foreign students and scholars have engaged in study and research in America have formed an extensive sustainable network of relationships that provides an important infrastructure for public diplomacy. Through study abroad and academic exchange, such as the Fulbright Program, the United States has developed a deep reservoir of mutual understanding and goodwill with opinion leaders in other countries. It has served as a vital aspect of America's ability to present and explain itself to the rest of the world.

The U.S. Motivation in International Education

One reason for America's successful role in higher education worldwide is the lack of central government planning and the presence of diversity. The federal government has sponsored a variety of initiatives—including well-known and successful programs sponsored by the U.S. Department of State and other programs under the auspices of the National Science Foundation, the Department of Defense, and other agencies. However, only a small minority of international students and scholars in the United States are funded by these or other government programs. Further, while there is a growing international outreach by the new for-profit sector in the United States, the large majority of international initiatives are sponsored and funded by either publicly supported state institutions or private nonprofit academic institutions—with the bulk of funding coming from those participating in the programs.

The interest of U.S. colleges and universities is not merely altruistic in nature. Foreign students, totaling more than 564,000 in 2005, are estimated to add about $13 billion to the U.S. economy. They contribute to the coffers of the universities that serve them and the communities in which they live. Indeed, many universities and colleges have designated staff whose sole purpose is to attract foreign students to their institutions. The huge exhibit hall at annual meetings of NAFSA: Association of International Educators is filled with academics who are competing to attract foreign students to their countries and institutions. Whether for monetary or intellectual capital, the value of attracting foreign students to U.S. higher education constitutes very serious business. In the quest to be more successful in enrolling foreign students at U.S. institutions, a number of national educational organizations have called upon the government to develop a national policy in this area (NAFSA 2000).

The motivations of the academic community vary, although most American colleges and universities define their main goals as academic rather than commercial. Committed to internationalizing their campuses, many institutions enroll international students as well as sending their own students abroad for study. Similarly, campus-based international programs, curricular offerings, and related undertakings are aimed at providing an international orientation for students. Some colleges and universities see internationalization as a key part of their academic programs. Foreign students, especially at the graduate and professional levels, also support the research and teaching programs of many universities—serving as teaching and research assistants. In some fields of study such as a few graduate engineering specialties, as well as some doctoral fields in computer science and management studies, foreign students constitute a significant part of enrollments. In fact, some departments and programs could not survive without them. A small number of schools depend on international enrollments to fill seats and balance the budget.

Direct commercial motivation increasingly serves as a stimulus for international programs and initiatives. Several of the new for-profit providers, such as Laureate Education (formerly Sylvan Learning Systems) and the Apollo Group, are active internationally in higher education. Traditional academic institutions are now more likely to see overseas activities as potentially profitable ventures. It is unclear how commercialization and a market orientation will affect the traditional norms and values of higher education, but there is little question that some changes will occur.

It is not possible to quantify the various goals for internationalization in American higher education, and there are certainly a mixture of rationales and motivations. However, if the motivation becomes largely commercial, as it is in many countries, it will in the long run weaken the academic enterprise of foreign study. Among the diverse motivations and policies, governmental initiative is without question only a minor factor.

The Impact of Foreign Study

It is possible to see many of these factors as elements of soft power—of the continuing impact of one culture on the thinking and behavior of people from different countries.

Without question, those who study abroad are influenced by their sojourn. They learn about the subjects they study, and many earn academic degrees that are useful at home. While science is of course universal, approaches to the curriculum, methodologies, and publications reflect particular countries. International students studying at American universities learn American approaches to science and scholarship, use American methods, and focus often on American data and problems. All these aspects of education shape lifelong perspectives on academic work.

Students also experience the academic cultures where they study. It is common for graduates of American universities to return home with a zealousness to alter their home institutions to resemble the American academic model—by promoting the departmental organization, the seminars, the course-credit system, and the availability of laboratory and library facilities. These arrangements may be effective, and feasible, in Wisconsin but may be impracticable in Niger or Cambodia. Students learn ways of engaging in scientific inquiry, specific methodologies, forms of interaction on campus, and the other subtle but nonetheless important norms of academic life. They get linked to specific networks of colleagues who remain relevant to them in later life, networks easy to maintain because of the Internet. Students master the use of specialized equipment—certain kinds of laboratory instrumentation, computers, and programming. The American university has a style of academic work that is often adopted by international students and scholars.

Nonacademic norms and values may also influence international students and scholars. Such effects may be as varied as a predilection for American fast food, an affinity for certain elements of U.S. popular culture, adoption of aspects of the American lifestyle, or even marriage to an American spouse.

Most international students return to countries that are not as academically developed as the United States, and a kind of center-periphery relationship takes hold. The graduates in their subsequent careers look to the United States as a central reference, working with American colleagues, using American scientific equipment, adopting American methodologies for work, and advising students to study in the United States. American universities and scholars help to maintain these links over time through alumni organizations, informal scientific networks, and international conferences, and in many other ways (Bureau of Educational and Cultural Affairs 2001). U.S. universities even seek to raise funds from wealthy overseas alumni. In a number of cases, returning scholars have provided the impetus for their own higher education institutions to adopt American models for substantial reform. The 1993 higher education act in Hungary reflected this kind of change. Hungarian university rectors were very influential in the law's passage. Six of the rectors involved in this reform movement had studied in America as Fulbright Scholars.

The Present and the Future

In the latter half of the twentieth century, the United States became the world leader in attracting foreign students and scholars to its shores. The United States is widely admired for its renowned scholars and Nobel laureates, an enviable record of scientific discovery, as well as the institutions that spawn the research. The beginning of the twenty-first century, however, represented a period of significant transition in international higher education. The key factors are the impact of September 11, 2001, on the United States, especially in the area of immigration policy and the general openness of the society, and the simultaneous emergence of competitors in the field of international higher education, the advent of distance education, and the rise of new for-profit academic providers.

The essential elements of American higher education's role in the world did not change as a result of September 11. The U.S. academic and research systems remain the strongest in the world, and students worldwide still see the United States as a major academic attraction. Yet shifts are evident—some obvious, some subtle, and some as yet uncertain. While the total numbers of international students worldwide continue to grow, increases in foreign-student enrollments in the United States stopped in 2002–3 and actually decreased by 2.4 percent in 2003–4, at a time when most major competitors were seeing significant growth in their overseas enrollments (Koh 2004; Altbach 2004).

These countries, increasingly entrepreneurial in their pursuit of graduate enrollments, are benefiting from the progressively more inhospitable environment for foreign students in the United States. Coming to study in the United States has become an obstacle course, and prospective students abroad are increasingly leery of stringent, changing, arbitrary, and sometimes inconsistent government regulations regarding visas, reporting to government agencies, and the like. Students from developing countries, especially those from the Islamic world, report being treated in their countries with disrespect by U.S. consular officials at American embassies. American university administrators responsible for international students also express concern that a significant number of students are denied visas or are forced to wait so long for their visas that they are unable to study in the United States, although government statistics do not show a significant number of visa denials.

A report from the Council of Graduate Schools documented a 28 percent drop from the previous year in applications for 2004 graduate school enrollments from foreign students in a survey of 125 top graduate schools in the United States (Council of Graduate Schools 2004). While applications for 2005 did not decline as steeply, they were down by 5 percent from 2004. They have, however, shown some signs of rebounding since then—2006 numbers were significantly up. The Council of Graduate Schools has sounded the alarm by indicating that such a trend may signal a change in the nation's status as the destination of choice for international students. This has prompted American university administrators to ask U.S. government officials to examine what can be done to ameliorate the situation. The implementation of the Student and Exchange Visitor Information System (SEVIS), a computer-based tracking system, by the Department of Homeland Security and the imposition of new fees charged to students from abroad constitute additional barriers. News of the difficult visa process has spread rapidly through foreign student populations and their families. The stories and myths concerning these difficulties have combined to create a new reality for the attractiveness of American higher education. Student applicants and their parents hear about these difficulties, and some choose not to come to the United States—particularly now that other countries are laying out welcome mats.

It is not only students who may experience a chilling effect. Recent examples, such as that of Tariq Ramadan, also add to concern about the openness of American society and its institutions. Professor Ramadan, a Swiss theologian who was born in Egypt, is a well-known and respected authority on Islamic religion. His invitation to be the Henry

Luce Professor of Religion, Conflict, and Peace at Notre Dame University became a casualty of America's new immigration policies. The revocation of his visa has been seen as a prime example of the decreasing openness of the American government and, by extension, academic institutions to a broad spectrum of visiting scholars. Professor Ramadan's recent appointment at Oxford University poses an interesting juxtaposition of the U.S. and UK responses to terrorism.

According to a 2002 survey conducted by JWT Communications, students considering studying abroad see the United States as a less safe place to study compared to such competitors as Australia and the United Kingdom (but such safety concerns do not yet loom very large, at least in the absence of additional major terrorist attacks in the United States). Although American international study administrators have noted an increase in concerns about safety, foreign students currently studying in the United States report feeling quite safe—security is seen as a greater problem from outside the United States than it is by students actually studying in the country. Many foreign students are more concerned about the safety of American students studying in some countries and regions in light of anti-Americanism. Only a small number of foreign students went home immediately following September 11, and most of them later returned to the United States to complete their studies.

The world of international higher education is not static. Key competitors have placed much greater emphasis than they have in the past on attracting students to their universities and see that increased American barriers to foreign students work to their advantage. Even before the effects of 9/11, there were indications that competitors were eroding some of the U.S. king-of-the-hill status. In 1970, the United States enrolled about 30 percent of the world's college students, but by 2000 its market share of the global college student population had fallen to 14 percent. This decline is apparent in the area of science and engineering. For example, in 1999, Europe surpassed the United States in its production of PhDs in science and engineering, and Asia is rapidly increasing its percentage as well. Over the past thirty years, America's leading role in educating scientists and engineers has been steadily falling (Freeman 2005). This decline is entirely natural as other countries build up their own higher education capabilities and competitors for international students strengthen their programs and enhance their marketing.

Other regions are successfully competing with the United States for foreign students. Australia is an especially aggressive recruiter of foreign students, with the United Kingdom and New Zealand not far behind. The Canadian government recently announced that it was altering its immigration policies to help its colleges and universities recruit foreign students. All of these countries see attracting students to their institutions as a major source of revenue and a way to perhaps increase their soft power through higher education. They are all in a position to take advantage of English as the lingua franca of international education. Their governments have stimulated an active foreign-provider education policy as a means of reducing local expenditures on higher education.

Other countries may also begin to see their own higher education systems as strong enough to warrant less support of studying abroad for their students. For example, in 2004 the Mexican government decided to provide less funding for graduate study in the United States. The announcement was accompanied by a statement indicating that the action was justified due to the increased strength and status of graduate programs at Mexican institutions. The governments of Singapore and Malaysia have announced their intentions of becoming attractive higher education centers in Asia and of offering first-class higher education to a broad clientele. Countries such as Qatar and Dubai are building "education cities" to attract students from the region who might otherwise be lured to the United States.

Japan is the largest host country for international students in Asia. Its academic system remains the strongest in the region. Prime Minister Nakasone's call, several decades ago, to enroll 100,000 international students by 2000 was not quite met at the time, although more than 118,000 international students are now studying in Japan. More than 90 percent come from Asia, and the large majority are Chinese. Japan identified international higher education as a source of soft power and devoted modest resources to attracting students from other countries, with a special emphasis on its major Asian trading partners. Scholarships are available for well-qualified international students to study at the top national universities. Japan has been less successful in attracting students from North America and Europe, with fewer than 5 percent of Japan's international student population coming from these regions. Japan faces several challenges in attracting international students—the most important of which is the Japanese language. Japanese is difficult to learn, and it is not used internationally. Students from China and Korea find it easier to learn Japanese than Westerners do, and this has helped boost enrollments from these countries. Facilities for international students have been limited, although improvements have been made recently.

While Japan has historically been a major force in international education in Asia, other nations in the region, such as Singapore, Malaysia, and China, are posing a challenge by making significant efforts to position themselves to be educational destinations for Asian students. China and India are traditionally the largest senders of students to the United States. Both countries show some variations in flow rates. In 2004, both sent fewer students to the United States than they had previously, with China's number declining by 5 percent—reflecting perhaps difficulties encountered in obtaining clearances and visas to study in the United States (Koh 2004). Statistics from 2005–6 show that numbers have again picked up, so the decline seems to have been temporary.

The Chinese, however, aspire to having a world-class system of higher education, and this may in the long run keep Chinese students at home. For example, Tsinghua University, often referred to as "China's MIT," is becoming a powerhouse for scientific research with the Chinese government's strong support. In just a decade, the data on top undergraduate students from Tsinghua's science departments have changed from the majority pursuing graduate education in the United States to the majority remaining in China for further education. China is rapidly closing its science and technology gap. It is projected that by 2010, Chinese universities will graduate more students with science and engineering doctorates than their U.S. counterparts (Freeman 2005). Thomas L. +Friedman's book *The World Is Flat* has also drawn increasing attention to the fact that countries such as China and India are moving significantly ahead in the development of their knowledge-based economies (Friedman 2005). These trends will lead to a reduced dependence on U.S. higher education for achieving their national ambitions.

Another indication that China's patterns of student mobility may be changing is the increase in the number of foreign students, primarily from Asia, choosing to pursue study in China. The number was up 11 percent in 2004 and hit a record high. The Ministry of Education has stated a goal of attracting foreign students to study in China. The ministry reported that the dramatic progress in attracting students from overseas could be attributed to outreach to countries by the government ("Overseas Students" 2005). Services for foreign students have improved, adding to the attractiveness of Chinese universities. Newly developed institutions patterned on American models, such as Shantou University, and the development of more innovative programs of study for international students at Peking University are signs of new trends.

Views of China's role in the region and its international behavior may also be making it a more attractive destination. A poll of twenty-two countries by the BBC World Service revealed that China is viewed as playing a more positive role in the world than the United States. Particularly significant are the favorable views of neighboring countries where China has traditionally been regarded with suspicion and dislike. Also enhancing China's attractiveness to students from Asia and beyond is that young people are more prone to view China positively (BBC World Service 2005).

While China's institutions may be making progress in the exercise of soft power, European institutions historically performed a significant role in Europe's influence on the United States, particularly in the development of U.S. institutions. Over time, Europe's influence waned, and the roles were reversed. It is thus noteworthy that Europe—both its individual countries and the European Union (EU)—is taking steps to regain its influence. This trend can be readily seen in Germany's efforts to increase the strength of its scholarly community and research prowess vis-á-vis that of the United States. A significant "brain-gain" campaign is under way among Germany's elite universities. In 2005, former chancellor Gerhard Schröder pledged to inject $250 million into five institutions to attract world academic talent. Among other things, this campaign is seeking to bring back German scholars who have settled in at U.S. institutions ("To Halt Brain Drain" 2005).

The changes taking place in Europe as a result of the EU Bologna process are equally important, although they are headed in a different direction. More European students will probably choose to study within the European Union, where costs are low and the "common academic space" makes cross-border study easy. Once the procedures are fully implemented, which should happen in the next five years or so, the European Union might well turn abroad to lure students from outside Europe, both to earn income and to contribute to the European Union's foreign policy goals. At present, EU debates seem to be focused mainly on the complexities of implementing the Bologna initiatives rather than on Europe's academic impact abroad. A few countries, such as Spain, are implementing international programs to expand the influence of Spanish higher education abroad, specifically to Latin America.

The New Transnationalism

Not only are students on the move—so, too, are institutions. We are at the beginning of the era of transnational higher education, in which academic institutions from one country operate in another, academic programs are jointly offered by universities from different countries, and higher education is delivered through distance technologies. These developments will affect flows of students from one country to another.

Transnational initiatives operate within the north-to-south dynamic and are almost without exception dominated by the partner institutions in the North—in terms of curriculum, orientation, and sometimes the teaching staff. Frequently, the medium of instruction is the language of the dominant partner, very often English, even if the local standard language of instruction is not English. There is often little effort to adapt offshore programs to the needs or traditions of the country in which the programs are offered—they are simply exported intact. A McDonald's hamburger in Malaysia is the same as one in Chicago—even if the beef is halal, to meet Muslim religious requirements.

Australia and the United Kingdom have been pioneers in transnational higher education, with the United States only now becoming a force in this area. In some cases, transnational arrangements are made between universities and postsecondary institutions abroad, and in others, the "partners" are corporations or entrepreneurs interested in entering the new education industry. Australian universities have, for example, linked up with academic institutions and private companies in Malaysia, and more recently in South Africa and Vietnam, to offer Australian degrees "offshore." A student can earn an Australian degree in Malaysia or Vietnam, for example, without ever setting foot in Australia. There are also franchising agreements that permit local providers to use educational programs of offshore institutions, for which they give their own degrees. Governments see transnational education, like attracting foreign students, as a way to increase higher education's revenues and, perhaps, their soft power. At the campus level, too, international initiatives produce significant income for a small but growing number of institutions. Indeed, the primary goal of many of the branch campuses and transnational programs is to enrich the home campus.

Although their presence has not historically been a significant part of the overall picture, some American academic institutions have been involved in transnational enterprises for a long time. A few U.S. universities—Boston University, the University of Maryland, and Widener University, for example—have been operating offshore branches for many years, to serve Americans (including those in the armed forces) overseas as well as an international clientele. A few foreign institutions have operated under the umbrella of American accreditation and sponsorship—the American University of Beirut is a prime example. In the 1970s, more than a dozen American colleges and universities opened branch campuses in Japan, hoping to benefit from Japan's booming economy and academic market at the time. But with one or two exceptions, the U.S. institutions in Japan were not among the more prestigious American academic institutions—several were in fact toward the bottom of the hierarchy. The American branches had problems with recognition by the Japanese education authorities and, after the Japanese economic bubble burst, with finances and enrollments. In 2005, just one of those branches continues to operate. The Japanese case illustrates the risks of expanding offshore higher education.

But the past few years have witnessed a new and more sophisticated approach to global expansion on the part of American institutions. The University of Chicago's business school established a branch campus in Barcelona, Spain, offering an MBA, and the curriculum includes a period of study at the main campus in Chicago; it is soon moving to London to better position itself in the European market. Both Chicago and the Wharton School of Business at the University of Pennsylvania are establishing branches in Singapore. American universities have also assisted in the development of a growing number of institutions called the "American University of . . ." in Bulgaria, Azerbaijan, Tajikistan, and some other countries. These schools typically seek and are often granted accreditation by agencies in the United States.

American overseas expansion is in some cases taking on an unabashedly entre-preneurial design. When Israel opened up its educational market more than a decade ago, several U.S. schools set up programs in teacher education and other fields in cooperation with Israeli entrepreneurs to meet a local need. The American institutions all consisted of low-prestige and in several cases quite marginal schools in need of a financial boost from overseas enrollments. Israeli authorities have since partially re-stricted such foreign collaborations, in part because of concerns about low quality and the lack of adequate supervision from the sponsoring institutions. Laureate Education, a for-profit higher education provider, is pursuing a different strategy for its overseas expansion. Laureate has purchased several foreign institutions (e.g., in Mexico and Spain). It is not clear if these schools will have links with U.S. institutions or will be accredited in the United States. The University of Phoenix, the largest private for-profit university in the United States, is also working to expand its overseas network. It has a small campus in China and will open another one in Mexico. Without question, U.S. higher education exports will grow and have an as yet undetermined impact on American higher education generally and on the United States' soft power.

The prospect for expanding trade in higher education services worldwide through the implementation of a version of the General Agreement on Trade in Services (GATS), which is part of the current negotiations of the World Trade Organization, may ac-celerate both the opportunities and the problems associated with transnational educa-tion. GATS, if implemented, would remove some restrictions on cross-border higher education initiatives, making it easier for U.S. academic institutions and corporations to offer programs and set up branches abroad. How this would affect international student flows or the specific policies of American universities is unclear.

The U.S. government, through the Department of Commerce, and the for-profit private higher education providers have favored GATS, while organizations including the American Council on Education and the academic community generally have opposed it. The opponents are concerned that the increased emphasis on competition and markets produced by GATS would affect the traditional values of American colleges and universities. There is a general feeling that higher education is not a commodity to be traded in international markets like steel or bananas. Some people in higher education also worry that GATS would jeopardize academic autonomy in the developing nations, in that governments would no longer be able to control education imports to their own countries. The debate continues, and the effects of GATS remain unclear.

Distance education is also part of the transnational picture. So far, cross-border distance higher education remains a small part of the total picture, but the number of students seeking Internet-based degrees is growing rapidly and will continue to expand. Will distance degrees be accepted in job markets around the world? If so, will students choose to study on the Internet in large numbers rather than traveling overseas? Distance education along with the provision of U.S. degrees in other countries through joint-degree or franchise arrangements with foreign universities will affect the numbers of students choosing to go abroad to study and will raise many questions about how America's soft power will be exercised in this context.

Conclusion

The United States faces significant competition in the rapidly expanding world of international study. While American higher education remains attractive to foreign students and scholars, competitors have several major advantages. These countries have instituted national policies relating to international study and cross-border higher education initiatives. They have been setting goals, putting policies into place, and giving incentives to academic institutions to attract foreign students. The United States, in contrast, has never developed a national approach concerning international higher education, an area of low priority for the Department of Education at the federal level. Now, whatever national policies do exist have been erected in the cause of national security, not international education. These policies have resulted in a myriad of new regulations that make it more difficult than ever before for foreign students and scholars to come to the United States. Further, the number of federally funded scholarships for overseas students recently showed a decline. The states, traditionally responsible for higher education policy in the United States, are quite focused on local issues such as the financing of higher education and have exhibited little interest in international students, despite the fact that those students bring significant amounts of money into local economies and provide needed help as low-paid teaching and research assistants in public universities. These circumstances leave an open field for the competition and may be the prelude to changing patterns and destinations of students seeking higher education, particularly those from developing countries.

The story of international student flows includes the significant expansion in worldwide numbers, increased competition among the major host countries, and the growing but as yet unclear impact of technology on the delivery of academic programs. The United States will remain a major player in all of these developments because of the size and excellence of its academic system. Whether the United States will be able to maintain its competitive edge and its leadership is another matter.

As noted at the beginning of this chapter, America's soft power has rested primarily on the attractiveness of its ideas and institutions. For the past half century, U.S. institutions of higher education have played an increasingly active and vital role in shaping and sustaining positive relationships with other nations. At this point in the twenty-first century, the United States stands at a challenging crossroads in terms of its image in the world and its exercise of public diplomacy.

The debate in the United States about how to improve international relationships has been intense. One school of thought proposes treating the United States like a brand with a bad image that could be improved with a well-planned advertising campaign. Building media networks that function with a propagandistic slant is also suggested as a winning strategy. Other variations on the theme involve sending high-profile basketball players and rock stars to the Middle East to convert teenage populations into admirers of the United States. The common bond linking all these schemes is that they seem to ignore higher education and the elite groups educated in universities. This includes not only the academic profession but also public intellectuals and other opinion leaders.

Juxtaposed with these suggestions is a deeper and more thoughtful vein of advice, some of which was noted earlier. This perspective focuses on the importance of educational exchange and the engagement of elites, as well as the general citizenry. The American government has been counseled that its ideas and values about democracy, human rights, freedom of speech, religious tolerance, and respect for national sovereignty are critical components of the relationships between the United States and the rest of the world. In a recent discussion about the challenges to America's ongoing attractiveness, a former Singaporean ambassador reminded his listeners that American universities educated elites who flocked as young students from all over the world to study in the United States. Many of them learned the language and ideas of American democracy and its philosophical underpinnings. As leaders in their countries, they now hold the government of the United States to the same high standards abroad to which Americans hold their own government at home (Mahbubani 2005). When America's admirers perceive the country to be less open or more dismissive of the rights of others than it has been in the past, meeting the challenge to the attractiveness of America and its institutions may be the biggest test of the soft power of the United States.

These issues of defining and acting on principles of democracy from a multicultural perspective and on an international scale will necessarily involve higher education. As opposed to defining the "American brand" in a monolithic way, the principles upon which American colleges and universities have been built foster free and open engagement of ideas and diversity of opinion. These are the traits that have made U.S. higher education institutions such an attractive destination for study and research for generations of foreign students and scholars and a central part of the nation's soft power.

References

Altbach, Philip G. 1971. "Education and Neocolonialism." *Teachers College Record* 72 (May): 543–58.

Altbach, Philip G. 2001. "The American Academic Model in Comparative Perspective." In *In Defense of American Higher Education*. Ed. P.G. Altbach, P.J. Gumport, and D.B. Johnstone, 11–37. Baltimore: Johns Hopkins University Press.

Altbach, Philip G. 2004. "Higher Education Crosses Borders." *Change* 36 (March–April): 18–25.

American Academy of Diplomacy. 2004. *Report of a Special Task Force of the American Academy of Diplomacy*. Washington, DC: American Academy of Diplomacy.

Ashby, Eric. 1966. *Universities: British, Indian, African*. Cambridge, MA: Harvard University Press.

Barber, Elinor G., Philip G. Altbach, and Robert G. Myers, eds. 1984. *Bridges to Knowledge: Foreign Students in Comparative Perspective*. Chicago: University of Chicago Press.

Basu, Aparna. 1974. *The Growth of Education and Political Development in India, 1898–1920*. Delhi: Oxford University Press.

BBC World Service. 2005. *BBC World Poll: Twenty-two Nation Poll Shows China Viewed Positively by Most Countries Including Asia Neighbors*, March 5. http://www.pipa.org/OnlineReports/China/China_Mar05/China_Mar05_rpt.pdf (accessed December 1, 2007).

Bureau of Educational and Cultural Affairs. 2001. *Outcome Assessment of the U.S. Fulbright Scholar Program*. Washington, DC: SRI International.

Chomsky, Noam, ed. 1997. *The Cold War and the University: Toward an Intellectual History of the Postwar Years*. New York: New Press.

Coombs, Philip. 1964. *The Fourth Dimension of Foreign Policy: Education and Cultural Affairs*. New York: Harper and Row.

Council of Graduate Schools. 2004. *International Graduate Student Survey*. Washington, DC: Council of Graduate Schools.

Council on Foreign Relations. 2003. *Finding America's Voice: A Strategy for Reinvigorating U.S. Public Diplomacy*. Report of Independent Task Force. New York: Council on Foreign Relations.

Djerejian, Edward P. 2003. *Changing Minds, Winning Peace: A New Strategic Direction for U.S. Public Diplomacy in the Arab and Muslim World*. Report submitted to the Committee on Appropriations, U.S. House of Representatives. Washington, DC: Advisory Commission on Public Diplomacy.

Freeman, Richard. 2005. *Does Globalization of the Scientific/Engineering Workforce Threaten U.S. Economic Leadership?* Cambridge, MA: Labor Studies Program, National Bureau of Economic Research.

Friedman, Thomas L. 2005. *The World Is Flat: A Brief History of the Twenty-first Century*. New York: Farrar, Straus and Giroux.

Gonzalez, Andrew. 2004. *The Philippines: Past, Present, and Future Dimensions of Higher Education*. In *Asian Universities*. Ed. P.G. Altbach and T. Umakoshi, 279–300. Baltimore: Johns Hopkins University Press.

Haskins, Charles Homer. 2002. *The Rise of Universities*. New Brunswick, NJ: Transaction.

Koh, Hey-Kyung. 2004. *Open Doors: Report on International Student Exchange*. New York: Institute of International Education.

Lutz, Jessie Gregory. 1971. *China and the Christian Colleges*. Ithaca, NY: Cornell University Press.

Mahbubani, Kishore. 2005. *Beyond the Age of Innocence*. New York: Public Affairs.

NAFSA: Association of International Educators. 2000. *Toward an International Education Policy for the United States*. Washington, DC: NAFSA: Association of International Educators.

Nye, Joseph S., Jr. 2004. *Soft Power: The Means to Success in World Politics.* New York: Public
    Affairs.
O'Malley, John W., Gauvin Alexander Bailey, Steven J. Harris, and T. Frank Kennedy, eds.
    1999. *The Jesuits: Cultures, Sciences, and the Arts, 1540–1773.* Toronto: University of
    Toronto Press.
"Overseas Students' Number Hits Record High." 2005. *China Daily,* May 24.
Pew Research Center for the People and the Press. 2003. *Views of a Changing World.* Wash-
    ington, DC: Pew Research Center for the People and the Press.
Public Diplomacy Council. 2005. *A Call for Action on Public Diplomacy.* Washington, DC:
    Public Diplomacy Council.
"To Halt Brain Drain, Germany Adopts 'Competition' Mantra." 2005. *Christian Science Moni-
    tor,* February 1.

4

Facing Crisis

Soft Power and Japanese Education in a Global Context

Yonezawa Akiyoshi

This chapter considers the history, current condition, and future vision of Japanese education, focusing on its own attractiveness, or soft power, for both Japanese and non-Japanese citizens in a global context. Distinguishing three types of powers, namely, military power, economic power, and soft power, Nye (2004, pp. 5–6) stated that "soft power rests on the ability to shape the preference of others" and that "soft power is attractive power." Approaches to discussing the relationship between soft power and education in Japan can be based on (1) the soft power or attractiveness of Japanese education itself and (2) the contribution or influence of the education sector in relation to Japanese soft power in general.

As a diplomatic concept, soft power is inevitably linked with the international context when it is applied to the field of education. Accordingly, the views toward Japanese education of actors both inside and outside of Japanese society must be taken into consideration.

In general, direct international exchanges in the field of education are more frequent in higher education, because of students' mobility, language skills, and intercultural skills. Teichler (1999) developed a typology of internationalization contexts of higher education systems based on degrees of necessity and respective situations within the global system. The contexts of this typology are characterized as follows: (1) *would-be internationalization:* wanting to be partners in international communication and cooperation but facing problems that prevent partnership on equal terms; (2) *life-or-death internationalization:* viewing internationalization as indispensable; (3) *two arenas:* being limited to striving for either more national, or more international, visibility; and (4) *internationalization by import:* hosting foreign students and considering international research only if published in the host country's dominant language.

Teichler categorizes Japan as a type 3 and the United States as a type 4 country, reflecting the different positions held by these two countries in the broader, global higher education power structure. The U.S. higher education system is regarded as the center of the world, protected by the hard and soft power of the country as well as the English language and the quality of American higher education itself. The Japanese higher education system, for its part, has assumed a central position in the East Asian region at least, and has attracted a significant number of high-profile international students who have managed to learn through instruction in the Japanese language. However, Japanese academics and students are aware that they are not at the global center, and they feel the necessity to further internationalize Japanese higher education to improve linkages with the global community.

In contrast to the U.S. example, the soft power of Japanese education in the domestic context and that in the global context are clearly distinguishable. Type 3 countries such as Japan, France, and Germany face difficulty in transforming their systems into type 2 systems because of the parallel yet separate existence of the international and domestic arenas. Even if the international arena gradually becomes larger and the domestic arena gradually becomes smaller, public sectors will remain largely domestic in orientation. Nevertheless, ongoing globalization will provide an impetus for these nations to eventually become type 2 countries.

In 1987, the U.S. Department of Education issued a report identifying the Japanese education system as one of the best models to examine, mainly in light of its perceived efficiency in human resource development. Even at that time, however, the international reputation of Japanese education was limited to primary and secondary education, which produced well-trained and homogeneous workers suitable for a rather domestic-oriented labor market. Japanese higher education has thus received more attention as a mechanism for producing a trainable and talented workforce, rather than an example of quality in teaching and learning (Dore 1997).

As is the case with its higher education, Japanese basic education is also losing its appeal. Although the academic achievement of Japanese students until the end of secondary education is relatively high, Japanese education does not have any outstanding merits compared with neighboring East Asian countries. Indeed, Japanese education seems to be losing its soft power in all respects.

Overall, Japanese education as a source of soft power is in crisis. Reflection on history and current conditions is indispensable to the development of a future vision. The report "Japan's 21st Century Vision" (Council on Economic and Fiscal Policy 2005) clarified the danger that Japan will be left behind in the process of globalization, and specified human resource development and education as priority areas for policy action. In September 2005, the Ministry of Education, Culture, Sports, Science, and Technology (MEXT) also published a proposal outlining its international strategy. Focusing on human resource development and academic and cultural exchanges, the MEXT proposal stated the following four objectives: (1) the strengthening of Japan's international competitiveness in an age of great global competition, (2) the improvement of Japan's soft power, (3) contribution for the solution of various global tasks, and (4) the strengthening of partnerships with Asian countries.[1]

Education is inevitably a core factor in developing the future soft power of Japanese society, because humans are the only resource available to increase its attractiveness. At the same time, Japan is no longer the only Asian country that can be proud of high academic achievement and technological advancement. Although the government and society in general recognize the importance of education, the future vision for improving the soft power of Japanese education and for utilizing the education sector to improve the soft power of Japanese society is unclear at this time.

To understand the nature of the soft power of Japanese education itself and the function of the Japanese schooling system to develop the soft power of Japanese society, this chapter analyzes historical change and current reality within Japanese schooling and its relationship to the soft power of Japanese society. Future visions of Japanese education are then discussed, with particular emphasis on potential contributions to the development of Japan's soft power from a global perspective.

History of Japanese Education and Soft Power

A look at educational development in Japan readily reveals that education itself has functioned as a device to transform military and economic power into soft power over relatively recent decades. Three stages in the transformation of the relationship linking education and the military, the economy, and soft power can be identified, namely: (1) education supported by military power (1868–1950); (2) accumulation of soft power in education through economic development (1950–80); and (3) utilizing soft power for transformation to a postindustrial society (1980–2007).

Education Supported by Military Power (1868–1950)

The Meiji government espoused the idea of *fukoku kyohei* (a rich country with a strong military) as a basic policy for national development. Under this policy, the development of military and economic power became dual national challenges, with people being the only resource that Japan could utilize to strengthen its power. Naturally, therefore, school-based education played a key role for national integration and human resource development. The dissemination of a standardized Japanese language and modernized lifestyle were implemented through school-based education and other modern, administrative hard power.

The national integration function of education was stressed not only in the original territory of Japan, but also in newly colonized territories such as Okinawa, Taiwan, and Korea. In other newly acquired territories and protectorates of the Japanese Empire, such as Indonesia, local languages were allowed, but instruction in and of the Japanese language was also promoted (Momose 2003). Japanese military occupation throughout East Asia and Southeast Asia in the 1930s and 1940s produced significant portions of whole populations who somehow learned basic Japanese language and culture.

This dissemination of Japanese language and culture was compelled through military power. Certainly, modern technology and knowledge, which were associated with the Japanese way of life, attracted neighboring peoples. Significant numbers of modernist elites were attracted to Japanese higher education and modern thought, and some studied in prewar Japan of their own volition. Tsurumi (1977) pointed out the positive effects of Japanese colonization in Taiwan, for example, technology transfer. Kim (2001) mentioned that South Korean academics utilized Japanese texts until around the 1970s. However, this having been noted, the colonization policy in many cases functioned negatively for developing Japanese soft power. Anti-Japanese sentiment in colonized Korea grew because the Korean language was prohibited and Korean names were changed into Japanese ones.

After its defeat in World War II, the Japanese position in the region was reversed. The U.S. occupational government reduced the power of the Ministry of Education (Monbusho)[2] in recognition of its use by the Japanese prewar government as a tool for supporting militaristic nationalism. Postwar "education reforms" based on American military power were implemented under strong initiatives and pressures by a committee of American experts. An American-type higher education system and decentralized education committee system at the primary and secondary education levels were introduced. The contents of the education curriculum were also changed drastically, and many parts of school textbooks were edited by having students themselves delete prohibited portions of text. The Education Basic Law, enacted in 1947, has been controversial, partly because it was enacted under the American military occupation authority, and partly because it places greater emphasis on individual human rights than it does on social cohesion and patriotism. In Japan, these two have come to be considered opposing ideals because of lingering memories of the role that prewar education policies emphasizing allegiance to the nation had in facilitating the rise of militarism. In 2006, the Education Basic Law was amended through an initiative of Prime Minister Abe Shinzo, following discussions based on the inclusion and expression of patriotism. Both individual human rights and social cohesion values including patriotism are now promoted as important aspects of the country's soft power.

Accumulation of Soft Power in Education Through Economic Development (1950–80)

The recovery of independence and the beginning of the Korean War in 1950 spurred the revival of Japan's economic power, while the country lost its military autonomy and power almost completely. Agricultural reform and other social and economic system changes, some of which had already been introduced during the Pacific War period, led to a massive movement of the population from the agricultural sector to the industrial and service sectors. The school system functioned as a meritocratic screening device for this intersector population movement. This meritocracy and the diffusion of a new middle-class lifestyle based on school education proved quite attractive to the Japanese; in many respects, the school system itself became a key component of Japanese society's soft power. Cummings (1980), analyzing the daily life of this new Japanese school system, noted that its screening function had a strong influence on the development of Asian school systems in general, especially those of Taiwan, South Korea, and Singapore.

Japanese economic development and the increasing competitive power of Japanese products fostered the cultivation of a consumption market and both direct and indirect links with Asian countries, although anti-Japanese movements sometimes presented obstacles during this transformation. In the 1970s, for example, the then–Japanese prime minister, Tanaka Kakuei, met with anti-Japanese demonstrations while visiting Indonesia, which had been occupied by the Japanese military during World War II.

Japanese Official Development Aid to Asian countries was initiated as partial reparation for its role in World War II, with technology transfer and human resource development being among the more visible results of international collaboration. However, international collaboration in education has sometimes been controversial, given its integral role in the formation of national identity. While most countries welcomed foreign investments in infrastructure and collaboration in such fields as science education, they were more hesitant to accept input from "former colonizers" or "Westerners" in the social sciences out of concern that it might interfere with the development of students' national identity. Some countries such as Malaysia have welcomed the influence of Japanese social and cultural components as a part of their "Look East" policy, aimed at counterbalancing the strong influence of Western countries and their cultures. In general, however, Asian countries exercise extreme caution when Japanese instructors become involved in core issues of national identity and culture.

Japanese contributions in the field of education are most evident in science and mathematics at the basic and secondary levels, and in engineering and the natural sciences in higher education. In general, developing countries are continuously short of trained teachers and experts in the sciences, mathematics, and technology. While Japanese technological skills and expertise have therefore been attractive to other countries, most have tried to keep the humanities and social sciences under their own control.

Utilizing Soft Power in the Transformation to a Postindustrial Society (1980–2007)

The policies of Prime Minister Nakasone Yasuhiro's cabinet on building the soft power of Japan, under his idea of "healthy internationalism," reflected a more strategic approach than had been pursued in previous years. "Healthy internationalism" was the combination of the idea of global citizenship and clearly stated nationalism (Hood 2001). At that time, Japanese automobile exports and other cultural and linguistic differences perceived as transport barriers served to increase conflicts between the U.S. and Japanese governments. Education and culture were strategically utilized as soft powers to smooth the relationship between Japan and other countries, including the United States. One key initiative under this new strategy was Nakasone's plan to attract 100,000 foreign students by 2000. While this target was realized in 2003, most foreign students are from China and Korea, and government scholarships have altogether supported only around 10 percent of international students. Most students are therefore from developing and middle-income countries without public financial aid, and have difficulty surviving without engaging in some form of employment during their study in Japan. In many cases, students are attracted by job opportunities themselves during and after higher education study in Japan as much as they are by the country's high academic standards and course offerings.

The Japanese government has also supported technology transfer and capacity development among higher education faculties in developing countries (JICA 2004). Jomo Kenyatta University in Kenya and King Monkut's University in Thailand are outstanding examples of higher education institutions whose development has benefited from Japanese international cooperation. These universities were funded by the Japanese Official Development Aid fund, and their staffs have received more than twenty years of training and support from Japanese higher education institutions. Such networks continue to contribute to the formation of effective links among Japanese, other Asian, and African academic communities. Currently, the African Institute for Capacity Development (AICAD), independent from the Jomo-Kenyatta University but located within the Jomo Kenyatta University campus, supports research activities and dissemination for poverty reduction in East African countries under a joint scheme with JICA. The ASEAN (Association of Southeast Asian Nations) University Network/Southeast Asia Engineering Education Development Network (AUN/SEED-Net), which supports capacity development of postgraduate training courses in ASEAN engineering education, is also an important example of how long-term collaboration between Japanese universities and other Asian universities can foster the soft power of Japanese higher education. In this project, future ASEAN elites in engineering education are studying together in both top institutes in Southeast Asian countries and partner Japanese universities (JICA 2004).

Although it is true that collaboration based on contributed economic prominence significantly fosters positive sympathies toward Japan, this does not indicate that Japanese higher education itself has invariably been attractive for international students and researchers. Japan tends to be chosen second or third as a destination for study. Offering scholarships is an important strategy to attract top students, as is the provision of rewarding learning environments in which these students can excel. The Japan Society for the Promotion of Science provides various scholarship schemes to draw the "best and brightest" students from both developing and developed countries. Some higher education institutions also offer scholarships to non-Japanese students. Through these measures, Japanese universities can also indirectly attract Japanese students who wish to study in an international learning and research environment. However, these opportunities for financial support are still very limited, and a majority of international students face great difficulty in acquiring Japanese-language skills sufficient to keep pace with course materials.

The Japanese government and many universities have established international student dormitories and centers for supporting international students in their study life and Japanese-language training. Adding to this, Japan combined efforts with more than ten American state universities to set up offshore programs; however, almost all failed to find stable markets (Chambers and Cummings 1990). At least until quite recently, Japanese higher education itself has continued to be protected from the international student market by low incentives for Japanese students to study seriously in foreign countries to obtain employment abroad, and the strong internal orientation of Japanese labor customs.

In short, the soft power of education has been given high priority in Japanese macro–policy planning. Throughout the twentieth century, Japan has tried various means to achieve a position of international influence, once through military power, and later through economic power. In both cases, Japan experienced resistance to or refusal of its efforts to push these hard powers into other countries. Beginning in the 1980s, the Japanese government changed its policy toward the active usage of educational soft power to facilitate its transformation into a postindustrial society. However, the Japanese education system itself has not yet succeeded in gaining sufficient soft power to attract international learners and researchers without relying on economic hard power.

The Current Decline in the Attractiveness of Japanese Education

At present, is difficult to find clear evidence that the broader appeal of Japanese education is increasing. While Japan continues to be one of the largest developed economies in the world, the impact of globalization is certainly contributing to pressure on the country to restructure its education system.

First, Japanese education policy has only a weak connection to the current boom in Japanese pop culture as a core part of contemporary Japanese soft power. While animation, television games, and "Shibuya-style" teenage fashion are regarded as representative exports of Japanese soft power in both the Western and Eastern worlds, these have long been targeted enemies of Japanese primary and secondary school education. Japanese primary and secondary schools have frequently attempted to prohibit these youth pop culture activities because they are thought to destroy the imagination, creativity, and morals of young people. South Korea had all but banned the influx of Japanese pop culture for many years, not only because it had been thought to pose a risk to the development of original Korean pop culture, but also because it was regarded as hindering the development of healthy personalities among Korean youth. In 2006, Kyoto Seika University, a private university, started a new comprehensive program of *manga* (Japanese comic book) study. However, this and other similar programs focusing on the study of Japanese pop culture command only a minimal following at this time.

Second, the academic achievement of Japanese students is under question. In primary and secondary education, the Japanese education policy of the past two decades—to foster individuality and creativity by reducing emphasis on the core "3Rs" training and by encouraging a more holistic approach to learning—is now being criticized. Recent statistics on the academic achievement of primary and secondary school children show that Japanese basic achievement in schools is in crisis (Kariya and Shimizu 2004). Trends in International Mathematics and Science Study (TIMSS)[3] 2003 indicated that while the mathematics and science achievement of Japanese eighth-grade students is at a high level, it is no longer the best in the world as shown in the result of TIMSS

Table 4.1

TOEFL Total Score Means (Computer Based) in Major Asian Countries

	Total Score Mean	Number of Examinees
Singapore	255	456
Philippines	238	6,389
India	236	72,973
Malaysia	232	1,998
South Korea	218	128,445
China (mainland)	216	9,107
Hong Kong	216	5,947
Indonesia	214	4,641
Taiwan	206	33,327
Thailand	200	13,162
North Korea	193	4,203
Japan	192	78,635
Afghanistan	182	99

Source: Educational Testing Service, *Test and Score Data Summary for TOEFL Computer-Based and Paper-Based Tests: July 2005–June 2006 Test Data* (Princeton, NJ: Educational Testing Service, 2007).

1999. The results of the Organization for Economic Cooperation and Development's (OECD) Programme for International Student Assessment (PISA) 2003, an international standardized assessment, indicated that the achievement of Japanese students was significantly high in mathematics and science literacy and problem-solving skills, but only average in reading skills among OECD countries. Fujita (2001), a leading educational expert, criticized the government's policy to reduce the amount of study in formal education in the past decade as "educational disarmament." Furthermore, and despite ever-increasing resources being dedicated to improve the situation, foreign-language proficiency among Japanese youth continues to be very problematic: In terms of English-language proficiency, mean TOEFL (Test of English as a Foreign Language) scores show Japan to be next to last, not only among Asian countries (see Table 4.1), but also among all countries worldwide.

Third, while certain Japanese universities still hold top positions in Asia, this lead is gradually diminishing relative to institutions in neighboring countries. Two world rankings of universities, released by QS and the *Times Higher Education Supplement* (*THES*), a British newspaper on higher education issues, and the Institute of Higher Education of Shanghai Jiao Tong University, a Web-based university ranking on academic performance,[4] indicate that top Japanese universities such as the University of Tokyo and Kyoto University hold very high positions globally. However, *THES* (2005) ranked Peking University the top university in the Asia-Pacific region in 2005, replacing the University of Tokyo, which had occupied the top position in Asia in almost every international ranking until 2004, and Singapore National University gained a position equal to the University of Tokyo in the 2006 *THES* ranking. The

Table 4.2.

Rankings of Top Asia-Pacific Universities, 2006 and 2007

QS THES Ranking				Shanghai Jiao Tong Ranking			
2007		2006		2007		2006	
Asia-Pacific	World	World		Asia-Pacific	World	World	
1	16	16	Australian National University	1	20	19	Tokyo University
2	17	19	University of Tokyo	2	22	22	Kyoto University
3	18	33	University of Hong Kong	3	57	54	Australian National University
3	25	29	Kyoto University	4	64	60	Hebrew University Jerusalem
5	27	22	University of Melbourne	5	67	61	Osaka University
6	31	35	University of Sydney	6	76	76	Tohoku University
7	33	45	University of Queensland	7	79	78	University of Melbourne
8	33	19	National University of Singapore	8	94	98	Nagoya University
9	36	14	Peking University	9	99	89	Tokyo Institute of Technology
10	38	50	Chinese University of Hong Kong				

Source: QS Top Universities http://www.topuniversities.com/
Academic Ranking of World Universities (ARWU) http://www.arwu.org/ranking.htm.

methodology of *THES* rankings relies heavily on peer review, an approach that has been questioned because it does not reveal details of who the peers are, as well as because some indicators and the weighting methodology are highly subjective. The domination of Japanese universities in the 2007 Shanghai Jiao Tong ranking, which is based on research performance indicators, suggests that top Japanese universities are still very strong in research among other institutions in the Asia-Pacific region. As to the THES rankings, its 2007 result ranked the University of Tokyo at the top among universities in non-English speaking coutries again, but this change is mainly based on the radical alteration of data sources of rankings. At the same time, as the data in Table 4.2 clearly indicate, Japanese higher education does not have distinguished academic performance globally.

Fourth, the fact that Japanese higher education is attracting large numbers of students does not necessarily indicate that its education and research content is globally

Table 4.3

Origins and Destinations of Incoming and Outgoing Students

International Students in Japan, 2006			Japanese Students Abroad, 2004		
	Number	% of Total		Number	% of Total
1 China	74,292	63.0	1 United States	42,215	50.9
2 South Korea	15,974	13.5	2 China	19,059	23.0
3 Taiwan	4,211	3.6	3 United Kingdom	6,395	7.7
4 Malaysia	4,156	1.8	4 Australia	3,172	3.8
Total	117,927	100.0	Total	82,945	100.0

Source: Japan Student Services Organization (JASSO), *International Students in Japan 2006.* http://www.jasso.go.jp/study_j/scholarships_sfisij_e.html.

competitive. In 2006, Japan attracted 117,927 international students, 90 percent of whom were from Asian countries (see Table 4.3). The *Asahi Shinbun* issues rankings of Japanese universities every year with various indicators, including the number and share of international students in both undergraduate and postgraduate programs. It is to be expected that in these rankings the majority of postgraduate students are found in prestigious, mainly national research-intensive universities. However, it is rather surprising that in these rankings the majority of students in undergraduate programs and in both undergraduate and postgraduate programs are found in less prestigious private universities, which are having difficulty attracting even Japanese students (see Table 4.4).

There are at least two possible explanations for what seems to be a disproportionate share of international students studying at the smaller and less prestigious universities. First, private universities have strong economic incentives to attract Japanese government subsidies, which are determined by considering the ratio of available student places to actual student enrollment figures. Should a private university fail to enroll more than half of the government-allocated study places, it is not eligible for public subsidization. The government also provides incentive funds to private institutions enrolling foreign students, an indication that the internationalization of higher education has become a national policy priority. Second, it is easier for non-Japanese students to gain entrance into smaller and less prestigious universities than into prestigious universities, because competition for student seats is not as high. There are also private agencies that arrange for students to be enrolled in Japanese universities, with some placing more emphasis on employment opportunities that can be capitalized on while studying in Japan than on the merits of any given educational program. In this sense, student visas are utilized as easily obtained working visas, a situation the Japanese government has been struggling with for some time. However, it is also true that most international students have to work to support themselves, since 90 percent of international students are supported financially neither by the Japanese government nor by their home governments (Yonezawa 2005).

Table 4.4

Number and Share of International Students by Institution, 2007

Number of International Students (Undergraduate)		Share of International Students (Undergraduate, %)	
1 Ritsumeikan Asia Pacific University*	1,733	1 Ritsumeikan Asia Pacific University*	38.1
2 Kokushikan	1,026	2 Keiai	33.8
3 Osaka Sangyo	1,021	3 Aichi Bunkyo	32.4
4 Takushoku	798	4 Osaka Kanko	25.3
5 Ryutsu Keizai	787	5 Eichi	25.2
6 Teikyo	776	6 Kyoto Sosei	24.8
7 Nihon*	707	7 Niigata Sangyo	24.5
8 Tokyo International	633	8 Chukyo Gakuin	23.9
9 Keiai	621	9 Takamatsu	23.8
10 Waseda*	599	10 Kyushu Joho	20.8

Number of International Students (Postgraduate)		Share of International Students (Postgraduate, %)	
1 Tokyo†	1,621	1 Ryutsu Kagaku	94.9
2 Waseda*	1,067	2 Ritsumeikan Asia Pacific University*	90.6
3 Kyoto†	822	3 Hiroshima Keizai	88.2
4 Tsukuba†	786	4 Hamamatsu	86.0
4 Nagoya†	786	5 Niigata Sangyo	85.7
6 Tohoku †	778	6 Asia	80.2
7 Kyushu†	730	7 Aichi Bunky	80.0
8 Kobe†	667	8 Ryutsu Keizai	79.4
9 Osaka†	637	9 Hannan	78.4
10 Tokyo Tech†	571	10 Hokkaido Bunkyo	77.8

Source: Asahi Shimbun Daigaku Ranking 2008 (Asahi Shimbun University Ranking 2008). Tokyo: Asahi Shimbun, 2007.
Notes: *Prestigious private universities
†National universities
No symbol: Private universities and colleges

Lastly, the quality control of grading, credits, and degree-granting status of a significant number of universities and colleges in Japan is under question. The famous "exam hell" that students must endure to gain acceptance to elite schools and universities is clearly based on the fact that the school system, and especially entrance to the top universities, has been utilized as an effective channel for the upgrading of social and economic status. An OECD review team once observed that the futures of Japanese youth seemed to be determined in a single day at the age of eighteen, namely, on the day of the university entrance examination (OECD 1972). At that time, there were clear incentives for children to study hard, or for families to make their children study hard, because educational achievement appeared to be a gateway to a comfortable and secure middle-class life. However, the typical characterization of university life in Japan as "leisure land" indicates that preparation for the entrance examination in itself does not ensure that students continue to study hard upon entering the university. Nor does it appear that they are being asked to; according to the OECD (2003), the graduation rate of Japanese higher education was 94 percent in 2000, the highest among OECD member countries, which clearly means it is easy to graduate Japanese universities and colleges. However, it is also true that many students, especially in the field of engineering and natural sciences, continue to apply themselves diligently to their laboratory work and in preparation for postgraduate entrance examinations. Other students study in private night schools to upgrade their professional qualifications and language skills. Based on their survey of more than 1,000 students in twelve Japanese universities from 1997 to 2003, Takeuchi (2005) argued that the attitudes of Japanese students toward learning and study habits, as measured by indicators such as class attendance and involvement in actual study, are improving.

All considered, with the exception of relatively isolated examples in the sciences, neither is the current condition of Japanese education what might be deemed "attractive," nor is it sufficient to contribute to the soft power of Japanese society. Again, a clear and strategic vision is necessary, because this country's only resource is its human resource.

Future Vision: How Can the Soft Power of Japanese Education Be Developed?

Soft power is an important tool for national prosperity, yet it is very difficult for most countries with minority-status languages and cultures to create it in the field of education. Japan's history of imposing Japanese education and culture on neighboring countries still functions as an especially severe negative factor. How, then, can the soft power of Japanese education and, by extension, that of Japanese society be developed?

Japanese primary and secondary education is now drastically changing or, to describe the situation more accurately, trying to catch up with trends of internationalization commonly seen in Asian countries. Although the Japanese government has been strengthening English-language education at the primary and secondary levels, progress in these areas lags far behind that seen in neighboring East Asian countries. At the same time, multicultural-oriented education and education for newcomers (those who do not have a Japanese family background) are hot topics in Japanese education (Shimizu and Shimizu 2001), while nationalism is also strongly stressed in ongoing educational reforms.

Among these issues, the internationalization of higher education is the most influential and strategically important, given that the number of international students is very high and directly related to the labor market in the global knowledge economy. Many Asian countries are now producing sophisticated industrial and service products, design, and culture. The development of the Asia-Pacific region has produced a significant number of new middle-class consumers. Soft power should be targeted to these new customers, based on a clear understanding and respect for their tastes and values. At the same time, the Japanese schooling system has an important function to foster good global citizens to make Japanese society more attractive. International students who choose to study in Japan are a very influential medium through which to measure and disseminate the soft power of Japanese society to the world.

Following are four case studies of Japanese universities[5] with recent and unique experiences in attempts to internationalize. These cases were chosen because the universities studied were front-runners in terms of educational provisions aimed at global student marketing. Although top comprehensive universities in Japan have been successful in attracting graduate students based on their research excellence, teaching methods and educational curricula do not meet the demands of students wishing to build on their abilities to survive in the global knowledge economy. Although there are many so-called international universities and colleges in Japan, most classes are taught in Japanese, and the majority of foreign students do not have sufficient language abilities to study in English. The diffusion of English-based transnational education, including offshore education programs by U.S., UK, and Australian higher education institutions, among Asian host countries has redefined the meaning of "internationally competitive education program." Especially in the social sciences, high-level English communicative competence is becoming almost prerequisite in many countries, not only within the Asia-Pacific region, but also in Europe and Africa. Countries facing "life-or-death internationalization" according to Teichler's categorization, such as Singapore, Malaysia, and the Netherlands, are now trying to be higher education "hubs" by providing education programs in the English language. Countries in "would-be internationalization" or "two arenas" contexts, such as China and Korea, are now increasing higher education programs in the English language, mainly targeted toward domestic students with intentions to study abroad.

There are two extreme scenarios for the future of Japanese higher education: (1) the provision of globally competitive education programs in English to attract anyone wishing to receive globally competitive education services, regardless of location or nationality, and (2) the provision of unique Japanese education programs to capture niche global markets both in Japanese and in English. While the following cases illustrate attempts to provide globally competitive social science education programs at universities located in Japan, all actually rely on the niche market of those wishing to learn something from Japanese society. These case studies can yield information regarding the future potential and possible limitations of Japanese higher education.

Case 1: Temple University Japan

The first case involves not a Japanese higher education institution, but an American one that is operated in Japan. This university is considered because transnational education services are too widely present to be ignored, and they attract students not only from inside the country in which the institutions are located, but also from other countries where there are international education branches. Temple University, a state university in Pennsylvania, has five domestic campuses within the state, overseas campuses in London, Rome, and elsewhere, and a total of around 36,000 students. Temple University opened its Tokyo branch (Temple University Japan; TUJ) as the first branch campus of an American university in Japan in the late 1980s. TUJ offers a comprehensive education system, including English training programs, undergraduate, master, and doctoral courses (for teachers of English to speakers of other languages, masters of business administration [MBA], and law), as well as continuing education programs and corporate education classes. TUJ's student body numbers about 2,100; 500 are undergraduate students and almost 60 percent are Japanese. Its campus is located in formerly commercial buildings in a downtown area.

The primary mission of TUJ is to provide Japanese students with education at the same level as that offered by the main campus in the United States. It is accredited by the Middle States Commission on Higher Education, a regional accreditation association in the United States, and its curricula are identical to those of the main campus. All programs are taught in English and given in classes comprised of small groups of students. Although students can freely select courses, depending on their own interests and enthusiasm to some extent, TUJ offers fewer courses than its parent campus. Students who prefer studying at a higher level or selecting from a wider range of study areas are encouraged to study at the main U.S. campus. In fact, at the TUJ undergraduate school, almost forty students move to the main campus every year. International students who come to study at TUJ, however, seem to be attracted by a system whereby American university degrees are conferred in Japan.

TUJ is building educational merit through a positive combination of the compact and flexible systems adopted by the Japanese campus, and the numerous programs offered at the main U.S. campus. TUJ is not without its own unique problems and challenges, however. There were many cases where graduates of TUJ who applied for jobs in Japan were simply rejected because of the university's low profile in Japan. TUJ faces a reality in which the branch campus in Japan cannot improve the disadvantageous job placement situation until it gains wider recognition as a university. In contrast, American university degrees continue to represent an advantage for students who hope to find employment or move to foreign universities overseas.

Case 2: Kansai Gaidai University

Kansai Gaidai University, which has been committed to promoting exchange programs since the 1970s, is widely known for the size of its international network, not only in Japan but also worldwide. The Asian studies program plays an important role in accepting international students. With regard to Japanese students applying to other institutions worldwide, the university implements various initiatives to promote successful applications.

In 1971, Kansai Gaidai University initiated an exchange program by inviting faculties and students from the University of Arkansas, and subsequently opened an Asian studies program conducted in English for international students in 1972. Since this time, it has worked to strengthen its status as a pioneer university in terms of exchange programs. As of 2004, the university was engaged in exchange agreements with 280 universities in fifty countries, under which credits could be mutually transferred. It provides exchange programs both for short-term study abroad (ranging from four to twenty-two weeks), mainly aimed at language training, and for long-term overseas study abroad (for one to two years), targeting mainly the upgrading of professional knowledge and the earning of degrees. In 2004, the number of Japanese students sent out under long- and short-term study abroad programs was 1,468 in total, 784 and 684 in each respective category, while the number of international students received from overseas institutions was 615. The numbers, for both outgoing and incoming students, have increased annually, almost in proportion to the rise in affiliation with overseas institutions. The university, with 9,925 students, is the largest to offer foreign studies in Japan.

In addition to regular university courses at Kansai Gaidai University, the Asian studies program offers courses of study exclusively for international students from all over the world. Under the programs provided by Kansai Gaidai University, many courses are taught by non-Japanese faculty members, with curricula designed so that international students can further their understanding of the societies and cultures of Japan and other Asian countries. Forty-three Asian studies courses are offered in various areas, including politics, economics, social science, and business. All credits earned in these courses can be transferred to students' home universities.

University degrees from Japanese universities are less attractive to international students from North America and Europe than they are to Asian students. Generally speaking, although hoping to study about Japanese culture and society in the short term, the vast majority of North American and European students will eventually return to their native countries to seek employment and therefore prefer degrees from universities more commonly recognized there. In recognition of this, Kansai Gaidai University is unique in Japan in providing Japanese and Asian studies programs that can meet a broad range of practical student needs. Specifically, the Asian studies program represents a "central attraction" for international students, allowing the department to develop other, more diverse exchange programs. Japanese students with sufficient English-language capabilities can participate in these programs to prepare to study in foreign universities.

Many Japanese students enter Kansai Gaidai University, attracted by the wealth of opportunities to study abroad; of this group, about 40 percent actually capitalize on such opportunities while at the university. Regardless of the extent to which universities offer sufficient opportunities for overseas study, students must somehow bring their language skills up to the level required for such study. Kansai Gaidai University's agreements with affiliated universities stipulate that the sending institutions are fully responsible for selecting students who are eligible to partake in study abroad opportunities; if language requirements are not satisfied, students may be sent back to their home countries.

Case 3: Ritsumeikan Asia Pacific University

Ritsumeikan Asia Pacific University (APU) was founded in 1999 and boasts one of the largest international student bodies in Japan. As of April 2005, the total number of students was 4,417, of which about 42 percent were international. International students come from seventy-five nations in Asia, North America, Europe, and Africa. The university is also said to be successful in attracting competent students; its graduates are highly valued by corporations, and 383 of the 390 international students (or 98.2 percent) who were set to graduate in 2004, and who applied for jobs, received informal job offers before graduation. APU comprises two colleges: the College of Asia Pacific Studies (APS), for learning diverse cultures and the social structures of Asian nations, and the College of Asia Pacific Management (APM), which includes a graduate school, for learning international management.

As is the case at other Japanese institutions, many international students whose standard language is English are not proficient in the Japanese language upon entering the university. APU provides Japanese-language training courses, so that students can improve their Japanese skills to the level needed to find employment in Japanese companies. Capable students who are interested in the Asia-Pacific region come from all over the world and study on campus. This international campus environment, in turn, attracts students from all over Japan; hence, international and domestic students can develop their respective potential by interacting with one another. APU aims to attract a wide range of instructors and students, mainly from the Asia-Pacific region, and foster internationally viable human resources, harnessing the potential of an on-campus international environment. Many APU students hope to move on to graduate schools elsewhere and work in international institutes.

Indeed, this mutually beneficial relationship serves to create an ideal model environment for universities wishing to internationalize. Domestic students have an opportunity to gain a global perspective and participate in international cooperative activities, such as mine-cleaning operations, and extracurricular activities related to international understanding, such as clubs that reflect on the issues surrounding history textbooks. Inspired by a multicultural environment, students may find the personal motivation to develop themselves. An international student from India commented, "The attraction of APU is its diversity of students and faculty members," which endorses the following statement from an APU official: "Internationalization led by American universities seeks to 'Americanize' students and faculty members. However, the internationalization sought by APU is not Americanization. The university stresses friendly exchange among international faculty members and students with different cultural backgrounds on the same stage."

Case 4: The Graduate School of International Corporate Strategy

The campus of the Graduate School of International Corporate Strategy (ICS), Hitotsubashi University, is located in the National Center of Sciences, constructed in central

Tokyo in 2000. ICS aims to develop specialists who are capable of contributing to society in the disciplines of administrative legal affairs, international administrative strategies, and financial strategies at a global level. Among the ICS programs, the full-time MBA program in international business strategy is taught entirely in English and became a professional degree program in 2004.

In the MBA program in international business strategy, international students account for approximately 60 percent of a total of ninety-three enrolled students. Faculty members number sixteen, including visiting lecturers and professors. The proportion of newly enrolled students in 2005 to faculty members was three to one, while tuition levels were comparable to those of other national universities. In comparison to other business schools, ICS has established a relatively favorable educational environment for the students of the program.

The graduate school, which offers classes taught in English to develop internationally viable business leaders, inevitably faces the challenge of competing with overseas business schools. Students are required to have a highly practical command of English, including knowledge of business terms, manners, and humor.

Since the establishment of the graduate school, in an effort to raise its profile as an internationally viable business school, ICS dean Takeuchi Hirotaka has underlined the importance of research outcomes on Japanese corporations. At present, with regard to method education, the majority of Asian cases taken up by so-called prestigious business schools have focused on the experience of Chinese corporations. Although Japanese corporations are only recently back on the path to economic recovery, they have performed poorly for a relatively long period, and are hence only rarely selected for case study in business school classes. ICS, in contrast, decided to concentrate exclusively on Japanese corporations for its research and introduced analyses of Japanese business models within domestic and international business circles, aiming to further establish the unique presence of ICS.

In recognition of its various initiatives, numerous domestic and overseas media, including the *Financial Times,* a British international economic publication, have covered the story of ICS as a model of an internationally viable Japanese business school since its founding. Recently, John Wiley and Sons published *Hitotsubashi on Knowledge Management.* The publishing company has handled books introducing the world's prestigious business schools, with titles including the areas of their strengths. The book was written in English by Professor Ikujiro Nonaka, a leading researcher in knowledge management, and eight colleagues as an effort to introduce Japanese knowledge management to an international audience.

One of the attractions of studying at ICS is its inexpensive tuition as a national university, ¥535,800 per year in 2006 (1 US = 117JPy at the end of March 2006). In addition, all international students receive scholarship awards. For example, the participants in the Young Leaders' Program, which is a national scholarship program, are exempted from the payment of admission and tuition fees and receive a stipend of ¥270,000 per month. An original ICS scholarship program for international students, supported by Daiwa Securities Group and other companies, provides ¥1 million to ¥2 million per student every year. The financial resources for the scholarship programs are not limited to government and alumni. ICS is known for the fact that some faculty members serve as board members of ORIX, Fujitsu, Vodafone, and other leading companies. These faculty members contribute 20 percent of their income from these companies to the scholarship programs.

Remarkably, when asked how students are recruited to study at ICS, Dean Takeuchi simply answered, "Just by word of mouth. . . . As for ranking or accreditation, we threw it off." ICS concluded that efforts to pursue a good position in the world rankings of business schools, such as those of the *Financial Times,* were not a productive use of time, so long as ICS remained the same size, because only business schools where the number of annual graduates reaches a certain level are nominated—ICS graduates about fifty per year at best. This stance is also applied to their approach to accreditation. Many business schools in other countries receive internationally recognized accreditations, such as by the Association to Advance Collegiate Schools of Business in the United States for seeking recognition by international students and business firms To be accredited, it is necessary to invest significant time and large sums of money as well as add more courses to the curricula. The ICS leadership determined, based on a cost-benefit analysis, that the school did not need to struggle to be accredited, despite the fact that some business students indicated that accreditation was a key factor in school selection. Meanwhile, ICS was ranked as high as fifth in the world (first among Japanese business schools) for business schools in 2004, as compiled by the MBA Tomono-Kai, an association of Japanese MBA holders, students, and recruiters, after surveying 1,028 members and other MBA holders.

ICS is strongly dependent on the power of name recognition, which has been built up over the long history of Hitotsubashi University and the networks of university faculty members and graduates; in other words, ICS did not begin, and then later come to thrive on its own devices.

The above four cases show that while Japanese higher education has not been successful in establishing "American-compatible" full-scale higher education programs, the attempts to make Japanese education more internationally attractive are ongoing. The official governmental authorization of foreign university programs such as that offered by Temple University Japan will stimulate the Japanese higher education market and could facilitate the further establishment of international university environments for both Japanese and non-Japanese students. The increase of exchange and partnership programs as observed at Kansai Gaidai University will also foster channels for student exchange, again for both Japanese and non-Japanese students. APU is a very interesting pilot project that encourages both faculties and students to introduce the Japanese way of higher education to the global academic community, despite the latter's increasingly competitive nature. ICS of Hitotsubashi University is regarded as an example of the "best educational practice in English" in Japan, with the quality of its education on par with international standards. Instead of focusing on world rankings or international accreditation, however, ICS puts its strategic impetus on research inherent in Japanese business studies. In all four cases, the idea of "mutual respect" is prevalent; this will be a key factor in developing truly international learning environments and in successfully building a uniquely Japanese soft power.

Conclusion

Japanese education has assumed an important role in transforming the country's military and economic power to soft power. However, Japanese education is losing its attractiveness, and a clear future vision is needed if this situation is to be redressed in a global context.

The examination of recent attempts to build the global competitiveness of Japanese higher education programs in the social sciences indicates that it is almost impossible to expect the emergence of large-scale, globally competitive English-language education programs in Japan. Despite their respective successes in other areas, every university considered in this chapter reveals a tendency to stress a unique identity as a higher education institution located in Japan. The attractiveness, or soft power, of Japanese education will be enhanced not through augmented academic profiles alone, but through capacities to foster the development of citizens with characteristics and a culture that can be admired by the global community.

Nye (2004) argued that Japan does not enjoy the full admiration of its Asian neighbors, due largely to the manner in which it used its military and economic power in the past. He further observed that the Japanese lifestyle is not regarded as a desirable model, and the general image of the Japanese is "arrogant." In that soft power is an intangible attraction that persuades one to go along with another's purpose without explicit threat or exchange, it is imperative that the Japanese education system find a unique approach to attracting students by inspiring "the dreams and desires of others."

To support and develop the soft power of Japanese society, the internationalization of Japanese education must be accelerated drastically. Considering Japan's strong social customs based on cultural homogeneity, the introduction of different schooling and academic cultures may raise conflicts, or merely reproduce a "two-arenas" structure of internationalization. However, dialogue based on mutual respect can only develop more harmonized communication as a resource to increase the soft power of the Japanese education community. If there is to be strength in Japanese education, the country must move closer to building an atmosphere of mutual respect with foreign participants; such values and attitudes are important and inevitable components of Japanese soft power. This will be realized only through the intensive involvement of the government, educational institutions, and individual stakeholders. Provided these conditions are met, Japanese education can work to build social capital to ensure the well-being of citizens living both inside and outside of Japan. However, if the Japanese fail in their efforts to establish such educational environments, the soft power of Japan's educational institutions and therefore of Japanese society itself will face very challenging international circumstances in the not-too-distant future.

Notes

1. *Monbu Kagaku Sho ni Okeru Kokusai Senryaku (Teigen)* (International Strategies at MEXT), 2005.
2. Monbusho was transformed into MEXT by a merger with the Ministry of Science and Technology in 2001.
3. TIMSS is an international study by the International Association for the Evaluation of Educational Achievement for providing comparative data of academic performance of fourth and eighth grades in mathematics and science. TIMSS assessments were implemented in 1995, 1999, and 2003. The next TIMSS assessment will be administered in 2007. http://timss.bc.edu/.
4. Academic Ranking of World Universities (ARWU) http://www.arwu.org/ranking.htm
5. These case studies are based on interviews with authorities of universities considered in articles written by the author, published in the Japanese journal *Between* (in Japanese) in 2005 and 2006.

References

Chambers, Gail S., and William K. Cummings. 1990. *Profiting from Education: Japan–United States International Education Adventures in the 1980s.* New York: Institute of International Education.
Council on Economic and Fiscal Policy. 2005. *The Report of the Special Board of Inquiry for Examining "Japan's 21st Century Vision."* Tokyo: Cabinet Office, Government of Japan.
Cummings, William K. 1980. *Education and Equality in Japan.* Princeton, NJ: Princeton University Press.
Dore, Ronald. 1997. *The Diploma Disease: Education, Qualification and Development.* 2nd ed. London: Institute of Education, University of London.
Fujita, Hidenori. 2001. *Shin jidai no kyoiku wo do koso suruka* (How to plan education in the new age). Tokyo: Iwanmi Shoten.
Japan International Cooperation Agency (JICA). 2004. *Approaches for Systematic Planning of Development Projects: Higher Education.* Tokyo: Japan International Cooperation Agency.
Hood, Christopher P. 2001. *Japanese Education Reform: Nakasone's Legacy.* New York: Routledge.
Kariya Takehiko and Kokichi Shimizu, eds. 2004. *Gakuryoku no shakaigaku* (Sociology of academic achievement). Tokyo: Iwanami Shoten.
Kim, Terri. 2001. *Forming The Academic Profession in East Asia: A Comparative Analysis.* New York: Routledge.
Momose, Yuko. 2003. *Shitte okitai senso no rekishi: Nihon senryoka no Indoneshia no kyoiku* (History of war worthwhile to know: Education under the Japanese occupation). Tokyo: Tsukubanesha.
Nye, Joseph, Jr. 2004. *Soft Power: The Means to Success in World Politics.* New York: Public Affairs.
Office of Economic Cooperation and Development (OECD). 1972. *Nihon no kyoiku seisaku* (Education policy in Japan). Tokyo: Asahi Shimbun.
OECD. 2003. *Education at a Glance.* Paris: Office of Economic Cooperation and Development.
Shimizu, Kokichi, and Mutsumi Shimizu. 2001. *Newcomer to kyoiku* (Newcomers and education). Tokyo: Akashi Shoten.

Takeuchi Kiyoshi. 2005. *Daigaku to campus life* (University and campus life). Tokyo: Sophia University Press.

Teichler, Ulrich. 1999. "Internationalisation as a Challenge for Higher Education in Europe." *Tertiary Education and Management* 5:5–23.

Times Higher Education Supplement (THES). 2005. *World University Rankings.* London. Times Higher Education Supplement.

Tsurumi, E. Patricia. 1977. *Japanese Colonial Education in Taiwan, 1895–1945.* Cambridge, MA: Harvard University Press.

Yonezawa Akiyoshi. 2005. "The Impact of Globalisation on Higher Education Governance in Japan." In *Globalization and Higher Education in East Asia.* Ed. Ka Ho Mok and Richard James, 125–36. New York: Marshall Cavendish Academic.

5

Nurturing Soft Power

The Impact of Japanese-U.S. University Exchanges

Ellen Mashiko and Horie Miki

The key to building and sustaining soft power, as conceptualized by Joseph S. Nye, Jr. (2004), is public diplomacy; that is, "conveying information and selling a positive image is part of it, but public diplomacy also involves building long-term relationships that create an enabling environment for government policies" (p. 107). In addition to daily and strategic communication, Nye cited the "development of lasting relationships with key individuals over many years through scholarships, exchanges, training, seminars, conferences, and access to media channels" (p. 109) as the third dimension of public diplomacy.

The primary purpose of this chapter is to examine the nurturance of soft power through the internationalization of Japanese higher education from macro and micro perspectives. That is, this chapter first discusses Japan's efforts to internationalize its universities. It focuses on the Japanese-U.S. relationship and presents background information relevant to current Japanese-U.S. exchange programs implemented by Japanese universities.[1] Second, it explores the outcomes of a preliminary research project on the impact of participation in Japanese-U.S. university exchange programs on undergraduate students' perceptions of the host country. The project was conceived and implemented vis-à-vis Nye's concept of soft power, notably the importance of building lasting relationships. Last, suggestions are put forward for further policy making regarding Japanese higher education that will enable universities, through their international programs, to nurture soft power and thereby contribute to the soft power of Japan as a nation.

Universities as Viable Sources of Soft Power

In Japan and the United States, universities have been traditionally viewed as learning and knowledge-generating centers that produce an educated citizenry and contribute to nation building. However, as Nye pointed out, universities and other independent sources also "develop soft power of their own that may reinforce or be at odds with official foreign policy goals" and "are likely to become increasingly important in the global information age" (2004, p. 17).

The presence of large numbers of international students and scholars in the United

States, Nye further observed, serves as a social index of American soft power. While not explicitly set in the context of soft power, discourse in Japan has also referred to the attraction of international students and scholars to its institutions of higher learning as an effective approach to cultivating individuals who will develop an understanding of Japan and therefore support it (Kokusai Bunka Koryu Kondankai 2003; Bunka Gaiko no Suishin ni Kansuru Kondankai 2005). Furthermore, dialog within and between Japan and the United States (and with other countries) has invariably supported the belief that the exchange of students, scholars, professionals, and members of grassroots organizations results in positive outcomes for the individual and promotes mutual understanding between the two countries. In Nye's words, "Exchanges . . . help create an attractive image of a country and can improve its prospects for obtaining its desired outcomes" (2004, p. 110).

The increase and expansion of exchange opportunities, however, does not automatically guarantee better understanding and cordial relationships among exchange participants. As is mentioned later, the Japanese higher education system and its services were strongly criticized by international students during the early stages of governmental policy implementation to increase the numbers of incoming overseas students (Horie 2002). As McConnell also points out in Chapter 2, some scholars of intercultural relations have concluded that the increase in the number of contacts between different cultures also increases the possibility of cultural conflicts and psychological stress (Paige 1993). Therefore, in order for universities to function as viable sources of soft power, they must be aware, in planning and implementing international programs, of pedagogical sequence, in other words, appropriate consideration of how people learn from intercultural experiences and develop positive interpretations of their experiences, including those of their host country and its people.

Japanese-U.S. Exchanges Within the Context of Global Student Mobility

The global map of student mobility has changed and expanded in recent years, and further growth is forecast. In 2000, the United Nations Educational, Scientific, and Cultural Organization estimated that more than 1.7 million students were studying at institutions of higher learning outside of their home countries. By 2025, it is estimated that this number will rise to between 7.5 million (Knight 2006) and 8 million (Davis 2003).[2]

University-to-university exchange programs play an important role in this milieu, particularly between Japan and the United States. The belief in and commitment to exchanges are being translated into an increasingly wider range of programs by governments, national and local organizations, universities, private foundations, and entrepreneurs in both countries.

For a growing number of Japanese and American students, degree- and nondegree-seeking study in another country is no longer unusual. Participating in short-term language training, academic study abroad, or both, on an individual basis or under the auspices of an exchange program organized by one's university or other organization is more commonplace than ever before, and seeking a degree abroad is also considered and pursued by a growing number of students. Multi-institutional attendance, too, is beginning to take hold among Japanese students.

Growth in the numbers of American students studying in Japan and Japanese students studying in the United States has been exponential, albeit in different numbers.[3] In 2004–5, 4,100 U.S. students studied in Japan, a 10.6 percent increase over the previous year; in comparison, the numbers in 1955 and 1983 were 112 and 276, respectively. These students studied at Japanese universities as nondegree-seeking students for limited periods (maximum of one year). During the same academic year, 38,712 Japanese students pursued higher education in the United States, 35.5 and 3.1 times more than in 1951 (1,150) and 1983 (13,010), respectively (Institute of International Education [IIE] 2005, 2006). About one-fourth of the Japanese students enrolled in an intensive English-language program, and approximately 70 percent studied at the undergraduate level, including degree- and nondegree-seeking students.

These statistics indicate that the number of Japanese students studying in the United States is more than nine times the number of American students studying in Japan. However, this significant difference requires closer examination, particularly in considering the role of university-to-university exchanges in cultivating soft power. What are some of the factors affecting the reported numbers of students exchanged between Japan and the United States? First, the number of Japanese students includes those who were admitted to U.S. degree programs and language-training courses, independent of any Japanese institution of higher education. In contrast, the majority of American students who studied in Japan did so through study abroad programs offered by their home institutions. The difference in the numbers of students exchanged between Japanese and U.S. universities is, no doubt, less dramatic than available data indicate, since bilateral exchange agreements help to assure a balance in the numbers of students exchanged. Second, U.S. students are increasingly seeking shorter study abroad opportunities, some as brief as four weeks, whereas the vast majority of Japanese universities offer programs not less than one semester (IIE 2005). Third, in the broad context of global student flows, the United States receives almost five times more international students than Japan; the largest numbers of international students received by both Japan and the United States come from Asia—China, Korea, and Taiwan in the case of Japan, and India, China, and Korea in the case of the United States. In contrast, the majority of Japanese students study abroad in the United States (followed by China and the United Kingdom), while the largest numbers of U.S. students study in European countries such as the United Kingdom, Italy, Spain, and France; Japan ranks eleventh among U.S. students' destinations (MEXT 2007; IIE 2006).

The disparity in the numbers of U.S. students in Japan and Japanese students in the United States still requires explanation. Language is, no doubt, the major factor impacting this difference. English continues to be the international language of communication across all sectors in the world, whereas Japanese is a minor language used by only 2 percent of the world's population. Furthermore, while the number of universities offering degree and nondegree programs in which the language of instruction is English is increasing, this number is still minute.

Statistics also indicate that over the past fifty years, study in the United States by Japanese students has changed from an "elitist" to a "popular" pursuit. Until 1964, the Fulbright Program, initiated by U.S. Senator J. William Fulbright shortly after World War II to promote international understanding between the United States and other nations, including Japan, provided one of the few opportunities for Japanese to pursue graduate study in the United States. Fulbright scholarship candidates were elites or future leaders, such as graduate students, faculty members, researchers, government officials, and company employees, who were selected on a highly competitive basis. The list of former Japanese Fulbright Scholars is remarkable for the names of leaders in various fields (Kondo 1992). However, while the Fulbright Program remains a prestigious source of funding for Japanese who wish to pursue graduate study in the United States, it is no longer the only option. There are many more sources of funding, including self-support, for high school, undergraduate, and graduate study in the United States as well as in other countries. As Altbach and Peterson note in Chapter 3 of this volume, U.S. higher education remains in a preeminent position, but they warn of "significant competition in the rapidly expanding world of international study."

Another change in the flow of students is the increasing diversification of students' motivations. Study abroad by the so-called elites in earlier times emphasized the acquisition of knowledge and technologies to bring back to Japan to further national development. Accordingly, Japanese students felt responsible for or were at least aware of bridging gaps between their host and home countries. American students' motivations, on the other hand, shifted from cultural learning to career enhancement, and will probably evolve into a complex configuration of motivations as many more, from diverse backgrounds, study in Japan.

Recent literature illustrates a global trend of students going wherever there are opportunities to use their creativity better and more freely, and indicates that countries must compete for talent by providing better learning and professional environments (Florida 2005). In the Japanese context, unlike in the pre- and immediate postwar periods, nowadays many university students do not perceive themselves as elites; nor do they have an inclination to become leaders or public intellectuals. Among those who pursue graduate degrees abroad, a good number seem to fit Florida's definition of the creative class, the growing numbers of individuals throughout the world who engage in "highly creative occupations—from architects to aesthetic workers, engineers and scientists to artists and writers, high-end managers, planners, and analysts to health care, finance, and law professions" (2005, p. 28).

There are many individual cases that can be cited to illustrate multiple institutional attendance and what Florida (2005) so aptly described as the "flight of the creative class." It may no longer be atypical of a younger Japanese to participate in a university exchange program in the United States, then serve as a summertime volunteer in Northern Thailand, work in Bangladesh following graduation on assignment from his or her Japanese employer, resign from full-time employment to pursue a graduate degree in the United States, and then seek a position with an international organization anywhere in the world.

The popularization of study abroad leads to the question of how soft power can be most effectively nurtured among nonelites. Nye (2004) has pointed out that educating "elites" (or future leaders) of another country might be viewed as a direct investment in building soft power by the host country. Educating greater numbers of nonelites can significantly impact the building of soft power "infrastructure," the peripheral system of nonelites who hold positive views of and favorably support the host country. In this context, university-to-university exchange programs are one of the most easily accessible opportunities for students to first experience study abroad. Therefore, institutional policies on study abroad programs, including the selection of partner universities and location, program content, and other pedagogical issues, such as intercultural learning, ought to be carefully considered because these factors impact the quality of the learning experience and the perceptions and attitudes that students develop vis-à-vis the host country.

Internationalization of Japanese Higher Education

The internationalization of Japan and its educational system dates back to the sixth century. However, it was only in the 1980s that various internationalization efforts gained the focused attention of policy makers and implementers. These efforts included curriculum reform, employment and integration of large numbers of non-Japanese faculty members, and modification of inter- and intra-university policies and practices to promote and facilitate international education. During this same period, the numbers of Japanese students, scholars, and professionals going abroad began to increase rapidly, as did the number of international students and scholars received by Japanese universities, albeit in smaller numbers. Concurrently, the establishment of university linkages became widespread, and campuses were founded abroad by Japanese universities and by U.S. institutions in Japan (Mashiko 1989).

In subsequent years, Japan carried out its so-called 100,000-by-2000 plan, which intended to increase the number of international students in Japan from about 10,000 in the early 1980s to 100,000 by the year 2000.[4] The plan initially emphasized quantitative expansion and later shifted to improving the quality of college and university education for international students (Horie 2002). During the early years of the plan's implementation, international students expressed strongly negative views of their living environments and educational services offered by their host institutions (Ogita 1986). In other words, at the beginning of the implementation stage, government investment in international students' education at Japanese universities was not successful in leading to students' positive perceptions of Japan and its higher education, or, in other words, nurturing soft power.

However, since then, some Japanese universities have made noteworthy progress in building infrastructure, programs, and activities directly related to internationalization, as Japanese international education professionals, with knowledge and skills obtained through their own study abroad experiences and from experienced U.S. counterparts, have assumed university positions directly related to international programming

(Horie 2003). The Japanese government and universities, both national and private institutions, have moved beyond the traditional approach of recruiting and educating degree-seeking international students to a broader strategy that includes sending many more domestic students abroad; increasing and strengthening university-to-university exchange programs; and implementing other short-term opportunities for international and domestic students, such as internships and service learning, twinning programs, and dual-degree programs.

More recently, the Ministry of Education, Culture, Sports, Science and Technology (MEXT) established the Strategic Fund for Establishing International Headquarters in Universities to facilitate the further internationalization of selected universities (Strategic Fund 2006). For example, Nagoya University, one of the pilot institutions, proposed four internationalization-specific categories—education and student services, research collaboration, international cooperation, and reform of its administrative system—for review and planning. That only twenty universities among sixty-eight applicants were selected no doubt reflects MEXT's strategy to focus its resources on the few universities that it believes have the best chance of achieving their goals and objectives, and thus becoming viable sources of Japanese soft power. MEXT's strategy is in line with Yonezawa's conclusions that "the internationalization of Japanese education must be accelerated drastically" (Chapter 4, this volume). It is noteworthy that almost all of the selected universities have many years' experience in implementing university-to-university exchange programs as well as research collaboration with multiple partners.

Survey of Selected Universities and Exchange Students: Approach and Outcomes

This interpretive survey was conducted to elicit responses to two main research questions: What changes did Japanese universities experience regarding exchange programs and their future outlook regarding international programs? How did participants in Japanese-U.S. exchange programs at the undergraduate level interpret their experiences, and what were their attitudes toward the host country? In this section, the research approach and outcomes are discussed from the perspectives of the collaborating universities and exchange students.

The rationale for the focus on exchange opportunities at the undergraduate level is as follows. First, both governments have long supported and promoted student exchange programs, including government-initiated and sponsored exchanges, such as the Fulbright Program, as well as university-based initiatives. An increasing number of universities in Japan and the United States have launched new or strengthened existing international student exchange programs to enrich their students' learning and, at some Japanese universities, to attract and recruit domestic students.

Second, there are large numbers of undergraduates in Japan and the United States; thus, the potential to nurture positive perceptions of the other country is greater than with graduate students, who are fewer in number, particularly in Japan.[5] Moreover, undergraduate students are more likely than graduate students, who often have predetermined academic or professional objectives, to seek a wider range of careers following completion of the first degree, including employment in business firms related to the host country and participation in the Japan Exchange and Teaching (JET) Program (see Chapter 2), and possibly to pursue graduate education in the host country or in an academic field related to the host country.

Third, for students, university-to-university exchange programs are easily accessible and help assure completion of a first degree at the home university within the prescribed number of years. That is, these exchange programs are designed to meet student needs and priorities, such as program length, and combine language, culture learning, and discipline-specific courses. Also, the credit earned (or time spent) at the host university is usually transferable to (or recognized by) the home university.

Fourth, undergraduate university exchange programs are oftentimes the first step for partner universities to develop further student-centered programs as well as scholarly activity among faculty members. In other words, these exchange programs serve as springboards for expanded activities that strengthen the collaborating universities as resources of soft power.

Two national and five private universities in Japan were selected as collaborating universities on the basis of their long-standing commitment to and implementation of international exchange programs and other forms of international activity.[6] Six of the seven collaborating universities completed a questionnaire designed to obtain basic information about their respective exchange programs, trends in their international activity over the past decade, and forecasts for the next five years. The collaborating universities electronically disseminated questionnaires to students in Japan and the United States who had participated in an exchange program between 2001 and 2005. Twenty-five Japan-based and seventy-one United States–based students replied directly in Japanese or English.[7] The general profile of students is summarized in Appendix 5.1.

Responses from the collaborating universities and students were collated and analyzed in two ways. First, basic information about universities and students was calculated as percentages to generate general profiles. Second, the thematic analysis method was applied to the narrative data to identify essential meanings from emerging themes and to present students' actual voices rather than generalizing their ideas and thoughts.

Universities' Perspective

Over the ten-year period under review, collaborating Japanese universities not only increased the number of universities with which agreements were concluded[8] but also diversified the countries in which these partner universities were located, reflecting universities' intent to broaden the learning opportunities for their students, focus on a specific region of the world, such as the Asia-Pacific region, and pursue internationalization on a wider scale. This, however, led to a diminished presence of the United

States.[9] All agreements related to students in part or as a whole, and all led to the actual implementation of student exchange programs with all partner universities. Among the collaborating universities, those that had many agreements and exchange programs, and sent and received larger numbers of students in 1995, grew even more during the ensuing decade, and already had plans to further enhance their international exchange and related programs from 2006 onward.

The numbers of students sent to the United States under exchange agreements by collaborating universities did not decrease, while exchange students received from the United States increased.[10] As with the increases in exchange agreements and countries, collaborating universities that were more active than others in 1995 further increased the numbers of students sent to and received from the United States over the ten years under consideration.[11]

All of the collaborating universities provide basic information on educational opportunities in the United States and other countries to their students, and on exchange programs to U.S. students considering study in Japan. The differences among collaborating universities emerge when the numbers of all exchange students are considered. That is, in general, the larger the number of students sent and received, the more comprehensive and sophisticated were the universities' information and advising services. However, with the exception of involving returned exchange students in the orientation of newly selected exchange students, none of the collaborating universities reported the implementation of follow-up activities, such as providing sources of new information and facilitating networking via the Internet, which would contribute to the sustainability and enhancement of their university-generated soft power.

Several patterns emerge among collaborating universities when their reports on significant changes over the past decade and in looking beyond 2005 are examined, as summarized below.

First, collaborating universities reporting more exchange agreements in many countries, and sending and receiving larger numbers of undergraduate students in 1995 and 2005, appear to be proactive, strategic, transnational, and issue focused in their planning and program development. In contrast, those reporting fewer exchange agreements in fewer countries, and sending and receiving smaller numbers of undergraduate students in 1995 and 2005, tend toward a reactive, problem-focused approach.

Second, proactive collaborating universities are pursuing or already implementing other learning options such as incorporation of study abroad into the curricula of new academic programs, transnational programs, dual-degree programs, facilitating study abroad outside the rubric of exchange agreements, promoting the learning abroad of languages not offered by the home institution, service learning, overseas fieldwork with faculty members, and volunteer work. Others are considering shifting from "à la carte menus" of social sciences and humanities study abroad course options to specialization-specific opportunities, and offering both short-term (several weeks) and long-term (up to three years) study abroad programs.

Third, all collaborating universities reported the need to secure adequate funding to support the participation of as many as possible of their students in study outside Japan. In addition, proactive collaborating universities are exploring new credit-transfer and tuition-payment schemes, new assessment mechanisms that will lead to improved study abroad programs, and effective risk-management practices.

Fourth, there were differences between the national and private universities in the sample, such as in the scope and scale of exchange programs. However, it appears premature to assess these differences at this time given the acquisition of "National University Corporation" status by national universities in April 2004, which will, no doubt, affect all aspects of academic and administrative planning, including internationalization-related initiatives and programs.

Fifth, by enrollment and comprehensiveness, as indicated by the numbers of undergraduate and graduate schools, the size of collaborating universities does not appear to be a key variable in assessing the strength of their exchange and other international programs and activities.

Students' Perspectives

The general characteristics of students' patterns of thinking and subjective meanings in relation to their study abroad experiences as semester or one-year exchange students have been summarized into three major points associated with the soft power–related discussion: casual attraction to the host country as the primary motivation for participating in a Japanese-U.S. exchange program, personal growth and human networking as the biggest gain and main source of appreciation for their experiences, and mixed feelings of longing and helplessness in searching for another opportunity to return to the host country or become involved in host country–related activities. These characteristics agree with McConnell's discussion of JET participants' reflections on their experiences in Japan (Chapter 2). Cited below are students' voices (excerpts below are labeled according to the country and sample numbers), which reflect a positive tone overall and an appreciation for the opportunity to speak about their overseas experiences. Specific survey questions and corresponding tables appear in Appendix 5.2.

First, the primary reason why students chose to study in Japan or the United States was casual attraction and general interest in various aspects of the host country's culture; academic perspectives were not emphasized. Learning the language of the host culture and having firsthand cultural experiences were general motivations for the majority of exchange students, as illustrated below:

> I already had a lot of exposure to Europe and European culture and was looking for something different. Japan was appealing in . . . its language, history and culture. . . . I also wanted to challenge myself by living in a different environment and speaking a new language. (U.S. #6)

> I wanted to study social problems such as racism. America is a multiethnic society and I wanted to experience firsthand such a society. (J. #18)

I liked American English the best and wanted to learn it. I also thought it would be easier for me to be integrated into U.S. society because the country has accepted many international students. (J. #7)

The general motivations expressed by these students have an orientation very different from the primary reasons expressed by Japanese who went to study in the United States in the 1950s, which was to catch up with an advanced country by acquiring knowledge and technologies that were missing in Japan (Kondo 1992).

Second, both Japan- and United States–based students highly valued their study abroad experiences and were eager to return to their host countries in the near future. They observed that they had fulfilled their personal study abroad goals, which were primarily language and cultural acquisition and personal growth, or at least they expressed satisfaction with their experiences.

Overall, I greatly appreciated the chance to study abroad in Japan. It gave me a chance to see the world in a completely different way. I can see that things are not always just the way they are in the U.S. . . . Not how the physical world acts, but how people act. (U.S. #12)

American students get to experience a culture that is extremely different from their own, and I believe this can open their eyes to the diversity in our world, so they can see that they have a role as a member of the greater global community. (U.S. #64)

America is full of diversity. I had opportunities to see people with various cultural backgrounds, and such experiences broadened my worldview. Also, I realized that nothing would be given to you if you do not take it. The environment does not matter; everything is up to you. (J. #9)

Besides personal growth, both United States– and Japan-based students valued the human networks that they developed during the study abroad period. The significance of human networks has already been pointed out by U.S. Fulbright Scholars in the early 1970s (Kondo 1992), and remains the same even if the patterns of study abroad have changed. The students observed:

I met so many amazing people and learned a lot about other cultures, as well as more about my own. The group of people whom I was acquainted with . . . were such a dynamic and intelligent group of individuals and I miss them all. Some of the connections I made will be lifelong and I am so grateful to have been part of this incredible experience. (U.S. #44)

The biggest gain that I had was friends from various countries. Most of them were students . . . in various specializations, and I believe that our human network will expand even more when each of us, in the future, has pursued a higher level of professional development in various fields. (J. #8)

Students' views toward the host countries as nations, accordingly, were very positive on both sides. However, a difference was found between Japan- and United States–based students regarding their confidence in better knowing their host country.

That is, United States–based students were more confident about their knowledge of Japan and expressed a heightened responsibility to share their firsthand knowledge and correct the misperceptions of persons without experiences of Japan. For example:

> Having had firsthand experience, I love being able to help others understand more about Japan. Many Americans have skewed perceptions of Japan, and I take every opportunity I have to help those perceptions more accurately reflect the reality. (U.S. #11)

In contrast, Japan-based students studying in the United States realized that they knew only a part of the United States.

> Even though I spent one year there, I cannot say that I understand everything about the U.S. I guess some people living in Japan have much more interest in the U.S. and study harder than I did. Also, characteristics are so different from state to state, and I . . . experienced only a little part of the whole. (J. #9)

Students also learned to understand a nation separately from its people through their firsthand human relationships. Some Japanese students expressed their growing awareness of various political ideas and attitudes toward U.S. international diplomacy expressed by the Japanese government and people around them. This shift in perspective made them more positive toward the United States as whole. That is, their critical attitudes toward U.S. national policy did not interfere with their feelings about and relationship to U.S. society.

Third, in spite of the fact that both Japan- and United States–based exchange students were eager to return to their host countries, the majority had no particular plans and some expressed helplessness in finding another opportunity to return to the United States or Japan. Others expressed a strong interest in pursuing a cultural experience in a different country.

> As much as I love Japan, I would choose another country because the world is a huge place and there's much I haven't seen yet. I would also like to learn more languages as well, and living elsewhere would give me that opportunity, as living in Japan did. (U.S. #4)

The majority of students did not directly connect their study abroad experience to career planning. Rather, they perceived a strong relationship between their study abroad experiences and personal growth, including development of better communication skills, broader perspectives, and greater self-confidence.

> Yes. I came to think that I should pursue whatever I want to do instead of keeping a stable job. I feel less insecure about changing jobs, and I believe I should change jobs if necessary. My current idea is that it is most important for me to make my own way to satisfy myself with everyday life. (J. #24)

Some reported still living with the experience of study abroad. Their learning continues by relating occurrences around them to what they discovered about themselves, the host country, or both, but they also felt isolated from others because of not being fully understood by friends who did not share their study abroad experience.

> Japan became a home I think about every single day. Its meaning in my life changes every day as well, as I make it mean something new to me with each experience I have now related to it. (U.S. #32)

> It's been odd that people have asked so little about my time abroad. Sometimes it feels as if it never happened. No one seems interested, but I suppose they just can't relate and instead feel inclined to tell me about their year here. I hope I don't forget all the amazing things I did and saw. (U.S. #56)

These aspects of students' retrospective and ongoing experiences revealed the potential to nurture soft power among U.S.-Japanese exchange students. The students placed the highest value on personal growth and human network building; in other words, they expressed great appreciation for what and how they learned as individuals. The survey results of collaborating universities indicated that institutions also highly valued these effects of students' study abroad experiences, and incorporated these impacts into the assumptions underlying their institutional policy in expanding study abroad programs.

Such strong positive student reflections, however, tended to be acknowledged by students as individual matters. The students indicated a strong willingness to keep abreast of and contribute to host country–related matters, but such motivation and determination were not recognized institutionally. Although many of the student respondents will probably not follow so-called elite career paths, they have the potential to be influential in policy making or leading public opinion at the local, national, or global levels.

Moving Forward

In spite of the limited parameters of the preliminary research project on which this chapter is based, the findings point to a range of interconnected soft power–related issues for the immediate attention of all stakeholders in Japan—university communities, including administrators, faculty and students; government policy makers and decision makers; and professional organizations, foundations, corporations, and other sources of financial and nonfinancial support—and their partners abroad.

Building and Sustaining Soft Power vis-à-vis Higher Education

The potential role of Japanese universities in building and sustaining soft power is clear but largely unfulfilled. It is essential that universities increase the attractiveness of higher education by providing learning opportunities that meet current and future global needs. A research project of selected Japanese educators with extended firsthand experience with international students supports this assertion. These educators defined internationalization of Japanese higher education as essentially to improve the level of instruction in order to fulfill international students' educational goals and expectations (Horie 2003). This result is supported by the findings of the survey described in this chapter. U.S. students did not refer to their academic learning but rather emphasized the value of their experiential learning.

Other unfulfilled aspects of Japanese universities' potential include various forms of cross-border joint programs, curriculum reform, updated teaching methods, and delivery of instruction in languages other than Japanese. Another unfulfilled potential is the development of alumni networks that not only provide a mechanism for social interaction among alumni and occasionally with the Japanese alma mater, but also engage international graduates in ways that sustain and build soft power vis-à-vis the university and, thus, Japan. This requires significant changes in the structure and priorities of Japanese higher education as well as a major shift in universities' recruitment strategies.

There appear to be at least three fundamental issues that impact the building and sustaining of soft power in relation to Japanese higher education. First, the modus operandi of these universities is generally based on a dichotomous model of education and research, on one hand, and service, on the other. The former is the responsibility of faculty and administrators with faculty rank, and the delivery of the latter is left to administrators and staff without faculty rank. Moreover, little attention is paid to the interconnectedness of academic and nonacademic matters and how linkages with international students following their completion of a program or degree can be created and sustained for the benefit of the individual, the institution, and ultimately the nation. While faculty members may maintain strong ties with at least some international students, individual academicians cannot be expected to bear primary responsibility for sustaining relationships between students and the institution.

Second, even Japanese universities that attract larger numbers of international students by reputation, active recruitment, or both do not appear to fulfill their institutional potential in maintaining substantive and meaningful linkages with exchange students and degree-seeking students who graduate and return home or move on to a third country. The research findings clearly indicate that former exchange students seek additional opportunities to strengthen their ties with the host country. However, the Japanese government and universities are not paying sufficient attention to this important matter and thus fail to build soft power. Building on Nye's observation on the potency of independent sources of soft power, particularly in the global information age, Japanese universities ought to place international student follow-up not on their lists of matters for future consideration but high among their immediate priorities.

Third, the creation and nurturing of soft power over the long term are major tasks that not only require but can be better accomplished by the formation of viable linkages among stakeholders in Japan rather than by perpetuating top-down, central government–driven practices. Altbach and Peterson argue in Chapter 3 that decentralization is a strong catalyst for the vitality of U.S. higher education. The same, no doubt, is applicable to Japanese higher education.

Moreover, these linkages should not be relegated to the sharing of information, liaison activity, or handling of problematic issues, as has been common practice in Japan, but should lead to collaborative activity that is proactive and productive. An example is the Nijuisseiki Daigaku Keiei Kyokai (University Management Association for the Twenty-first Century). A nonprofit organization established in 2004, the association brings together university administrators, the corporate sector, and other individuals and organizations that are committed to and jointly working on concrete ways to strengthen university management. While it is still too early in the association's life to make a determination about its success in these endeavors, it will be interesting to see whether it becomes a significant player in transforming university management in Japan.

Seeking and Supporting Diversity

Japan's post–World War II educational system has been remarkable in its quest to educate all citizens by, for example, providing equal access to education from the primary through the tertiary level. While the overall results have been generally positive, the drastically declining college-age cohort and increasing number of universities have changed the complexion of the higher education scene so that the tendency for most institutions to offer similar programs is not efficacious from either the domestic or the international perspective. As in other nations, there are a range of universities in Japan—large and small, comprehensive and specialized, research- and education-oriented, competitive and less competitive—with varying institutional missions and strengths.

In the current milieu of increasing national competitiveness for domestic students, global competitiveness for international students, fast-emerging cross-border education, and "the prospect for expanding trade in higher education services worldwide through the implementation of a version of the General Agreement on Trade in Services" (Chapter 3), it is incumbent on Japanese universities to reexamine their missions and institutional strengths and to determine and prioritize what kinds of educational and research programs and activities that they can best implement.[12] The next crucial task is to communicate these outcomes to both potential domestic and international students to enable prospective students to make appropriate choices that fit their needs and priorities. This point is also supported by Florida's definition and argument that potential members of the creative class pursue what they determine as the best education, wherever it is offered, and then the best employment, wherever it is available. Japan, as a nation, must also rethink its strategy to attract both domestic and international students, and then develop and implement effective means to sustain and nurture relationships with these students.

Competitive research-oriented universities and less competitive education-oriented universities need not compete on the same grounds for similar cohorts of students. However, this requires an overall transformation of the higher education system to make it easier, for example, for an international student acquiring Japanese-language proficiency and a solid grounding in social sciences at a smaller, regional university to then compete for and earn a place in a larger, urban graduate school in Japan. Moreover, it is crucial for government and independent sources of support to provide funding and in-kind support in flexible ways that support diversity. Soft power is surely better created and nurtured by university-initiated activity that results in diversity, because institutions know or ought to know best what they want to and can deliver most effectively. If institutions are successful in delivering quality programs, this will likely lead to increased attractiveness of Japanese universities, an area in which Yonezawa (Chapter 4) postulates Japan has been losing ground.

Responding to Local and Global Challenges

Local and global challenges are oftentimes presented and approached as diametrically opposing forces, a simplistic and uncreative stance. For example, universities are sited in various kinds of localities that have specific strengths and needs, and they can partner with, for example, municipalities in fulfilling needs and priorities that can be shared with international students who also come from a variety of locales. An international student coming from a medium-size port city with the goal of becoming a port manager upon his or her return home will surely benefit more from a maritime management program at a Japanese university in a port city of a similar size than from a program in a Japanese university in a large metropolis. The learning opportunities in and outside of the classroom for the student are greater and the potential of long-term relationships is limitless.

Universities, as sources of soft power, ought to be encouraged to think outside the proverbial box. For example, a jointly planned midcareer professional training program for Japanese municipal employees is being collaboratively implemented over five years by a three-way partnership comprising a Japanese university, a U.S. university, and a private foundation. Both universities had a more than thirty-year agreement under which undergraduate students were actively exchanged but which did not evolve into other areas of exchange. Collaboration on the midcareer professional training program, which is conducted at and by both universities, led to the establishment of exchange programs for degree-seeking graduate students, faculty exchange, launch of joint research, and the commercial publication of a bilingual project management tool kit.

The "big" and "changing picture" of participants in higher education, such as attendance at multiple institutions, the increasing transnational mobility of the creative class referred to earlier, growing competition for students, and the projected dramatic increase in young people seeking access to higher education in countries that are unable to provide it, require the attention and foresight of all stakeholders in Japan. Undergraduate student exchanges are only one aspect of this large, evolving collage but this group will no doubt continue to be a primary pool of future leaders, the creative class, and the many others who will participate in an increasingly active civil society and thus impact soft power. The potential of these exchanges has not been exhausted and requires long-term commitment and investment for the long-lasting relations that Nye (2004) advocated. The desired outcome is soft power that is about nation building and, irrespective of tradition or culture, is best achieved by effective strategy and determination.

Notes

1. In this chapter, so-called island programs, in which students take classes only with their cohort from the same home institution, are not included. The exchange programs that are referred to in this chapter are programs in which courses are offered by the host institutions and students take classes with other domestic and international students.

2. According to Knight, "student mobility cannot satisfy the hunger for higher education within densely populated countries wanting to build human capacity and thus fully participate in the knowledge society—hence the emergence and exponential growth of cross-border education programs and providers. These new types of providers, forms of delivery, and models of collaboration will offer students education programs in their home countries" (Knight 2006, p. 4). In Chapter 3 of this volume, Altbach and Peterson discuss "cross-border education" and related issues under the rubric of "the new transnationalism."

3. *Open Doors* (Institute of International Education 2005) cites statistics of U.S. students participating in programs arranged by U.S. institutions, while the Japan Student Services Organization (JASSO) reports 1,646 U.S. students studying at Japanese institutions of higher learning (JASSO 2005). It may be inferred that the difference in numbers announced by JASSO and IIE refers to students enrolled in summer school, so-called island programs, or other types of nonregular programs.

4. The "100,000-by-2000 plan" refers to then prime minister Nakasone Yasuhiro's 1983 announcement of the goal to increase the number of international students in Japan to 100,000 by the year 2000. The goal was met in 2003, when the number of international students reached 109,508.

5. In 2004, there were 2,505,923 students enrolled in bachelor's and 244,483 students enrolled in master's and doctoral degree programs in Japan (MEXT 2005a). In 2002, the equivalent statistics in the United States were 7,922,926 (full-time only, or 13,155,393 full- and part-time students) and 1,086,674 (full-time only, or 2,156,896 full- and part-time students), respectively (MEXT 2005b).

6. The two national universities (undergraduate/graduate enrollments as of May 2004 shown in parentheses) were Nagoya University (9,818/5,993) and Osaka University (12,230/7,702); the five private universities were Asia University (5,895/67), Kansai Gaidai University (12,900/100), Nanzan University 9,066/425), Ritsumeikan University (35,327/2,836), and Waseda University (45,451/7,357). This ratio of national to private universities (2:5) approximates the ratio of all national and private universities in Japan; as of May 2004, there were 87 national, 73 public, and 716 private universities (*Zenkoku Daigaku Ichiran* 2005).

7. Participants in exchange programs from Japan to the United States are referred to as "Japan based," and students sojourning in the opposite direction as "United States based." These terms are used to establish the national identity of students, which included one non-Japanese national and sixteen non-U.S. nationals who participated in the survey.

8. The numbers of exchange agreements increased overall, with the largest proportional increase by a collaborating university that reported six agreements in 1995 and forty-seven in 2005; in absolute numbers, however, the most dramatic increase was from 96 to 306. University-to-university agreements increased by 1.69 to 7.83 times per collaborating university over the ten-year period; agreements with consortia were 1 percent to 11 percent of the total.

9. In 1995, the number of countries ranged from five to nineteen; in 2005, the range was sixteen to seventy-five. The number of agreements with U.S. universities was 0 percent to 71 percent in 1995 and 10 percent to 50 percent in 2005.

10. In 1995, collaborating universities sent zero to 589 students to the United States; in 2005, this range was one to 300, primarily for one, but up to two, academic years.

11. Nevertheless, there is potential for growth. The percentage of Japanese students studying in the United States was less than 1 percent of the total enrollments of five of the six collaborating universities (4 percent at the remaining university); the percentage of American students studying in Japan was 1.9 percent of all American students studying abroad.

12. UNESCO and the Organization for Economic Cooperation and Development (OECD) have issued a set of guidelines (UNESCO 2005) to protect students from low-quality higher education services. These include guidelines for governments, higher education institutions and providers, student bodies, quality assurance and accreditation bodies, academic recognition bodies, and professional bodies.

References

Bunka Gaiko no Suishin ni Kansuru Kondankai. 2005. *Bunka koryu no heiwa kokka, nihon no sozo wo* (A report on cultural exchange by a peaceful nation submitted to the Prime Minister's Office). Tokyo: Bunka Gaiko no Suishin ni Kansuru Kondankai.

Davis, Todd M. 2003. *Atlas of Student Mobility.* New York: Institute of International Education.

Florida, Richard. 2005. *The Flight of the Creative Class: The New Global Competition for Talent.* New York: HarperCollins Publishers.

Horie, Miki. 2002. "The Internationalization of Higher Education in Japan in the 1990s: A Reconsideration." *Higher Education* 43:65–84.

———. 2003. "International Students and Internationalization of Higher Education in Japan: Interpretive Study with Policy Makers and International Educators." PhD diss., University of Minnesota.

Institute of International Education (IIE). 2005. *Open Doors: Report on International Educational Exchange, 1948–2004.* CD-ROM. New York: IIE.

———. 2006. *Open Doors 2006 Fast Facts.* http://www.opendoors.iienetwork.org/ (accessed November 28, 2006).

Japan Student Services Organization (JASSO). 2005. *Ryugakusei ukeire no gaikyo (Heisei 17 nendo ban)* (Outline of international students education [2005]). http://www.jasso.go.jp/statistics/intl_student/data05.html/#4 (accessed February 10, 2006).

Knight, Jane. 2006. "Cross-Border Education: Not Just Students on the Move." *International Educator.* Washington, DC: NAFSA: Association of International Educators, pp. 4–5.

Kokusai Bunka Koryu Kondankai. 2003. *Kongo no kokusai bunka koryu nosuishin ni tsuite* (A report on the future of international cultural exchange promotion submitted to the Agency for Cultural Affairs). Tokyo: Kokusai Bunka Koryu Kondankai.

Kondo, Ken. 1992. *Mouhitotsu no nichibei kankei: Fulbright kyoiku koryu no 40 nen* (The other side of Japan–U.S. relations: 40 years of the Fulbright Program). Tokyo: Japan Times.

Mashiko, Ellen E. 1989. *Japan: A Study of the Educational System of Japan and a Guide to the Academic Placement of Students in Educational Institutions of the United States.* Washington, DC: American Association of Collegiate Registrars and Admissions Officers.

Ministry of Education, Culture, Sports, Science and Technology (MEXT). 2005a. *Statistics.* http://www.mext.go.jp/english/statist/index.htm (accessed December 19, 2005).

———. 2005b. *2004 International Comparison of Education Index.* http://www.mext.go.jp/b_menu/houdou/17/01/05012102.htm (accessed December 19, 2005).

———. 2007. *Wagakuni no ryugakusei seido no gaiyo* (Outline of the student exchange system in Japan]. Tokyo: MEXT.

Nye, Joseph S., Jr. 2004. *Soft Power: The Means to Success in World Politics.* New York: Public Affairs.

Ogita Sekiko. 1986. *Bunka "sakoku" nippon no ryugakusei* (International students in Japan: A culturally closed country). Tokyo: Gakuyo Shobo.

Paige, R. Michael. 1993. "On the Nature of Intercultural Experiences and Intercultural Education." In *Education for Intercultural Experience.* Ed. R.M. Paige, 1–19. Yarmouth, ME: Intercultural Press.

Strategic Fund for Establishing International Headquarters in Universities. 2006. *Program Outline.* http://www.u-kokusen.jp/index_e.html (accessed May 19, 2006).

United Nations Educational, Scientific, and Cultural Organization (UNESCO). 2005. *Guidelines for Quality Provision in Cross-Border Higher Education.* Paris: UNESCO.

Zenkoku Daigaku Ichiran, Heisei 17 nendo ban (National directory of universities, 2005 edition). 2005. Tokyo: Zaidan Hojin Bunkyo Kyokai.

Appendix 5.1 **Students' Profiles**

1. Nationality

	U.S.	%	J.	%
U.S./Japanese	55	77.5	24	96.0
Other	16	22.5	1	4.0
	71	100.0	25	100.0

2. Gender

	U.S.	%	J.	%
Male	30	42.3	5	20.0
Female	41	57.7	20	80.0
	71	100.0	25	100

3. Length of program

	U.S.	%	J.	%
1 semester	47	66.2	1	4.0
1 year	23	32.4	18	72.0
Other	1	1.4	6	24.0
	71	100.0	25	100

4. Requirement or optional

	U.S.	%	J.	%
Requirement	5	7.0	0	0.0
Optional	66	93.0	25	100.0
	71	100.0	25	100.0

5. Group or individual?

	U.S.	%	J.	%
One or few	52	73.2	20	80.0
Group	19	26.8	4	16.0
Other	0	0.0	1	4.0
	71	100.0	25	100.0

6. Expenses

Tuition fees	U.S.	%	J.	%
Scholarship or waived	50	70.4	18	72.0
Personal funds	18	25.4	7	28.0
Other (loan)	3	4.2	0	0.0
	71	100.0	25	100.0
Living expenses	U.S.	%	J.	%
Scholarship	23	32.4	5	20.0
Personal funds	44	62.0	20	80.0
Other (loan)	4	5.6	25	100.0
	71	100.0	25	100.0

7. Prior international sojourn

	U.S.	%	J.	%
Yes	40	56.3	19	76.0
No	31	43.7	6	24.0
	71	100.0	25	100.0

8. Year of study abroad

	U.S.	%	J.	%
2001–2	3	4.2	1	4.0
2002–3	15	21.1	0	0.0
2003–4	17	23.9	3	12.0

9. Prior language proficiency

	U.S.	%	J.	%
None	9	12.7	0	0.0
Very low	10	14.1	1	4.0
Low	20	28.2	5	20.0
Fair	21	29.6	9	36.0
Good	7	9.9	10	40.0

Appendix 5.1 **Students' Profiles** *(continued)*

2004–5	34	47.9	12	48.0		Excellent	3	4.2	0	0.0
NA	2	2.8	9	36.0		NA	1	1.4	0	0.0
	71	100.0	25	100.0			71	100.0	25	100.0

10. Satisfaction level

Overall evaluation	U.S.	%	J.	%		Living environment	U.S.	%	J.	%
1 (Highly satisfactory)	45	63.4	11	44.0		1 (Highly satisfactory)	36	50.7	7	28.0
2	17	23.9	7	28.0		2	15	21.1	5	20.0
3	2	2.8	3	12.0		3	10	14.1	8	32.0
4	1	1.4	0	0.0		4	2	2.8	0	0.0
5	2	2.8	2	8.0		5	3	4.2	3	12.0
6	2	2.8	0	0.0		6	3	4.2	1	4.0
7 (Unsatisfactory)	1	1.4	1	4.0		7 (Unsatisfactory)	1	1.4	0	0.0
NA	1	1.4	1	4.0		NA	1	1.4	1	4.0
	71	100.0	25	100.0			71	100.0	25	100.0

Academic program	U.S.	%	J.	%		Personal development	U.S.	%	J.	%
1 (Highly satisfactory)	18	25.4	6	24.0		1 (Highly satisfactory)	39	54.9	9	36.0
2	30	42.3	7	28.0		2	14	19.7	9	36.0
3	13	18.3	5	20.0		3	10	14.1	2	8.0
4	3	4.2	1	4.0		4	5	7.0	0	0.0
5	3	4.2	2	8.0		5	0	0.0	1	4.0
6	2	2.8	1	4.0		6	1	1.4	2	8.0
7 (Unsatisfactory)	1	1.4	2	8.0		7 (Unsatisfactory)	1	1.4	0	0.0
NA	1	1.4	1	4.0		NA	1	1.4	1	4.0
	71	100.0	25	100.0			71	100.0	25	100.0

Note: J. = Japanese.

Appendix 5.2. **Students' Responses**

1. Reason for choosing Japan/United States (multiple responses)

United States	No.	%
Japanese language and culture	38	53.5
Japanese major	32	45.1
Challenging environment	10	14.1
Japanese friends	8	11.3
Economy/business major	6	8.5
Japanese ancestor/relatives	3	4.2
Prior experience in Japan	2	2.8
Availability	2	2.8

Japan	No.	%
U.S. characteristics/strength	16	64.0
Availability	8	32.0
Prior experience in the United States	2	8.0
Recommendation of others	1	4.0

2. Components of human network (multiple responses)

United States	No.	%
Classmate (mainly international students)	54	76.1
Japanese students	28	39.4
Host family	23	32.4
Club members	19	26.8
Dorm mate (both international and Japanese)	18	25.4
Language partner	17	23.9
Outside of university	8	11.3
University staff	4	5.6

Japan	No.	%
Dorm mate	17	68.0
Classmate (mainly U.S. students)	15	60.0
Japanese learner	8	32.0
Japanese students	8	32.0
International students	8	32.0
Partnership program	5	20.0
Church member	3	12.0

3. Influence of study abroad over career choice

United States	No.	%
Yes/Yes, indirectly	47	66.2
No	16	22.5
NA	8	11.3
	71	

Japan	No.	%
Yes/Yes, indirectly	22	88.0
No	0	0.0
NA	3	12.0
	25	

4.1.Have your view of host country changed?

United States		No.	%
Yes		54	76.1
	Positive	*24*	
	Negative	*2*	
	Neutral/Realistic	*16*	
	NA	*12*	
No		9	12.7
NA		8	11.3

Japan		No.	%
Yes		19	76.0
	Positive	*5*	
	Negative	*6*	
	Neutral/Realistic	*8*	
	NA	*0*	
No		5	20.0
NA		1	4.0

Appendix 5.2. **Students' Responses** *(continued)*

	71	100.0

	25	100.0

4.2. Has your interest in accessing information on your host country increased?

United States	No.	%
Yes	50	70.4
No	14	19.7
NA	7	9.9
	71	100.0

Japan	No.	%
Yes	19	76.0
No	3	12.0
NA	3	12.0
	25	100.0

4.3. Are you able to and do you explain Japan-related issues to others?

United States	No.	%
Yes	62	87.3
No	3	4.2
NA	6	8.5
	71	100.0

Japan	No.	%
Yes	22	88.0
No	2	8.0
NA	1	4.0
	25	100

5. If given an opportunity to study abroad again, would you choose Japan/the United States again?

United States	No.	%
Yes	65	91.5
No	2	2.8
NA	4	5.6
	71	100.0

Japan	No.	%
Yes	16	64.0
No	5	20.0
NA	4	16.0
	25	100

III

Popular Culture

6

The Attractions of the J-Wave
for American Youth

Anne Allison

In the 2003 Hollywood hit *Lost in Translation,* Tokyo is the backdrop for a story about two Americans as lost in a foreign culture as they are in their lives back home. Strangers when they first meet as travelers in the same hotel, the two connect over shared insomnia and the mutual recognition of anomie in the other. Japan—a place neither wanted to visit and in which neither is particularly interested—is utterly strange, yet it is a strangeness that, when ventured into together, inspires intimacy between the two. The storyline of *Lost in Translation* is one of being oddly in place while displaced from home and culture. Director Sofia Coppola shoots scene and after scene of a searingly beautiful Tokyo that, unreadable by the Americans, mystifies and amuses them. It is as strangers "lost in translation" that the audience, too, is positioned to view Japan: a place signifying displacement—a not altogether uncomfortable state, as the story tells us. In this, Japan is treated less literally than metaphorically—a signifier of foreignness about which the Americans remain uncomprehending.

In summer 2004, ABC aired an episode of the children's television show *Abarangers* (the seasonal name of the long-running *Power Rangers*) titled "Lost and Found in Translation." An obvious reference to the previous year's adult-targeted movie *Lost in Translation,* the show replayed its theme of cultural difference with a significant twist. The scene opens in the United States with the rangers working on homework—a social science project studying two cultures. Switching on a TV, they discover a Japanese program that turns out to be the Japanese version of *Abarangers* dubbed into English. The plotline is standard for the series: confronted by a strange-looking alien, the rangers morph into cyberwarriors, battle with stylistic moves and newfangled weapons, and defeat the foe. Amusingly, the story also includes an American: an athlete caricaturized as vulgarly money hungry who has come to Japan in search of a good chiropractor (and is saved in a double sense by the Japanese black ranger, who cures his back and also his drive for money). Two of the Americans watching the show are riveted. The third, however, is dismissive. Saying "they got it all wrong," Conner discounts the enemy as a "guy in a rubber suit" and is offended by the portrayal of the American. "To make fun of our sports heroes? This represents what they think of us in Japan!" As his pals tell him that it's just a show and to use his imagination, Conner relaxes and gets into the action. By the end of the program, all three are excited and Conner admits that "it was kinda cool." The episode ends with a message about cultural difference voiced by the new convert: "We're not so different after all; just a slightly different interpretation." Completing his homework assignment, he announces the title to the others: "Japanese Versus American Culture—Closer Than We Think."

Lost in Translation and "Lost and Found in Translation" are U.S.-made popular productions that juxtapose Americans and Japanese. Both reflect, as I argue here, a new fad or fetish for Japan in the American imagination, particularly among youth. But the two would seem to be at odds; one features adults who get "lost" in a Japan they fail to "translate," and the other features American rangers who see in their Japanese counterparts a "different interpretation." Though the messages are not as divergent as they first appear (more on this later), what is most immediately striking for my subject here—how to make sense of the current J-wave in U.S. youth culture and how to measure this in terms of soft power—is the *Abarangers* episode and its proclamation of Americans getting "lost and found" in a pop cultural production at once foreign and familiar, different and not. The airing of this episode is significant, for it came at a time—2004—when (pop) cultural goods from Japan were circulating globally with a currency of trendy coolness—what Douglas McGray (2002) has called Japan's GNC (gross national cool). For more than a decade now, the global prominence of Japanese creative or fantasy goods—comic books (*manga*), animation (anime), video and electronic games, youth fashion, Hello Kitty, and Pokémon collectible card games—has been on the rise, making Japan world-renowned as the producer of cutting-edge "cool."

Japanese influence on the global imagination is hardly new, of course. Japanese imports have impacted American pop culture throughout the postwar period, with *Godzilla* movies, television shows such as *Speed Racer* and *Astro Boy,* toys such as Transformers, which were a big hit in the 1980s, and cultural technology such as the Sony Walkman and Nintendo video-ware (both software and hardware). Since the 1990s, though, there has been a palpable shift to a greater mainstreaming of not only Japanese properties but also the way in which Japan or "Japaneseness" gets encoded in the popular imagination of American kids. The example of "Lost and Found in Translation" is illustrative. Broadcast in 2004 as *Abarangers,* this constituted the twelfth season of *Power Rangers* on U.S. television: a show based on the Japanese *renjā* series that has been produced by Tōei Studios since 1975. Acquiring rights to its U.S. broadcast in 1985, Haim Saban—a U.S.-based entrepreneur—tried for eight years to interest an American television network in the show. All refused on the grounds that it had a foreign flavor and a kitschy aesthetic that would fail to catch on with American kids. When Margaret Loesch, who had been raised on Japanese television shows, signed it for the Fox Kids network, however, *Power Rangers* became an immediate success, outranking all other children's television programs in the United States within a scant five weeks and soon becoming the number one children's program internationally. But in order to appeal to American kids, it was thought necessary to transform the show.

Utilizing the Japanese footage of the action scenes when the rangers have morphed into warrior costume, Fox Kids reshot all the scenes where the rangers are in everyday mode (and their bodies thus revealed) with American actors. The Japanese and American footage was spliced together to create a hybrid renamed *Mighty Morphin Power Rangers*. The show was not only reinvented; it was also Americanized. An executive at Saban told me in 1996 that it had become "an American classic." As a number of people in the children's entertainment business confirmed, a Japanese show like this could not have been mainstreamed on American network TV with actors who were Asian instead of American or with credentials that openly announced their origins as "made in Japan." What needed to be excised, in other words, was its Japanese identity. And, indeed, most of the American youth I interviewed about the program in the late 1990s were unaware that it originally came from Japan.

Power Rangers started airing as an American, or Americanized, show in 1993. It is still airing today in 2007, one of the longest-running children's series in the history of American kids' television. But, as the episode "Lost and Found in Translation" would seem to indicate, while the U.S. version is still being cast with American actors and culturalized to appeal to American tastes, the reluctance to credit its Japanese roots is beginning to fade. And the case of *Abarangers* is hardly singular. For example, in Saturday morning television these days, there are a host of shows made in Japan (such as *Shaman King,* broadcast on Warner Brothers) with not only Japanese credits but also scenes and characters clearly reflecting a Japanese, or at least Asian, identity (with temples and spirits, and characters drinking tea, eating with chopsticks, and writing Japanese script). Indeed, as a Saban executive told me recently, such signs of Japaneseness no longer need to be excised because they *are* what now makes a show cool with American youth: a cultural identifier that sells precisely because it signals a style, a fashion, and a culture that is *not* American. This J-trend in America is also reflected in the craze over Japanese *manga* and anime (often called "Japanimation" in America), shelves of which can be seen in bookstores and video stores; the continuing and growing interest in Zen, karate, ki-aikido, sushi, and green tea; the commercial cult faddism of Hello Kitty and Kitty-ish spin-offs; the rise in toy trends such as Digimon, Yu-Gi-Oh!, and Pokémon; and the "Japanization" of even U.S.-made pop culture, as seen in the movies *The Matrix* and *Kill Bill* and with pop stars such as Gwen Stefani and her Harajuku Girls.

When doing fieldwork on the Pokémon craze that peaked in the States in 1999, I was struck by the fact that virtually all of the fans I interviewed—girls and boys ages four to sixteen—were well aware that the property originated in Japan. Many also said that the image they had of Japan was positive and, further, that they wanted to visit there one day and even study the language and culture. Indeed, Japanese classes in U.S. universities and high schools are filled these days with students driven by their enthusiasm for anime or *manga* and an interest in being able to consume made-in-Japan comics or animation in their original form. (By contrast, few American youth studied Japanese in the 1960s and 1970s; in the 1980s, when Japanese studies and classes increased across the country, those who enrolled were largely business and law majors interested in working in Japan's bubble economy.)

In this sense, the popularity of Japanese fantasy goods—among youth in the United States and other postindustrial settings across the world today—is generating an attraction of some kind to Japan. And, as the *Abarangers* episode depicted this—in contrast to the adults of *Lost in Translation*—youth do not want to be lost in this foreign terrain but rather to find their way in a different cultural terrain that becomes comfortable and familiar to them. I heard such sentiments voiced by several fans of J-pop. As one twenty-two-year-old man put it, Japanese cool is so popular with American youth these days precisely because of its utter difference. "The fantasy worlds portrayed could be Mars" for the strangeness of the setting, story lines, and characters. But equally important, he continued, is knowing that this all comes from a real place: from a Japan that actually exists, which inspires at least some fans to learn about Japanese culture, language, and history. "Japan" signifies something important in this context, but the signifier is shifting: a marker of phantasm and difference, yet one that gets anchored in a reality of sorts—a country that Americans can study and visit. So fantasy and realism alternate here, the one serving as the alibi for the other in what Roland Barthes (1957) described as the construction of myth. Japan's role in the current J-boom is mythic: a place whose meaning fluctuates between phantasmic and real, foreign and familiar, strange and everyday. Fans of Japanese anime, *manga,* card games, and toys I have talked with in the States voice their attraction in similar terms: having their imaginations piqued by the complexity and strangeness of an alternative (non-American) fantasy world, enjoyable for the fluency they strive to master in it (by learning some Japanese, downloading pirates of the Japanese originals, or acquiring knowledge about the cultural references). The first part of this attraction is not so different from the depiction of foreignness in *Lost in Translation*—a quirky and bizarre otherworld. But, in contrast to the adult perspective taken in the film, American youth who are fans of J-pop want to be "found" rather than "lost" in this terrain, by keeping the edginess of its difference yet acquiring the savvy—of a global traveler or global citizen—to speak the language.

Soft Power and Cultural (De)odorization

How does this jibe with Joseph Nye's (2004) notion of soft power, which he defined as an attractive power: the ability to get what you want through attraction (rather than coercion or payment) that arises from the attractiveness of a country's culture, ideals, or policies? As he noted, popular culture does not, in and of itself, equate with soft power. Rather, soft power rests primarily on three resources: a country's culture, political values, and foreign policy. The more universal the values it adheres to and the more global (or globally shared) its national policies, the greater a country's potential for influencing the behavior of others (i.e., exerting soft power), according to Nye (2004, p. 11). When such conditions are compromised, however—as when a culture is more parochial than universal and its values are narrow rather than broad—there is less potential for the generation of soft power even when a country's cultural goods are trafficking well outside national borders. As Nye observed, "Excellent wines and cheeses do not guarantee attraction to France, nor does the popularity of Pokémon games assure that Japan will get the policy outcomes it wishes" (2004, p. 12).

As an example of popular culture that succeeds in generating soft power, Nye cited the United States, particularly when—prior to recent moves such as the Iraq war—its national policies were viewed with less hostility or resentment around the world. The image the United States has implanted of itself through the attractiveness of its popular culture is of a country "exciting, exotic, rich, powerful, trend-setting—the cutting-edge of modernity and innovation" (Rosendorf 2000, p. 123, cited in Nye 2004, p. 10).

Pointedly, this is *not* the image Japan has been able to project of itself or incubate in others despite the increasing popularity of its cultural products in global traffic, according to Iwabuchi Kōichi. In his important book *Recentering Globalization: Popular Culture and Japanese Transnationalism* (2002), Iwabuchi argued that while Japan's cultural power has certainly increased in recent years, it is of a nature far different from that associated with "Americanization." Working primarily with the trade of J-pop in East Asia ("inter-Asia") since the 1980s, he characterized the transnational cultural power in operation as "decentered" from a definitive place and "dispersed" away from a central location. In fact, this has become the tendency of cultural power and global culture in this millennial era, even that produced and disseminated by (the once hegemonic) United States. In terms of Japanese pop culture more specifically, Iwabuchi also traced the very particular history of postwar Japan, where corporations adopted a policy of *mukokuseki*—erasing national identity from cultural products sold outside Japan. The reason for this was very practical: to diminish or "deodorize" unsavory associations with Japan. In Southeast or East Asia, these associations involved the brutal history of colonization and militarism that lasted throughout World War II. For the Euro-American market, the images were of Japan as a secondary or second-rate cultural producer, fostered by the cheap carnival goods and kitschy monster movies it sold in the early postwar years. The policy adopted by the Japanese company Sony to remove such cultural odors was typical. Attempting to fashion its corporate image and products as culturally global rather than Japanese, it assumed an aesthetically cosmopolitan and culturally neutral style for everything from its corporate name—Sony—to the colors of its goods—tones of gray and black (Kuroki 1995). And the stamp "made in Japan" was imprinted on its products in the smallest letters possible.

As Nye pointed out, Sony has become one of the top twenty-five multinational brand names in the world today, and two others on this list come from Japan as well: Toyota and Honda (2004, p. 86). The success of these Japanese brand names has occurred despite, or precisely because of, what Iwabuchi and others described as their culturally odorless nature. But, as Nye also noted, the cultural capital of Japan has dramatically changed over the course of the postwar period. While the image of its wartime imperialism still remains in neighbors including China and South Korea, even in these countries—as in the rest of the world—Japan's prestige as an industrial powerhouse started growing by the 1970s. Particularly in the fields of consumer electronics and automobiles, the imprimatur "made in Japan" has acquired a positive rather than negative connotation today, signifying high-quality workmanship and technological sophistication. In these arenas—of digital cameras, high-resolution TVs, camcorders, automobiles—Japanese products have become much more clearly marked with their manufacturers' national identity. As Nye acknowledged, the image of Japan carried by such goods is attractive: the manufacturing prowess of a technological superproducer, an image that, particularly before the bubble burst in 1991, generated worldwide interest in Japanese management techniques and business practices (2004, p. 86). Still, as the designer of Sony's Walkman, Kuroki Yasuo, has lamented (1995), consumers around the world eagerly buy their made-in-Japan Sony Walkmans, but few outside the country ever play Japanese music on them. In his mind, there is a distinction between what he calls hard technology and soft technology. The former, consisting more of machines—cars, VCRs, televisions, Walkmans—is where Japan has achieved global recognition. In the latter, however—the realm of images, music, films, and storytelling that he, and others, treat as "culture"—Japan is far less influential. In Kuroki's estimation, Japanese culture fails to translate or transfer to the global imagination. Or, as Nye has put it in terms of soft power, the culture is parochial and has cultural values that are narrow rather than universal.

This is the image portrayed in the Hollywood movie *Lost in Translation.* The American travelers to Japan are intrigued, but befuddled, by the foreign culture they come into contact with. They can never make sense of the people, places, or situations they encounter, which generates a series of comedic gaffes and cultural miscommunications. But these Americans also never really try to understand, lost as they are, not so much in a place that does not or cannot make sense, but, rather, in their own cultural ethnocentrism: an Americanism they assume is (or should be) universal. It is from this perspective that the Japanese culture depicted in *Lost in Translation* comes across as utterly bizarre. Significantly, this is precisely the reaction many American adults have had to the recent fad of Japanese play goods. For example, when the mass media empire of Pokémon—comics, cartoons, video and Game Boy games, trading cards, toys, tie-in merchandise and campaigns—peaked in the States in 1999, I interviewed countless parents of Poké-fans who were totally mystified as to the appeal of the property. Most had no concept of what a pocket monster was—an attitude that was widely shared even among the corporate executives who became the marketers of the product in the United States. The logic of the fantasy was elusive, as a toy industry veteran admitted. He could understand the superhero concept of *Power Rangers*, with its good-versus-evil mythology so familiar to American mass story making, but Pokémon seemed too abstract, complex, and open-ended to appeal widely to American youth. As he noted, it is a diffuse and endlessly transforming play world that requires vast investments of time, energy, and commitment in order to achieve the game's objective—acquiring all 151 (now more than 300) Pokémon residing in this virtual universe. Such a construction of play seemed patently alien to him: an assessment based, in part, on the fact that Pokémon was a foreign creation and lacked American sensibilities.

This attitude—of adult bewilderment over Pokémon—was spoofed in the sharp-edged *South Park,* a television show that runs on the Comedy Central network. In an episode titled "Chinpokomon" that aired in 2000, the parents of Poké-fans struggle to understand what a pocket monster is. "What *are* those things? Animals? Robots? I don't know, but suddenly I want to own them all!" Realizing that the hold these made-in-Japan creatures have over their children is being manipulated by Japanese to colonize the minds of American kids and help foment a Japanese takeover, the parents come up with a strategy to break the spell: they learn Pokémonology. And this works, for once the adults become savvy about the game and master the monsters' names, the kids lose interest and find Pokémon not that cool anymore. Needless to say, the *South Park* episode was a parody, and what it parodied was not only the cluelessness of American adults about the nature of Japanese playthings so popular with their kids, but also the geopolitical effect such attraction could yield: the terrain, we could say, of soft power—gaining influence for a country through the attractiveness of its soft technology. In the context of "Chinpokomon," this becomes the "brainwashing" of American kids by a toy fad that is programmed by its producers with nationalist ideology, turning players against their own country and into Japanese clones. But this possibility—of a political effect brought about by the influx of Japanese pop culture into the United States—is so exaggerated and lampooned in the show as to make it seem utterly ridiculous. It is as if the show is making fun not only of the ineptitude of American adults in understanding the J-wave in their country but also of any association made between this pop cultural trend and "real" geopolitical influence by Japan in the United States (or the rest of the world). Indeed, by the end of the show, American kids have abandoned their Japanese toys, and in the sigh of relief breathed by their parents is a message about the transience of popular trends and the shallowness of the cultural influence (soft power) the J-wave holds in the United States.

But is this assessment correct? It is one that reflects what I found to be the general attitude of American adults regarding the Pokémania that captivated U.S. youth for at least two years: that, though a popular fad of immense proportions, Pokémon (and through it Japan) influenced American youth in terms of their goals, actions, or aptitudes in a way that was judged to be relatively benign. As one mother put it to me, "I don't understand the game and I don't understand the hold it has on my children. But Pokémon are cute and there is no killing or blood. To me, it seems benign. And the fact it comes from Japan, well—that doesn't matter one way or another. In the end, it's only a toy." We could translate this understanding of the impact of J-cool on American youth into Nye's terminology of soft power in the following way: the globalization of Japanese pop culture does not equate to Japanese soft power, failing, as it does, to become anchored in something in the culture or country itself—social policies and practices, for example, that could fuel a yearning or attraction for the so-called real Japan. Interestingly enough, Iwabuchi said something similar in speaking about *mukokuseki*—the long-standing policy of Japanese corporations to "deodorize" national identity from their cultural products sent abroad.

> We find a basic contradiction: the international spread of *mukokuseki* popular culture from Japan simultaneously articulates the universal appeal of Japanese cultural products and the disappearance of any perceptible "Japaneseness." . . . If it is indeed the case that the Japaneseness of Japanese animation derives, consciously or unconsciously, from its erasure

of physical signs of Japaneseness, is not the Japan that Western audiences are at long last coming to appreciate, and even yearn for, an animated, race-less and culture-less, virtual version of "Japan"? (Iwabuchi 2002, p. 33)

New Global Imagination: A Different Model from Americanization

The assumption being made by the parent cited above that, in the global fad of Japanese cool today, the properties evoke little if anything of a real Japan and produce a yearning for something that, *because it is virtual and artificially constructed,* yields little soft power—in Nye's definition—for the producing country. But, again, is this assessment correct? Not exactly, I would say. Rather, I argue that at work here is a new kind of global imagination, or at least new in the way it differs from the older model of Americanization. The latter, of course, conforms to Nye's notion of soft power in the sense that its ability to attract "arises from the attractiveness of a country's culture, political ideals, and policies" (2004, p. x). Power of this nature comes from inspiring the dreams and desires of others by projecting images about one's own culture that are globally appealing and transmitted through channels of global communication (such as television and film). As has been generally agreed, only the United States has had the soft power—in the strength of its cultural industries and the appeal of a culture that has translated around the world as rich, powerful, and exciting—to dominate the global imagination throughout the twentieth century.

But not only is America's soft power ebbing today due in part to the global unpopularity of such U.S.-led initiatives as the Iraq war; so, too, is the desirability—even in the States—of a monolithic, monochromatic fantasy space. As A.O. Scott wrote recently about the 2004 Toronto film festival, the global currency in films made in India, China, South Korea, and Japan is increasing, defying the prediction that Hollywood "would take over with its blockbuster globalism dissolving all vestiges of the local, particular and strange" (2004, p. 86). As Scott sees it, Hollywood is stuck in making movies that, while technologically impressive, project "counterfeit worlds" that spectacularize fantasies out of sync with the lived emotions of people in the twenty-first century. By contrast, some recent movies set and produced elsewhere (the example he gives is *The World,* by Chinese director Jia Zhangkhe) may be smaller in scale but are more emotionally real. Stories of ordinary people struggling to make it in cities in jagged transition (Beijing, Seoul, Calcutta, Taipei), where they are both dislocated and at home, project "the anxious, melancholy feeling of being simultaneously connected and adrift" (Scott 2004, p. 86)—a state deeply recognizable to postindustrial subjects the world over. Of course, the fantasy making of Hollywood filmmaking, embedded with attractive images of American culture, remains ever popular both in the United States (though theater attendance has been slipping) and, perhaps even more, outside (where revenues for films such as *Titanic* are much greater than at home). But, as film critic Charles Taylor put it, what characterizes the emotional condition of the new millennium is "being in a world where the only sense of home is to be found in a constant state of flux" (quoted in Scott 2004, p. 86)—a state conjured through mobility, nomadism, travel, the foreign. This is a descriptor, in fact, of *Lost in Translation,* and also of the Japanese pop cultural products that are appealing to the tastes and sensibilities of global youth, including those in the United States.

With this, I make three final observations. The first (well-known already) concerns the ebbing, if hardly collapse, of American soft power as the hegemonic center of global culture. I concur, as do so many others, with Iwabuchi's observation that national power and global influence are congealing in a different direction these days from the Cold War times of U.S. world dominance. This is to say not that the United States has lost its ability to wield worldwide power but rather that the form power takes in the twenty-first century, particularly within the realm of soft power—ideas, images, information, and trend making—is becoming decentered away from any single place, including the United States.

The second observation is about new models of the global imagination today that, in the case of Japanese cool and its popularization around the world, carry an attractive power but not one that is driven by, or generates, an attraction in others for the actual place or culture of the producing country. "Japan" does register in all this, in a recent shift from the time when Japanese cultural products were marketed around the world by "deodorizing" their roots—a cultural influence that a number of Japanese critics have referred to as invisible colonization and Iwabuchi as cultural deodorization (Iwabuchi 2002, p. 33). But, as described above, it is not so much Japan itself as a compelling culture, power, or place that gets signified (despite the fact that this is precisely what the Japanese government is trying to capitalize on in all the rhetoric and attention currently given to Japan's new soft power in the globalization of J-pop). Rather, "Japan" operates more as signifier for a particular brand and blend of fantasy-ware: goods that inspire an imaginary space at once foreign and familiar and a subjectivity of continual flux and global mobility, forever moving into and out of new planes, powers, terrains, and relations. What is created, in other words, is less a product that crystallizes some essence (or odor) of a particular country or culture and more an experience that yields an effect—the product of what Hardt and Negri (2000) have recently argued is immaterial labor and the direction of global capitalism in the twenty-first century.

To put this more concretely, the current popularization of Japanese cool around the world is best understood in terms of its fantasy formation, which, in turn, lends itself so productively to capitalistic marketing in the new millennium. As I have argued elsewhere (Allison 2006), key here are two qualities. The first I call polymorphous perversity—a universe in which characters, plotlines, and play products continually morph or extend into something new. This is true of the Power Rangers, whose characters start off as ordinary teenagers but then transform into cyberwarriors aligned with special spirits, high-tech weapons, and fanciful flying gear, and then, by the end of the show, revert back to street clothes. It is also true of Pokémon, where, in the Game Boy iteration, players aim to catch wild monsters that, once caught and therefore "pocketed," become an entity with multiple identities: weapons, capital, pets, friends, and genies. Pocket monsters (Pokémon) also accrue powers, values, and secrets the more that they fight; many also evolve. Not only do these play creatures morph and expand, but so do the lines of Pokémon toy products. So what started out as a Game Boy game in February 1996 soon expanded into a media-mix empire of comic book, animated cartoon, trading cards, video game, movies, toy merchandise, and tie-in campaigns (such as the ANA *poketto* jets). The other quality key to the global craze of J-wave, in my estimation, is what I call "techno-animism": technology that gets animated with spirits, creatures, and intimacies of various sorts. The virtual pet *tamagotchi,* manufactured by Bandai, is an example of techno-animism where players raise "pets" by manipulating icons on a digital screen that become "lifelike," generating affective bonds of companionship. On the basis of these two qualities of techno-animism and polymorphous identity, what emerges is a fantasy of perpetual transformation (humans who morph into rangers, pocket monsters who become both weapons and pets) that, extended into the cyberfrontier, promises (new age) companionship and connectedness, albeit in a commodity form. Resonant with the fluctuation, fragmentation, and speed-up facing postindustrial youth across the world, such a fantasy also becomes addictive, compelling players to keep changing and expanding their play frontiers through a capitalism of endless innovation, information, and acquisition. All of this makes a play product like Pokémon not only pleasing but also compelling: an attractive commodity that sells—and sells big.

The third observation I make about the global trend of J-cool is about place: the place of production of J-cool and also the role of place in Nye's model of soft power. In this age, when global soft power is becoming increasingly decentered, the place assumed in geographies of power—both real and imaginary—becomes correspondingly deterritorialized—delinked from a firmly bounded territory (Hardt and Negri 2000). Take, for example, one of the newest Japanese properties to become popular with American youth: *Duel Masters*—a media mix of card game, cartoon, comics, toys, and video games that was launched in the United States in March 2003. Based on the popular *manga* and anime in Japan, the story features an adolescent boy, Shobu Kirifuda, who loves to play a special trading game called *Duel Masters.* While the game is set in a totally fantastic universe—five separate civilizations inhabited by monsters who are battling it out for total domination—human players of the *Duel Masters* game are enjoined to use a form of martial arts called by its Japanese name—*kaijudo*—even in the American version. As one of the official guidebooks put it, "To become a Kaijudo master you have to achieve a very high level of self-awareness. There is even a Kaijudo code that states: 'I make no excuses. My actions are my voice. . . . My character is my sword. . . . My courage is my secret weapon. . . . My experience becomes my strength'" (Wizards of the Coast 2004, p. 5).

According to the way *kaijudo* is then laid out in the guidebook, it sounds reminiscent of a Japanese traditional art such as *karate* premised on a code of strict discipline, training, and form. As the guidebook further explained about the cartoon, "When most anime is imported to the U.S., nearly anything Japanese gets changed or dubbed over. This is untrue with *Duel Masters.* While battling, characters shout out their commands in Japanese, giving *Duel Masters* a much more distinct Eastern flavor" (Wizards of the Coast 2004, p. 5).

Quite distinctive here is the juxtaposition of different cultural codes. The *Duel Masters* guidebook claimed "a distinct Eastern flavor" in its inclusion of Japanese commands. But immediately before this, it noted that the card game resembles the U.S.-made *Magic: The Gathering* and adds that the same American company, Wizards of the Coast, has, in fact, produced it. As the anime and *manga* come from Japanese creators (produced by Shōgakukan and Mitsui-Kids), *Duel Masters* is a joint production, distributed—as is now commonplace for such Japanese products that get globalized—differently in Japan and Asia versus in the United States and "all territories outside of Asia." In terms of production, this (as well as other U.S.-Japanese fare such as Power Rangers and Pokémon) represents a model of global power different from that associated with Americanization. The property is jointly produced, differentially distributed, and culturally mixed. Unlike McDonaldization, with its Fordist formula of one size fits all or even with the glocalization it now travels with—a global commodity that gets localized differently in differing locales—a property like *Duel Masters* is both "Eastern" and not, a globalized fantasy whose intermixture of the foreign and the familiar is not localizable in or to any one place.

As an effect of the craze of Japanese properties in the orbit of American pop culture in recent years, there are an increasing number of such joint or mixed productions—movies, cartoons, comic books, and video games—that, made jointly in the United States and Japan, adopt cultural codes both American and Japanese, and U.S.-made properties that project a "Japanese" cultural air. This is true, for example, of the Hollywood films *Kill Bill* and *The Matrix;* Arthur Golden's fictionalized memoir of a Japanese geisha, *Memoirs of a Geisha,* which was made into a Hollywood blockbuster starring three Chinese actresses as the lead geishas; a new "*manga*" running in the American teen magazine *Cosmo Girl!* (written by an American girl, a longtime fan of *Sailor Moon* who has never visited Japan); and the cult fad of *Powerpuff Girls* (a popular cartoon featuring three girl superheroes designed by an anime-inspired American artist). An article in the *New York Times* characterized another such "Japanish" property, *Avatar,* Nickelodeon's cartoon hit released in spring 2005, as "Kung Fu Fightin' Anime Stars, Born in the U.S.A." (Lasswell 2005, p. 19). In the case of *Avatar*—the story of a twelve-year-old boy who learns to channel his supernatural powers to help protect the peace-loving Air, Water, and Earth nations against the evil Fire nation—the cartoon is called "Asian influenced," though it was created by two American men. As the *New York Times* article joked, "The creators of six-year-old boys' favorite cartoon figures aren't actually Asian. But, they say, they have tried yoga."

In all the above cases, projected are images and auras of Japan (or, as *Duel Masters* puts it, "a distinct Eastern flavor"). But production comes either partially or entirely from non-Japanese; in this case, Americans. What does this mean for the notion of soft power and for Nye's formulation of it? The concept, at the very least, needs to be complicated, given that the lines of power operating here are as much postnational and transnational as national, and the cartographies of place have become virtual, constructed, and phantasmic (an anime of a Japanese boy designed by an American who may nevertheless capture something poignant about "Japan"). There is a powerful attraction at work, nevertheless. And for American youth attracted to J-cool (wherever it is made), the allure is for a cultural coding at once different and foreign that is within their capacity to master and grasp. This differs from the relationship the American adults have to Japan in the movie *Lost in Translation*. There, Japan is forever foreign (if also a so-called real place) because, when traveling there, the Americans do so within the shell of their own cultural ethnocentrism. For the American youth who embrace a Japanese ranger ("Lost and Found in Translation") or even an American-made "anime," precisely for its cultural difference, I see an attitude that is much more promising: a willingness to go beyond the cultural orbit of "Americanness" and the hegemony of the global imagination it once held. This, surely, should be part of the way we assess and measure soft power: not (merely) in terms of the interest it holds for a producing country such as Japan but also (and more important, perhaps) for what it means in terms of the way globalism gets imagined as multi-odored and decentered from bounded places.

References

Allison, Anne. 2006. *Millennial Monsters: Japanese Toys and the Global Imagination*. Berkeley: University of California Press.

Barthes, Roland. 1957. *Mythologies*. Trans. Annette Lavers. New York: Noonday Press.

Hardt, Michael, and Antonio Negri. 2000. *Empire*. Cambridge, MA: Harvard University Press.

Iwabuchi Kōichi. 2002. *Recentering Globalization: Popular Culture and Japanese Transnationalism*. Durham, NC: Duke University Press.

Kuroki Yasuo. 1995. "Nihon no monotsukuri wa sekai ni eikyō o ataete iru ka?" (Does the Japanese way of producing things have an influence on the world?). In *Sekai shōhin no tsukurikata* (The making of world products). Ed. Akurosu Henshūshitsu, 10–16. Tokyo: Parco.

Lasswell, Mark. 2005. "Kung Fu Fightin' Anime Stars, Born in the U.S.A." *New York Times*, August 28, p. 19.

McGray, Douglas. 2002. "Japan's Gross National Cool." *Foreign Policy* 130 (May–June): 44–54.

Nye, Joseph S., Jr. 2004. *Soft Power: The Means to Success in World Politics*. New York: Public Affairs.

Rosendorf, Neal M. 2000. "The Life and Times of Samuel Bronston, Builder of Hollywood in Madrid: A Study in the International Scope and Influence of American Popular Culture," Ph.D. diss. Harvard university, 2000, "Appendix: The Power of American Pop Culture—Evolution of an Elitist Critique," pp. 402–15 and passim.

Scott, A. O. 2004. "What Is A Foreign Movie Now?" *New York Times Magazine*. November 14, 79–86.

Wizards of the Coast. 2004. *Duel Masters*. Wizards of the Coast/Shogakukan/Mitsui-Kids.

7

Shared Memories

Japanese Pop Culture in China

Nakano Yoshiko

When I read Japanese comics, I don't think about the Rape of Nanjing.
—A university student in Nanjing commenting on
his favorite Japanese comic, *Slam Dunk*, in 1999

*With all due respect to Mickey and Donald, whether you look at J-pop,
J-anime, or J-fashion, the competitiveness of any of these is much
more than you might imagine. . . . [These are] bringing about a steady
increase in the number of fans of Japan. We have a grasp on the hearts
of young people in many countries, not the least of which being China.*
—Aso Taro, minister for foreign affairs, speaking to producers and
distributors of Japanese pop culture, April 28, 2006

Is "Japan" really winning the hearts and minds of young people in China, as Foreign Minister Aso seemed to imply? The press reports from the past few years suggest otherwise. In April 2005, we witnessed young Chinese people joining anti-Japanese protests across major Chinese cities for two weeks, triggered mainly by Japan's efforts to gain a permanent seat on the United Nations Security Council and by the latest government approval of a controversial history textbook. Digital messages mobilized tens of thousands of young Chinese protesters, who took to the streets. The resulting vandalization of Japanese premises was visible to all: Shattered glass surrounded the embassy in Beijing and the consulate in Shanghai, and Japanese restaurants, convenience stores, and cars. At the Shanghai consulate alone, more than 5,000 plastic bottles were thrown, along with rocks, eggs, tomatoes, and waste. Prime Minister Koizumi Junichiro, who had stirred up emotions with his repeated visits to the Yasukuni Shrine, was burned in effigy, along with the Japanese national flag. Banners on the street screamed, "Face up to History!"; "Beat Japanese Militarism!"; and "Boycott Japanese Goods!"

And yet, at convenience stores in Shanghai, copies of the Japanese comic books *Slam Dunk* and *Detective Conan* (also known as *Case Closed*) fill the shelves. At bookstores, you can find stacks of *Leili*, the Chinese-language version of the Japanese fashion magazine *Ray*. And a Japanese drama series featuring heartthrobs Kimura

Takuya and Domoto Tsuyoshi reaches students' computers through illegal downloads whether or not the Chinese censors have approved them for broadcasting. Students who are not studying Japanese often wave good-bye to me not with an accompanying bookish "*Sayōnara*" but using the casual "*Jyaa-ne!*" that they have learned from pirated Japanese animation or drama discs.

The influence of Japanese pop culture is often measured by its commercial success in the United States. Pokémon's first American box office release in 1999 earned more than $80 million and became a symbol of Japan's improved soft power. Joseph Nye, referring to Pokémon to illustrate how Japanese cultural influence has grown, wrote that "Japanese images dominated children's dreams quite handily over the last five years with their mix of cuteness and power" (Nye 2004, p. 132). As Anne Allison describes in Chapter 6, children in the United States basically have a monopoly on Japanese *anime* (animation), *manga* (comic books), and games, which are gradually moving from the foreign category to mainstream, leaving many of their parents puzzled.

In contrast, in Asia, Japanese children's shows have been nothing but mainstream for the past few decades—for the past twenty-five years in China, and for the past thirty-five years in Hong Kong, the gateway to China. As viewers have become older, their tastes have evolved, as have the tastes for the types of Japanese pop culture imported, legally and illegally, to the region. The children who spent afternoons watching Japanese anime have gone on to become consumers of anime and *manga* for teenagers and adults, computer games, Japanese television dramas for single women and men, salmon *sashimi, ramen,* and *tako-yaki* octopus balls, and Japanese fashion magazines. In Asia, Japanese pop culture icons are not just pastel-colored monsters and superheroes in rubber suits without apparent nationality. Japanese singers and actors sell fantasy, fill the pages of tabloid papers and magazines, and draw students to Japanese-language classes because they want to understand the lyrics of Japanese songs or the dialogue in drama series. These Japanese stars are foreign but not so foreign to Chinese students.

What role does Japanese pop culture play in China? Is it a soft power resource for Japan? Nye defined soft power as "the ability to get what you want through attraction rather than coercion or payment" (2004, p. x) and pop culture as "a source that produces soft power" (2004, p. 12). He also pointed out that "soft power resources . . . sometimes take years to produce the desired outcome" (2004, p. 99). In other words, this model of soft power places the nation in the center, takes the unilateral perspective of the nation, and regards pop culture as a tool for persuasion in international politics.

This model, however, does not seem to correspond to Japanese pop culture in China. First, although Japanese pop culture is definitely attractive to many younger Chinese, especially in affluent coastal cities, as I discuss farther on, Japan as a nation-state does not seem to be winning these consumers' hearts and minds. Second, in Asia, Japanese pop culture products have been crossing borders largely at the initiative of the Asians on the receiving end, often in the form of pirated products (Shiraishi 1997; Iwabuchi 2004; Nakano and Wu 2003). In other words, the government in Tokyo has not participated in the diffusion, and the much-hyped "Cool Japan" has largely been an unintended outcome. In addition, while there are devoted fans of J-pop music and TV drama who knowingly choose Japanese products, many Chinese consumers of anime or *manga* seem to judge products in terms of quality and their particular interest, and not necessarily in terms of their country of origin.

This is not to say that Japanese pop culture does not have power. I tend to believe that Japanese pop culture in China is most powerful when we take an interactional approach, and consider it not just as a resource for Japan, but as a resource for interaction among Chinese, Japanese, and people of other Asian countries, as it provides much-needed shared memories. Memories are at the core of who we are and how we see others, and divergent memories of the Asia-Pacific War often disturb the relationship between China and Japan. Although pop culture is under strict state control in China, an insufficient supply of domestic children's entertainment programs in the 1980s and digital piracy in the 1990s opened up channels for Japanese pop culture to reach the younger generation in China and to be a part of their memory. In this chapter, I look back to 1980, when Japanese TV anime was first introduced in China, consider how consumer tastes evolved, and examine how anime and TV drama have added new dimensions to Japan, a country often seen as an aggressor nation.

The Anime and the Sword

What do Chinese university students think of Japan? How have they developed their views? What kind of pop culture images do they remember? With these questions in mind, in 1998 I began a project to interview university students in Beijing, Nanjing, and Guangzhou with three colleagues at the City University of Hong Kong, and later expanded the project to include Shanghai and Suzhou with Wu Yongmei of the Beijing University of Foreign Studies in 2002.[1] These students were China's first generation—they grew up with a carefully filtered influence of foreign entertainment once condemned as poison for the minds and still treated as a possible threat to Chinese national identity.

I soon learned that most of the students we interviewed had antagonistic images of Japan. The majority of them embraced Japanese pop culture while they rejected the way Japanese remembered and commemorated the experiences of the Asia-Pacific War. "If you ask me," a female student in Beijing commented on Prime Minister Hashimoto's visit to the Yasukuni Shrine in July 1997, "I would say that the shrine represents the souls of fascism." And she reiterated the Chinese government's official line—"The Japanese government should face up to history"—and explained how Japanese leaders should emulate German chancellor Willy Brandt, who fell on his knees in front of a Holocaust memorial in Warsaw.

On the other hand, this same student has happy memories of running home to watch Japanese anime. She spoke fondly of *Ikkyu-san* (Little Monk Ikkyu), one of the most popular anime series in China, which has been repeated numerous times since it was first broadcast in 1984. Ikkyu is a fifteenth-century Zen master, but in the anime he is depicted as a whiz kid who looks no more than eight years old. In each episode, Ikkyu meditates and solves problems with brilliant wit and humor. When he tries to come up with ideas, he circles his index fingers around his head with the sound "*kulu kulu.*" "Even now," the student in Beijing said, "I still circle my fingers around my head—'*kulu kulu*'"; she feels that this might give her better ideas when she needs them.

Under the open-door policy, children have grown up watching more Japanese anime than American or local programming. This is because Japanese children's shows had been de facto standard in neighboring Hong Kong when China opened up. In addition, China's broadcasting technology was up and running before locally produced TV animation series were ready—China's first animated series did not go on the air until 1993. Thus, Japanese and American animated series were imported to fill the void in TV programming. In December 1980, two years after Deng Xiaoping announced his open-door policy, China's state television, CCTV, began to broadcast fifty-two episodes of the Japanese anime *Astro Boy* (Tetsuwan Atomu), featuring a wide-eyed boy robot with a nuclear-generated heart who saves a futuristic world.

Another lovable robot, Doraemon, may be the most memorable Japanese export for Asians under the age of thirty. The moon-faced robot from the twenty-second century has a round bright turquoise body. He and his friends fly by means of low-tech propellers attached to their heads, and travel to beaches and jungles through Doraemon's "Anywhere Door." Doraemon made his debut in a Japanese monthly comic magazine in 1970, and the anime was first exported to Hong Kong in 1981. As the *Doraemon* anime, *manga,* and countless toys and T-shirts spread to cities across Asia, the vision of *Doraemon*'s friendly future captivated children of an "emerging consumer class" (Shiraishi 1997, p. 265). Doraemon lives with a middle-class family in a two-story suburban row house, the kind that a 1979 European Community document once ridiculed as a "rabbit hutch," a symbol of the low living standard of the new economic superpower in the East. However, many children in Hong Kong admired the same house as a "very big house" and found the neighborhood in *Doraemon* clean and orderly. By the time its anime appeared on CCTV in 1991, approximately 60 percent of urban households in China had replaced their black-and-white TVs with color TVs.

"Of course, I love Doraemon," said a Chinese woman who works for Toyota in Beijing. "Doraemon always helps out his friend Nobita with new gadgets out of his pouch. I guess a part of the reason I enjoyed *Doraemon* so much is because Nobita didn't do so well in school." The main character, Nobita, is an antihero—the fourth-grader is slow, lazy, and always getting into trouble—he makes the dream world more accessible to the viewers. In addition to the state-approved anime on TV, pirated *manga* of *Doraemon* and another favorite, *Dragon Ball,* were sold at newsstands throughout the 1990s, fascinating children who were growing weary of lessons on the Communist Revolution. The pirated *manga* were smaller than passports, so some students were able to hide them inside history or political science textbooks and read them during class.

When Chinese children were watching anime, most of them knew that they were Japanese programs from the theme songs, names, fashion, credits, and style of drawing. Some of the grandparents supervising them, however, may not have recognized them as Japanese programs. "My grandmother hated the Japanese so much," recalled one male student in Guangzhou. "Every time there was a Japanese drama on TV, she immediately switched to another channel. But not Japanese cartoons; she didn't know they were Japanese." At least in some households, Japanese anime escaped adult censorship because the adults did not recognize its Japanese origin. And even if the adults knew that the programs were Japanese and switched to another channel, there were virtually no Chinese domestic cartoon series playing. Their children's favorites were Japanese anime and American cartoon classics such as Mickey Mouse, Donald Duck, and Tom and Jerry.

As *Doraemon*'s viewers grew up, so did the less-than-perfect Japanese anime characters. In 1998, *Slam Dunk,* an anime about a high school basketball team, was the rage in high schools and universities in Chinese cities. In Nanjing, male students hung posters in their dorm rooms of Sakuragi Hanamichi, a good player with bad grades and a wild hairdo, and rented the thirty-one volumes of its *manga* imported from Taiwan at *manga* rental shops on campus, devouring them one after another.

CCTV's cartoon producer Li Jianping explained that Japanese anime characters connect with the Chinese students because they go through the same kind of problems and disappointments that the viewers would go through (Li 1999). "High school students," said Li, "think that American animated stories are good, but the characters are not what they aspire to be. But Japanese cartoons are different. When the students see them, they want to be like the characters." In other words, the Chinese young people identified with the Japanese anime characters and felt that they could be a part of the story.

Through extended exposure to Japanese anime and *manga,* Chinese children unconsciously experienced "Japan" in action. Some began to recognize everyday Japanese rituals such as bowing and taking off their shoes inside the home. Some formed the opinion that the status of Japanese women was low because the mothers in anime stayed home and the fathers did not do any housework. But above all, they learned to appreciate Japanese visual narratives.[2] They became familiar with Japanese story lines, characters, pace, body movements, relationships, and customs in the shows they watched. This would serve as the basis for appreciating other forms of visual entertainment from Japan. It is the *Doraemon* generation that reached out for Japanese dramas designed for single women, dramas that were not shown on Chinese television but were sold and rented as pirated video disks.

How-to Videos of Middle-class Lifestyles

When the first *Doraemon* generation in China became university students, their country was involved in a brand-new search for affluence. The proletarian society was history; a better lifestyle became a central concern for many. A 2002 best seller, *Xiaozi qingdiao* (Petit-bourgeois sentiment), asked a new question: "Do you know which class you belong to?" To talk about "class" in public in China was less of a taboo than it had been a decade before. Members of the "petit bourgeois," with little wealth, were condemned during the Cultural Revolution and sent to the countryside for "reeducation." In 2002, however, the Chinese Academy of Social Sciences published a study of the Chinese social classes (Lu 2002), which was considered the Communist Party's approval to discuss class in the public arena. Now it officially became a wonderful thing to be middle class. *Xiaozi qingdiao* (Petit-bourgeois sentiment) was one of many publications suggesting to the emerging middle class how they might spend their time and money in style.

Back in the mid-1990s, Chinese people in coastal cities began to get a glimpse of the affluent lifestyle. As China shifted from a planned economy to a market economy, foreign supermarkets and department stores began to open and to display massive quantities of products on store shelves. For many Chinese urbanites, this was the first encounter with consumerism. At the same time, university students in metropolitan areas began to enjoy greater freedom on campus, to have opportunities to choose careers for the first time, and to gain more control over their futures. In the midst of this transition, in 1995 the Japanese TV drama *Tokyo Love Story* was first broadcast in Shanghai.

"Trendy drama," as it is labeled in Japan, usually stars single twenty-somethings living in Tokyo. In these stories, an attractive man lives alone in a chic apartment, with no sign of his parents. He falls in love with a woman whose apartment is equally chic; there is no sign of her parents, either. These Japanese dramas (J-dramas), the products of the bubble economy and niche marketing, marked a departure from the one-program-for-all mentality of TV producers. Second TV sets and VCRs freed young Japanese women from the need to share TVs with their parents and enabled them to watch series about family problems involving sisters and in-laws (Schilling 1997, p. 272). The commercial networks Fuji and (later) TBS then created love stories featuring single men and women, which revolved around their own issues and aspirations. In other words, J-dramas were stories of carefree individuals, to be consumed alone or with friends.

One of the first mega-hits in this genre, *Tokyo Love Story,* was based on a *manga* series for girls. It is a story of a young graduate from the southern island of Shikoku, who struggles to find his place in Tokyo and its modernity. He falls in love with an American-educated colleague who knows exactly what she wants, but he then goes back to his high school sweetheart, who needs him by her side. This eleven-part series was originally broadcast in Japan in 1991, in Mandarin by the Pan-Asian satellite broadcaster Star TV in 1992, and in Cantonese in Hong Kong in 1993. The program created a sensation among young people in Taiwan and Hong Kong—two "overseas" Chinese societies, which have been the most important source of entertainment for mainland China. "Although American films and television have made some headway in China," wrote anthropologist Mayfair Yang in 1997, "they cannot compare with the influence of Hong Kong and Taiwan pop culture." Yang argued that Hong Kong and Taiwan pop culture represented "a faster-paced, prosperous life-style outside of the borders of the mainland" that young Chinese people aspired to (Yang [1997] 2002, p. 335). In fact, Hong Kong drama has been a fixture on mainland Chinese TV since the early 1980s. Female students cried while they read Taiwanese romance novels in the 1990s. And CDs of Taiwan pop and Canto pop (Hong Kong pop in Cantonese) occupy a lot of space in music stores across China. With stamps of approval from

Hong Kong and Taiwan, *Tokyo Love Story* crossed the border and was broadcast in Shanghai in 1995. It became truly popular, however, when it spread as a set of pirated VCDs (lower-resolution cousins of DVDs) in the late 1990s.

In the spring of 1999, a college freshman in Nanjing told me that he had seen *Tokyo Love Story* on pirated disks eight years after it was originally broadcast in Japan. He was taken by the lifestyle of college graduates and medical students, and watched about ten hours of programs over a weekend with a classmate: "I don't remember any parts of the story that impressed me. The only thing that I remember is the lifestyle of today's young people in Japan. I had no idea how young people lived before I watched this TV drama."

In fact, the distributors of pirated disks and tapes in China also featured the lifestyles of young people in their promotions. For example, an unauthorized script and cassette tapes of *Tokyo Love Story* that were sold as a Japanese-language learning aid were accompanied by the following introduction: "Today's hottest idols in Japan act in a story that shows *young people's lifestyle,* love, work, and life in a modern metropolis, Tokyo" (emphasis added). "Young people's lifestyle" comes before "love" and "work." There is a certain parallel between J-drama in China and how Japanese read the *Blondie* comic strip in the late 1940s or watched the TV drama *Bewitched* in the 1960s and were struck by affluent American lifestyles exemplified by thick sandwiches and huge refrigerators.

Subsequent J-drama series also became immensely popular in the form of pirated VCDs in 1999–2001, without being broadcast and without marketing campaigns. The VCD boxes were standardized and the disks were openly sold at the state-run Xinhua Bookstores. As of spring 2001, Shanghai video rental stores stocked more than fifty titles of pirated J-drama series. "The J-dramas are very hot," said a shopkeeper. In Nanjing, one of the video stores on a campus that had been occupied by the Japanese Imperial Army stocked more than forty pirated J-drama series, including a title whose last episode had aired in Japan only three weeks before. Rental was no more than US$1.50 for three nights for a complete series. For Chinese students, the pirated J-drama series were digital fast food: pervasive, fast, cheap, often predictable, but filling (Nakano 2002).

These J-drama series, suggested my colleague Wu Yongmei, functioned just like the 2002 best seller *Xiaozi qingdiao* (Petit-bourgeois sentiment), which made recommendations to the emerging middle class on how they might spend their time and money in style. Unlike the Hollywood blockbusters and Hong Kong action movies that were more popular on campus, Japanese dramas were not just entertainment. They were often seen as how-to videos, which illustrated a comfortable, independent, and liberal lifestyle.

Urban Dreams

Why did Chinese students see J-dramas as urban-lifestyle how-to videos? They perceived them this way probably because although such lifestyles had come within their reach, there were not enough models within China for the younger generation to emulate. Chinese campuses went through massive changes as China began to shift from a planned economy to a market economy. Until 1994, university students were treated like pawns of the planned economy. Jobs were not for them to choose; the government assigned jobs to them. But as the market economy began to penetrate more deeply into the society, the students began to have the freedom to choose their jobs. As they gained more control over their futures, they began to dream about their careers. When we asked university students in 2002 what they would like to be in the future, we heard traditional answers, such as "public servant," "lawyer," and "teacher." But we also heard students express a desire to take on what are considered "new middle-class" positions—"engineer at a foreign company," "IT entrepreneur," and "public relations manager." One female student in Shanghai told us that she would like to get her master's degree overseas, find a job there, and return to China with an ex-pat package (which is a package with a housing allowance and other perks for those who are posted overseas). In the early 1990s the norm was not to stand out from one's peers; it would have been unthinkable for a university student to dream of being an entrepreneur, a manager, or an ex-pat assigned back to China.

When students in Shanghai and Suzhou explained the attraction of J-drama, many of them used the phrase, "It is a story based on everyday life, but on an idealized life." Meiyu, who majored in tourism at Suzhou University, told us in 2002 that she would like to be a manager at a travel agency in Suzhou and have a comfortable life, hopefully reaching the level of "middle class." "The middle class," she continued, "has money to spare, and I could think about what kind of lifestyle I want, like what to display at home." Meiyu came to the interview in a stylish gray dress and brought along her boyfriend, who was in law school. Their cellular phones kept ringing throughout the interview. They both loved J-drama and had rented a number of pirated disks including *Tokyo Love Story, Long Vacation, Hero,* and *Beautiful Life,* but Meiyu and her boyfriend paid attention to different things. While he was interested in what the Japanese characters went through, she was interested in the latest fashion trend. "I first look at fashion—what they wear—and then their living standard."

When Chinese students watched J-drama, they took note of not only what characters wore but also where they lived, what kind of jobs they had, what kind of office they worked in, what they had in their bags, which model cellular phones they carried, whom they dated, where they went after work, and where they stayed at night. On Chinese campuses, until 1985, dating was banned. Even as late as 1992, if students had premarital sex, their names would be posted on a bulletin board and they would be expelled from school (Liu 1992, p. 239). J-drama, however, often showed Tokyo singles who spent their nights together but did not spend their lives together. This indeed was a new concept for many Chinese university students in the 1990s.

Memory Wars

How did hours of exposure to J-drama images affect the viewers? They helped to project contemporary images of Japan, and as a result some Chinese viewers revised their impression of Japanese people. Here is one example from *Shanghai Dianshi* (Shanghai TV weekly) magazine, published in 1999. A female university student commented on how J-drama made her realize that her image of Japanese was outdated: "Before [I began watching J-dramas], I didn't understand Japan. I used to think Japanese girls would wear *Kimonos* and walk in small steps while singing 'Sakura Sakura,' and Japanese men were short, have little mustaches, and bow three times. But I saw J-dramas and I learned I was completely wrong!" (Jian 1999).

This indeed is an extreme example. What is interesting about her comment, however, is that her Japanese girls "walk in small steps" and her Japanese men "bow three times." These are not static images from books but dynamic ones from screens. My guess is that the girls in kimonos are from the anime *Ikkyu-san* or the Japanese drama *O-shin*. The latter is a lifelong journey of a peasant's daughter born at the turn of the century and her rise from live-in maid to supermarket owner. She was a member of the last generation of Japanese who wore kimonos all their lives. Broadcast as a public TV drama for housewives, *O-shin* was a megahit in Japan in 1983. It was first broadcast in China in 1984 and had repeat runs numerous times, attracting the older generation of Chinese.

The men with little mustaches are probably based on Tojo Hideki, who remains one of the most familiar Japanese characters, even among young people in China. If not on Tojo, they were probably based on all the Japanese military commanders who appear in the anti-Japanese war documentaries, and docudramas that are frequently broadcast during the summer months to celebrate the victory over Japan in 1945. According to a 2005 survey in *The 21st Century,* a youth English-language weekly in China, the most familiar Japanese figure in China was then–prime minister Koizumi Junichiro, followed by wartime general Tojo Hideki and admiral Yamamoto Isoroku.[3] These two military "aggressors" still provide the dominant images of Japanese in China sixty years after the Asia-Pacific War. This survey conducted by a Communist Party newspaper, starting in April 2005, also showed that, among the young Chinese people who responded, only 2.8 percent said that they liked Japan, and "more than half said they hated or disliked the country" (*China Daily* 2005).

This result seems hardly surprising in the aftermath of the anti-Japanese protests in 2005. At the center of the memory wars between China and Japan are the visits of former prime minister Koizumi to the Yasukuni Shrine, where people come to pay their respects to the souls of some 2.5 million veterans, among whom are fourteen people convicted in the International Military Tribunal for the Far East as Class A war criminals. From the time he took office in May 2001, former prime minister Koizumi visited the Yasukuni Shrine six times between August 2001 and August 2006, whereas he visited Beijing only once, for one day, in October 2001. A popular phrase in Chinese describes Sino-Japanese relations as "cold politics, hot economics."

The prime minister's Yasukuni visit is a highly divisive issue in Japan. After Koizumi's sixth and last visit as prime minister on August 15, 2006, *Asahi Shimbun* conducted a telephone poll: the result was that 49 percent of the respondents supported the visit while 37 percent opposed it. And yet when asked whether or not the next

Table 7.1

Chinese Evaluation of Prime Minister Koizumi's Visits to Yasukuni Shrine
(in percent)

1. It is Japan's domestic issue; he can visit.	5.0
2. After Japan apologizes for its aggression, he can visit.	18.9
3. After moving the souls of war criminals such as Tojo Hideki, he can visit.	17.4
4. He should not visit under any circumstances.	42.0
5. Other	1.2
6. Not sure/no response	15.5

Source: Jiang 2004.

prime minister should visit Yasukuni, the respondents reacted differently: 47 percent answered that he should not visit, whereas 31 percent answered that he should (Asahi 2006b). While the debate in Japan centers on national identity, Chinese young people often link it to Japanese militaristic ambitions. A 2004 poll conducted by the Institute of Japanese Studies at the Chinese Academy of Social Sciences after Koizumi's fourth visit to Yasukuni asked approximately 3,000 people across China how they evaluated the Japanese prime minister's visit to the Yasukuni Shrine (see Table 7.1).

The results, shown in Table 7.1, indicate that nearly 80 percent of the Chinese people polled were opposed to the visit. The respondents were also asked if they were concerned that Japan would once again pursue the road to militarism. More than half responded that the revival of Japanese militarism was a concern, while only 13.5 percent answered that they were not concerned (Jiang 2004).

In 2000, the controversial mayor of Tokyo, Ishihara Shintaro, made the following remark in reference to the growing Japanese pop culture influence in Korea: "Recently, the young generation [of Koreans] has moved beyond history and is interested in Japan's new pop culture" (March 15, 2000). I believe, however, that pop culture will not wash away different interpretations of history, but rather add other dimensions to the images and soften the sharp edges of Japan. Many of the student fans of anime and J-drama in China hardened their attitudes when we asked about their views of the Asia-Pacific War and Japan. In other words, many of these young people embrace Japanese pop culture but at the same time reject the way in which the Japanese remember and commemorate the Asia-Pacific War. In a 1999 interview, a student in Nanjing said, "I don't think about the Rape of Nanjing when I read *Slam Dunk*." He simply enjoyed reading a riveting story about a high school basketball team.

Is it a contradiction to embrace one part of Japan while rejecting another? In fact, both Chinese literary giant Lu Xun and Chairman Mao Zedong advocated that Chinese people be selective when they import foreign culture. A 1934 Lu Xun essay suggests that one should not refuse what is useful even when it comes from a person with whom one disagrees. Mao's 1940 essay criticizes "wholesale Westernization" and urges taking only what can nourish Chinese national culture. Many of the students interviewed quoted from these school texts and referred to Japanese pop culture as falling into the category of "what is useful" for China. A female student in Guangzhou explained, "We have to separate history from the present. We don't judge culture from the historical point of view. There are still a lot of things that we can learn from the Japanese. We like watching cartoons or TV dramas because they are really excellent. We don't think about the history or the Rape [of Nanjing] when we are watching TV dramas."

Since the American journalist Douglas McGray published "Japan's Gross National Cool" in *Foreign Policy* (2002), there has been continuous self-congratulatory discourse in Japan. "Cool Japan" has been a popular phrase, linking the global presence of Japanese pop culture directly to Japan's national power. This line of argument, however, looks only at the effects of globalization from Tokyo and does not consider the process of distribution and the role that local distributors as well as consumers have played in it. Viewed from the Chinese perspective, Japan, as a nation-state, does not seem to be central in the discourse of pop culture. What is cool here—Japanese pop culture or Japan as a nation?

The Japanese pop culture market is highly competitive, and anime and J-drama are often results of meticulous research and considerable investment. One conclusion could be that Chinese young people are smart and pragmatic consumers who choose highly competitive pop culture products. As social scientist Michael Billig reminded us, "National identity no longer enjoys its preeminence as the psychological identity that claims the ultimate loyalty of the individual. Instead, it must compete with other identities on a free market of identities" (1995, p. 133). It is as if the labels "consumers" and "Chinese" were in different compartments, reflecting this generation's multiple and fluid identities.

Comic Book Diplomacy

In the meantime, the Japanese Ministry of Foreign Affairs is determined to use Japan's pop culture resources to enhance the image of Japan in China (Asahi 2005). In an unprecedented speech in April 2006 on the role of pop culture in Japanese public diplomacy, Foreign Minister Aso Taro, who reads more than twenty *manga* books a week, announced that the Ministry of Foreign Affairs—not the Agency for Cultural Affairs—would introduce the International MANGA Award. In addition, he proposed building a solid partnership between the ministry and the producers of Japanese pop culture: "I think we can safely say that any kind of cultural diplomacy that fails to take advantage of pop culture is not really worthy of being called "cultural diplomacy." Then he spoke of the need for an "all-Japan" partnership between Japanese public and private sectors to "market" Japanese contemporary culture. He explained that the ministry would work on the "frameworks through which content originating in Japan can more easily be spread around the globe." This would include protection of intellectual property rights in Asia.

Copyright infringement is still rampant in China. Stall after marketplace stall sells pirated versions of the latest Hollywood and Hong Kong blockbusters, including banned titles. For example, the Chinese authorities originally gave the green light to *Memoirs of a Geisha,* which was scheduled to open in theaters in February 2006, but reversed its decision and banned it for unspecified reasons right before its release. The film's three lead actresses, Zhang Ziyi, Michelle Yeoh, and Gong Li, are ethnic Chinese, and the speculation was that it was not acceptable to some people to have Chinese superstars playing the roles of Japanese *geisha.* However, after its ban, pirated DVDs of *Memoirs of a Geisha* were widely available in Chinese cities for as little as 63 cents (5 yuan).

As for J-drama series, the boom had subsided in China by 2002, as Korean dramas replaced J-dramas in popularity. In February 2006, in Shenzhen, the city right across the border from Hong Kong, a DVD shop carried 222 sets of pirated Asian drama disks. Among them, 114 were Korean (51 percent), eighty-four were Japanese (38 percent) and twenty-four were Taiwanese (11 percent). The pirated DVD sets were available for 60 yuan—approximately US$7.50—for an entire season's episodes, while the official box sets in Japan go for ¥19,950 (US$178.55), or more than twenty times the price, and are usually only released three months after the last episodes are aired. According to an estimate by Japan's Copyright Research and Information Center, during 2000 and 2001, 3.18 billion pirated disks of Japanese games, music, anime, drama, and movies were circulating in China, leading to an economic loss of more than ¥2 trillion (US$17.6 billion) (Sugiura 2005). The estimated loss is highly debatable because many of the Chinese consumers would not have bought the disks had they been distributed at the higher price months or even years after their original release in Japan. However, the fact remains that Japanese pop culture is actively traded on the underground market.

As a result, Japan is tightening its grip. In 2005 the Content Overseas Distribution Association, whose members include Japanese content producers and copyright watchdog groups, conducted investigations in China, Hong Kong, and Taiwan that led to confiscation of 2.28 million pirated disks of Japanese pop culture and 515 arrests by the local authorities (Asahi 2006a).

While the tendency is to continue to combat the piracy, it is equally important, if not more so, to keep Japanese images flowing at an affordable price and at the fast pace that Chinese consumers have become accustomed to. Although this may create a potential economic loss, it will be a huge cultural gain to project multiple images of Japan at a time when Japanese programs, especially anime, are losing ground to Chinese TV. The Chinese government is determined to raise Chinese children with Chinese animation rather than with the popular Japanese animation. The Communist Party sees animation as a propaganda medium that can be used to tell Chinese stories that showcase Chinese heritage and teach values such as patriotism and socialism.

In reaction to the 1989 student protest in Tiananmen Square, President Jiang Zemin emphasized the need for the media and entertainment sectors to provide good "food for the minds" of children (Zhonggong Zhongyang Zhengce-yanjiushi 1999), and as a result China began to broadcast domestic TV animation in 1993. Figure 7.1 illustrates how successfully China has carried out its plan to develop its domestic TV animation

Figure 7.1 **Total Length of TV Animation Produced and Approved in China** (in hours)

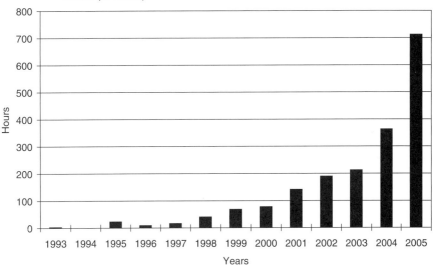

Source: Based on data from the SARFT 2006d.

production, as revealed by the total length of animation produced and approved by the State Administration of Radio, Film and Television in China (SARFT).

As the production of domestic TV animation grew, China began to tighten quotas on foreign animation. In 2000, foreign animation was cut back to less than 40 percent of overall animation programs in order to "protect the well-being of the children" and "establish spiritual civilization based on socialism" (SARFT 2000). In April 2004, the Chinese government issued a further directive to intensify efforts to produce more domestic animation. In the following two years, the overall number of hours of approved Chinese domestic animation nearly quadrupled: from 364 hours in 2004 to 713 hours in 2005, and to more than 1,350 hours in 2006. In addition, in September 2006, SARFT took the policy one step further and banned all foreign cartoons between 5 P.M. and 8 P.M (China View 2006).

Among the imported TV animation programs, Japanese programs were the hardest hit by China's staunch protectionist policy. Figure 7.2 shows the countries from which China imported TV programs (including drama, movies, and animation) during the period 2003 to 2006:

In 2005, ninety-nine programs, most of which were Hollywood movies, were imported from the United States, while only two programs, both of which were J-dramas, were imported from Japan. While there were eight Japanese anime series approved for broadcast in 2003, there were none in 2005. Japan thus fell from the sixth-largest source of foreign TV programs in 2004, behind the United States, Hong Kong, Taiwan, the United Kingdom, and Australia, to the thirteenth in 2005 and to the fifteenth in

Figure 7.2 **TV Programs Imported to China 2003–2006** (Drama, movies, and animation, including drama reruns)

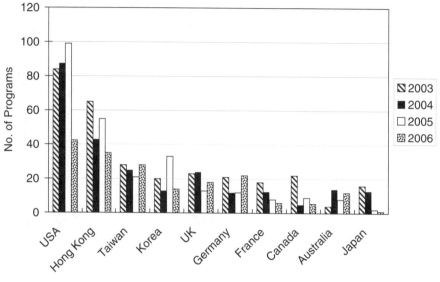

Countries/Territories

Source: Based on data from the SARFT 2003–6a, 2003–6b, 2003–6c.

2006, behind countries such as Korea, Canada, and India. In the meantime, newer Japanese anime circulating in the underground market remain the favorite of young Chinese consumers.

This is why it is important to keep the latest Japanese TV programs available in digital formats such as DVDs and VCDs, to enable file downloads for computers and cellular phones, and to move the programs gradually from piracy to authorized distribution. Foreign Minister Aso emphasized that to "sell" Japanese pop culture, it would be necessary to make "all-Japan" efforts by forming a partnership between the Japanese government and private sectors. Although this speech was addressed to the Japanese, "all-Japan" does not seem to be the solution. In fact, the distribution process is not a unilateral action by Japan for China. After all, Japanese pop culture has been spreading in China largely at the initiative of the Chinese, including those in Hong Kong and Taiwan, often in the form of pirated products, without the involvement of the Japanese. We might say that it has been a highly localized system that fits the needs of Chinese consumers.

What Japan needs is not unilateral action but an interactive process involving Chinese people: Japanese producers and Chinese distributors need to form a partnership, define mutually beneficial terms, and search for production and distribution methods that work in China without forcing Japanese ways onto the Chinese market. Japanese pop culture provides opportunities to enhance the image of Japan, but the distribution process also provides opportunities to enhance or reduce its attractiveness.

There is a deep-rooted belief in China that the Japanese look down on the Chinese. As commercial exchanges involving Japanese pop culture grow, how Japanese industry treats its Chinese workers and partners and how it responds to their aspirations are critical.

Asian Memories

Exposure to Japanese pop culture does not wash away negative memories of the past, but it has been creating positive memories across East Asia. Hong Kong is one of the few territories in East Asia that has not put a ban on Japanese pop culture, and it was the first Chinese city to broadcast Japanese television series. In 1970, *Sain wa V* (V is our sign), a drama series about a women's volleyball team celebrating the "can-do spirit," won the hearts of people in Hong Kong. Nearly thirty years later, in January 2005, a senior government official from the Home Affairs Bureau spoke at the opening ceremony for the Hong Kong–Japan Year. She recalled how she had looked forward to the program and how she had run home from school to watch *Doraemon* on TV. This brought smiles to the faces of both Chinese and Japanese audience members.

The early consumers of Japanese pop culture are turning out to be opinion leaders in Hong Kong, while the younger generation tends to see Japan as a source of pop culture and a posh shopping destination. We cannot readily compare China to Hong Kong, where people, products, and information flow freely; but Japanese pop culture has been building shared memories between Chinese and Japanese since 1980. Those who dreamed of *Doraemon* and shed tears over *Tokyo Love Story* will be China's opinion leaders in the coming decades.

Notes

1. I conducted four rounds of interviews with university students in Greater China:
    1. From November 1998 to March 1999, a total of 156 students (thirty-two in Beijing, forty-six in Nanjing, twenty-six in Guangzhou, twenty-six in Hong Kong, and twenty-six in Taiwan) in a group discussion format with three former colleagues at City University of Hong Kong: Yuling Pan, Maggie O.Y. Leung, and David C.S. Li;
    2. From February to April 2001, a total of fifty-nine students (eighteen in Beijing, twelve in Nanjing, twelve in Guangzhou, and seventeen in Hong Kong) in a group discussion format;
    3. From June to July 2002, a total of twenty-four students (twelve in Shanghai and twelve in Suzhou) in individual interviews with Wu Yongmei of Beijing University of Foreign Studies, Beijing Center for Japanese Studies; and
    4. From December 2005 to June 2006, thirty students in Hong Kong in individual interviews.
2. Shiraishi Saya calls this ability "literacy" (1997, pp. 240–45).
3. A similar poll conducted by *Asahi Shinbun* and the Chinese Academy of Social Sciences in 2002 showed the following results, with Tojo in the fourth and Yamamoto in the fifth position. This result, however, includes four pop stars and one soccer player (*Asahi Shinbun*, September 27, 2002, pp. 8–9):

If You Were Asked to Identify a Japanese Person, Who Would Come to Your Mind?

1. Koizumi Junichiro	292	Prime minister, 2001–6
2. Tanaka Kakuei	181	Prime minister, 1972–74, who restored Sino-Japanese relations in 1972
3. Yamaguchi Momoe	163	1970s pop star/actress
4. Tojo Hideki	159	World War II general
5. Yamamoto Isoroku	99	World War II admiral
6. Nakata Hidetoshi	38	Soccer player
7. Sakai Noriko	37	Pop star/actress
8. Takakura Ken	34	Actor
9. Miura Tomokazu	24	Actor; starred with and married Yamaguchi
10. Okamura Yasuji	23	World War II commander in China who signed the instrument of surrender

Note: 1,432 respondents with multiple answers.

References

Asahi. 2005. "Hannichi kanj ōkanwa ni anime ya hitto-kyoku: Gakumusho ga taichu k ōho kyoka" (Anime and J-pop music to mitigate anti-Japanese feelings: Foreign Ministry strengthens its public diplomacy efforts in China). December 21. http://www.asahi.com (accessed December 21, 2005).

———. 2006a. "Chūgoku taiwan no kaizokuban ōshu, 228-man mai ni, taiho-sha 515-nin" (Pirate disks confiscated in China and Taiwan: 2.28 million disks and 515 arrests). June 1. http://www.asahi.com (accessed June 1, 2006).

———. 2006b. "Abe-shi wo shush ō ni 53 percent: Honsha yoron ch ōsa" (Our poll shows 53 percent supported Mr. Abe as the next prime minister). August 23. http://www.asahi.com (accessed November 30, 2006).

Aso, Taro. 2006. "A New Look at Cultural Diplomacy: A Call to Japan's Cultural Practitioners." Speech at Digital Hollywood University, Tokyo, April 28. http://www.mofa.go.jp/mofaj/press/enzetsu/18/easo_0428.html (accessed May 24, 2006).

Billig, Michael. 1995. *Banal Nationalism.* London: Sage.

China Daily. 2005. "51 percent of youths want to have Japanese friends" July 6. http://www.chinadaily.com.cn/english/doc/2005-07/06/content_457476.htm (accessed December 10, 2007).

China View. 2006. "China produces 81,000 minutes of cartoons in 2006" December 30. http://news3.xinhuanet.com/english/2006-12/30/content_5551054.htm (accessed December 10, 2007).

Iwabuchi Koichi, ed. 2004. *Feeling Asian Modernities: Transnational Consumption of Japanese TV Dramas.* Hong Kong: Hong Kong University Press.

Jian, Ping. 1999. "Riben qing chun ou xiang ju: mei li de 'pan duo la mo he'" (Japanese young idol drama: Beautiful Pandora box). *Shanghai Dianshi* (Shanghai TV weekly). February C, pp. 14–17.

Jiang, Lifeng. 2004. "Zhongguo minzhong dui riben de buqingan xianzhe zengqiang" (The Chinese public's negative feelings towards Japan became even stronger). Institute of Japanese Studies, Chinese Academy of Social Science. http://www.ijs.cn/files/xuekan/2004-6/2thdiaocha.htm (accessed January 15, 2006). Originally published in *Riben Xuegan* (Journal of Japanese studies) 6.

Li, Jianping. 1999. "Donghua-pian ye ying you 'qingchun ouxiang-ju'" (Animation also needs "young idol drama"). *Zhongguo Dianshi* (Chinese television) 155 (December): 34–36.

Liu, Dalin, ed. 1992. *Zhongguo dangdaixing wenhua: Zhongguo er wan li "xing wen ming" diaocha baogao* (China's culture today: China's 20,000 examples from Sex Civilization Research Report). Shanghai: Shanghai Sanlian Shudian.

Lu, Xueyi, ed. 2002. *Dangdai Zhongguo shehui jieceng yanjiu baogao* (Research report on today's China's social stratification). Beijing: Shehui kexue wenxian chubanshe.

McGray, Douglas. 2002. "Japan's Gross National Cool." *Foreign Policy* 130 (May–June): 44–54.

Nakano, Yoshiko. 2002. "Who Initiates a Global Flow? Japanese Pop Culture in Asia." *Visual Communication* 1 (2): 229–53.

Nakano, Yoshiko, and Yongmei Wu. 2003. "Puchiburu no kurashi-kata: Ch ūgoku no daigakusei ga mita Nihon no dorama" (Aspirations for a middle-class lifestyle: Japanese pop culture on Chinese campuses). In *Gur ōbaru purizumu: Asian dorimu to shiteno Nihon no terebi dorama* (Global prism: Japanese TV drama as an Asian dream). Ed. K. Iwabuchi, 183–219. Tokyo: Heibon-sha.

Nye, Joseph S., Jr. 2004. *Soft Power: The Means to Success in World Politics.* New York: Public Affairs.

Schilling, Mark. 1997. *The Encyclopedia of Japanese Pop Culture.* New York: Weatherhill.

Shiraishi, Saya. 1997. "Japan's Soft Power: Doraemon Goes Overseas." In *Network Power: Japan and Asia.* Ed. P. Katzenstein and T. Shiraishi, 234–72. Ithaca, NY: Cornell University Press.

State Administration of Radio, Film and Television (SARFT). 2000. "Guanyu jiaqiang donghuapian yinjin he bofang guanli de tongzhi" (Announcement of tightened regulation regarding importation and broadcast of cartoons). http://www.sarft.gov.cn/ (accessed March 1, 2001).

———. 2003–6a. "Tongyi quanguo faxing de yinjin dianshiju muci" (List of imported TV drama agreed to be broadcast throughout the nation). http://www.sarft.gov.cn/ (accessed July 12, 2007).

———. 2003–6b. "Tongyi quanguo faxing de yinjin donghuapian muci" (List of imported animation agreed to be broadcast throughout the nation). http://www.sarft.gov.cn/ (accessed July 12, 2007).

———. 2003–6c. "Tongyi quanguo chongbo de yinjin dianshiju muci" (List of imported TV drama agreed to be rebroadcast throughout the nation). http://www.sarft.gov.cn/ (accessed July 12, 2007).

———. 2006d. "Guangdianzongju guanyu 1993 zhi 2005 niandu quanguo dianshi donghuapian faxing xukezheng hefa qingkuang de tonggao" (SARFT: Report on the situation of permit issued for TV animation production throughout the nation from 1993 to 2005). http://www.sarft.gov.cn/manage/publishfile/168/3467.html (accessed July 14, 2007).

Sugiura, Tsutomu. 2005. "Chizaiken wa inobeshon wo unagasu ka sogaisuru ka" (Would the intellectual property rights promote or prevent innovation?). *Invitation.* June.

Yang, Mayfair Mei-hui. [1997] 2002. "Mass Media and Transnational Subjectivity in Shanghai: Notes on (Re)cosmopolitanism in a Chinese Metropolis." In *The Anthropology of Globalization.* Ed. J. Inda and R. Rosaldo, 323–49. Malden, MA: Blackwell.

Zhonggong Zhongyang Zhengce-yanjiushi (Chinese Communist Party Central Policy Study Section), ed. 1999. *Jiang Zemin lun shehui-zhuyi jingshen-wenming jianshe* (Jiang Zemin discusses the establishment of spiritual civilization based on socialism). Beijing: Zhongyang Wenxian Chubanshe.

8

Japan's Creative Industries

Culture as a Source of Soft Power in the Industrial Sector

Sugiura Tsutomu

Soft Power and Culture

According to Joseph S. Nye, Jr. (2004, p. 1), power is the ability to get the outcomes one wants. And soft power is the ability to get what you want through attraction rather than coercion or payment. Nye (2004, p. 11) also told us that the soft power of a country rests primarily on three resources: cultural attractiveness to others, political values, and foreign policies seen as legitimate and having moral authority.

Usually soft power is thought to pertain primarily to the world political scene and to the relationships among countries. A country's hard power—such as military power or economic power—is not enough for it to get what it wants. To gain the respect of other countries or to become a leader in the world, a nation needs to have soft power; in particular, cultural attractiveness as a source of soft power.

Here, however, I would like to suggest that culture as a source of soft power is also necessary for businesses. As is the case for countries, hard power such as capital and a dedicated workforce is not enough for a company to become a leader in the world. For a company to be excellent, it needs soft power. A company's soft power rests, I believe, on such cultural attractiveness as its innovation power, design power, and brand power—in short, on creative and talented people.

An Era in Need of Soft Power

In the political arena, world leaders have shown a marked trend toward too much reliance on hard power since the attacks of September 11. The intention of the United States' Bush administration to democratize such countries as Afghanistan and Iraq was plausible, but it seems to have been lacking in sensitivity, because it has given the impression that only military hard power was used to accomplish the mission. War kills civilians in greater or lesser numbers, and the families and friends of the victims usually develop a grudge against the attackers or invaders. Such resentment may linger for generations. Based on the principle of action and reaction, if one person uses hard power against another, the latter tends to use hard power, too. And the world becomes locked in a vicious circle. By contrast, soft power, if used intelligently (sometimes with self-controlled hard power), can avoid useless confrontation and alleviate lingering rancor, though it will take some time before the effects can be seen. The current era is in great need of soft power.

In the business arena, it is widely believed that since the 1990s, Japan, as well as some of the other developed countries, have undergone revolutionary changes in their economic structure. With the increasing transfer of production offshore, Japan is developing into a postindustrial and service-oriented society. In addition, with the aging of the baby boomers, Japan is rapidly becoming an aging society. These trends suggest, first, that Japan's economy will be formed more through personal contact with other people. In such a society, the source of economic activities or businesses is not financial capital but rather talented people. Madsen Pirie (2002) has dubbed such an economy, driven by talented individuals, the "people economy." In the people economy, most of the new companies contend not so much for capital as for talented and creative workers. Their accomplishments are often evaluated by their creation of services or software instead of physical products.

Second, due to the mass production system and economic development, argued Michael H. Goldhaber (1997a/b), our priority in everyday life has shifted from a desire for material gain, which dominated the old economy, to a desire for spiritual satisfaction. In the developed countries, people have enough goods to live on, and many people now make a living by engaging in information processing instead of agriculture or textile production. Some people may describe the situation as the coming of the information economy, but, as Goldhaber reminded us, information is not scarce. Therefore, it is more appropriate to say that the "attention economy" is approaching, because it is attention that is truly scarce. We cannot concentrate our attention on many things at the same time. Therefore, attention cannot be distributed equally among people. Some people or some goods attract more attention than others. Sometimes attention is monopolized by a few people. There are innumerable ways to draw the attention of others, such as unique ideas, inventions, self-displays, performances, artistic creations, attractive attire, petitions, and so on. One of the conditions for success in a society of intense competition is, therefore, to draw the maximum attention toward ourselves, our products, and our services.

Third, as Kieran Healy (2002, p. 91) pointed out in his excellent paper, nonconventional skills are required of workers in a globalizing world of advanced information technology. In a highly competitive global marketplace, a premium is placed on creativity and the capacity for innovation. According to Healy, the idea of the creative sector or creative industries has emerged over the past thirty-five years, with a big push in the past fifteen. By the 1990s, cultural policy advocates in the United States began to push for a new definition of the cultural sector that embraced commercial cultural goods and emphasized the role of arts and culture in promoting innovation and economic growth. And in the early 2000s, some official reports and studies promoted this new view of the creative sector and creative industries in many countries worldwide.

The Blair administration in the United Kingdom, for example, introduced a new national project called "Cool Britannia" in 1997 with the objective of promoting creative industries, making the nation attractive, heightening the motivation of the British people, and revitalizing the country's economy. The creative industries in that project are defined as those industries that have their origins in individual creativity, skill, and talent. They include advertising, architecture, the art and antiques market, crafts, design, designer fashion, film and video, interactive leisure software, music, the performing arts, publishing, software and computer games, television, and radio.

According to the Department of Culture, Media and Sport of the United Kingdom (2004), the result of the project after five years (1997–2002) was that British creative industries had an annual growth rate of 6 percent, while the UK gross domestic product (GDP) grew only 3 percent annually. In 2002 creative industries made up nearly one-eighth of the United Kingdom's total GDP. The annual growth rate of the number of employees from 1997 to 2003 was 3 percent for creative industries compared to only 0.9 percent for the United Kingdom as a whole.

The same phenomenon can be observed in Japan. According to Yoshimoto Mitsuhiro (2003), in the 1990s, when the Japanese economy had long been in depression, the number of employees in all creative industries increased by 16 percent from 1.2 million in 1996 to 1.4 million in 2001, while that of all industries decreased by 4.3 percent from 60.9 million to 58.3 million. In terms of revenues, creative industries as a whole earned 28 trillion (US$280 billion) in 1999, a robust gain of 86 percent from ¥15 trillion (US$150 billion) in 1989, whereas all service industries earned ¥202 trillion (US$2,020 billion) in 1999, a gain of 69 percent from ¥119 trillion (US$1,190) in 1989. These figures show that creative industries are gaining a stronger position in the Japanese economy (see Table 8.1).

Not only in the United Kingdom and Japan, but also in China, creative industries have already begun to take the lead in the Chinese service industry. As can be seen from Figure 8.1, the most rapidly growing industry group is post and telecommunications; the second group is education, culture and arts, and radio, film, and television, on a par with social services; and the third group is scientific research and polytechnic services.

What do people, attention, and creativity have in common? The answer is culture. Culture is one of the most important and influential elements of soft power in the new economies. Culture can be linked to something broadly spiritual, value added, and knowledge based, which enriches the quality of everyday human life.[1] Culture is cultivated by people. People are fascinated by culture. And culture is closely connected with creativity. Creative industries need cultural resources such as creative and talented people. Creative people like to live or work in a "creative and cultural atmosphere" that drives them to new challenges. Therefore, it is desirable for countries, cities, and businesses to provide them with a creative environment filled with cultural stimulation. In that sense, creative industries draw on cultural resources that are different from those in the traditional industries, though the latter also need to rely more and more on creative industries to compete effectively in a global environment. I would like to

Table 8.1

Growth in Creative Industries in Japan

	Number of Employees			Revenue (¥ million)		
	1996	2001	% Change	1989	1999	% Change
All industries	60,931,256	58,280,751	-4.3	n.a.	n.a.	
1. Advertising	149,996	154,381	2.9	7,174,991	10,189,829	42.0
2. Antiques and curiosities retailing	26,041	45,166	73.4	n.a.	n.a.	
3. Lacquered ware manufacturing	14,814	10,762	-27.4	n.a.	n.a.	
4. Design	47,068	46,861	-0.4	450,116	665,150	47.8
5. Movies and video	65,153	75,288	15.6	1,059,630	1,806,595	70.5
6. Music and film recording, sales and lease	134,842	119,002	-11.7	269,166	445,131	65.4
7. Music and performing arts	76,948	77,542	0.8	606,856	1,099,409	81.2
8. Publication	177,569	169,395	-4.6	n.a.	n.a.	
9. Computer software	397,886	584,253	46.8	3,217,981	10,334,381	221.1
10. TV and radio	69,782	67,438	-3.4	2,100,981	3,436,257	63.6
11. Organization of arts and sciences	11,704	10,810	-7.6	263,487	236,986	-10.1
Total creative industries	1,171,803	1,360,898	16.1	15,143,208	28,213,738	86.3
Total service industries				119,311,683	201,715,241	69.1

Source: Yoshimoto 2003.

Notes: I exclude the construction and engineering industry from the creative industries originally included in Yoshimoto's list. It is debatable whether the whole of construction should be included in creative industries, though I think architectural design and engineering are to be included.

Revenue figures are not adjusted for inflation.

100 yen = $1

Figure 8.1 **Value Added of the Tertiary Industry in China**

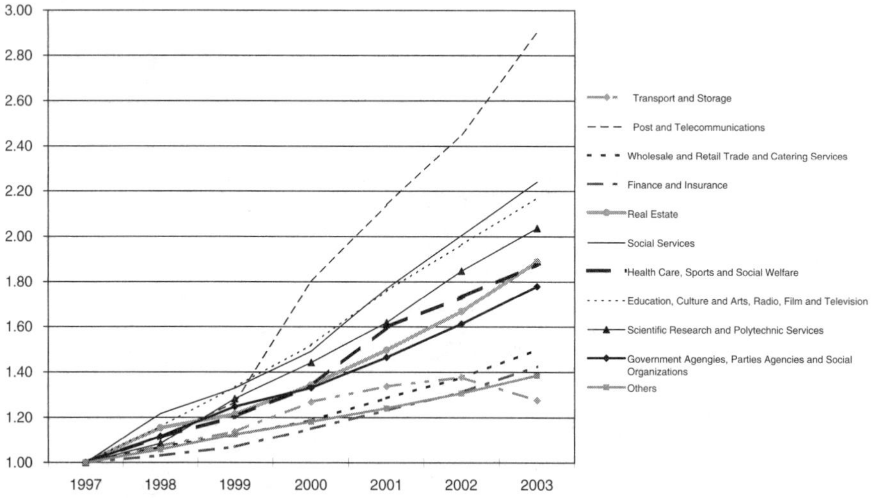
3.00
2.80
2.60
2.40
2.20
2.00
1.80
1.60
1.40
1.20
1.00
1997
1998
1999
2000
2001
2002
2003
Transport and Storage
Post and Telecommunications
Wholesale and Retail Trade and Catering Services
Finance and Insurance
Real Estate
Social Services
Health Care, Sports and Social Welfare
Education, Culture and Arts, Radio, Film and Television
Scientific Research and Polytechnic Services
Government Agengies, Parties Agencies and Social Organizations
Others

Source: National Bureau of Statistics of China, *China Statistical Yearbook 2005.*

stress again that cultural attraction is very important for countries, cities, industries, and individuals. I call such cultural attractiveness "cultural power."

World Popularity of Japanese Pop Culture

In recent years, Koda Kumi, Hamasaki Ayumi, Amuro Namie, Utada Hikaru, PUFFY, SMAP, Kinki Kids, and other Japanese singers and entertainers have acquired a wide fan base overseas, especially in other Asian countries. Millions of teenagers in Hong Kong, Seoul, and Bangkok avidly follow the latest Japanese trends, a phenomenon also responsible for the illegal circulation of bootleg copies of Japanese products in Asia. It is pop culture that has recently emerged as a source of Japan's soft power.

Two young Frenchmen, friends of my son, visited Japan in the first year of the twenty-first century. Though they had traveled all the way from France, they returned home without seeing Kyoto or Kamakura. They did, however, visit Tokyo's Akihabara, Shibuya, Shinjuku, and Ikebukuro, carrying back with them around fifty books of *manga.* To my surprise, I learned from my son that their reason for coming to Japan was specifically to buy Japanese comic books.

Their case is just one example, but some statistical data explain the background of their passionate behavior. According to *Le Monde* (December 12, 2004), there are 1,300 comic book artists (*manga-ka*) in France, and 50,000 new book titles were published there in 2004, of which 3,070 were *manga* (of these, 754 were Asian and 163 were American). The *Financial Times* (February 4, 2004) also reported that the sales of Japanese comic books increased at an annual rate of 20 percent in 2003, whereas

Table 8.2

**Per Capita Spending on Japanese Pop Culture in the
United States and France** (US$)

	Year	United States	France
Animation films	2003	0.01	0.19
Manga	2004	0.52	1.07
DVDs	2004	0.62	1.87

Source: Based on data estimated by JETRO 2005.

the total book market was static. Another document reveals that French people spend more money (though still a modest amount overall) than Americans on Japanese pop culture content, as shown in Table 8.2.

Japan has long been known by a narrow group of intellectuals and Japanophiles in other countries for its traditional culture, such as pottery, lacquerware, tea ceremony, flower arrangement, bonsai, haiku and tanka poetry, calligraphy, martial arts, and kimonos. In recent years, however, as the above example shows, Japanese contemporary pop culture has made notable strides in world popularity. Japanese animation (anime) and video games in particular are forms of entertainment shared by young people not only in France but also around the world.

The smash hit *Pokémon* (Pocket monsters) series became a sensation as soon as it was aired nationwide on U.S. television in 1998, with revenue from the U.S. release of the *Pokémon* movie the following year topping $85 million. The series has been broadcast on TV in nearly seventy countries around the world. Children in the four- to twelve-year-old age range account for 40 percent of the audience. Four thousand related products amounting to ¥700 billion (US$7 billion) have been sold worldwide. More than 13 billion Pokémon trading cards have been sold globally, and when the market for all character-related goods is considered, Pokémon is an economic force said to be worth some ¥2 trillion (US$20 billion) worldwide (¥1 trillion (US$10 billion) in Japan. A similar phenomenon has occurred for other TV anime series, such as *Dragon Ball Z, Bishojo senshi sailor moon* (Pretty soldier sailor moon), and *Hello Kitty.* Miyazaki Hayao's *Sen to chihiro no kami-kakushi* (Spirited away) was the first animated film to win the Grand Prize at the Berlin International Film Festival, going on to win an Academy Award in 2003 for Best Animated Feature Film.

Japan's best-selling *manga* weekly, *Shonen Jump,* which sells not less than 3 million copies per issue domestically, was first published in the United States in November 2002, and more than 500,000 copies per issue per month have already been printed there. The Japanimation (Japanese animation) market, which increased from ¥4.6 billion (US$46 million) in 1975 to ¥200 billion (US$2.0 billion) in 2002, is said to represent more than 60 percent of the world market of animation now (Marcadal 2006).

In addition to the popularity of the Japanese sensibility inherent in these forms of entertainment, Japanese comics (*manga*), animation, and video games are highly acclaimed for their extremely well-developed narratives and realistic depiction of speed in motion, attracting the attention of foreign artists, designers, and other cultural communicators. Japanese anime have also been used in music videos by Western rock groups. The French group Daft Punk uses anime by Matsumoto Leiji, creator of *Uchu senkan Yamato* (Space battleship Yamato), and the British group the Orb uses *Doraemon* as a character in its single "From a Distance." Even such Hollywood films as *Kill Bill*, directed by Quentin Tarantino, pay homage to, and take their inspiration from, Japanese comics.

The craze over Japanese *manga* and anime among young people is also evident from the Web sites created for anime fans around the world. These sites are filled with photographs of young people dressed in the outfits of characters that appear in anime, a type of role-playing, if you will. *Power Rangers* and *Sailor Moon* character costumes are apparently popular as Halloween costumes among an increasing number of children in the United States. One English Web site devoted to the popular video game Final Fantasy has received more than 59 million hits as of June 27, 2007, an indication of how many fans this game has attracted.[2] In fact, according to *BusinessWeek* (Rowley 2005), more than 35 million copies of the Final Fantasy series have been sold, and its online version has more than 300,000 subscribers worldwide.

Table 8.3 shows the number of Web sites for various groups such as Japanese anime and game sites, Japanese traditional culture sites, Disney sites, and miscellaneous others,[3] excluding the corresponding Web sites written in Japanese. It shows that animation and game software have as many Web sites as traditional culture in Japan. Google searches reveal even more Web sites featuring Japanese anime than for *Peter Pan, Beauty and the Beast, The Jungle Book, Cinderella, Mickey Mouse,* and other Disney animation, though it is fair to say that the latter's copyrights are under stricter surveillance.

I call the phenomenon described above "third-generation Japanism," a phenomenon resembling the first generation of Japanism, which emerged at the end of the nineteenth century, and the second, which emerged during the 1950s and 1960s. The latest generation, however, differs from the first two in one key component: The current wave has brought Japanese culture to the general public in other countries, where it has found a more widespread appeal, particularly among young people. And it is through the personalities and lifestyles of the characters featured in these media that young people around the world are exposed to, and may come to know, the soul and culture of Japanese people, though as Allison points out in Chapter 6, the meanings attributed to Japanese pop culture (J-pop) can vary considerably. There is no question, however, that J-pop has created a large number of new Japanophiles in the world.

There are four elements behind the sudden surge in the popularity of modern Japanese culture in the 1990s. First, a stagnating domestic economy led to the saturation of the market in Japan, and culture-related industries began to make serious efforts to move into overseas markets. Second, higher-quality products and software gained a stronger foothold amid the international competition. Prior to the success of Suzuki Ichiro and Matsui Hideki in the arena of professional baseball, the *manga* and anime

Table 8.3

Number of Google English-Language Web Sites for Different Cultural Industries, as of June 27, 2007

Selected Japanese Manga, Anime, Game Titles, and Others	Number of Web Sites	Japanese Culture in General	Number of Web Sites	Disney Animated Features	Number of Web Sites	Selected Non-Japanese Anime, Movies, Novel Titles, and U.S. Popular Food Brands	Number of Web Sites
1 Game Boy, computer game	19,338,000	Manga	132,170,000	Make Mine Music, animation	5,808,400	Superman, movie	29,558,000
2 Final Fantasy, computer game	16,377,000	Karaoke	86,930,000	Peter Pan, animation	3,339,500	Harry Potter, movie	26,089,000
3 Naruto, manga	10,212,000	Ninja	65,020,000	Oliver and Company, animation	2,835,000	Lord of the Rings, movie	24,486,000
4 Dragonball Z, anime	10,010,000	Sushi	45,930,000	Beauty and the Beast, animation	2,482,700	Disney animation	22,492,000
5 Gundam, anime	8,782,000	Samurai	42,820,000	The Jungle Book, animation	2,423,600	King Kong, movie	18,050,000
6 Sailor Moon, anime	7,345,000	Karate	32,607,000	Cinderella, animation	1,781,300	Da Vinci Code, novel	16,198,000
7 Evangelion, anime	6,097,000	Anime, Japan	25,480,000	Mickey Mouse, animation	1,745,200	Fantastic Four, movie	15,696,000
8 Inu-Yasha, manga	5,650,000	Judo	23,541,000	The Little Mermaid, animation	1,575,900	Da Vinci Code, movie	15,321,700
9 Yu-Gi-Oh, manga	4,545,900	Bonsai	17,245,000	Sleeping Beauty, animation	1,559,800	X-men, movie	15,270,000

(continued)

Table 8.3 *(continued)*

10 Bleach, manga	4,529,000	Sumo	16,993,000	Aladdin, animation	1,518,100	Harry Potter, novel	10,371,300
11 One Piece, manga	4,230,000	Haiku	14,859,000	Melody Time, animation	1,446,600	Coca-Cola, drink	8,672,800
12 Dragon Quest, computer game	4,200,000	Geisha	13,612,000	Bambi, animation	1,389,040	Superman, animation	7,198,400
13 Ghost in the Shell, anime	3,869,000	Japanese sushi	13,471,000	Hercules, animation	1,329,084	Hulk, animation	7,136,500
14 Akira, manga	3,431,000	Ramen	12,951,000	Tarzan, animation	1,286,700	X-men, anime	5,485,900
15 Fullmetal Alchemist, manga	2,794,300	Tofu	12,038,000	Robin Hood, animation	1,239,083	Coca-Cola, drink	4,933,900
16 Hello Kitty, anime	2,789,000	Aikido	9,352,000	Fun and Fancy Free, animation	1,207,000	KFC	3,761,000
17 Pokémon, anime	2,105,800	Futon	8,621,000	The Sword in the Stone, animation	1,193,300	Zorro, movie	3,748,900
18 Astro Boy, anime	1,779,000	Kimono	8,410,000	Fantasia, animation	1,115,400	Fantastic Four, animation	3,223,200
19 Rurouni Kenshin, manga	1,606,500	Soba	7,978,000	Alice in Wonderland, animation	932,900	Walt Disney, anime	2,404,100
20 Oh My Goddess, manga	1,591,200	Tea ceremony	7,716,000	The Great Mouse Detective, animation	808,420	McDonald's hamburger	1,919,667

Notes: Web sites listed here have been selected as they occur to the author, and the list order does not show ranking. Various top ten rankings can be seen on the Web site http://www.animenewsnetwork.com/encyclopedia/ratings. The numbers of Web sites are subject to change every access moment and therefore are for reference only.

industry focused on exporting products that had already proven extremely competitive in the domestic market. Third, as fashion in general has become increasingly homogenized due to young people around the world interacting on the Internet and through other channels, the groundwork has been laid for a more open acceptance of other cultures. Fourth, though there is no political unification in East Asia comparable to the European Union, an informal "Asian Union," as Edward Gresser (2004) termed it, has been formed in certain economic and educational arenas such as trade, investment, and cultural exchanges; for example, aggregated export amounts in the East Asian region increased by 3.5 times from US$333 billion in 1991 to US$1,164 billion in 2004. As a result, regional trade now makes up almost 55 percent of the region's total exports, compared with 66 percent in the European Union and 45 percent for NAFTA countries. And mutual cultural exchanges as well as student exchanges have been quite active in the East Asian region in recent years, as shown in Tables 8.4 and 8.5. Therefore, the popularity of Japanese pop culture is not a singular phenomenon in Asia. South Korean and Chinese films, dramas, and music are becoming more and more popular in Japan, as can be observed at video rental shops.

Preliminary Evaluation of Japan's Cultural Power

For signs that indicate that a third wave of Japanism has appeared as a worldwide phenomenon, one need look no further than the American writer Douglas McGray (2002), who has noted that Japan, from the viewpoint of culture, became the world's new superpower during the 1990s. He coined the term "gross national cool" (or GNC), a takeoff on the term gross national product (or GNP), as a way to explain Japan's cultural power. "Cool," which corresponds to the Japanese word *kakkoii,* basically means hip, or, for lack of a better word, attractive; and GNC can be thought of as the degree of a country's appeal, or to put it another way, the extent of its cultural power.

As "culture" is born of the spiritual (see note 1), it is, by its very nature, almost impossible to measure the cultural power inherent in GNC in the same fashion as GNP is measured. For a thorough comparison, statistics would have to be garnered completely from scratch and would be a most time-consuming undertaking. So I will make a simple evaluation of Japanese cultural power.

First, for the sake of comparison, I estimate the scale of Japan's cultural power as a whole by assuming that GNC is made up of mostly culture-related activities.

Domestic Culture Market

Domestically, one industry that is plainly an integral part of the culture market is the leisure industry, because it gives people pleasure and spiritual satisfaction. The Japan Productivity Center for Socio-Economic Development has estimated that the scale of Japan's leisure industry was some ¥81.3 trillion (US$813 billion) in nominal terms in 2004. The individual sectors yielded the following totals: the recreation category was a ¥54.8 trillion (US$548 billion) market, the hobbies and creativity category was worth ¥11.6 trillion (US$116 bil-

Table 8.4

Change in Exports of Culture-Related Goods in Asia, 1994–2004 (US$1 million)

	1994	2004	Multiple Increased By (2004/1994)
India → China	0.05	2.5	50.0
India → Japan	0.9	15.0	16.7
China → India	1.1	12.2	11.1
China → ASEAN-4	2.0	20.5	10.3
ASEAN-4 → China	0.5	4.6	9.2
NIEs → India	28.6	247.8	8.7
Japan → India	1.5	11.4	7.6
India → NIEs	22.6	161.5	7.1
China → NIEs	95.2	513.3	5.4
NIEs → Japan	273.6	1,350.3	4.9
India → ASEAN-4	2.6	12.5	4.8
NIEs → China	100.1	422.3	4.2
Intra–ASEAN-4	4.4	16.6	3.8
Japan → China	40.0	144.5	3.6
China → Japan	25.9	83.3	3.2
ASEAN-4 → India	1.6	3.6	2.3
Japan → NIEs	271.1	586.6	2.2
ASEAN4 → Japan	10.3	20.9	2.0
Intra-NIEs	332.7	521.8	1.6
NIEs → ASEAN-4	163.0	254.9	1.6
Japan → ASEAN-4	61.3	73.2	1.2
ASEAN-4 → NIEs	96.6	101.1	1.0
Total	1,535.7	4,580.4	3.0

Source: Japan's Ministry of Economy, Trade and Industry, *2006 White Paper on International Economy and Trade,* pp. 71–74. http://www.meti.go.jp/english/report/g_main.html.

Notes: Culture-related goods: Goods of HS codes HS3705/3706, HS49, HS97, HS8524 (films, books, art works, music, and related goods).

ASEAN-4, Association of Southeast Asian Nations-4 (Indonesia, Malaysia, the Philippines, and Thailand); NIEs, newly industrializing economies.

lion), the tourism and outings category totaled ¥10.5 trillion (US$105 billion), and sports accounted for ¥4.4 trillion (US$44 billion), as shown in Table 8.6.

Some might criticize the automatic inclusion of pachinko and gambling in the culture market. But since Roland Barthes ([1970] 1993, pp. 40–43) paid special attention to pachinko, *"un jeu collectif et solitaire* (a collective and solitary play)," which is played with "a hand of an artist," I don't think it strange to include it in the culture market. Sometimes, state-of-the-art technologies and leading pop culture trends are in evidence in the pachinko and game industry.

Table 8.5

Change in Numbers of East Asian Foreign Students, 2000–2002

From	To	2000	2002	Multiple Increased By (2002/2000)
China	ASEAN-4	921	6,455	7.01
ASEAN-4	ASEAN-4	1,358	5,200	3.83
ASEAN-4	China	2,614	5,763	2.20
South Korea	China	16,787	36,093	2.15
China	South Korea	1,182	2,407	2.04
Japan	ASEAN-4	254	444	1.75
China	Japan	28,076	41,180	1.47
ASEAN-4	South Korea	96	136	1.42
South Korea	ASEAN-4	794	1,098	1.38
Japan	South Korea	613	721	1.18
Japan	China	13,806	16,084	1.17
South Korea	Japan	18,237	18,899	1.04
ASEAN-4	Japan	4,548	4,603	1.01
Total area concerned		196,235	257,323	1.31

Source: Conditions of Acceptance of International Students (Japan Student Services Organization) is used for acceptance into Japan. The Ministry of Education of the People's Republic of China is used for acceptance into China, and other countries are based on the Education at a Glance, and Education Database (OECD). Japan's Ministry of Economy, Trade and Industry, *2005 White Paper on International Economy and Trade*, p. 303. (http://www.meti.go.jp/english/report/index.html).

Note: ASEAN-4, Association of Southeast Asian Nations-4 (Indonesia, Malaysia, the Philippines, and Thailand).

Other industries that might be considered to be in the domain of culture are education and research, a ¥36.2 trillion (US$362 billion) market,[4] and the information and communications industry, including broadcasting but excluding information and communication-related manufacturing and construction industries, at ¥93.3 trillion (US$933 billion) (in 2003).[5] Together, these industries (including the leisure market) make up the culture market or overall culture industry and are estimated to reach ¥210 trillion (US$2,100 billion) in scale in 2004, equivalent to approximately 21 percent of Japan's total output (not value added).[6]

Unfortunately, due to Japan's long-lasting economic stagnation, Japan's domestic culture-related industry has, as a whole, failed to achieve growth in recent years. During the ten years from 1994 to 2004, Japan's leisure industry, the mainstay of Japan's culture-related industries, saw its market shrink by 9 percent in inflation-adjusted real terms.

Looking at the overall domestic culture market in a broad sense, we cannot recognize the expansion of Japan's cultural power. Figure 8.2 shows that Japan's media soft market, that is, the culture market in a narrower sense, is in a similar condition.

Table 8.6

Japan's Leisure Market, 1994–2004 (¥ trillion)

	1994	2000	2001	2002	2003	2004	2004/ 1994 (%)
Sports	5.8	5.0	4.8	4.6	4.5	4.4	−24.0
Hobbies and creativity	11.3	11.8	11.7	11.7	11.5	11.6	3.3
Hobby and creative goods	1.2	1.7	1.7	1.7	1.7	1.6	34.7
Art appreciation goods	3.9	3.7	3.7	3.7	3.6	3.8	−1.4
Journals and books	4.7	4.7	4.6	4.6	4.5	4.5	−3.4
Learning and practicing service	1.0	1.1	1.1	1.1	1.1	1.1	9.4
Art appreciation	0.5	0.6	0.6	0.6	0.6	0.6	13.8
Recreation	61.0	57.2	55.2	56.1	55.3	54.8	−10.3
Pachinko and other games	32.0	30.0	29.1	30.4	30.8	30.6	−4.2
Gambling	9.2	7.8	7.5	7.2	6.8	6.5	−29.8
Eating and drinking	19.3	18.9	18.1	18.1	17.3	17.3	−10.3
Karaoke box	0.6	0.5	0.5	0.5	0.4	0.4	−31.6
Tourism and outings	11.7	11.1	11.0	10.8	10.4	10.5	−10.2
Car-related expenditures	3.1	3.2	3.1	3.1	3.0	2.9	−6.5
Domestic tourism	7.9	7.1	7.0	6.9	6.7	6.8	−14.9
Overseas travel	0.6	0.8	0.8	0.8	0.7	0.8	30.4
Total leisure market	89.8	85.1	82.7	83.2	81.8	81.3	−9.4
Consumer price indices (2000 = 100)	98.6	100.0	99.3	98.4	98.1	98.1	−0.5
Inflation-adjusted leisure market	91.1	85.1	83.3	84.6	83.3	82.9	−9.0

Sources: Japan Productivity Center for Socio-Economic Development (JPCSED), *2005 White Paper on Leisure*; Bank of Japan, *Financial and Economic Statistics Monthly*, June 2005 is used for consumer price indices.

Note: The figures in the table are based on sales amount for each category, compiled and estimated by JPCSED.

Cultural Influence Abroad

Japan's cultural influence abroad, however, seems to have become stronger in recent years. I have attempted to take a look at the growth in Japan's cultural influence abroad by using merchandise and service trade statistics from the industries that make up the GNC formula. These exports cover such technology and service-related trade as patent royalties and income from culture and entertainment (performances, events), as well as such products as recorded tapes and records, books, magazines, newspapers, painting and picture books and other publications, exposed and developed plate and film (photos, illustrations, etc.), exposed and developed film for movies, art and handicrafts, collector's items, and curios.

Included in patent royalties are industrial processes, franchises, copyright payment, and the like. The increase of patent royalties reflects the increase in industrial processes' royalties received from overseas production and sales of Japanese cars and electronics. I have included patent royalties in the amount of

Figure 8.2   **Market Trends in Japan's Media Soft Industries**

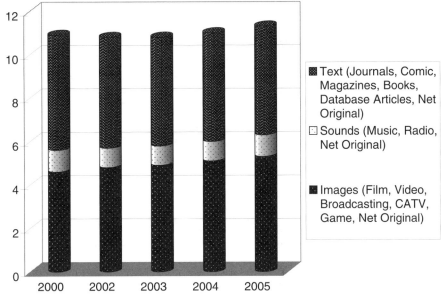

■ Text (Journals, Comic, Magazines, Books, Database Articles, Net Original)

☐ Sounds (Music, Radio, Net Original)

■ Images (Film, Video, Broadcasting, CATV, Game, Net Original)

Source: Institute for Information and Communications Policy, June 2007.

cultural exports because the growth of patent royalties means the diffusion and popularization of Japanese brands, and it sometimes reflects exports of innovative or creative technologies.

Export amounts and income from these culture-related products and services more than tripled from a combined total of ¥837 billion (US$8.37 billion) in 1996 to a combined total of nearly ¥2,539 billion (US$25.4 billion) by 2006. During the same timeframe, Japan's total merchandise exports grew by around 68 percent, from ¥44.7 trillion (US$447 billion) to ¥75.2 trillion (US$752 billion). So, by simple comparison, Japan's culture-related export growth was much greater than its total merchandise trade (scc Figure 8.3).

For these culture-related exports, patent fees rose by 3.2 times to reach ¥2,330 billion (US$23.3 billion), and plate and film already used for photos and the like increased by 7.4 times to ¥55.8 billion (US$558 million). Likewise, total exports for art and handicrafts, collectors' items, and curios rose three times between 1996 and 2006. The categories of recorded tapes and records, recorded movies, and books, magazines, newspapers, and other publications fared less well than total merchandise exports, with combined exports growing by only 58 percent.

In fact, it might even be inferred from this data that "hard," merchandise-related cultural exports of film, publications, and tapes are moving over in favor of "soft," service-related exports of knowledge rights.

Figure 8.3   **Japan's Cultural Exports and Imports (GNC Trade), 1993–2006**

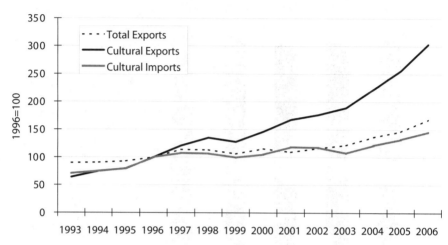

Sources: Japan Tariff Association, *Japan Exports & Imports*, 2005 and Bank of Japan, *Balance of Payments.*

The Economic Influence of Cultural Power

What influence, then, can culture have on economic activities? Those who are interested in another country's culture will also be interested in the country itself: its language, its products, and its people. They will want to learn its language, visit the country to acquire better knowledge, and buy its products.

A field study conducted by Yagi (2003–5) supports the hypothesis that international cultural exchange might stimulate interest in foreign culture, preference for foreign design, and willingness to pay (WTP) for products with foreign design. To measure the amount of increase in WTP for products with foreign design through a cultural exchange program, Yagi compared the WTP of respondents who attended a Japanese music concert and the WTP of randomly selected respondents in the region where the concert was held. In addition to the measurement of the WTP through a Japanese music concert, Yagi measured the WTP of attendees at a workshop on Japanese music. The same questionnaire was distributed to all three groups. The questionnaire asked the ordering of preference of the combinations of three prices and three designs. Yagi used Japanese design, European design, and standard American design for lamps, and applied "conjoint analysis"[7] in calculating the WTP.

Yagi's analysis shows that expansion of Japanese cultural influence increases the marginal utility of the lamp with Japanese design and would increase demand for it. The result that the marginal utility of the Japanese-design lamp is larger for the respondents who attended the concert or workshop than for residents of the area where the concert or workshop took place implies that deeper understanding of Japanese culture increases the demand for products that embody the essence of its culture. This gives some foundation for promoting workshop programs on Japanese culture, to strengthen the competitive power of Japanese products in the global marketplace.

Although Yagi's findings must be interpreted cautiously because concert attendance and preference for Japanese items may be the result of the same impulse, his study has important implications for other countries when they devise strategies to improve their competitive power in the global marketplace, especially by creating new markets. The demand for a country's products increases as the understanding of its culture deepens.

Yagi's analysis also suggests that not only major cultural events, such as the Olympic Games, international expositions, and the World Cup, but also bilateral cultural exchange programs and the spread of popular films, dramas, and music could greatly affect the flow of trade and tourists between the countries concerned. A separate study by the Research Institute of Economy, Trade and Industry in 2005 did, in fact, find a significant positive correlation between cultural exchange and economic exchange in East Asia (Ministry of Economy, Trade and Industry of Japan 2005, pp. 208–9). That is to say, active cultural exchange in a region accelerates mutual trade and direct investment in the region, and vice versa.

A typical example of this phenomenon can be observed in the powerful influence of South Korean culture in attracting Japanese tourists. Chuncheon City, where the South Korean TV drama *Winter Sonata* was filmed, attracted 370,000 foreigners, of which 60 percent were Japanese, in 2004, 2.6 times more than in the previous year. The ripple effects of *The Da Vinci Code,* written by Dan Brown, which is a worldwide bestseller with more than 60.5 million copies in print, extend to 53 million related Web sites, and translations in forty-four languages.[8] It is luring many more people than ever to the Louvre in Paris and to other places highlighted in the novel.

Cultural Power and Profits in Industrial Sectors

The English word "strategy" corresponds to the Japanese "*sen-ryaku,*" which is written with two Chinese characters as (戦略). As Tasaka Hiroshi (2006) reminded us, *sen* (戦) means a war or a fight, and *ryaku* (略) means elimination or omission. From this original meaning of the compound word, *sen-ryaku* (戦略) is the strategy to get the outcomes we want without doing unnecessary battles with competitors. Thus, *sen-ryaku* power can be regarded as soft power in a certain sense.

Because businesses need strategies, they need soft power, particularly cultural power, to attract prospective buyers without being drawn into a price war. Kevin Roberts (2005), CEO worldwide of Saatchi and Saatchi, has invented the word "Lovemarks" to express sustainable and loyal attachment to a product or a brand.[9] Lovemarks could be considered a sublimate of cultural power.

Now, then, how can "cultural power" or "degree of cultural inclination" be measured from the standpoint of a business or industry? Recognizing the difficulties in quantifying this concept, we can nevertheless attempt to do so in the following way. By selecting three balance sheet items from the Bank of Japan's official industry

Figure 8.4 **Cultural Proclivity and Profit Rates by Industry in Japan, Average for FY 1991–1995**

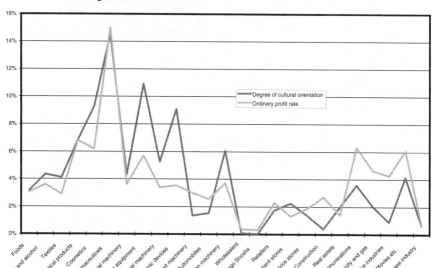

statistics—research and development expenditures, advertising expenditures, and net additions to intangible assets—and totaling them against sales revenue, we can arrive at an industry's degree of cultural proclivity.

Under this formula, pharmaceuticals with high expenditures in research and development rank as the manufacturing sector with the highest degree of cultural proclivity, at 14.5 percent. They are followed by three industries whose cultural proclivity index hovers around 10 percent: resin products, cleansers, and the cosmetics industry, with high outlays on advertising, office and home equipment, and communications and electronic devices. Precision machinery stands at 6 percent, with beer and alcohol and textiles at around 4 percent each. In nonmanufacturing industries, the most culturally oriented sectors are movies and entertainment and telecommunications, at around 4 percent each, followed by department stores, real estate, and electricity and gas, each of which scores 2 percent or higher.

Interestingly, most of the industrial sectors with high cultural orientation scores also posted high levels of profit. Pharmaceuticals, the sector with the highest cultural orientation score, posted a 15 percent profit rate,[10] followed by chemical products, telecommunications, and movies and entertainment, all with profit rates of 5 percent or higher. Finally, electricity and gas, precision machinery, and beer and alcohol had profit rates of 3 percent or higher.

From this analysis we could proffer a tentative theory that industries that have high levels of cultural proclivity will also tend to have higher profit returns. Figure 8.4 and Table 8.7 show the results of these calculations. The figures provided cover the period from fiscal year 1991 through fiscal year 1995. Unfortunately the Bank of

Table 8.7

Cultural Proclivity and Profit Rates by Industry in Japan, Average for FY 1991–1995
(¥ million and %)

	Sales Amount	Net Additions to Intangible Assets	Advertising and Marketing Expenditures	Experimental Research Expenditures	Total Culture-Related Expenditures	Degree of Cultural Orientation (%)	Ordinary Profit Rate (%)
Industry total	331,716,331	128,798	1,854,242	3,560,438	5,543,478	1.7	2.4
Manufacturing industries	136,466,398	7,332	1,179,796	3,151,028	4,338,156	3.2	3.6
Foods	9,322,913	626	241,366	52,588	294,580	3.2	3.0
Beer and alcohol	3,666,764	817	126,228	32,076	159,121	4.3	3.6
Textiles	4,446,960	1,078	41,427	140,030	182,535	4.1	2.9
Chemical products	12,756,000	-1,372	214,040	658,717	871,385	6.8	6.8
Cosmetics	1,564,398	-2,704	99,367	48,076	144,740	9.3	6.2
Pharmaceuticals	2,444,221	1,166	61,924	291,907	354,997	14.5	15.0
General machinery	7,530,935	57	36,900	288,813	325,770	4.3	3.6
Office equipment	2,030,560	-144	19,513	202,376	221,745	10.9	5.7
Electrical machinery	33,513,689	3,248	285,189	1,469,839	1,758,276	5.2	3.4
Electronic devices	7,785,415	534	61,789	645,116	707,439	9.1	3.5
Transport machinery	34,067,597	-1,094	265,439	197,529	461,874	1.4	3.0
Automobiles	23,056,007	273	263,662	91,632	355,567	1.5	2.6
Precision machinery	1,196,563	742	17,002	54,709	72,453	6.1	3.7
Wholesalers	113,300,157	6,392	77,909	0	84,301	0.1	0.4
Sogo Shosha	96,789,016	4,900	14,443	0	19,343	0.0	0.3

(continued)

Table 8.7 (continued)

Retailers	15,944,216	9,259	267,952	0	277,211	1.7	2.3
Department stores	4,924,188	5,865	105,234	0	111,099	2.3	1.3
Self-service stores	9,931,057	3,841	133,969	0	137,810	1.4	1.9
Construction	20,963,286	656	54,944	25,935	81,535	0.4	2.7
Real estate	3,447,578	−531	69,801	0	69,270	2.0	1.4
Telecommunications	7,288,950	45,767	52,695	162,325	260,787	3.6	6.3
Electricity and gas	16,951,415	41,462	88,135	215,112	344,709	2.0	4.6
Service industries	3,601,057	38	31,048	1,469	32,555	0.9	4.3
Movies, etc.	334,170	450	13,400	0	13,850	4.1	6.1
Lease industry	1,877,018	10,185	1,785	0	11,970	0.6	0.7

Source: Bank of Japan, *Management Analysis of Major Corporations*, 1991–1995. Analysis averages 651 corporations (377 in manufacturing industries and 274 in nonmanufacturing industries) that include listed and unlisted corporations with minimum capital of ¥1 billion.

Note: Intangible fixed assets: Know-how and other expertise purchased or developed by a company, which include operating licenses, patent rights, leaseholds, trademark rights, utility model patents, design rights, mining concessions, and fishing rights.

Japan stopped publishing these statistics from fiscal 1996 onward, so the most recent trend is not available for comparison.

It is worth mentioning that research and development and high-quality advertising (including public relations) are also important in the development of brand prestige, though advertising costs can be greatly minimized by raising the value of a brand. In addition, it could be said that research and development costs, that is, the expenditures used in the development of new products or new technology, or both, are central to creating high-quality goods and services and are thus a starting point or source of brand power. Investments in advertising are used to disseminate the message of high-quality products and services to a wide audience, bearing in mind the company's culture, in order to catalyze brand power.

According to a *BusinessWeek* article, the best global brand builders are intensely creative in getting their message out.[11] A new generation of brands, including Amazon, e-Bay, and Starbucks, has amassed huge global value with little traditional advertising. They use culture to make their brand messages enjoyable and to encourage consumers to see them as entertainment instead of an intrusion.

Path to a "Country Built on Culture"

Language is a weapon of mass attraction. Matthew Frazer (2005, p. 24) observed that the Romans were so cognizant of the influence of their language in national affairs that they took serious care to extend, along with the progress of their arms, the use of the Latin tongue.

Japan is steadily becoming a soft power middleweight, owing mainly to the recent world popularity of Japanese pop culture. Just look at the number of people worldwide who have taken an interest in the Japanese language. In 2006 the number of people studying the Japanese language overseas was estimated at nearly three million, an increase of 83.5 percent over 1993 (see Figure 8.5). It is said that the increase could be explained mostly by the popularity of Japanese *manga* and anime among young people overseas, as the aforementioned anecdote about French young men shows.

While Japan has been experiencing a decade-long economic slump, it has, over the same ten-year span, witnessed the worldwide permeation of Japanese culture. Highly profitable Japanese products and services that have made their way across the globe also reflect Japan's culture, and as a result Japan's cultural appeal is being felt by ever-more people.

Of course, trends forever change with the times. Throughout the modern period, Japanism has been an on-again, off-again affair. Even though current Japanese animation and comics are considered by many the ultimate of "cool," it must be remembered that interests tend to quickly fade, and as generations change, so do tastes. So, for continuity's sake, it is very important not only for Japan but also for all other countries not to antiquate their traditional culture.

The present has its origins in the past. Most of modern culture has its roots in tra-

Figure 8.5   **Number of Persons Studying Japanese Language Overseas, 1979–2003**

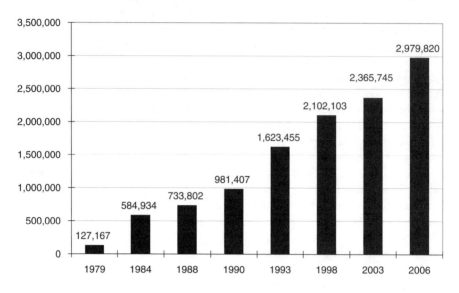

Source: Japan Foundation.

ditional culture. New cultural practices often emerge from traditional culture flowing just below the surface. I call this phenomenon *kongen-genjo* (根源現成), the origin's renaissance. This is to say that traditional culture often remains just behind the scenes, but when outside influences are present it may reappear in different shapes, with the result being new cultural forms. The rise of Japanese animation and comics owes more or less to such traditional Japanese popular cultural works as *e-maki* (scroll pictures), *ukiyo-e,* and *kibyoshi* (chapbooks). They will, in turn, accumulate as traditional culture for the next generation. In order to remain "cool," it is important for us not to forget our underlying traditions.

Moreover, innovations are created at the intersection of tradition and modernism or from exchanges of ideas with other people or other countries, just as many fish can be found at the *shio-me* (潮目), the point where a cold current and a warm current cross in the sea. Matthew Fraser (2005, pp. 196, 218) referred to this effect as "cross-fertilization" or "creative alchemy." In other words, the importance of international cultural exchanges cannot be stressed enough.

More than sixty years ago, a famous art historian, Yashiro Yukio (2004, pp. 26–27), gave a memorial speech at the inauguration of the Japan-U.S. Cultural Foundation in Kyoto. In the speech, he stressed that the obligation of Japan, which was defeated in World War II, was to contribute to the happiness of the world's people as a peaceful and cultural nation and that "cultural power" was one of the *raisons d'être* of Japan in the world.

Keeping Cultural Soft Power Soft and Sustainable

In April 2005, the Japanese government suggested in *Japan's 21st Century Vision* (The Report of the special board of inquiry for examining "Japan's 21st Century Vision") that toward 2030, Japan should become an "open, culturally creative nation" using tradition, creative power, and technology to bring out its attraction and strength. Making Japan's economy and society wide open to the world, the *Vision* says, would increase vitality through the free and active exchange of goods, people, capital, and culture. Japan seems to have begun to take the right course.

However, policy makers should pay careful attention to Matthew Frazer's caution (2005, pp. 37–38) that if there is a smell of cultural intrusion or imperialism in promoting a country's cultural policy, it will more often than not stir up fear and hostility. We therefore must be sensitive to the possibility that there might be a saturation point where excessive cultural popularity and monopolization bring about repulsion. As Nye (2004) pointed out, attraction can turn to repulsion if we act in an arrogant, self-centered, and unilateral manner and destroy the real message of our deeper values. Converting resources into realized power in the sense of obtaining desired outcomes requires well-designed strategies and skillful leadership.

The *Wall Street Journal Asia* (May 12–14, 2006) reported, "The Japanese Foreign Ministry plans to sell the Japanese 'brand' by marketing national treasures like manga (Japanese comics), animation and music abroad. This new initiative will include an international prize awarded to manga artists and may even certify Japanese animators as 'ambassadors of animation culture,' showcasing their work at embassies worldwide. Foreign Minister Aso Taro . . . used a historical example to show how comics help heal wounds in his April 28 speech."[12]

As the article shows, Japan's government is now carrying out a national policy or a public diplomacy focusing on such Japanese popular culture as animation and game content. It should be noted, however, that one of the reasons why Japanese animation has become so popular in the world is that it has long been out of reach or control of the government, left to take its own course and enjoy freedom of expression. Too much government emphasis on "Japan cool" might put people off.

In that sense, concerns must be raised about the recent somewhat excessive emphasis on Japan cool as a tool of Japanese soft power. This tight focus might in fact hinder the development of Japan cool and its soft power. The promotion of soft power by the government could be embarrassing for those concerned. Otsuka Eiji (2005), an author of *manga* and a writer of junior novels, showed his displeasure over such promotion.[13] Referring to traditional culture, Yashiro (2004, pp. 61–62) said that we should restrict ourselves to increasing the pleasure of the world's people only by letting them look at and understand Japanese culture, the last national treasure of Japan, without using it rashly and shortsightedly for political purposes and without expecting a good result overnight.

To keep cultural soft power effectively soft and persistent, therefore, emphasis should be put mainly on construction of the infrastructure for the industry concerned, such as

Japanese-language education abroad; international broadcasting of Japanese dramas, anime, and music; well-balanced[14] protection of intellectual property rights; and provision of more opportunities to new talents both at home and abroad for presentation of their work. Again, to keep cultural soft power effective and sustainable, constant support and promotion of both traditional and contemporary culture by both public and private sectors are much more important than sporadic or ephemeral efforts.

Notes

1. Derived from its roots, which mean "to cultivate" and "to respect," the English and French word "culture" had come by the mid-sixteenth century to denote "developing spiritual capacity through germane intellectual training. (*Developpement de certaines facultés de l'esprit par des exercices intellectuels appropriés. Ensemble des connaissances acquises qui permetent de développer le sens critique, le goût, le jugement*) (*Le Petit Robert* dictionary). "*Bunka*," the Japanese word for culture, is also defined in the *Kojien* dictionary (広辞苑) as the "composite of modes of behavior or patterns of living acquired, shared and communicated among people," as well as "that which is born of spiritual activities, mainly in the areas of academia, art, religion and morality." The root of the character "*bun*" (文) in the Japanese word "*bunka*," however, originated from the crisscrossed rope patterns in the Jomon style of pottery and denotes a beautiful pattern or decorative touch that is externally beautiful. Our ancestors could have enjoyed watching the patterns while waiting for cereals or legumes to be boiled. It is from this root meaning that I define culture as that which enriches the qualities of day-to-day human life and as that which appeals to the five senses of a human being and the human spirit. Therefore, culture is something that can provide all of us with love (愛), smiles (笑), tenderness (優), pleasure (楽), peace (安), beauty (美), humanity (仁), harmony (和), and virtue (徳), among others. (Japanese characters can be read as "I show you luck" and "*bi-jin- wa-toku.*")

2. Final Fantasy Online—An Unofficial Guide to Final Fantasy, http://www.ffonline.com/ (accessed June 27, 2007).

3. It would be relevant to refer to numbers of foreign visitors rather than numbers of sites, but it is difficult to get the numbers because a large majority of Web sites do not show numbers of site visitors.

4. The market estimation is based on the *2000 Input-Output Tables* published by Japan's Ministry of Public Management, Home Affairs, Posts and Telecommunications, Tokyo, in 2004.

5. The market estimation is based on the *2005 Information and Communications Industry White Paper* published by Japan's Ministry of International Affairs and Communications.

6. According to the *Daily Sunshine* (晶報) (May 22, 2006, A2) and the *Shenzhen Special Zone Daily* (深圳商報) (May 19, 2006, A10), the culture industry accounted for 17 percent of GDP in Japan, 18 percent to 25 percent in the United States, and 2.15 percent in China in 2004 (Shenzhen: 5 percent; Beijing: 14 percent in 2005).

7. "Conjoint analysis" is the technique of measuring the taste of a consumer for a product or service, and it has been used as a market research tool to come up with effective product design.

8. http://en.wikipedia.org/wiki/The_Da_Vinci_Code (accessed June 15, 2006).

9. In May 2007 the Japanese government introduced a similar concept called "Kansei (感性) Value," a special type of value based on a high-order function of the brain, including inspiration, intuition, pleasure and pain, taste, curiosity, aesthetics, emotion, sensitivity, attachment, and creativity. It thinks that in a mature economy, manufacturing and service centered on the concept of Kansei Value will stimulate new demand. (See http://www.meti.go.jp/english/ information/downloadfiles/PressRelease/080620KANSEI.pdf.)

10. The pharmaceutical industry's high profit rate can be attributed partly to the government's drug price regulation.

11. For example, Apple Computer launched a special iPod MP3 player in partnership with the band U2. "Not only did the 'U2 iPod' say 'U2' on the front and have brand signatures etched into the back, but the band starred in a TV ad and buyers got $50 off a download of 400 U2 songs." Likewise, "McDonald's Corp.'s sponsorship of a tour by R&B group Destiny's Child means that fans who want access to exclusive video and news content about the band have to click first on the company's Web site." Also according to the *BusinessWeek,* Samsung has posted the biggest gain in value of any Global 100 brand, with a 186 percent surge, over the past five years. "It focused on building a more upscale image through better quality, design, and innovation." Samsung was a lead sponsor of the year 2004's "much-hyped movie, *The Fantastic Four,* in which a variety of Samsung gadgets played a part" (*BusinessWeek,* September 5–12, 2005).

12. The whole text of Aso's speech is available in Japanese online at: http://www.mofa. go.jp/mofaj/press/enzetsu/18/easo_0428.html#01.

13. "What in America might be called the culturally strange or even abnormal [*hentai*] the Japanese government has opted to label 'Japan Cool,' and in the process attempted to turn this cultural industry genre into a collective national crusade in and of itself to bolster Japan's pride. This all came about due to the fragility of the Japanese economy and long period of economic stagnation following the bursting of the economic bubble. Japan's national identity, heretofore closely associated with its economic prowess, was thus linked to the cultural industry almost solely on the back of Japan's very successful comic and animation industry. However, politicians and industry in general have actually exaggerated this cultural industry's economic importance based on the industry's growing popularity overseas. It goes without saying, therefore, that as the Japanese economy emerges from the doldrums, the current 'Japanimation' fever running rampant in the political and business worlds will soon run its course.

"For those of us connected to comics and animation, the national promotion of booming 'Japanimation' as a kind of successful mutant strain in the poor Japanese economy has really not been all that meaningful to us. As far as we are concerned, as a subculture we take pride not in dubious recognition at the national level by the government but in creating comics that delight and are supported by readers. Furthermore, we question the motives of a national polity trying to cozy up to a sub- or even counterculture.

"This kind of market falls completely outside the realm of what the Nikkei might consider a normal or mainstream market or industry. So, although the government may be trying to insert this market into the current framework of markets or industries due to its vitality, I'm afraid that government recognition and the accompanying system of approvals and protection will only lead to the decline of this counterculture" (Otsuka and Ohsawa 2005; translation by the author).

14. I say "well-balanced" because, as Nakano and Sugiura discussed at the CGP-SSRC seminar conference held on February 25–26, 2005, illegal copies of Japanese dramas and software have sometimes been pivotal for the diffusion of Japanese culture and for gaining fans, suggesting that accessibility rather than inherent attractiveness also determines the popularity of a country's cultural product. Overly strict protection of intellectual property rights might weaken cultural soft power.

References

Barroux, David. 2005. "Japon: La nouvelle usine à rêves" (Japan: The new factory of dreams). *Enjeux les echos* 211 (March): 66–70.
Barthes, Roland. [1970] 1993. *L'empire des signes* (The empire of signs). Paris: Editions d'Art Albert Skira.
Brown, Dan. 2003. *The Da Vinci Code.* New York: Doubleday.
Chozick, Amy. 2007. "The Cool Factory: How Japan Made Hip a Business." *Wall Street Journal,* March 16–18, pp. W6–W7. Weekend Journal.

Cornell, Andrew. 2006. "Gross National Cool." *Australian Financial Review Magazine,* December, 38–43.

Faiola, Anthony. 2003. "Japan's Empire of Cool." *Washington Post,* December 27, A1, A20.

Fraser, Matthew. 2005. *Weapons of Mass Distraction: Soft Power and American Empire.* New York: Thomas Dunne Books, St. Martin's Press. Originally published in Toronto: Key Porter Books, 2003.

Frederick, Jim. 2003. "What's Right with Japan." *Time,* August 11, 23–25.

Goldhaber, Michael H. 1997a. "The Attention Economy and the Net." Draft of a talk presented at the conference Economics of Digital Information, Cambridge, MA, January 23–26. http://www.well.com/user/mgoldh/AtEcandNet.html (accessed January 28, 2004).

———. 1997b. "Attention Shoppers!" *Wired* 5.12 (December). http://www.wired.com/wired/archive/5.12/es_attention_pr.html (accessed January 28, 2004).

Gresser, Edward. 2004. "The Emerging Asian Union?" In *Policy Report* (May). http://www.ppionline.org/documents/China_trade_0504.pdf (accessed June 20, 2004).

Healy, Kieran. 2002. "What's New for Culture in the New Economy?" *Journal of Arts Management, Law and Society* 32 (2): 86–103.

Howkins, John. 2001. *The Creative Economy: How People Make Money from Ideas.* London: Allen Lane.

Japan External Trade Organization (JETRO). 2005. "Furansu ni okeru Nihon no anime wo chusin tosuru kontentsu no shinto jokyo" (The permeation of Japanese content focusing on Japanese animation in France). March. http://www.jetro.go.jp/biz/world/europe/reports/05001223. (accessed May 14, 2006).

Kjær, Esben. 2004. "Japan er bruttonational-cool. (Japan is gross-national-cool)." *Berlingske* (August 1): 6–7.

Marcadal, Raphaëlle. 2006. "Le 'Japan cool' inonde la planète." (The "Japan cool" is in flood on the planet.) http://japancool.typepad.com/japan_cool/2006/03/_soft_power_cul. html.(accessed June 25, 2006).

McGray, Douglas. 2002. "Japan's Gross National Cool." *Foreign Policy* 130 (May–June): 44–54.

Ministry of Economy, Trade and Industry of Japan. 2005. *Tsusho Hakusho* (White paper on international economy and trade).

Nye, Joseph S., Jr. 2004. *Soft Power: The Means to Success in World Politics.* New York: Public Affairs.

Otsuka, Eiji, and Ohsawa Nobuaki. 2005. *Japanimation wa naze yabureruka* (Why does Japanimation lose?). Tokyo: Kadokawa Shoten.

Pedroletti, Brice. 2003. "Le Japon, nouvelle référence du consommateur asiatique. (Japan, new reference of Asian consumers). *Le Monde,* December 8, 14.

Pirie, Madsen. 2002. *The People Economy.* London: Adam Smith Institute and Academy of Enterprise. http://www.adamsmith.org/images/uploads/publications/people-economy.pdf (accessed April 30, 2004).

Roberts, Kevin. 2005. *Lovemarks: The Future Beyond Brands.* New York: Powerhouse Books.

Rowley, Ian. 2005a. "Tired of the Pummeling: Can Once-Mighty Japanese Video Game Makers End the Rout by U.S. Rivals?" *BusinessWeek,* April 4, 8–19.

———. 2005b. "The Anime Biz." *BusinessWeek,* June 27, 20–25.

Special Board Of Inquiry For Examining "Japan's 21st Century Vision." 2005. "Japan's 21st Century Vision: A New Era of Dynamism," 9–12. www.kezai-shimon.go.jp/english/publication/pdf/050419visionsummary_fulltext.pdf.

Sugiura, Tsutomu. 2003a. "Bunka-ryoku to Kigyo-senryaku" (Cultural power and corporate strategies). *Nikkei,* September 18–October 10.

———. 2003b. "Hi wa mata noboru: Pokemon kokokuron" (The sun rises again: Pokemon hegemon). *Bungei Shunju,* September, 186–93.

————. 2004a. "Hitobito no itonami ni miryoku wo soeru 'bunkaryoku' no jidai" (The era of cultural power that gives an additional charm to the human life). *CUC (*View & vision*)* 17 (March), 6–11.

————. 2004b. "Japanese Culture on the World Stage." *Japan Spotlight* 23 (2): 6–10.

————. 2004c. "Nyu-ekonomii to bunka-ryoku" (The new economy and cultural power). *Sekai Keizai Hyoron* (World economic review) 48 (9): 32–43.

Tasaka, Hiroshi. 2006. "Kaze-no-Tayori." Message Mail 186. http://www.hiroshitasaka.jp/tayori/index.php (accessed November 30, 2006).

Tepper, Steven Jay. 2002. "Creative Assets and the Changing Economy." *Journal of Arts Management, Law and Society* 32 (2): 159–68.

UK Department of Culture, Media and Sport. 2004. *Annual Report 2003–2004.*

Yagi, Tadashi. 2003–5. "Effect of Cultural Influence on Expansion of Market: Empirical Evaluation of Economic Benefits of Cultural Social Infrastructure." *Keizaigaku Ronso* 57 (2): 117–43.

Yashiro, Yukio. [1988] 2004. *Sekai ni okeru Nihon bijutsu no ichi: Kokusai bunka to Nihon bijutsu* (The position of Japanese arts in the world: International culture and Japanese arts). Tokyo: Kodansha.

Yoshimoto, Mitsuhiro. 2003. "Sozoteki sangyo-gun no choryu" (Trends of the group of creative industries). *Nissei Kiso Ken REPORT.* NLI Research Institute, November, 8–13.

9

Baseball in U.S.-Japanese Relations

A Vehicle of Soft Power in Historical Perspective

Sayuri Guthrie-Shimizu

> *Originated sometime ago by Americans*
> *This wondrous thing called Baseball*
> *One can never get enough of it*
>
> —Tanka by Masaoka Shiki (1898)

In 1953, the arrival of Matthew Perry and his naval squadron in the Bay of Edo ended Japan's two-century-long diplomatic seclusion, and the United States has closely entwined itself with modern Japan's historical trajectory ever since. The commodore's high-pressure tactics compelled the Tokugawa shogunate to open its doors to the wider world, and it inflamed the jingoistic sensibilities of Japanese firebrands. Yet due in no small part to the diplomatic aptitude of its first consul general, Townsend Harris, the United States won over Japanese officialdom and positioned itself as a singular friend of Japan in the world of predatory Western colonial powers. As Japan stumbled its way through the turbulent closing years of the Edo period and the Meiji Restoration, the idea of the United States as a benign and in many respects inspirational nation retained its sway in Japan's official circles (Kamei 1979, pp. 68–134).

Evincing modern Japan's attraction to the young republic across the Pacific, the shogunate dispatched its first diplomatic mission to the United States. The Meiji oligarchs followed in its footsteps by making the United States the first stop in their inaugural ambassadorial tour of the Western world, headed by plenipotentiary Iwakura Tomomi. Outside the corridors of power, denizens of modern Japan just as eagerly sought out America. Castaways who had reached the shores of the United States in the late Edo period, such as Nakahama (John) Manjiro and Hamada Hikozo, made America their adopted home even before the commencement of formal diplomatic exchange between the two governments. Following these unwitting pioneers were willful stowaways who defied the state ban on overseas travel to pursue their personal quest of imagined America. Nijima Jo, the latter-day founder of Doshisha University, was one such early admirer. The allure of the United States to modernizing Japan was such that, when the Meiji state lifted its ban on overseas travel to usher in the "civilization and enlightenment" period

154

in Japanese history, the plurality of study abroad students seeking to acquire Western knowledge chose the United States as their destination (Kamei 1979, pp. 70–71).

Historic U.S.-Japanese encounters, however, were not a story of uninterrupted admiration. Japanese attitudes toward the United States have oscillated between adulation, sometimes bordering on infatuation, and revulsion, often approaching visceral hatred. In the 1880s, the Meiji oligarchy's embrace of things American waned as it shifted its gaze toward Europe, particularly the newly unified German state, to gain expertise and practical know-how for its modernization project. Reflecting this official trend, the number of Japanese students heading for the United States dropped relative to those bound for Europe. And yet the United States continued to occupy a unique place in Japan's popular imagination, especially among renegades in government and literary circles, reform-minded elites, and those in the country's economically marginal regions, a reservoir of America-bound unskilled laborers. The United States still beckoned the Japanese on the margins as a shining city upon a hill. It remained a metaphor for freedom, equality, democracy, openness, and unbounded possibilities in life (Kamei 1979, pp. 83–98).

It was not just such abstract visions of an egalitarian and expansive society, dreams of material abundance, or scientific and technological progress that enticed early Meiji Japan to the United States. Avatars of American culture that permeated Japanese society also captured the hearts and minds of the citizens of the modernizing nation. Baseball, an athletic form and a diversionary activity that was gaining in popularity in the United States in the late nineteenth century, was exported to Meiji Japan and drew many Japanese, elite and plebian, to the country of its origin. The short verse by the era's preeminent haiku poet, Masaoka Shiki, cited at the opening of this chapter evokes this heartfelt affection for the game and the country that fathered it. Students of the elite Ichiko, an institutional forerunner to Tokyo Imperial University, where Masaoka Shiki studied, enthusiastically embraced *besuboru* and took pride in their college's unrivaled excellence in it. The game also embodied "America" and all that was liberating and ennobling about its values in the eyes of those Japanese who played or watched it in the Meiji period (Guthrie-Shimizu 2004, p. 5).

In his acclaimed 2004 book, Joseph S. Nye, Jr., defined "soft power" as a nation's "ability to shape the preference of others" through its values, culture, and institutions. Nye also described soft power as a nation's capacity to guide others' behaviors through attraction and approbation, instead of coercion or explicit quid pro quo (Nye 2004, p. 5). In wielding soft power, the United States can, as can other nations, draw on three resources: its culture (both high culture and popular culture), its political values, and its foreign policies (Nye 2004, p. 11). Soft power thus defined by Nye entails reciprocal dynamics between a nation that projects it and another that responds to it. When the United States exercises soft power in the world, it needs to articulate and translate into action attractive and inspirational ideas through its social and cultural practices and public policies, both domestic and foreign. The effectiveness of America's soft power depends on the reception, appreciation, and affirmation of American ideas, practices, and institutions by the recipient countries.

Elsewhere in *Soft Power,* Nye also noted that popular sports can play an important role in communicating American values (Nye 2004, p. 47). In this chapter I suggest that, viewed in the context of U.S.-Japanese relations, baseball, a bodily regimen, a modern competitive sport, the stuff of popular recreation and mass entertainment that attained an iconic status as "America's national pastime" by the dawn of the twentieth century, affords a particularly elucidatory validation of this thesis. By becoming a highly popular sport and successful commercial enterprise on both sides of the Pacific, baseball also highlights soft power's long-term potential for drawing its wielder and receiver closer in vision, making their practices more compatible, and transforming their institutions into more mutually reliant and receptive entities. How has baseball been transmitted to Japan and functioned as a vehicle through which the United States has projected soft power? How has Japan responded to or against America's soft power at this site of enduring intersocietal interaction? Has Japan come to exercise its own soft power through this shared vehicle? Has the sustaining mutual engagement through baseball made the two countries' values, practices, and institutions more compatible? And finally, how has the mutual attraction to this form of soft power mediated the relations between the two countries, whose hard power resources were once violently and tragically deployed against each other? To address these interlocking questions, this chapter first examines baseball's early history when the metaphorical amalgamation of baseball and American virtues began.

Baseball as a Resource of Soft Power: Incipient Years

In postbellum America, architects of seminal professional baseball such as Albert G. Spalding and his cohorts in the nascent National League tried to establish its legitimacy as a respectable popular recreation and profitable and stable commercial enterprise in Gilded Age America. They did so in part by touting the game's supposed attributes befitting industrious and self-disciplined citizens of the industrializing nation. Through this marketing process, the newly codified and rapidly commercializing sport began to be associated with such hallowed American values as democracy, freedom, and open and fair competition (Levine 1985, pp. 67–70).

Similarly, Americans who sought to propagate the public discourse of intersectional reconciliation and national unity after the bloodletting Civil War also engineered the conflation of baseball and all-American values by evoking the lore, often embellished, of Union and Confederate soldiers temporarily laying down the arms in battlefields to play "America's game" together (Kirsh 2003, pp. iv–xiv; Goldstein 1989, pp. 10–14). As white settlement penetrated the American West in the late nineteenth century, the U.S. Army used baseball as an administrative tool with which to establish rapport with the local settler communities and integrated the game into its program to "civilize" the pacified Plains Indian tribes through everyday practices and reeducation. In these historical instances, baseball worked as a launching pad of soft power, targeting domestic individuals and groups to draw them into the orbit of the emerging national culture.

When the United States attained overseas colonial possessions as a result of the

Spanish-American War, the U.S. military and civilian administrators in the newly acquired colonies again enlisted baseball in their self-assigned mission to "Americanize" and "civilize" the indigenous populations. Arguably, the United States used baseball as an instrument of a more coercive (decidedly so) version of present-day "public diplomacy" in these colonial territories. In the Philippines as well as in Puerto Rico and (quasi-independent) Cuba, baseball, the sport of choice of the new colonial master, became a staple of the local administrative and educational regimen. In the case of the Philippines, the first locals to adopt baseball were laborers on the U.S. Army bases, and the sport became a favorite pastime of Filipino children in public schools established under U.S. colonial rule (Perez 1994, pp. 493–517).

Baseball was not imposed on these conquered territories as an unwanted outsider practice, however. Many among the indigenous populations readily abandoned the cockfights and bullfights introduced by the Spanish colonial master in favor of the America's game because it came to them as an antidote to vestigial Spanish colonial influences and a metaphor for a better life under the supposedly more benevolent suzerain. The Americans were able to turn baseball into a source of soft power largely because of this local receptiveness and unforced acceptance. Nye is right: Power, soft or hard, always depends on the context in which the relationship takes place (Reaves 2002, p. 92; Nye 2004, p. 2).

In the United States, baseball emerged as a form of popular culture, became commercialized as the nation became industrialized, and morphed into a staple of mass entertainment with the advent of new communications and transportation technologies. But this plebian genealogy should not mask the contrastingly "high culture" pedigree of the game's transmission to and initial dissemination in Meiji Japan. Nye's conceptual formulation divides culture into high and low (popular) culture. He further holds that high culture's soft power manifestations consist of aesthetic expressions such as literature and art, as well as education (Nye 2004, p. 11). But it was through the channels opened by state-driven enterprises in higher education that this popular American cultural form initially penetrated Japan.

The first American to introduce the fundamentals of baseball to Japan was Horace Wilson, a Civil War veteran who was hired by the Meiji government as an *oyatoi* (hired hand) college instructor to teach math and English at Keiseiko, an elite preparatory program later reorganized into Tokyo Imperial University (Ikei 1977, pp. 2–4; Watanabe 1996, pp. 21–22). Others in the pool of *oyatoi* teachers recruited to educate Japan's best and brightest helped popularize baseball in Mikado's empire. Albert Bates, an instructor at Kaitakushi Karigakko, the technical school adjunct to the Hokkaido Development Agency, was another early baseball missionary. Leroy Lansing Janes, a West Point graduate and a Civil War veteran, came to Kumamoto Yogakko (the Western Studies Institute) in Japanese government employ to teach English, science, and math. He also tutored his intellectual disciples in the provincial city in baseball and other Western competitive sports. Among the band of Janes's students in Kumamoto was Abe Isoo, the revered father of Japanese collegiate baseball who would spearhead Japan's first baseball tour to the United States in 1905 (Oshima 1958, pp. 22–27, 64–66; Kumamoto Nichinichi Shinbunsha 1967, p. 7).

These examples call into question the high culture/popular culture dichotomy implicit in Nye's conceptual model as applied to baseball's early years in Japan. Baseball's initial infiltration of Meiji Japan's elite and intellectual circles illustrates that a popular cultural form can often come in tandem with, or as a rider to, what Nye categorized as high culture. Because culture is a synergy of metaphysical imaginings and real-life practices, participants of that complex system of human exercise frequently practice its diverse components in multiple social roles and capacities, as did those young *oyatoi* American teachers and their Japanese charges. The Meiji government's attraction to the United States' superior institutions and rich human tradition in higher education and technical training thus yielded unintended yet profound social consequences: It "turned the Japanese on" to a form of American popular culture that was baseball. An overly clear-cut distinction between "high" and "popular" culture when considering this font of America's soft power would obfuscate the osmotic and boundary-breaching potential of culture.

Flowering of U.S.-Japanese Baseball Exchange: Early Twentieth Century

The genesis of Japanese baseball as an elite privilege faded as the sport spread to the general population by the late Meiji period. The game owed its popularization partially to those who introduced "clubs" to Japan in the late 1870s as a venue of diversionary activity and organized play. Hiraoka Hiroshi, a railroad engineer trained in the United States, was one such cross-cultural emissary. He organized Japan's first private baseball club, named the Shinbashi Athletic Club, after he returned from studies in Boston and a subsequent apprenticeship in railroad engineering. It was also Japan's earliest dues-charging private association devoted solely to a nonoccupational activity. This Japanese apostle of participatory recreation modeled his fraternity of athletic fun seekers after baseball "clubs" of all sizes flush in Gilded Age America.

While similar amateur baseball clubs began to dot Japan's urban social landscape, the advent of collegiate baseball and the broad fan base it came to command in the late Meiji period spurred baseball's nationwide proliferation. Between the 1880s and early 1900s, several private institutions of higher learning were founded in Japan. Pioneer private colleges, such as Keio, Waseda, and Meiji Gakuin, organized extramural baseball teams and challenged Ichiko's heretofore uncontested reign in the sport. Again, the new entrants adopted an American model of intraregional athletic competition to bring rationality to its structure in line with the game's evolution into a mass spectator sport. In 1903, Waseda and Keio baseball squads began to meet regularly in a manner patterned after the annual Harvard-Yale football game. In the face of the growing baseball prowess of other colleges in the Tokyo metropolitan area such as Hosei and Meiji, this exclusive format expanded first into multiteam tournaments and then, in the mid-1920s, to a six-team league running on a fixed schedule similar to Ivy League or Big Ten athletic competitions among major colleges in the U.S. Midwest. In the absence of professional baseball, intercollegiate baseball was *the* object of baseball spectatorship and fandom in Japan in the Taisho and early Showa periods (Guttman and Thompson 2001, p. 183).

The Japanese college squads did not only play regularly among themselves and against teams of American expatriates in Japan and the visiting U.S. naval fleet. With the advent of transoceanic travel in the early twentieth century, the Japanese collegians' playing field expanded to reach the shores of the U.S. mainland and America's colonial outpost in Asia, the Philippines. Top-tier Japanese college squads began barnstorming against American collegiate and semiprofessional teams on the U.S. mainland and in Hawaii, or Filipino and U.S. military teams in Manila, with Waseda's 1905 West Coast tour paving the way (Kiku 1993, pp. 113–14). Its faculty manager, Abe Isoo, a Christian socialist, had imbibed key ideological tenets of Victorian-era reform movements during his studies at Hartford Seminary. As a reform theorist, Abe opposed concubinage and licensed prostitution and advocated female suffrage during the Taisho Democracy period, another era in modern Japanese history when American values and institutions commanded the high esteem of Japanese parliamentarians, intellectuals, and literati (Kamei 1979, p. 78).

In 1905, Abe and his student players sailed for the United States amid the Russo-Japanese War and played twenty-six games in San Francisco, Los Angeles, Seattle, and Tacoma. The financial basis of the tour was tenuous at best, yet on-site donations from Japanese immigrant communities on the West Coast permitted the tour's completion. The tour also received a promotional gift of baseball equipment from A.G. Spalding Company, a leading American sporting goods company then eyeing overseas markets (Abe 1905). After returning home, Abe and the team's captain, Hashido Makoto, disseminated information on "scientific baseball" then practiced in the United States. Cutting-edge playing techniques and training regimens such as pitcher rotation, warm-up, the squeeze play, bunt, and slide were explicated in a manual titled *Saishin yakujutsu* (Brand-new baseball techniques), fusing in the minds of Japanese baseball aficionados "America," baseball, modernity, and scientific rationality. The widely read text helped bring the Japanese style of play into closer conformity with the prevailing American practices. Again, local (Japanese) cultural intermediaries proved critical in the projection of American soft power via baseball (Hashido 1905).

Waseda's archrival, Keio, also learned the intricacies of scientific baseball firsthand. In 1908, Keio invited Hawaii's St. Louis College to Japan and received a reciprocal invitation to play in the U.S. outpost in the Pacific in the following year. This triggered a round of baseball one-upmanship among Japan's premier colleges in the following two decades. Waseda brought the University of Washington team and the University of Chicago team to Japan. Assistance rendered by the inaugural director of Chicago's athletic program, Amos Stagg, was instrumental in Waseda's barnstorming tour deep into the U.S. mountain, Midwest, and Mid-Atlantic states (Tobita 1950, pp. 102–4). Not to be outdone, Keio reached out directly to the doyen of scientific baseball, the manager of the New York Giants, John McGraw, and recruited Arthur Schaefer, the Giants' third baseman, and Tommy Thompson, another Giant, to coach its student players. In 1913, Keio also sponsored Stanford's barnstorming tour in Japan (Ikei

1977, pp. 76–82). Meiji University, a relative upstart, engineered the University of Washington's second tour of Japan and the all-Filipino team's barnstorming that same year (Kiku 1993, p. 114).

By sports sociologist Kiku Koji's counting, between 1905 and 1915 alone, twenty American, Japanese, and Filipino amateur baseball teams crossed the Pacific and engaged one another on the diamonds. The transpacific baseball traffic thickened as American semiprofessional and professional teams entered the stream in the 1920s and early 1930s. A Negro League team (the Philadelphia Royal Giants), a Native American team (the Sherman Indians), Japanese American teams in the U.S. Pacific Coast League and Hawaii (the Seattle Mikado and the Hawaii Asahi), and an American All Women's professional baseball team nicknamed "the Bobbies" met their matches among Japan's college and corporate-sponsored (*shakaijin*) baseball teams (Kiku 1993, p. 113). In the U.S.-Japanese baseball exchange efflorescing against the backdrop of relative harmony in the intergovernmental relationship, private individuals and groups largely autonomous from government policy intents and other types of public mandates delivered American soft power packaged in baseball. The emergence of the transpacific world as an increasingly integrated cultural sphere and a popular entertainment market became the infrastructure upon which these purveyors of American soft power wielded baseball's winning effects (Imada 2004, pp. 111–49).

Crosscurrents of Hard Power and Soft Power: 1930s

Nye noted that "hard and soft power sometimes reinforce and sometimes interfere with each other" (Nye 2004, p. 25). This precept certainly applied to baseball in U.S.-Japanese relations in the first half of the twentieth century. As the diplomatic and military relationship between the two governments underwent a series of cooling, souring, and inflaming through this period, baseball could not help being sucked into a maelstrom of hard power considerations. The first notable instance in which the deployment of this soft power resource intersected with hard power calculations by the governments took place in the fall of 1908.

The years immediately following the Russo-Japanese War saw one of several crises in twentieth-century U.S.-Japanese relations that would cumulate into World War II in the Pacific. When the Portsmouth Treaty, brokered in the summer of 1905 by U.S. president Theodore Roosevelt, failed to deliver the kind of peace terms with imperial Russia the Japanese believed were due them, the Japanese government and public opinion turned against the United States. Tokyo's relationship with Washington cooled further, for the two countries no longer appeared to see eye to eye on many issues once imperial Russia had retreated in the Far East. The dramatic rise in Japanese immigration to the United States and Americans' exclusionary response was another bone of contention. President Roosevelt launched the U.S. Navy's Great White Fleet into a practice cruise at this juncture as a way to impress Japan with the United States' growing naval capabilities and battle readiness in the Western Pacific.

Nye noted that popular culture as a soft power resource "does not always produce the exact policy outcomes that the government might desire because it is not under direct control of government" (Nye 2004, p. 52). This adage certainly held true in this instance. When the mighty American fleet of sixteen battleships plus auxiliaries arrived in Japan in the late fall of 1908, U.S. Navy baseball teams played a series of games with Japan's two premier college teams, Waseda and Keio. The Japanese student players held their own in the contests of masculine prowess embodied in baseball, sometimes literally beating the Americans at their own game. The final match between the All-Americans and the Waseda-Keio all-stars was a highly suggestive 1–1 draw. The whole enterprise, reinforced by requisite after-game libations, morphed into an occasion for reaffirming U.S.-Japanese friendship and brotherly camaraderie forged in a shared passion for baseball. To the extent that the ballyhooed cross-ocean naval maneuver was designed symbolically to shock and awe the increasingly recalcitrant Japanese, baseball as a medium of soft power helped muffle its menacing effects. It might well have been the first time the Japanese government noted the usefulness of this soft power resource in endearing itself to the Americans (Keio Gijuku Daigaku Yakyubu 1989, pp. 36–40).

As the reciprocal animosity over the United States' anti-Japanese immigration policy and less-than-compatible diplomatic priorities continued to simmer in the background, the economic prosperity of the 1920s continued to foster the baseball exchange across the Pacific. Even after the worldwide Depression hit both countries and intergovernmental relations deteriorated over the two nations' dueling hard power imperatives, the baseball exchange safeguarded an avenue of conciliatory bilateral transactions. In 1934, the United States even helped Japan venture into a new baseball enterprise: the launching of professional teams on the American model.

By this time, Japan had hosted several American major league exhibition tours. The first U.S. professionals to land in Japan were the Reach Reach-All American Stars. Its impresario, Albert Reach, was a professional player-turned-owner of a sporting goods company. Combining a Major League tour to "Americanize Filipinos" through "America's game" with a promotional campaign for his merchandise, Reach assembled a team of eighteen players from the Pacific Coast League and the nascent American League. The group played twelve exhibition games against Japanese amateur teams in Tokyo, Yokohama, and Kobe in late 1908 (Reach & Co. 1909, pp. 582–85).

In 1913–14, the New York Giants' manager, John McGraw, and the owner of the Chicago White Sox, Charles Cominsky, led a world tour of a combined National and American League team, with "the support and well-wishes of the President of the United States," the State Department and the National Baseball Commission. During the globe-trotting exhibition tour, encompassing Canada, Asia, Australia, India, Ceylon, Egypt, and the British Isles, the Major League stars played against Japanese college teams. In 1920 and 1922, a mix of Pacific Coast Leaguers and Major League players again barnstormed in Japan and Manchuria during its winter-season junket partially sponsored by the *Daimai* newspaper (Kiku 1993, p. 114).

By far the most significant of all American pro tours was the Major Leagues' two Japan trips organized with great fanfare by the newspaper *Yomiuri Shinbun.* In 1930, the company's helmsman, Shoriki Matsutaro, launched a coordinated publicity campaign to boost his paper's national circulation. One way he tried to attract public attention to his second-tier daily was to recruit an American media celebrity highly popular in Japan: Babe Ruth (Ikei 1977, pp. 108–11). Shoriki, using his political connections, persuaded the Foreign Ministry to throw its weight behind his company's publicity campaign. The Japanese Foreign Ministry tried to help broker a deal to bring the homerun king to Japan after the 1931 season to "further U.S.-Japanese friendship." Ruth ended up not coming because the minimum guarantee of $50,000 each required for Ruth and Lou Gehrig proved too much. The Major League tour still received red-carpet treatment nearly comparable to that granted an official state visit, including an audience with Prime Minister Wakatsuki Reijiro, then busy deflecting worldwide opprobrium over the Manchurian Incident only several weeks before. Tokyo appeared none too shy about using America's national pastime to worm its way back into Americans' good graces.[1]

Three years later, Shoriki succeeded in obtaining Ruth's postseason appearance in Japan. The Major League's second Japan tour included both Ruth and Gehrig and received a rapturous welcome by Japanese fans, who thronged to a ticker-tape parade on the thoroughfare of the Ginza. The team hobnobbed with high-level Japanese government officials and U.S. ambassador Joseph Grew (Grew 1948, p. 193). Ruth and company toured Japan for a month, leaving behind memories Japanese baseball fans would cherish well into the postwar years, among them, fresh-faced seventeen-year-old pitcher Sawamura Eiji's exploit in striking out Gehrig and Ruth in succession. The shared love of baseball endured through the turbulent 1930s, spinning off a thread, if increasingly tenuous, binding together the two nations, which were descending into a downward spiral of hostility in the realm of hard power.[2]

The 1934 Major League tour also shepherded in the birth of Japanese professional baseball. Two years prior, the Ministry of Education had banned college players from playing against professional baseball players (both Japanese and foreign) to combat the "banes of vapid commercialism and excessive materialism" (Sakaue 2001, pp. 117–19). This state intrusion into civil society, accompanied by an implied rejection of what American-style consumer culture symbolized, reflected the totalitarian ideology gripping Japan in the 1930s. Because of this government edict, the hosts of the 1934 Majors tour assembled on a crash basis, leading players from collegiate and high school baseball to create a team of "professionals" to play against the Major Leaguers. The founding members of Japan's professional baseball, including Sawamura, Mizuhara Shigeru, and a White Russian pitcher named Victor Starffin, would emerge from this pool of conscripts. The club owned by Shoriki's *Yomiuri Shinbun* adopted the nickname Giants after the New York Giants during its 1936 U.S. barnstorming tour (Suzuki 1983, pp. 61–123).

While the governments of the two nations drifted apart under the weight of seemingly irreconcilable differences, baseball precariously held together this well-trodden terrain of soft power. After Japan invaded north China in 1937, however, the U.S. baseball commission withdrew its support from, and forced cancellation of, the Major

League's Japan tour scheduled for that fall. The decision marked the beginning of an eight-year drought in the U.S.-Japanese baseball exchange. After the two governments broke off relations in that fateful December 1941, baseball, as did many aspects of civil society, morphed into an instrument of wartime morale building and a visual display of national mobilization on both sides of the Pacific. Sawamura's hurling prowess was recast at the hands of Japan's war propagandists into a rousing report of hand grenade throwing in the Chinese theater. The military service of major league greats, such as Joe DiMaggio and Jimmy Foxx, was touted by organized baseball and the U.S. government as a shining example of the citizen soldier defending the American way of life. "Wartime soft-power resources were created in part by the government and in part independently," Nye noted (Nye 2004, p. 102). It should be added that once the state becomes bent on wielding hard power, agents of soft power could just as easily be deployed as faithful servants of hard power and presented to the public as such.

Baseball During the U.S. Occupation: Soft Power Travels Both Ways

The war in the Asia-Pacific ended on August 15, 1945, and baseball returned to Japan immediately in the war's aftermath. On November 23, 1945, at Tokyo's Jingu Stadium, the Japanese enjoyed a long-awaited opportunity to satisfy their craving for what their militarist government had vilified as an "enemy sport" during the war. Six thousand residents of the flattened capital city gathered at Japan's oldest modern ballpark and savored an East-West game played by former Japanese baseball greats. Symbolizing the political realities of the nation under U.S. occupation, the use of the stadium, recently commandeered by the occupation forces and renamed Stateside Park, became possible only with the authorization of Lieutenant General Robert Eichelberger, commander of the U.S. Eighth Army.

The acute food shortage of the immediate postsurrender months did not stop enthusiastic Japanese baseball lovers from forking over ¥6 for a ticket to watch the game they had furtively missed during the war against *kichiku beiei,* "the devilish Anglo-Americans." The occupation headquarters even arranged for a live radio broadcast of the exhibition game. It was the first time the Japanese people had heard a baseball game over the radio waves since 1942 (Suzuki 1984, pp. 239–42; Suzuki 1978, pp. 211–12). Five months later, the first postwar pennant race among eight professional clubs pieced together from the remains of prewar organized baseball opened at the Korakuen Stadium, another public facility temporarily released from exclusive use by the U.S. military. The message was loud and clear: Baseball was back in, and the game returned to Japan with the U.S. occupation army with an avowed mission to democratize the defeated nation.

Key officials in the general headquarters indeed enlisted baseball as a tool of pacification and democratization. Eichelberger stated openly that sports, by providing wholesome distraction and healthful recreation, would facilitate the orderly governance of the former enemy country and facilitate U.S. efforts to reeducate the local population in the ways of self-directed, rule-abiding democratic citizenry. Officials under his command declared that learning the concept of fair play and sportsmanship was a key to Japan's reintegration into the "brotherhood of nations" and announced the occupation authorities' commitment to reintroduce Western competitive sports in "every college and school in the land." Baseball was deemed particularly important in this reeducation project, for America's favorite game had, in the words of a Supreme Commander of the Allied Powers (SCAP) officer, already become "Japan's national pastime prior to December 8, 1941."[3]

One area in which baseball was deployed for the occupation headquarters' larger reform agenda was the institutional overhaul of youth education in the Allied occupation's early years. In 1946, the Americans eliminated traditional Japanese martial arts from school curricula because of their place in wartime militarism and replaced them with Western team sports. Many of the American officials involved in this social engineering project had worked in community sports programs in the United States. Through their expertise and outlook, the idyllic notion of community-based sports and group recreation fertilizing grassroots democracy was infused into the blueprint for Japan's postwar reorientation through education and recreation (Kusafuka 1987, pp. 59–127).

That baseball occupied a central place in the reform of physical education was clear from the preferential treatment the sport received in the rationing of scarce goods and materials. The sports promoters within SCAP argued for the vaunted effects of "wholesome recreations" as inoculation against Japan's potential return to militarism. Their rhetorical strategy yielded a number of dividends for baseball boosters, American and Japanese. Among them was allocation of leather and rubber for the production of baseballs as one of the "emergency priority items" critical to implementing occupation mandates.[4]

Less formal ways of privileging baseball emerged in the everyday interactions between Japanese concerned with the resurrection of baseball and the Eighth Army. American officers not infrequently made a "special case" of releasing baseball equipment for Japanese civilian use. One SCAP report put the number of baseball equipment sets circulated in Japan this way at 8,000.[5] The memoirs written by members of Japan's organized baseball contain a plethora of anecdotal evidence of assistance accorded by SCAP officials in obtaining needed baseball equipment and securing playing fields in the early postwar years, including the benign neglect by the U.S. military police of intercity black market trafficking of baseball equipment.

In using baseball to help the Japanese relearn American-style democracy, the SCAP also promoted spectatorship. Soon after its arrival in Japan, the Eighth Army's top brass began channeling substantial resources into intramural athletic programs, in part to give U.S. military personnel a sense of normalcy amid the alien population. This mandate generated such officially sponsored events as the Thanksgiving Day football game called the Tokyo Rose Bowl and the U.S. Army's own baseball league, consisting of the North Japan League of six baseball teams and a twelve-team equivalent for southern Japan, complete with the postseason "Japan Series" between the two division champions. These baseball games were customarily open to the Japanese public free of charge, even though most U.S. military facilities were off-limits to the locals. The limited choice of playing partners forced U.S. Army teams to engage Japanese collegiate teams in practice games. With a dearth of public entertainment in war-devastated Japan, free amateur ball games often drew crowds in the thousands.[6]

Baseball's amazingly swift postwar reinstatement was also a product of astute lobbying and political entrepreneurship by the holdovers from the prewar Japanese professional baseball league. Shoriki and other baseball boosters strategically targeted officials in the Eighth Army whose love of baseball was well-known. They found a useful ally in Captain Tsuneo (Cappy) Harada, a California-born Japanese American serving as an aide to the director of the SCAP Economic and Science Section, William Marquat. Having played baseball professionally for a West Coast AAA team and almost joined the Tokyo Giants in 1936, Harada proved a useful conduit between Japan's baseball lobby and Marquat. Visual reminders of Japan's prewar allegiance to America's game, such as prewar photographs taken with Babe Ruth and Lou Gehrig, were dutifully presented to SCAP's high officials to garner their sympathetic hearing. Baseball came in handy in this type of backhanded use of soft power by the defeated Japanese (Sano 1994, pp. 376–80; Harada 1980, p. 77).

Under U.S. censorship, a spate of baseball magazines came into circulation in early 1947 amid the still-draconian paper rationing. In these popular venues, Japan's baseball commentators, such as Tobita Suishu, elegized baseball as the mainstay of "democratic people's sports" becoming of the New Democratic Japan. The inaugural issue of the magazine *Yakyu Shonen* (Baseball boys) is emblematic of this new invented orthodoxy. Along with Japanese professional baseball players and U.S. major league stars such as Bob Feller of the Cleveland Indians, the newly launched boys' magazine featured a photograph of young crown prince Akihito with the caption "His Imperial Highness loves all sports, but especially baseball. He tries to perfect his swing while taking a break from his school work. Let sports be the engine of Japan's rebirth." The Japanese knew that their American overlord had a soft spot for baseball.[7]

The symbolic connection between baseball and Japan's postwar redemption was concocted by both parties, and it received its most dramatic public display at Korakuen Stadium in October 1949. The occasion was the SCAP-sanctioned tour of Japan by the San Francisco Seals, the New York Yankees' AAA franchise in the Pacific Coast League. The team's manager, Lefty O'Doul, a former New York Giant, had participated in the 1931 Japan exhibition circuit. The nation's economy was then still stymied in a debilitating dollar shortage, and strict foreign exchange control remained in place. The Japanese baseball community's ability to host the undertaking, billed "the U.S.-Japan Friendship Tour," thus depended on whether requisite amounts of the now-almighty U.S. dollar could be secured for this commercial enterprise. With Marquat's intercession, the SCAP's financial adviser, Joseph Dodge, the stern gatekeeper of the Japanese currency reserves, authorized the use of dollar proceeds from ticket sales to U.S. military personnel to cover the costs of the Seals' six-week tour (Harada 1980, pp. 110–13).

Under a clear October sky, the Japanese public saw the Rising Sun flag hoisted next to the Star Spangled Banner and their national anthem played publicly and broadcast over the national radio for the first time since Japan's surrender. Mrs. Douglas MacArthur, with Marquat at her side, threw the ceremonial first pitch of the game between the Seals and the Yomiuri Giants. Only the presence of the supreme commander himself could have topped this carefully choreographed public ritual of Japan's postwar redemption and rebirth into a U.S. ally through baseball. The American military ruler further delighted the Japanese baseball fans by granting permission to purchase coveted post exchange (PX) food and beverages with the yen at the game's concession stands. A taste of Coca-Cola, hot dogs, and Hershey's chocolate bars indulged by the lucky Japanese baseball fans during the Seals' national tour undoubtedly taught them that the self-professed benevolent military ruler and the pastime it officially endorsed brought to their country benefits beyond democracy: They came with the seductive appeal of consumer abundance and material comfort promised in this sacred American creed.[8] If this is not soft power in play, what is?

Baseball in the Postwar World: A Shared Avenue of Soft Power

The Allied occupation of Japan ended in 1952, and Japan launched into a dizzying economic ascent soon afterward. Riding on the crest of the unprecedented postwar economic boom that began in the mid-1950s, Japanese professional baseball grew into a successful mass entertainment industry. With the two-league structure, the interleague postseason championship series, and the independent commissioner's office, Japanese organized baseball bore the unmistakable imprint of its American prototype. The sport also became a truly mass-appealing commercial enterprise with the advent and rapid diffusion of television. The Yomiuri Giants, the Tokyo-based titan, which boasted twin superstars on its roaster, the flamboyant Nagashima Shigeo and the introspective Oh Sadaharu, stood to gain from its parent company's tie-up with a leading national TV and radio network.

As professional baseball matured as an industrial sector, it mirrored some of the central features of "Japan Incorporated," chief among them insular labor recruitment practices. In its prewar fledging phase, Japanese professional baseball accepted onto its rosters American players of Japanese descent, but the prewar professional baseball association's bylaws stipulated that, except for specially approved cases, only Japanese nationals were allowed to play as professionals in Japan (Nagata 1994). In the early postwar years, Japanese Americans continued to fill the talent void left by the war deaths of many top players. After this brief transition, however, professional baseball became yet another Japanese business sector with a restrictive system of hiring foreign nationals. After 1953, the quota for players with non-Japanese citizenship was set at three per team. The new industrywide agreement adopted in 1966 reduced the number to two. In 1981, the restriction was relaxed ever so slightly, with the permitted number of foreign players restored to three, but only two could be placed on the active roster at any given time (Kitaya 1992, p. 167). In the halcyon days of championship glory in the 1960s and 1970s, the Yomiuri Giants famously excluded gaijin (foreign) players from its ranks in the name of *junketsushugi* (the pure blood principle). Besides the carefully controlled infusion of talent from the U.S. majors, Japanese professional baseball's engagement with its American counterpart was limited to the latter's biannual postseason exhibition tours of Japan. Fans were exposed only to scattered references to the major league's game results and player statistics in the print media. A career in the big leagues remained but a distant dream for Japanese baseball players, professional or amateur.

The globalization of commercialized baseball and Major League Baseball's aggressive player recruitment outside the continental U.S. in the latter half of the twentieth century, however, did not allow Japan to be an insulated enclave of play. A border-breaching trend in the major league's talent scouting originated in the Western Hemisphere and reverberated across the Pacific. Starting in the early postwar years, after Jackie Robinson broke the major league's once-impenetrable color barrier, the U.S. major league teams and some minor league teams began to draw in growing numbers prospects from Cuba, the Dominican Republic, Puerto Rico, and Venezuela, where "America's game" had long been an entrenched aspect of the local cultural landscape, a legacy of the northern colossus's ubiquitous military presence in the hemisphere over the previous century. In the Caribbean incubator of Major League Baseball (MLB) talents, youthful sandlot players would eagerly sign up for what to North Americans amounted to mere pocket change and pursued the American Dream with a Latin beat. Even Cuba's rabidly anti-American revolutionary leader Fidel Castro was nearly recruited into the New York Giants for a contract with a $5,000 signing bonus ten years prior to his triumphant march to Havana that installed a socialist state in America's background (Paterson 1994, p. 51).

Unlike the major league teams' hunting ground in the Caribbean basin, Japan, as a talent source, was considered neither cheap nor technically up to par through much of the postwar period. The singular exception to the absence of Japanese players on major league teams' rosters was Murakami Masanori. His stint with the San Francisco Giants in the 1964 season and an ensuing contractual dispute between the Giants and his Japanese home team, Nankai Hawks, led to a falling out between the national commissioner's offices and a thirty-year-long hiatus in U.S.-Japanese talent exchange. In the 1995 season, another Japanese native, by the name of Nomo Hideo, finally ended this draught and donned a Los Angeles Dodgers uniform. The Japanese rookie pitcher with a unique twirling delivery generated a minicraze among American baseball fans, dubbed "Nomomania." The Osaka native's venture onto baseball's home turf began when, after a salary dispute, he defied the player reserve system of the Japanese Major League (JML), whose field of vision did not quite anticipate cross-border player jumping. Nomo single-handedly scuttled the JML's unexpectedly fragile institutional confines, reflecting the proclivity of the Japanese X Generation to define work and weigh career options unencumbered by the existing conventions of corporate Japan. Once the levy was breached, America's big business, professional sports included, stood ready to tap into this new offshore reservoir of talent and began to entice premier Japanese players, such Sasaki Kazuyoshi and Irabu Hideki, with the glitz and glare of major league fame and megasize American professional sports salaries. In 2001, Suzuki Ichiro, the seven-time leading hitter in the Pacific League, became the first Japanese position player to break into the major leagues. Ichiro's fabulous first-year performance landed him a place on the All-Star Game roster for the American League and the Rookie of the Year title. Matsui Hideki's decision to seek his own glory in the majors soon followed (Whiting 2004, pp. 96–117). The transpacific migration of several top-tier Japanese talents necessitated that the two national ruling bodies of professional baseball formulate a *modus vivendi* on player recruitment in the integrating global baseball labor market. In effect since 1998, the current bilateral agreement requires that American clubs bid for rights to negotiate with their Japanese prospects and only then is permission or free agency status granted to Japanese players aspiring to a career in the U.S majors.

It was not just because of the individual pioneer spirits of players such as Nomo and Ichiro that the U.S.-Japanese cross-pollination of baseball talents accelerated in the past decade. Technological breakthroughs since the mid-1970s have also played a key role. New communication and transportation technologies have facilitated the integration of baseball spectatorship across national boundaries and helped create global sports icons who command a truly transnational mass following. Basketball superstar Michael Jordan readily comes to mind (LaFeber 1999, p. 2). Baseball was no exception to this technology-spurred globalizing trend in mass culture. Satellite and cable TVs, and, after the mid-1990s, the Internet made it possible for Japanese baseball fans to get instant and real-time coverage of major league games in their living rooms and on their desktops. The widespread household use of video players turned the once-insurmountable obstacle of differing time zones in the expansive transpacific world into only a minor inconvenience. Wired into these intersecting informational networks, Ichiro's fans can now watch their native son and hero break George Sisler's eighty-four-year-old single-season hit record against the backdrop of a throng of on-site Ichiro admirers consisting of Seattle locals and package tourists from Japan. Stateside fans of Godzilla—now given the new American epithet Big Matsui—have simply to point and click to read the Web version of the *New York Times* article anointing their hero the apotheosis of "Yankee Ingenuity via Japan" for his exemplary hard work, sportsmanship, and graciousness, the same litany of qualities that made him the darling of Japanese baseball lovers, Giants fans or not. Ichiro-viewing package tours to Seattle are now a major revenue source for the local economy. The field of dreams has now become transpacific for players and fans alike.[9]

In the new millennium, the commingling trend in American and Japanese baseball talent is no longer limited to the player pools. Just last year, JML watchers on both sides of the Pacific were treated to the rare spectacle of Bobby Valentine piloting the Lotte Chiba Marines to the pinnacle of the 2005 pennant race. The story of Valentine's initial recruitment ten years prior as the Lotte Marines' gaijin manager, his dramatic dismissal a year later, and his rehiring in 2003 for a three-year, $2.5 million-per-year contract, highlights the change, albeit at glacier speed, that Japanese professional baseball is now undergoing. More than player rosters, posts of field managing and coaching in Japanese professional baseball had remained closed to foreign nationals. Only two

Japanese Americans, Yoshio "Kaiser" Tanaka and Tadashi "Bozo" Wakabayashi, were deemed familiar enough with the Japanese way of doing things because of their Japanese ancestry and given a chance to manage a Japanese professional team in the early postwar years. Wally Yonamine, a second-generation Japanese American from Hawaii with ten years as a player for the Yomiuri Giants under his belt, managed the Chunichi Dragons and successfully led it to the Central League championship in 1974.

And yet in the following two decades, only a small handful of Americans, such as Don Blasingame (Blazer), rendered coaching and managerial performance ranging from abysmal to mediocre. After Valentine's forced departure at the end of the 1995 season, two Americans occupied managerial posts, both in the 2003 season: Trey Hillman for the Nippon Ham Fighters and Leon Lee as interim manager of the Orix BlueWave when his predecessor Hiromichi Ishige was fired in midseason (Whiting 2004, pp. 174–76). Valentine's return to JML to the delight of his Japanese admirers at the end of the same season and his managing feat two years later proved to skeptics that nothing innately Japanese is required for fielding a winning team in the JML after all. At the very least, Japanese kids on the grandstand of Lotte Marines Stadium cheering for *Barentain kantoku* seem to think so.

As a globalizing sport, baseball has become a soft power resource employable by many nations besides the United States, and what happened in March 2006 was telling proof of it. In the World Baseball Classic (WBC) held in the United States, Japan, and Puerto Rico, the U.S. team took an early exit after losing to Mexico in the tournament's second round, and the final game was played between Japan, whose roster included only two MLB players, and Cuba, whose participation was jeopardized at one point by the U.S. government's inveterately anti-Castro policy. MLB commissioner Bud Selig had presided for the previous two years over the planning and negotiations that culminated in the sixteen-nation, four-round baseball tournament. The MLB kingpin proposed the event to enhance baseball's worldwide visibility and develop a following in nations where the sport had yet to be popularized. From the planning stages, support of JML and its players' union was critical. During WBC, the mainstream U.S. media lavished praise on the Japanese team, which claimed the championship at the venue provided by MLB's ruling body. The *New York Times* bannered its report of the Japanese WBC victory with the title "For the Love of Yakyu." ESPN's Web report dubbed Japan's WBC title "The New World Order." Hardly any chagrin was openly expressed about the Japanese besting the Americans at their own game.[10]

How are we to make sense of all these remarkable developments in the U.S.-Japanese baseball exchange over the past 130-plus years? The enduring nature of baseball as soft power in U.S.-Japanese encounters offers one answer. Precisely because soft power purports to generate yearning, admiration, and resulting emulation, the longer it is exerted through an avenue, the more compatible, if not identical, both parties may grow in that particular site of long-term interaction. In this shared arena, it is thus no surprise if the exercise of soft power should become more reciprocal, mutual, and self-sustaining over time. Nye's theory of soft power seems to posit, at least implicitly, that this type of influence flows in one direction, but cannot the efficacy of soft power be measured in terms of the attainment of this reciprocity or mutuality as well as imperviousness to hard power pressures frequently exerted in the iron-clad units of the nation-state? In other words, the ultimate test of soft power depends on how stable and mutual that exercise of power will become. As Nye has noted, "soft-power resources often work indirectly by shaping the environment for policy, . . . although [they] sometimes take years to produce the desired outcomes" (Nye 2004, p. 99). The more durable and reciprocal a channel of soft power is, the more its constitutive members identify "the other side" as part of who they are and what they value. When such amalgamation takes place, they become capable of imagining the others' needs, interests, and aspirations as real, legitimate, and in need of fulfilling. Is this not the "environment of policy" that Nye said might be fostered through soft power? If so, baseball in U.S.-Japanese relations has attained many of the key attributes of a shared font of soft power. Hail to Pacific-straddling swatters and hurlers.

Notes

1. Telegram from Foreign Minister Shidehara to Consul General Sawada in New York, November 20, 1930, Foreign Ministry Archives.
2. *Yomiuri Shinbun,* November 3, 1934.
3. *Pacific Stars and Stripes,* November 2 and 22, 1945.
4. "Nippon no Taiiku," "Physical Education Projects," September 26, 1946, Box 5445, CIE Records, CIE Special Report (166-SR-A); "Conference on the Production of Athletic Equipment," Box 5727, CIE Records.
5. "Physical Education Officer: Conference Reports," Box 5734, CIE Records.
6. *Pacific Stars and Stripes,* October 8, 1945, February 17, 1946.
7. *Yakyu Shonen* 1, 1 (April 1947).
8. *Pacific Stars and Stripes,* October 17, 1949; *Yomiuri Shinbun,* October 16, 1949.
9. *New York Times,* March 20, 2005.
10. *New York Times,* March 22, 2006.

References

Abe, Isoo. 1905. "Waseda daigaku yakyu senshu tobeiki-20" (Waseda University baseball players American tour). *Tokyo Asahi Shinbun,* July 3.
Goldstein, Warren. 1989. *Playing for Keeps.* Ithaca, NY: Cornell University Press.
Grew, Joseph. 1948. *Tainichi Junen.* Tokyo: Mainichi Shinbusha.
Guthrie-Shimizu, Sayuri. 2004. "For Love of the Game." *Diplomatic History* 28 (5): 637–62.
Guttman, Allen, and Lee Thompson. 2001. *Japanese Sports.* Honolulu: University of Hawaii Press.
Harada, Cappy. 1980. *Taiheiyo no kakehashi* (A bridge across the Pacific). Tokyo: Besuboru Magajinsha.
Hashido Makoto. 1905. *Saishin Yakyujutsu* (Brand new baseball techniques). Tokyo: Hakubunkan.
Ikei, Masaru. 1977. *Hakkyu taiheiyo wo wataru* (White baseballs traverse the Pacific). Tokyo: Chuo Koron.
Imada, Adriana. 2004. "Hawaiians on Tour: Hula Circuits Through the American Empire." *American Quarterly* 56 (1): 111–49.
Kamei, Shunsuke. 1979. *Meriken kara Amerika e* (From meriken to America). Tokyo: Tokyo Daigaku Shuppankai.

Keio Gijuku Daigaku Yakyubu. *Yakyubushi* (The chronicle of the baseball club). 1989. Tokyo: Keiou Gijuku Taiikukai Yakyubu.

Kiku, Koji. 1993. *Kindai puro suportsu no rekishi shakaigaku* (A historical sociology of modern professional sport). Tokyo: Fumaido.

Kirsh, George. 2003. *Baseball in Blue and Grey.* Princeton, NJ: Princeton University Press.

Kitaya, Yukiya. 1992. *Puro yakyu no keiseigaku* (A study of how professional baseball was created). Tokyo: Tokyo Keizai Shinposha.

Kumamoto Nichinichi Shinbusha. 1967. *Kumamoto no tairyoku* (Athletic activity in Kumamoto). Kumamoto: Kumamoto Nichinichisha.

Kusafuka, Naoomi. 1987. "Taiiku Supotsu no Sengo Kaikakuni Kansuru Daiichiji Beikoku Kyoiku Shisetsudan Hokokusho no Sakusei Katei" (The making of the official report of the first post-war mission on postwar athletic reform). *Taiikugaku Kenkyu* [Keneology] 41:27–59.

LaFeber, Walter. 1999. *Michael Jordan and the New Global Capitalism.* New York: Norton.

Levine, Peter. 1985. *A.G. Spaulding and the Rise of American Baseball.* New York: Oxford University Press.

Nagata, Yoichi. 1994. *Besu boru no Shakaishi* (A social history of baseball). Osaka: Toho Shuppan.

Nye, Joseph S., Jr. 2004. *Soft Power: The Means to Success in World Politics.* New York: Public Affairs.

Oshima, Masatake. 1958. *Kuraku sensei to sono deshitachi* (Professor Clark and his students). Tokyo: Hobunkan.

Paterson, Thomas. 1994. *Contesting Castro.* New York: Oxford University Press.

Perez, Louis A., Jr. 1994. "Between Baseball and Bullfighting." *Journal of American History* 81 (2): 493–517.

Reach & Co. 1909. *The Reach 1909 Base Ball Guide.* Philadelphia: Reach & Co.

Reaves, Jose A. 2002. *Taking in a Game.* Lincoln: University of Nebraska Press.

Sakaue, Hiroyasu. 2001. *Nippon yakyuno keifugaku* (A chronicle of Japanese baseball). Tokyo: Seikyusha.

Sano, Shinichi. 1994. *Kyokaiden* (A portrait of a titan). Tokyo: Bungei Shunju.

Suzuki, Akira. 1978. *Showa 20nen 11 gatsu 23 nichi no Pureboru* ("Playball" on 23 November, 1945). Tokyo: Sogosha.

Suzuki, Ryuji. 1984. *Puro Yakyu to Tomoni 50-nen* (50 years with professional baseball). Tokyo: Besuboru Magajinsha.

Suzuki, Sotaro. 1983. *Fumetsu no Daitoshu Sawamura Eiji* (Sawamura Eiji, an invincible great hurler). Tokyo: Besuboru Magajinsha.

Tobita, Suishu. 1950. *Waseda daigaku yakyubu gojunenshi* (50-year chronicle of Waseda university baseball club). Tokyo: Waseda Daigaku.

Watanabe, Masao. 1996. *Oyatoi Beikokujin kagaku kyoshi* (Science teachers in government employ). Rev. ed. Tokyo: Hokuyosha.

Whiting, Robert. 2004. *Meaning of Ichiro.* New York: Warner Books.

10

American Pop Culture as Soft Power

Movies and Broadcasting

Matthew Fraser

Pop culture is arguably the most fascinating, and controversial, instrument of American soft power. It is fascinating thanks to the worldwide appeal of the American leisure and entertainment industries and their globally famous pop icons—from Madonna and MTV to McDonald's and Mickey Mouse. Nearly the entire population of the planet has ready access, as consumers, to the symbolic universe in which these pop icons exercise their influence. Their elevation to the complex realm of international diplomacy and geopolitics is inevitably intriguing.

The role of pop culture in this sphere is also controversial. Some claim that a focus on pop culture trivializes analysis of a complex dynamic that includes more important forms of soft power influence, such as public policy and educational programs. Soft power, it is argued, is more than Mickey Mouse, Madonna, McDonald's, and MTV. And yet American pop culture provokes deeply paradoxical reactions, inspiring awe and anger depending on the specific regional context. Terms such as "Coca-Colonization" and "McDomination" are not neutral (Kuisal 1993; Pells 1997). As former U.S. secretary of state Madeleine Albright observed at a White House conference shortly before leaving office in late 2000, "There are some who describe our country as hegemonic, equate globalization with Americanization, and say unkind things about our hamburgers" (Fraser 2005, pp. 18–19). The violent acts against McDonald's around the world provide graphic evidence that American mass culture is so powerful that its most recognizable logos are frequently regarded as symbols of America itself. Pop culture may trivialize the discussion of American foreign policy, yet its symbolic potency makes it a real and unavoidable force.

More substantively, it is difficult, if not impossible, to quantify the influence of pop culture. Whatever its appeal, pop culture does not produce measurable *effects,* let alone desired outcomes, where it is consumed around the world. Specifically, it cannot be demonstrated that the extension of pop culture—whether the export of Hollywood movies or the global popularity of Anglo-American pop songs—mobilizes action that promotes the conditions for pluralism, freedom of expression, and democracy. No one would seriously claim that North Korea's communist dictator, Kim Jong Il, is likely to end his country's nuclear arms buildup and open its domestic market to free trade merely because he is an avowed fan of Hollywood movies and hero-worships American basketball superstar Michael Jordan (Fraser 2005). A direct causal link between the consumption of American pop culture and democratic reform cannot be demonstrated.

Indeed, American pop culture is widely consumed in countries where populations live under authoritarian regimes. Even theocracies are sometimes powerless against the appeal of American pop culture. Iran's ayatollahs banned satellite TV in order to keep out proscribed channels such as MTV, but no fiat or fatwa could prevent countless thousands of satellite dishes from mushrooming on rooftops throughout Tehran's suburbs. Twenty years after the 1979 revolution, not only were Iran's satellite laws liberalized, but also a pop concert in Tehran was permitted by religious authorities (Nye 2004; Fraser 2005).

In his 1995 book, *Jihad vs McWorld*, Benjamin Barber observed that Islamic extremism and Western capitalism are paradoxically interdependent and have in common their hostility to democracy. Barber's McWorld is a vast shopping mall populated by soulless consumers who eat Big Macs and drink Coca-Cola. McWorld embraces free markets, but not necessarily democratic institutions (Barber 1995).

The attraction of pop culture may not lead directly to liberal reforms in countries whose regimes are hostile to freedom and democracy, but its messages, when consumed receptively, are often embraced as symbols of values associated with individualism and freedom of expression—and can lead to social and political change when these desires are mobilized into collective action. The German youths who smashed the Berlin Wall were wearing T-shirts emblazoned with the MTV logo. The chairman of the U.S. government's Board of Broadcast Governors even asserted that "it was MTV that brought down the Berlin Wall" ("Department of Propaganda" 2002).

It is also argued that, whatever the influence of pop culture, the U.S. government should not be involved in the dissemination of its messages in the execution of American foreign policy. Culture, it is argued, should be left to nonstate actors. The role of states in the dissemination of pop culture indeed is controversial. Those who argue against the role of states in cultural soft power projects have no shortage of examples where these efforts have failed. A recent example was the closure of the Arab-language magazine *Hi*, which the U.S. State Department had financed and targeted at youth in the Arab-speaking world (Pipes 2005). Similarly, two U.S. government–sponsored broadcasters in the Middle East—satellite TV network Alhurra and pop radio station Sawa—encountered criticism for their lack of credibility as American soft power resources (Riding 2005). These criticisms may have merit, yet they tend to focus on the Islamic world, which presents a challenge for American soft power due to the region's difficult adjustment to modernity, the hostility of religious elites, and the deep cultural divide between the West and the Arab world (Huntington 1996). The fact remains, however, that American pop culture—as we shall see with examples of movies and broadcasting later in this chapter—has been deployed, with varying degrees of effectiveness, as part of American foreign policy for nearly a century. Every U.S. president from Woodrow Wilson to George W. Bush has been aware of the strategic importance of American cultural power.

The American movie and broadcasting industries provide abundant evidence of the strategic importance of pop culture in the formulation of U.S. foreign policy. They also offer powerful examples of the profoundly contradictory reactions that American pop culture provokes around the world. As we shall see, the attraction of American soft power in the pop cultural sphere depends largely on the underlying *value systems* in regions where it is disseminated and received by local populations. In Western countries, where populations broadly share liberal and secular values associated with individualism and democracy, American movies and broadcasting signals generally have been success-ful and popular. Local elites in some Western countries, to be sure, have attempted to restrict the importation of American cultural products, and indeed often have evoked cultural justifications for their opposition, but these gestures have tended to be motivated by commercial protectionism. Beyond the West, hostile reactions to American cultural products have been motivated, on the contrary, by a profound antipathy toward the un-derlying values conveyed by American cultural messages. China's ruling communists and authoritarian leaders in the Middle East are not particularly concerned about the balance of payments when they restrict or ban American cultural imports. Rather, they feel threatened by the mobilizing—and potentially destabilizing—effects of American movies and satellite TV signals that reach their populations. At noted above, American culture is resisted with particular vehemence in Muslim countries governed by regimes whose authority is based on religious legitimacy.

From a theoretical perspective, analysis of American soft power is usually situ-ated within a neoliberal approach, which emphasizes the role of nonstate actors and the importance of ideas and values in the shaping of foreign policy. The export of American values and lifestyles via Hollywood and satellite TV indeed fits neatly into neoliberal models. Yet the commercial exportation of American cultural products has never been a purely moral mission undertaken by nonstate actors, whether Hollywood producers or CNN executives. The U.S. government has never been indifferent to the commercial advantages procured by American cultural exports. In like manner, America's trading partners have long been concerned about the negative impact on the national balance of payments when their markets are awash in American cultural products. It can be argued, therefore, that U.S. government behavior as a promoter of American soft power has been characterized not solely by high-minded idealism, but also by a more pragmatic approach that belongs squarely in the realist tradition in international diplomacy. Moral idealism and commercial realism may be strange bedfellows, but they are nonetheless constant companions in American foreign policy when domestically produced cultural products are being exported globally. They oper-ate simultaneously, symbiotically, even paradoxically.

Hollywood: Ambassador to the World

The United States was emerging as a global power at precisely the time, circa 1900, when movies were spreading worldwide as a new form of mass entertainment. The American movie market actually was dominated by French films at that time, but French dominance quickly faded as inventor Thomas Edison and his associates gained control of the domestic U.S. and international markets with a combination of monopolistic practices and populist American movies (Abel 1999). By the outbreak of the First World War in 1914, American movies had conquered the planet.

President Woodrow Wilson, a moral idealist, was predisposed to regard movies as a useful instrument of American foreign policy. Hollywood producers, too, saw the promise of movies as weapons of American soft power. The National Association of the Motion Picture Industry sent the following statement in a memo to President Wilson: "The motion picture can be the most wonderful system for spreading national propaganda at little or no cost." Wilson agreed. He believed Hollywood could serve as a vehicle for American values—the "Gospel of Americanism"—to take hold throughout the world. In a wartime speech, Wilson declared, "The film has come to rank as the very highest medium for the dissemination of public intelligence. And since it speaks a universal language, it lends itself importantly to the presentation of America's plans and purposes" (Rosenberg 1982, Chap. 4). Thus, the White House's moral idealism and Hollywood's commercial ambitions were married and consummated in a context of global conflict. The marriage would be enduring.

President Wilson set up the Congressional Committee on Public Information—known as the Creel Committee after its driving force, George Creel—whose mission was to promote the Wilsonian vision of a world peace and democracy. At the same time, Creel exercised tremendous power over Hollywood movies through the U.S. War Trade Board, which approved films for export. Creel banned for export any movie that portrayed "false" American values or conveyed negative images of the United States. One film singled out for censorship was *Jesse James,* which portrayed the larcenous career of the infamous American outlaw. President Wilson, meanwhile, summoned mogul Samuel Goldwyn to the White House and urged him to rush as many Hollywood films as possible to war-torn France so America could win the hearts of the French. Among Hollywood's anti-German movies of the period were *The Kaiser: The Beast of Berlin* and Cecil B. DeMille's *The Little American,* starring Mary Pickford, who was known as "America's sweetheart." Pickford, along with her husband, Douglas Fairbanks, and Charlie Chaplin, used her celebrity to promote the sale of wartime U.S. liberty bonds. The three Hollywood stars also conducted a world tour financed by the State Department. After one trip, Pickford declared, "The cheering crowds of the Far East were shouting not for me, but for the American motion picture and the American people and for the world of make-believe. Therefore, I hold that, in a large sense, we were ambassadors not only of the motion picture, but of our own country" (Seagrave 1997, p. 93). It was also during this period that Hollywood began producing anti-Japanese movies, drumming up fears about the so-called yellow peril. Perhaps the best-known of these films at the time was DeMille's 1915 movie *The Cheat,* in which Japanese movie star Hayakawa Sessue played a shifty Asian whose Zen-like charms seduce the gullible Fanny Ward. The following year, a film called *The Yellow Menace* was released. Hollywood was not only patriotic, but often xenophobic according to crass stereotypes of the era (Corliss 2001).

When World War I ended, the United States was the world's leading creditor nation. President Wilson, the most powerful player at Versailles in 1919, owed a great debt to Hollywood, whose motion pictures were now a mass cultural extension of America's newfound global power. The White House even declared movies to be an "essential industry" (Balio 1985). In 1922, the Hollywood studios established a lobby group called the Motion Picture Producers and Distributors of America, whose first president, Will Hays, was a longtime Republican political organizer who had managed President Warren Harding's successful election campaign in 1920. The most powerful Hollywood mogul of the era, Louis B. Mayer, also enjoyed proximity to political power. Mayer played a key role in Herbert Hoover's presidential election campaign in 1928. When Hoover won the election, his first dinner guests at the White House were Mr. and Mrs. Louis B. Mayer (Brownstein 1990, p. 35).

During the Depression, when capitalism seemed to have failed, communism began to loom as a serious threat to liberal democracy. Hollywood became a hotbed of radical politics, but the studio moguls used their powers to make movies that promoted capitalism and incited fear of the "red menace." Movies such as *The House of Rothschild* were unmistakable tributes to capitalism and banking. On a more populist note, the homespun optimism of child star Shirley Temple encouraged Americans to remain faithful to their basic values. During the Second World War, Hollywood was transformed into a propaganda factory. The U.S. Office of Wartime Information, created by President Franklin Roosevelt, worked closely with Hollywood to produce movies such as *Wilson,* which glorified Woodrow Wilson's crusade to create the League of Nations and create a new world order (Rosenberg 1982; Seagrave 1997). Walt Disney, whose Mickey Mouse cartoon character was now globally famous, also joined the war effort by churning out propaganda films featuring Mickey and Donald Duck. A memorable Disney cartoon of the era was *Donald Gets Drafted,* in which Donald Duck triumphs over petty irritations to fulfill his patriotic duty as a soldier. Another anti-Nazi cartoon was *Der Fuehrer's Face,* featuring Donald working at a munitions factory in a country called Nutziland. The Oscar-winning film, released in 1943, shows Donald Duck fighting against the torments of totalitarianism and, in the end, saluting the Statue of Liberty and shouting, "I am glad to be a citizen of the United States." By the early 1940s, roughly a third of the entire planet's population had seen at least one Disney film (Watts 1997, Chap. 12).

Since Japan was an Axis power allied to Nazi Germany, the war marked a resurgence of virulently anti-Japanese movies in which the enemy were portrayed as slit-eyed "Japs" with a malicious bent for torture. The advertisement for the 1943 film *China* exorted cinema-goers to see the movie with this teaser: "Alan Ladd and twenty girls—trapped by the rapacious Japs!" One film in this genre was the 1944 film *The Purple Heart,* about the cruel treatment of American soldiers captured by the Japanese. Japan's relationship with Hollywood had been ambivalent before World War II. When the Great Kanto Earthquake destroyed much of Tokyo in 1923, most of the nascent Japanese movie industry was decimated in the rubble. This tragedy created a cinematic vacuum for the importation of Hollywood and other foreign movies that would inspire a whole generation of young Japanese filmmakers. In the 1930s, the emperor's government took a hands-on approach toward the domestic movie industry as part of its policy of "national imperialism" that resulted in the invasion of China. During this period, many Japanese films were censored, and some filmmakers with Marxist inclinations were assassinated. Movie distribution was strictly controlled by a cartel of two Japanese companies, Toho and Shochiku. During the Second World War, Japan shut the door completely on American movies.

After the war, when a defeated Japan fell under American control, the Japanese entered a period of emulation of American institutions, values, and habits. In the wake of Hiroshima, Hollywood movies about Japan in the 1950s—such *Sayonara* starring Marlon Brando playing an U.S. Air Force pilot who falls in love with a Japanese actress—were more sentimental. In the real world, Japan—forced by Washington to adopt U.S.-style political institutions—also adopted Hollywood's model of the vertically integrated movie studio combining production, distribution, and theatrical exhibition. As in Hollywood, this industrial model was highly efficient and produced many superlative Japanese movies. Kurosawa Akira, arguably Japan's greatest movie director, emerged in Japanese cinema during this period. In 1950, Kurosawa made *Rashomon*—about the mysterious death of a samurai—which won the Oscar for best foreign film. Kurosawa's debt to American cinema was repaid when his *Seven Samurai* inspired the Hollywood movie *The Magnificent Seven.*

Following the Second World War, Hollywood increasingly turned its energies toward America's confrontation with Soviet communism. When the House Un-American Activities Committee arrived in Hollywood, Walt Disney belonged to a high-profile group of Hollywood anticommunists that included actors Ronald Reagan, Robert Montgomery, and Gary Cooper. Disney told the House Un-American Activities Committee that a labor strike at his studio had been concocted by "Commie front organizations," adding that the communist campaign against Disney extended well beyond America's borders. "Throughout the world all of the Commie groups began smear campaigns against me and my pictures," he stated. It was Walt Disney's abiding belief that America's destiny was, in his words, to "export values, institutions, and politics of democracy and capitalism to achieve a peaceful dominion over the rest of the world" (Watts 1997, p. 287).

In Europe, Hollywood provided a soft power component to the Marshall Plan. As part of the Marshall Plan's two-pronged strategy, economic aid and cultural exports worked in tandem. Accordingly, the Hollywood studios received roughly $10 million in direct subsidies as part of the U.S. European Recovery Plan. One American senator called on Hollywood to contribute to "a worldwide Marshall Plan in the field of ideas." A Hollywood producer put it more succinctly: "Donald Duck as World Diplomat!" (Puttnam 1998, p. 159). Hollywood's new chief lobbyist was Eric Johnston, who, like his predecessor, Will Hays, was well connected at the White House. Johnston had worked as an emissary for FDR and met frequently with President Harry Truman. Under Johnston, the Motion Picture Association of America was referred to as the "Little State Department" (Fraser 2005, p. 55).

Hollywood's postwar diplomatic skills were put to the test in France, which was in a ruinous state of economic collapse. The U.S. Army's Psychological Warfare Division flooded the French market with some 400 prints of the latest Hollywood movies in a campaign called "Arsenal of Democracy." The Hollywood movies were immediately popular with French audiences, who were eager to watch, for the first time, films such as *Gone with the Wind*. French elites were less enamored of the Hollywood product. In 1945, following national elections in which the Socialists and Communists won 50 percent of the popular vote, there was talk of nationalizing the French movie industry. Both Hollywood and the White House were alarmed. In an atmosphere of mutual suspicion, the French and U.S. governments instigated bilateral negotiations. According to an agreement reached in 1946, the United States agreed to wipe out France's war debt, to provide a $318 million loan, and to accord France $650 million in credits from the U.S. Export-Import Bank. Washington insisted on, and obtained, one trade-off as part of the accord: France must eliminate prewar import restrictions on American movies. Outraged, French Communist leader Maurice Thorez declared that American films "poison the souls of our children, young people, young girls, who are to be turned into the docile slaves of the American multimillionaires, and not into French men and women attached to the moral and intellectual values which have been the grandeur and glory of our nation." (Fraser 2005, p. 57)

Hollywood met similar resistance in other European countries, including Britain, where the domestic film industry was heavily unionized and interest groups lobbied for import duties. The British government, worried about a negative balance of payments, imposed a 75 percent ad valorem tax on Hollywood movies in 1947. The following year, however, Britain buckled under U.S. pressures and watered down its restrictions (Seagrave 1997; Fraser 2005).

In 1948, the U.S. State Department created a program called Informational Media Guaranty, which boosted Hollywood by giving movie studios dollars in exchange for soft foreign currencies earned in Europe. In effect, the State Department was subsidizing the distribution of Hollywood movies in foreign countries where local currencies were blocked by foreign exchange restrictions. There was one proviso: to qualify for the currency conversions, Hollywood studios were obliged to export movies that portrayed American life and values in a positive manner as part of the Truman administration's Cold War soft power campaign in Europe.

Some Hollywood movies of the period were explicitly anti-Soviet, such as the 1950 film *I Married a Communist,* starring Robert Ryan playing a radical who is blackmailed into working for the Soviet Union. In Washington, meanwhile, the House Un-American Activities Committee was stepping up its investigation into suspected Hollywood communists. Some Hollywood liberals, such as Humphrey Bogart, attempted to shame the House Un-American Activities Committee hearings, but theirs was a minority voice. Hollywood moguls were keen to send a message to Washington, and the world, that the American movie industry was not infiltrated by Soviet spies and leftist subversives. In November 1947, Hollywood moguls issued a "Waldorf Statement" declaring that suspected procommunist screenwriters would be blackballed. McCarthyism was just around the corner.

The Kremlin banned Hollywood movies, yet they still were popular in Russia and Soviet-bloc countries as a forbidden fruit. In the late 1950s, Washington and Moscow finally signed a cultural exchange agreement that allowed a limited number of Hollywood movies into Soviet bloc countries. The Soviet Union chose ten American movies for distribution, including *Oklahoma, Roman Holiday, The Old Man and the Sea, The 7th Voyage of Sinbad,* and *Man of a Thousand Faces.* Under State Department orders, however, Hollywood refused to sell the Soviets any movie that portrayed America in a negative light, such as *Elmer Gantry* and *Dr. Strangelove.* Still, other movies exported to Soviet-controlled countries—such as *Sunset Boulevard, All About Eve, On the Waterfront,* and *East of Ed*en—were hardly propagandistic testimonials to the virtues of American society (Pells 1997, p. 215). The export of these movies showed, if anything, that America was an open society where self-criticism was an accepted part of life in a liberal democracy.

In 1966, when Jack Valenti—an aide and close confidant of President Lyndon Johnson—became head of the Hollywood lobby, he boasted that "the motion picture industry is the only U.S. enterprise that negotiates on its own with foreign governments" (McDougal 1998, p. 320). Valenti lobbied Washington with great skill and finesse, but his attitude toward foreign markets owed more to realpolitik. Hollywood was becoming increasingly aggressive with foreign markets as its dependence on international revenues grew. Valenti was successful in convincing Washington that Hollywood's fortunes abroad were tied to American prestige around the world. The White House was particularly receptive to Hollywood's message in the 1980s, when the pervasive mood about U.S. power and prestige was bleak. There was a great deal of foreboding talk of American "declinism." Not even the figure of President Ronald Reagan—who personified Hollywood's rise to supreme political power—was sufficient to assuage concerns about America's inevitable decline.

Determined to reassert American supremacy, Washington began taking a tough, no-nonsense stance on bilateral and multilateral trade issues, especially in the media and entertainment industries. In 1984, a subcommittee of Congress issued a report titled *Trade Barriers to U.S. Motion Pictures and Television, Pre-recorded Entertainment, Publishing and Advertising Industries.* Canada, where anti-American rhetoric about U.S. cultural domination is frequently exploited by politicians, was at the top of Washington's list of countries whose trade policies were identified as hostile to American interests. Some bilateral issues were resolved when the United States and Canada negotiated the Free Trade Agreement in the mid-1980s. Canada's biggest concession to Washington was in the area of movie imports.

While America seemed to be in decline in the 1980s, Japan was soaring as an economic superpower. Indeed, many believed that Japan was poised to replace the United States as a global power. Japanese takeovers of large American corporations were making headlines with alarming frequency in the United States—particularly in the media and entertainment sectors. One of the biggest deals was Coca-Cola's sale of the Hollywood studio Columbia Pictures to Japanese consumer electronics giant Sony. Suddenly it seemed as if Japan, once a defeated nation occupied by the American army after the Second World War, was returning to a position of global power with a vengeance. The first Hollywood movie to exploit pervasive anxiety in America about the Japanese threat was the 1989 film *Black Rain,* starring Michael Douglas, who plays a New York cop caught in a Yakuza gang war with the Japanese mafia. Another Hollywood film in this genre was the 1993 movie *Rising Sun,* starring Sean Connery and Wesley Snipes, about an attempt by a Japanese conglomerate to take control of a major U.S. computer company. Nearly fifty years after Pearl Harbor, the "Japs" were the bad guys again.

On the commercial front, Hollywood faced formidable opposition in Europe. As in the past, cultural relations between the United States and France—both republics founded on universalistic values—were particularly tense. In 1981, Franco-American relations became strained when socialist François Mitterrand was elected president and appointed four communists to his first cabinet. Mitterrand's flamboyant culture minister, Jack Lang, was not a communist, but he espoused fiercely anti-American rhetoric. Shortly after the socialists took power, Lang called on the nations of the world to embark on a "crusade" against the American entertainment industries, which he denounced as a capitalist campaign of "financial and cultural imperialism that no longer, or rarely, grabs territory but grabs consciousness, ways of thinking, ways of living" (Fraser 2005, pp. 68–69).

The real irritant, however, was economic. By the mid-1980s, Hollywood movies had surpassed French movies at the domestic box office for the first time. While lushly produced French movies such as *Madame Bovary* found critical success, Hollywood movies such as *Jurassic Park* invariably crushed local competition at the box office. France took its campaign against Hollywood domination to the European Commission, pressuring the supranational body to insist on a "cultural exception" in General Agreement on Tariffs and Trade (GATT) negotiations with the United States. Carla Hills, who was President George H.W. Bush's special trade envoy, told European filmmakers, "Make films as good as your cheeses and you will sell them!" Hollywood nonetheless feared a "Fortress Europe" strategy in trade negotiations. Jack Valenti worked furiously behind the scenes to sabotage the European effort to carve out "audiovisual" products from GATT. Valenti's fears were well-founded. In late 1993, the Clinton administration accepted the European Commission's demands for a "cultural exemption." Valenti furiously lashed out against his European adversaries. "This negotiation had nothing to do with culture, unless European soap operas and game shows are the equivalent of Molière," he said. "This is all about the hard business of money" (Fraser 2005 p. 72).

Hollywood's battles in the non-Western world have been infinitely more complex than its skirmishes with America's industrialized trading partners. Western governments frequently have been forced to strike a balance between protecting domestic commercial interests and allowing freedom of choice in the marketplace. In non-Western nations, local tastes do not always clamor for Hollywood products. In some countries—Iran, China, India—values and cultural identities have been significantly shaped by different religious traditions, and consequently local tastes and preferences have tended to favor domestic cultural products. This gives local elites more autonomy vis-à-vis American diplomatic pressures on their governments. In Latin America, governments have reacted to Hollywood's grip on domestic movie markets with familiar measures such as taxes and quotas. Hollywood has retaliated with boycotts, though they have not always been effective. When Fidel Castro overthrew Cuba's pro-American government in the late 1950s, the U.S. embargo against communist Cuba actually exempted Hollywood movies. Washington evidently regarded Hollywood films not merely as consumer goods, but also as indispensable soft power weapons. Castro nonetheless seized Hollywood assets in Cuba and railed against American movies as "obnoxious, childish, and poison for the minds of young people" (Seagrave 1997, p. 227).

Hollywood's relations with the Arab world have been infinitely more complex. Historically, anti-Western hostility in Muslim countries was aimed at colonial powers, especially Britain and France. The United States actually benefited, to some degree, from Muslim disenchantment with their colonial past. Local Muslim populations often turned to America—a neutral noncolonial power—as a preferred model for modernity. Two events after World War II turned the Islamic world against America. The first was the creation of Israel in 1948. The second was the rise of Islamic fundamentalism. Following the birth of Israel, Arab nations embargoed Hollywood movies. Whatever the official rationale, anti-Hollywood attitudes were based on the widespread perception that Hollywood was controlled by Jews. In some cases, specific Hollywood movies were targeted because they starred actors known for their Zionist sympathies. Egypt, for example, banned all movies starring Danny Kaye and Mickey Rooney because both stars had contributed money to the cause of Zionism. The ten-nation Arab League compiled a list of Hollywood stars—including Frank Sinatra, Paul Newman, and Joanne Woodward—that it recommended be blacklisted in all Muslim countries. A second anti-Hollywood backlash came twenty years later, after the Arab-Israeli War broke out in 1967. Egypt again blacklisted all Hollywood movies, but this time cited "moral" reasons. The Egyptian government claimed that Hollywood movies featured excessive violence and sex and glorified wealth and luxury (Fraser 2005).

In the 1990s, Hollywood became an even more obvious target of pervasive anti-Americanism in the fallout of the Gulf War. In 1993, the Disney movie *Aladdin* triggered angry protests in several Muslim countries because of the movie's alleged racist portrayal of Arabs. Disney also met with a barrage of protest when it released a sequel to *Father of the Bride*, featuring a sleazy, detestable, Arab-looking character called Mr. Habib. Arab groups cited other Hollywood movies that, they claimed, portrayed Muslims as villainous characters. Movies made by Disney were frequently singled out: *The Return of Jafar, Kazaam, In the Army Now*, and *GI Jane*. In 2000, Arab-American and Islamic advocacy groups in the United States called for a boycott of the Hollywood movie *Rules of Engagement*, about the rescue of a U.S. ambassador and his family under siege by an angry mob of Islamic protestors in Yemen.

Less than a year after September 11, 2001, Hollywood and Washington were working together again. The blockbuster *The Sum of All Fears*, based on the Tom Clancy novel about nuclear terrorism, could have been billed as a Hollywood-Pentagon co-production. The Pentagon provided the producers with an arsenal of authentic military hardware—B-2 bombers, F-16 fighter jets, Marine Corps and U.S. Army helicopters, plus the nuclear-powered John Stennis aircraft carrier, including its crew of 5,000 soldiers. What's more, top military and CIA officials worked with Paramount Pictures as consultants on the film. *The Sum of All Fears* provoked complaints that the Pentagon was using American taxpayers' money to parade its military hardware in Hollywood movies. Others argued that the Pentagon was manipulating Hollywood to project a positive image of the U.S. military establishment. Philip Strub, the Pentagon's special assistant for entertainment media, put it differently: "We want an opportunity to communicate directly to the American public through that powerful medium" (Seelye 2002). Other recent Hollywood movies, such as *Syriana,* starring George Clooney as a CIA operative, have been sharply critical of U.S. foreign policy in the Middle East. *Syriana,* released in 2005, explores the power of giant oil companies over U.S. foreign policy. Movies like *Syriana* can ironically have a positive impact abroad, because they show to foreign audiences that open debate and criticism of governments are permitted in liberal democracies like the United States. There is no such freedom in Islamic theocracies.

Television Without Frontiers

Television is an indispensable instrument of global soft power. "I learn more from CNN than I do from the CIA," President George Bush once remarked. Media mogul Rupert Murdoch famously declared that satellite television represents an "unambiguous threat to totalitarian regimes everywhere." As noted, some have given the MTV Generation credit for bringing down the Berlin Wall. Theocratic regimes in the Middle East ban satellite TV dishes that pick up Western signals. Autocratic rulers in Africa rail against CNN because its news reports show images of repression inflicted on their local populations. With the global satellite systems and the Internet, video images are everywhere, ubiquitous, inescapable—and powerful.

Television exploded as a mass medium in the late 1940s, just in time for the Cold War. From its inception, American television was instrumentalized as an ideological weapon to promote liberal, democratic, procapitalist values. In the 1950s, millions of Americans watched reassuring television shows—*Ozzie and Harriett* and *Leave It to Beaver,* for instance—that celebrated the white-picket-fence ideals of Middle America. The U.S. networks conferred upon themselves the highest moral purpose: to bind America together against the communist threat. There was pervasive anxiety that the Soviets might gain a technological head start in television—as dangerous as a technological advantage in advanced weapons. It was this anxiety that brought Washington and the U.S. networks together to develop a global television strategy.

The U.S. government had already created Voice of America during the Second World War following the Japanese attack on Pearl Harbor. After the war, Voice of America—whose motto was "Telling America's story abroad"—became the State Department's official Cold War broadcasting weapon, producing programs in some fifty different languages. In the 1950s the U.S. government, via the CIA, created Radio Liberty and Radio Free Europe to target the Soviet Union and Eastern Europe. Voice of America supporters soon began lobbying in favor of a concerted U.S. strategy to ensure that the United States played a leading role in the spread of global television. The idea found eager support in Congress. U.S. senator Alexander Wiley asserted that television "would spread the truth concerning the epic battle of the forces of the free world against Communist dictatorship." In 1955, *Variety* reported that global television would "give the lie to Commies," adding that "it's Communism versus the American way." Pat Weaver, who headed NBC throughout the 1950s, proposed to construct an international network of transmitters and install some 10,000 TV sets in public places throughout the world to promote American values. If implemented, said Weaver, a U.S.-owned global television network would "leave the Russians gasping for breath and out of the running." Weaver's global television system was never built, but the rhetoric invested in its design revealed a well-concerted complementarity between the interests of U.S. foreign policy and the American television industry (Seagrave 1998; Held 1999).

Instead of building a global television system, the U.S. networks settled for the more lucrative option of exporting American TV shows. Given its massive economies of scale thanks to its large domestic market, the United States quickly became the world's biggest exporter of television programs. In the 1950s, foreign TV networks were only too happy to buy low-cost American shows such as *I Love Lucy*. It didn't take long before U.S. television producers were pushing for the creation of a Hollywood-style cartel to act as a unified "State Department" to negotiate sales with foreign governments. When the Television Program Export Association was born in 1960, its first president was John McCarthy, a former State Department official. The U.S. Information Agency supported television exporters with its Informational Media Guarantee, which protected television exports from currency devaluations and blockages. The U.S. government guaranteed convertibility by ensuring payment to TV producers in dollars at favorable rates. But there was a quid pro quo: American television shows, before they could be exported, had to portray the United States "in a favorable light" (Seagrave 1998).

The advent of satellite TV in the 1970s extended the influence of American television more powerfully. Now U.S. networks could beam their signals directly into foreign countries to reach their local populations. CNN was the first American television network to achieve a global reach. CNN's role as an intermediary in international politics became so important that UN secretary-general Boutros Boutros-Ghali once described the all-news network as the "sixteenth member" of the UN Security Council. CNN's global influence was often resented. During the first Gulf War, some chastised CNN for airing precensored raw video footage obtained directly from the Pentagon's Military Joint Information Bureau. Yet CNN was also criticized for broadcasting uninterrupted speeches by Iraqi dictator Saddam Hussein (Robinson 2002).

Al-Qaeda's attacks on the United States once again thrust CNN into the international spotlight as its images of the collapsing World Trade Center towers were beamed to the entire planet. When the United States invaded Iraq in March 2003, television viewers worldwide tuned in to CNN. This time, however, CNN had all-news rivals with their own satellite signals, such as Fox News in the United States and the BBC's World Service. But it was the launch of the Arab-language satellite network Al Jazeera that altered the soft power dynamic in the global information war. Based in the tiny Persian Gulf emirate of Qatar, Al Jazeera had been launched in 1996 and was beamed into more than twenty Arab countries. Al Jazeera instantly became successful—and notorious—because it eschewed the established model of state-controlled Muslim broadcasters. By launching Al Jazeera, Qatar became a small state banging a big drum. The Muslim world now had its own CNN: fast paced, slickly produced, and unafraid of controversy. Not surprisingly, neighboring governments in the region reacted angrily to Al Jazeera, calling the Qatar-based network an affront and deliberate provocation. Saudi Arabia, which had long considered itself the region's most powerful pan-Arab satellite television power, was particularly incensed by Qatar's broadcasting ambitions. Qatar's other neighbor, Bahrain, banned Al Jazeera on the puzzling pretext that its news reports were "Zionist." Ironically, even the United States was irritated by Al Jazeera, despite the fact that the Arab all-news network emulated the style of CNN and Britain's BBC. (Nevertheless, during the second Gulf War, the U.S. Army established its headquarters in Qatar.) Al Jazeera's dissemination of Osama Bin Laden's speeches and other material sometimes infuriated the White House and State Department (Zayani 2005; Lynch 2005). Thus, Al Jazeera found itself in the paradoxical situation of being hated in the Muslim world for its "Zionist" bias and pro-Western style, yet equally resented in the West as a conduit for pro-Islamic propaganda.

After September 11, 2001, the U.S. government decided to launch its own Arab-language news network, called Alhurra. Overseen by the Board of Broadcast Governors and based just outside Washington, Alhurra began broadcasting in early 2004. Regarded as a U.S. counterstrategy against Al Jazeera's allegedly anti-American bias, Alhurra was quickly dismissed in some quarters as "Al Jazeera lite" because of fluffy shows such as "Hollywood Couples," though it also broadcast serious documentaries from PBS and Britain's BBC. In late 2005, the State Department's inspector general investigated Alhurra for alleged management irregularities, including the allegation that viewership figures had been falsified (the network claimed to reach 21 million viewers weekly). The review also included wider questions about Alhurra's entire operations, and whether it was fulfilling its mission (Dinmore 2005). This scrutiny did not enhance Alhurra's image and credibility. In tandem with Alhurra, the U.S. Board of Broadcast Governors launched a pop music radio station, Radio Sawa, aimed at the Arab world's youth population, from which terrorists are often recruited. Like Alhurra, however, Radio Sawa came under fire when the State Department's inspector general questioned whether it was presenting American values effectively (Kessler 2004; Bayles 2005). Radio Sawa is, officially, a "liberty" radio station on the Voice of America model. Radio Sawa is a continuation of this soft power strategy, but with one important difference: it is aimed not at a population governed by a rival ideology, but rather at a population where cultural identities have been shaped by religion, often fanatically fundamentalist. Radio Sawa's challenge, consequently, is much more complex than VOA's mission in Eastern Europe during the Cold War.

As the United States continues its public diplomacy efforts in the Muslim world, it can be expected to encounter resistance to instruments such as Alhurra and Radio Sawa. It is true that the Muslim world is diverse—and must be distinguished from the "Arab" world, which is a linguistic rather than a religious category—and some populations, such as those of Qatar and Dubai, have been relatively open to American influence and cultural models. The Muslim world, however, remains largely hostile to American soft power, because local elites can exercise mobilizing power among their populations, especially among youth. As Joseph Nye has correctly observed, "Soft power depends on willing receivers" (Nye 2004, p. 120).

Conclusion

The United States—like Greece and Rome in ancient times and Britain and France more recently—has enjoyed the advantages of a dominant culture because its military power and economic performance have been superior to those of other nations. American soft power domination is also attributable to the efficiency of communications systems that serve as distribution channels, whether satellite broadcasting or, more recently, the Internet. The ability of the United States to build, control, and access an efficient communications infrastructure—like the Roman viaducts—has enhanced American soft power.

Still, the attraction of American popular culture cannot be explained by efficient distribution systems alone. As we have seen with the examples of movies and television signals, the strategic deployment of American pop culture achieves varying degrees of success depending on specific contexts and conditions. In nations that have been forged within the same broad tradition of liberal democracy as the United States, American popular culture is generally embraced, particularly in the Anglo-American world but also throughout most of Europe. Where there has been tension, it usually has been triggered by commercial issues related to trade imbalances, protectionism, and uneven distribution of economic benefits. Even in France, with its long cultural rivalry with the United States, *Rocky* and *Rambo* and *The Terminator* were box-office hits.

In countries that do not share a tradition of liberal democracy, American popular culture has not always been embraced with undiluted enthusiasm. If soft power co-opts rather than coerces, it would seem that America's co-optive powers are more seductive in countries with rival *ideologies* than in those with different *religious* identities. It might be an exaggeration to assert that MTV brought down the Berlin Wall, but there can be little doubt that, in the final analysis, the Soviet communist system was powerless to combat the attraction of American popular culture among its citizens. In countries where regimes based their legitimacy on communist ideology, the population's fascination with American culture was intensified by the longing to escape a political system whose economic performance was failing. In other words, the attraction of American culture was linked to the overall performance, and prestige, of the United States as a society.

This is manifestly not so in regions, notably the Islamic world, where cultural identities have been forged, and political power legitimized, by religion. Since ruling elites in the Arab world, including secular leaders, found their legitimacy on Islamic faith, it is not surprising that cultural messages from a powerful secular country like the United States are regarded as a threat—not only by elites, but also by mass populations whose behavior can be mobilized by rulers exploiting religious themes. The questionable effectiveness of U.S. government initiatives such as Alhurra and Radio Sawa only highlights these challenges.

It is nonetheless naive to believe that the U.S. government should play no role in the deployment of American cultural power in foreign policy. As we have seen, cultural power has been an instrument of U.S. foreign policy since the moral idealism of Woodrow Wilson. It was, to be sure, more effective during the Cold War, when America's main adversary was an ideological rival whose economic and military performance was unsustainable. Today, when the greatest threat to the United States is religiously based terrorism, American cultural power may not be as effective, especially against regimes whose treasuries are flowing with petrodollars. American military power may prevail in Afghanistan and Iraq, but so far soft power strategies in the cultural sphere have not been regarded as successful.

Still, in the information age of the Internet, the United States is well positioned to maintain its global dominance culturally. The United States is still the world's greatest military and economic power, and these advantages will continue to facilitate the spread, and attractiveness, of American culture globally. Soft power rivals are nonetheless emerging. The governments of other world powers—Russia, China, Japan, India—are now openly talking about harnessing the advantages of their own soft power. The global popularity of Nintendo and anime characters from Pokémon are signs of Japan's growing soft power. The challenge for U.S. foreign policy will be to deploy American cultural power as a positive normative model that is embraced as attractive and appealing, and, where it encounters resistance, to convey cultural messages in a way that contributes to the transformation of underlying values.

References

Abel, Richard. 1999. *The Red Rooster Scare: Making Cinema American 1990–1910.* Berkeley: University of California Press.
Balio, Tino. 1985. *The American Film Industry.* Madison: University of Wisconsin Press.
Barber, Benjamin. 1995. *Jihad vs McWorld.* New York: Ballantine.
Bayles, Martha. 2005. "Goodwill Hunting." *The Wilson Quarterly* (Summer): 46–56.
Brownstein, Ronald. 1990. *The Power and the Glitter: The Hollywood-Washington Connection.* New York: Pantheon Books.
Corliss, Richard. 2001. "Geishas and Godzillas." *Time Asia,* April 30.
"Department of Propaganda: The Sound of America." 2002. *New Yorker,* February 18.
Dinmore, Guy. 2005. "US-Backed Arab TV Network to Be Investigated." *Financial Times,* November 4.
Fraser, Matthew. 2005. *Weapons of Mass Distraction: Soft Power and American Empire.* New York: Thomas Dunne.

Held, David, Anthony McGrew, David Goldblatt, and Jonathan Perraton. 1999. *Global Trans-formations: Politics, Economics and Culture.* Stanford: Stanford University Press.

Huntington, Samuel. 1996. *Clash of Civilizations and the Remaking of the World Order.* New York: Simon and Schuster.

Kessler, Glen. 2004. "Role of Radio Sawa in Mideast Questioned." *Washington Post,* October 13.

Kuisel, Richard. 1993. *Seducing the French: The Dilemma of Americanization.* Berkeley: University of California Press.

Lynch, Marc. 2005. "Watching Al Jazeera." *Wilson Quarterly* (Summer): 36–45.

McDougal, Dennis. 1998. *The Last Mogul: Lew Wasserman, MCA, and the Hidden History of Hollywood.* New York: Crown Publishers.

Pells, Richard. 1997. *Not Like Us: How Europeans Have Loved, Hated, and Transformed American Culture Since World War II.* New York: Basic Books.

Pipes, Daniel. 2005. "Don't Waste the Dollars." *Jerusalem Post,* December 27.

Puttnam, David. 1998. *Movies and Money.* New York: Alfred A. Knopf.

Riding, Alan. 2005. "Rerun Our Cold War Cultural Diplomacy." *New York Times,* October 27.

Robinson, Piers. 2002. *The CNN Effect: The Myth of News, Foreign Policy and Intervention.* London: Routledge.

Rosenberg, Emily. 1982. *Spreading the American Dream: American Economic and Cultural Expansion 1890–1945.* New York: Hill and Wang.

Seagrave, Kerry. 1997. *American Films Abroad: Hollywood's Domination of the World's Movie Screens from the 1890s to the Present.* Jefferson, NC: McFarland.

———. 1998. *American Television Abroad: Hollywood's Attempt to Dominate World Television.* Jefferson, NC: McFarland.

Seelye, Katherine. 2002. "When Hollywood's Big Guns Come Right from the Source." *New York Times,* June 10.

Watts, Steven. 1997. *The Magic Kingdom: Walt Disney and the American Way of Life.* New York: Houghton Mifflin.

Zayani, Mohamed, ed. 2005. *The Al Jazeera Phenomenon.* Boulder: Paradigm Publishers.

IV

Public Diplomacy

11

Wielding Soft Power

The Key Stages of Transmission and Reception

Kondo Seiichi

Pokémon and Foreign Policy

For those foreign policy makers who intuitively acknowledge the growing importance of soft power, the biggest and perhaps most persistent question is no longer whether soft power exists but how and to what extent one can or should wield it for specific policy purposes. This is because in the case of soft power, more than in the case of hard power, it is difficult or impossible to establish a causal relationship between inputs and outcomes; furthermore, policies on occasion invite unintended consequences—often negative ones. On top of that, government involvement in the realm of soft power is liable to be seen as meddlesome intrusion by the authorities into matters of personal taste and beliefs, raising suspicions and causing an almost reflexive backlash. These challenges have kept policy discussions on soft power from maturing.

In this chapter I clarify what the government, facing these challenges, should do to wield soft power in such a way that its potential benefits to the public can be fully translated into reality. For this purpose, I examine subjectivity and the specific aspects of culture that play peculiar roles in soft power, thereby distinguishing it from hard power. I also highlight cooperative interaction between the subject and object as another distinctive feature of this type of power. I then attempt to analyze the secrets behind the popularity of "cool Japan," as expressed in the forms of Pokémon and anime, to discover hints for how to position soft power within public diplomacy.

These approaches might invite us to go beyond the framework of conventional social science, which excludes subjectivity and culture from the direct targets of its analyses. Such exploration is beyond the scope of this chapter, but it is a challenge that should be proactively addressed in the face of the reality that individuals and nongovernmental entities have started joining as influential actors in international politics, an arena where participation was traditionally limited to sovereign states assumed to be acting on the basis of rationally calculated self-interest.

Transmission and Reception in the Operation of Soft Power

The most important reason why traditional political scientists are hesitant to label soft power as a form of real power and policy makers are skeptical about its utility lies in the difficulty of establishing causal relationships between policy inputs and their outcomes, which are crucially important for predicting and measuring policy impact. However, Joseph Nye has noted that there is always a "gap" between the resources and outcomes of power, or more specifically, that the resources do not directly bear the desired outcomes, and this can be seen not only in soft power but in hard power as well. According to Nye, what connects resources to outcomes are well-designed strategies and skillful leadership. Although the number of tanks possessed by German forces in 1940 was less than the number possessed by the combined British and French forces, this disadvantage was not reflected in the actual fighting, and the result was France's fall. Nye also has said that whether the resources of power will bring about intended consequences or not depends on the "context"—who relates to whom under what circumstances. As Nye sees it, this gap is not unique to soft power, and the differences between soft and hard power are "matters of degree" (Nye 2004, pp. 3, 6, 16, 99).

However, the very low predictability of outcomes brought about by soft power seems to justify the attempt to develop a hypothesis that there are significant differences—whether qualitative or not—in the way soft power and hard power operate. It is easy to foresee that tanks may not function in a specific context, such as in dense forests, for example. But it is highly unlikely that they will be able to function in some dense forests and not in others. In the case of soft power, however, not only it is difficult to predict what outcomes certain resources will deliver, but also a particular approach often causes unintended consequences; furthermore, the same approach may produce different results depending on the recipient. Consequently, if one seeks to pursue effective public diplomacy policies taking full account of the characteristics of soft power, it is necessary to analyze the gap between resources and outcomes and the context in which the policies are implemented.

The main theme of the television drama series *Oshin,* produced by NHK (Japan Broadcasting Corporation), was originally intended to be an admonition about excessive materialism in postwar Japan. However, this drama, the story of an ordinary young Japanese girl who was toughened by the hardships she experienced during and after World War II and matured into a brave woman running a household and thereby contributing in her own way to the reconstruction of postwar Japan, evoked considerable sympathy among many people, especially women, when it was subsequently broadcast in more than sixty developing countries in Asia, the Middle East, and Latin America. The drama cheered up viewers suffering from the hardships of nation building by allowing them to overlap their own images with that of the heroine, thus leading to greater respect for Japan. This is one example of how soft power can produce unintended consequences—positive ones, in this case. In the United States, however, *Oshin* was not well received.

This series showed how traits such as diligence and perseverance were demonstrated by the protagonist's words and deeds, which appealed to people who shared these values, thereby enhancing their appreciation of Japan. Conversely, Americans who placed other values above these traits tended not to accept the drama. The implications are made clearer by comparing the poor reception of this drama with the fact that when the diligence and precision of the Japanese were transformed into high-quality cars, Americans extolled them in unison, turning these products into positive images for Japan.

These examples demonstrate that the operation of power (hard as well as soft) can be better grasped if divided into four stages: the *resources,* their *transmission,* their *reception,* and the *outcomes.* By adding the two stages of transmission and reception, which bridge the gap between resources and outcomes, as noted by Nye, one can complement and strengthen one's argument. Power brings about outcomes only after the four stages proceed in the proper manner. With malfunction at any stage, power cannot determine the outcome. It is only at these two added stages where *subjectivity,* a characteristic of soft power, becomes evident.

If we apply these four stages to hard power, we may take missiles, for example, to represent the resources, their firing the transmission, intrusion into an enemy's air-space the reception, and destruction of a target the outcome. Each of the stages can be measured objectively and scientifically, from the number of missiles to the destruction of the target. In this way, there is a high degree of predictability regarding hard power. Regardless of the target country—and irrespective of its political system, culture, and national creed—the same outcome can be expected. In the case of soft power, however, the method of transmission varies widely depending on individual tastes; also, the way people receive it in the target country (whether it is attractive or not, in Nye's words) can be completely different depending on their subjective responses. It is virtually impossible to make an objective forecast of what outcomes any given country's resources of soft power will have on a particular target country.

Generally speaking, what become the resources for soft power are the culture developed by and rooted in the people of a country and the ideas based on it. While these resources are not likely to change over a short period of time, there is considerable synchronic variety in the forms in which they are transmitted, which include political and social ideals, art and culture, institutions, policies, and economic goods. Although Nye cites culture, political values, and foreign policies as three components that constitute the resources (Nye 2004, p. 11), this chapter defines some of their elements as belonging to the transmission stage, distinct from the resources proper. In addition, strategy and leadership, which are regarded by Nye as elements that bridge the gap between resources and outcomes, are here also defined as elements of transmission. The operations that led to victory by the German forces that were outnumbered in tanks by the British and French forces were part of the work of transmission. And the elements to which Nye referred when he said that "soft power depends more than hard power upon the existence of willing interpreters and receivers" and "their effects depend heavily on acceptance by the receiving audience" (Nye 2004, pp. 16, 99) are defined here as belonging to the reception stage.

This categorization is neither abstract nor theoretical. According to it, among what Nye regards as the resources, only those that could be considered national assets and are fixed and not changeable over a short period are defined as "resources," and others (i.e., those that can be changed at the will of the subject) are included in "transmission." Moreover, regarding what he referred to as "the context" or "the gap," what is caused by the subject's actions is defined as "transmission," and what is caused by the object's actions as "reception." Dividing the operation of soft power into these four stages makes it possible to understand at what stage *subjectivity* appears and whose subjectivity it is, allowing the policy makers of public diplomacy to determine which policies are viable at what stage.

Projection and Presentation: Cultural Constraints Found in Comparing Japan and the United States

The transmission and reception of soft power are affected not only by subjectivity at the individual level but also by the culture of the societies to which the subject and object belong. Those who accepted *Oshin,* which exemplified Japanese culture at a time when holding firm to run a household while patiently enduring unfavorable surroundings was considered a virtue, were people with similar cultures. If the drama had presented a story in which the heroine fought courageously and emerged victorious in a struggle to overcome discrimination against women, it might have been well received in the United States—but a story based on that kind of mind-set could not have originated in Japan at that time.

The message transmitted reflects culture not just in its content but in its method of transmission as well. Although power is generally considered to be something that must be "projected," it is useful to distinguish two different modes of transmission, namely *projection* and *presentation,* the former being aggressive and the latter being reserved. A comparison of the transmission of soft power by Japan and the United States highlights the significance of this classification. The Japanese characteristically excel at—and prefer to focus on—indirectly and quietly presenting a value system, which represents their soft power resources, through artistic expression and the creation of objects, while they are weak in projecting their philosophy directly and aggressively in the form of ideas and words.[1] Both these characteristics can work either to their advantage or to their disadvantage. The resources of soft power, such as diligence and technical skills, were presented when Japan manufactured high-quality goods and achieved a phenomenal economic recovery in a short period after World War II. Consumers across the world extolled the Japanese, deepening their positive feelings and developing a sense of regard for Japan as the first non-Western nation to achieve modernization successfully. Japan was thus accepted by the international community, and as a result many governments responded affirmatively to the Japanese government's postwar diplomatic efforts to rejoin the international community at the earliest date possible.

In contrast, Japan's reflection on World War II was presented in the form of verbal expression (e.g., remarks by prime ministers and the Japan-China Joint Communiqué of 1972) and actions (e.g., reparations and official development assistance). These efforts failed to yield sufficient effects since they did not match the expectations of the victim nations, which had demanded that clear-cut apologies be projected by Japanese leaders without ambiguity.

Americans, meanwhile, characteristically excel at clearly and systematically projecting their value system in the form of ideals, which represent their resources; they tend not to be good at patiently taking time to gradually penetrate the recipient's mind through a reserved presentation. Although such values as respect for freedom and individualism are already well presented in the forms of democracy and the market economy, along with institutions to realize them, Americans go a step further to proactively spread these values to the rest of the world (Rothkopf 1997; Pei 2003). Christopher Ross, who served as U.S. ambassador to Syria, noted that the mission of public diplomacy is "projecting" U.S. values and to "articulate U.S. policy clearly in a short period" (Ross 2003).[2] The early resurgence of democracy in postwar Japan and the internal collapse of the Soviet Union were two prominent examples of success, where the aggressive projection of freedom and democracy by the United States was matched with its enthusiastic acceptance by the citizens of Japan and the Soviet Union, who had been battered by their rulers' militarism and communism, respectively. If the Americans had been content with a reserved presentation of these ideals, the collapse of the Soviet Union would have at least been delayed.

In regions where people still hold deep resentment against colonialism or have firm convictions that do not comply with Western values, however, the projection of democracy by the United States has set nerves on edge and has been rejected, since it has been construed as neocolonialism or as a violation of local culture. In the Middle East, unlike postwar Japan, there is an apparent mismatch between U.S. projection and the counterpart countries' reception. This U.S. projection of ideals often develops into an explicit link between values and coercion, such as the use of military and economic might, and becomes strongly associated with imposition. Moreover, as the projection gets stronger, any gap between the ideals the subject (the United States) espouses and its actual actions becomes susceptible to criticism as revealing a double standard. All these developments can result in strong or even explosive antipathy and a serious loss of the inherent efficacy of soft power resources. The rising tide of anti-Americanism in the Middle East is an example in point.

What a comparison of Japanese and U.S. public diplomacy implies is that even excellent resources can fail to deliver the intended effects—or worse, actually produce adverse effects—if the wrong method of transmission is employed because of cultural constraints. The effective practice of public diplomacy requires not only the use of the cultural strengths of each country in transmission but also the efforts to overcome cultural constraints. But the state, in general, is awkward, and cannot easily correct its own shortcomings.

When the state tries to step out of its cultural constraints, it often does it either so awkwardly that it invites negative reactions and is forced to withdraw, or does it too late with no significant impact. At one time, encouraged by Western educated public relations consultants to project the supposed excellence of the Japanese management system as the secret of Japan's miraculous postwar economic recovery, the Japanese started giving lectures about it to foreign audiences. But they repulsed many audiences with their arrogance and even became the butt of jokes. Taken aback, the Japanese immediately stopped. Also, though the Japanese government gradually realized that the presentation of Japan's apologies for World War II had not been accepted by victim countries, it was not until fifty years after the end of the war that it came up with the Murayama Statement (delivered by Prime Minister Murayama Tomiichi in 1995), an attempt to project an apology. Although it was the projection of an apology with a clarity no less than that of the famous speech delivered by West German president Richard von Weizsacker in 1985, it brought about only very limited effects, because a negative image of a "Japan unable to face up to history squarely" had been established by then. It took Japan too long to learn how to project its apology.[3]

The American tendency to appreciate projection of resources and seek visible results in a short time often creates cultural constraints by underestimating the importance of long-term presentation of resources, resulting in impeding full exercise of potential American soft power. The United States successfully created many friends through exchange programs, such as Fulbright scholarships. Although it takes time, such exchanges are the best method of effectively transmitting resources through presentation. The deep cuts in the U.S. State Department's budget for exchange programs after the end of the Cold War reflects the difficulty in getting out of this deep-seated American culture.[4]

In the wake of the 9/11 terrorist attacks and growing anti-American sentiment in the Middle East, the United States seems to have realized that its past projection of ideals was not accepted as expected, but instead provoked antagonism in that region. There is, however, a deep conviction among Americans that free and open debate, using all available rhetoric, offers society an open and dynamic mechanism essential to achieving justice. This belief tends to overreach itself as a result of fierce competition among the actors involved, causing them to get caught up in a game of forming perceptions favorable to their own convenience; it can become impossible to restrain this process even if it provokes foreign countries (Kondo 1997, 1998). Americans, believing that their ideals are universal and that expansion of freedom is an American mission, think it is a matter of course to project these ideals, and as a result their public diplomacy has traditionally been heavily ideology driven (Newsom 1988, pp. 6, 180). This has continued to be the case even since the disappearance of the Soviet propaganda machine. In this regard, the passage in President Bush's January 2006 State of the Union Address in which he declared, "We will act boldly in freedom's cause," might have left no room for doubt in the American mind in spite of the risk of further inflaming anti-American sentiment the world over. It appears difficult for the American leadership to acknowledge that in some cases it is the method of transmission of the message, not its contents, that leads to failure.

Interaction Between Transmission and Reception: Cooperation for Convergence or Confrontation for Surrender

Another advantage in dividing the gap between soft power resources and their outcomes into the separate stages of transmission and reception is that it brings to light the importance of the continuous interaction that takes place between the transmitter and the receiver. The resources of soft power transmitted in a certain form by the subject are not swallowed or rejected in their entirety by the recipient; rather, they are thoroughly scrutinized. The subject, upon evaluating the recipient's response, revises the shape of its expression. And the recipient, influenced by the continuous flow of transmission, changes its degree of acceptance in accordance with the subject's revisions. According to Anne Allison's chapter in this volume (Chapter 6), *Power Rangers,* for which the U.S. broadcast rights were initially obtained in 1985, was not able to take hold in the United States until eight years later, after going through the modification process known as "Americanization," which was necessary in order for it to be accepted by American children. But now, some thirteen years later, the original Japanese version of the TV program is being broadcast without modification. The conveying of cultural and artistic works, which at a glance appears to be a one-way transmission, in fact often reflects the processes and results of continuous interaction between creator and consumer—even if these sometimes take place only in the artist's mind, invisible to others.

Of course, interaction itself is not limited to soft power. In the implementation of hard power military strategies, for example, planners monitor the results of a first missile strike and alter subsequent operations accordingly. It is common sense in the military that "the premeditated strategy is bound to be changed at the first encounter with the enemy" (Takeda 2004, p. 18). A country that possesses interceptor missiles may attempt to use them to shoot down enemy missiles before they reach their targets. Just before the U.S. forces started bombing Baghdad, Saddam Hussein, along with his palace guards, fled from the center of the city. The United States changed its strategy accordingly and eventually captured him in his hiding spot. Here, too, continuous exchanges between transmission and reception took place.

This, however, is where soft power clearly distinguishes itself from hard power. While interaction in the operation of hard power is *hostile,* consisting of exchanges of attacks and defensive actions, with the transmitter seeking to achieve the surrender of the recipient in as unilateral a fashion as possible, the interaction in the operation of soft power is *cooperative,* seeking empathy and aiming for convergence through a dialogue between the parties. In other words, while the former is a zero-sum game of win-lose, the latter is a plus-sum game of win-win. It is precisely because of the working of this cooperative interaction that soft power takes considerable time to deliver its results—and that the effects on the recipient, once they take hold, far outweigh and outlive those of hard power.[5]

Furthermore, cooperative interaction also occurs among receivers. A fad such as the Pokémon boom is caused not by the simple build-up of individual consumers' preferences but by a sudden amplification instigated by their own interaction. The popularity of *Oshin* and *Power Rangers* was brought about through a process of subjective interaction, not only between the transmitter and the receiver, but also among receivers, thereby making it difficult for rational strategists to predict it in the traditional way. Reflected in these aspects of soft power is the current trend of the twenty-first century, when international relations are shifting from an authoritative and hierarchical structure composed of sovereign states to a horizontal one involving a diversity of actors.

In understanding these characteristics of soft power, it is useful to touch upon the oft-debated relationship between public diplomacy and propaganda. Propaganda, such as that practiced by the Soviet Union, clearly involves the application of soft power, in that it does not employ armed might or economic incentives in aiming to achieve specific purposes. One ought to recognize, however, that the working of soft power in this case has a substantial hard power coloration, inasmuch as it is not cooperative but intended to induce the recipient to take actions desired by the transmitter by manipulating the recipient's will in as unilateral a fashion as possible. Whereas public diplomacy tries to maximize its innate power by utilizing the characteristics of soft power in the form of cooperative interaction, propaganda can be considered a policy that runs counter to the characteristics of soft power (Melissen 2005, pp. 18–19). This explains why propaganda has become totally outmoded in today's international relations and why projection is becoming increasingly risky, because it is conducted without sufficient "market testing" through interaction with the receivers.

This cooperative interaction, or, in other words, two-way dialogue, is the best way to narrow cultural gaps and have different values accepted. There is already much U.S. commentary noting the importance of "listening, dialogue, and debate" (Council on Foreign Relations 2003, pp. 43–44), or "listening rather than a monologue" (Rugh 2006, p. 88). But dialogue alone is not enough. As British scholars have contended, in order to have others abandon some of their values, we need to be ready to "accommodate alternative views" (Riordan 2003, p. 124) and to "allow our values to change in the process" (Leonard and Smewing 2003, pp. 58–59).

Karen Hughes, who was appointed U.S. undersecretary of state for public diplomacy and public affairs in the summer of 2005, testified at her nomination hearing before the Senate Foreign Relations Committee as follows: "I am mindful that before we seek to be understood, we must first work to understand." Right after this statement, however, apparently she felt the need to show strong confidence in her country's ideals, probably because of the nature of the occasion and her nationalistic audience. She continued, "In the long run, the way to prevail in this battle is through the power of our ideals: for they speak to all of us, every people in every land on every continent. Given a fair hearing, I am sure they will prevail" (Hughes 2005). This indicates, once again, the difficulty of overcoming cultural constraints inherited from forebears and shared by compatriots. This is a crucial area for the success of public diplomacy, if it aims to win the battle for "hearts and minds" that has become a recent slogan of public diplomacy theory in the United States (Lennon 2003; Fukuyama 2006).

Cool Japan and Japanism: What Position Does Cool Japan Hold in Japan's New Public Diplomacy?

The current phenomenon of "cool Japan" seems to have elements inherently different from those of the Japanism that emerged in the West following the Paris Exposition of 1867 and again during the 1950s and 1960s. The spread of Japanese pop culture of late is attributable to elements in both the transmission stage and the reception stage. With respect to the former, the bursting of Japan's bubble economy early in the 1990s and the shifting of values due to globalization have served to break down the country's male-dominated, seniority-based hierarchy, thus allowing Japanese young people and women, who were previously relegated to a relatively low social status, to develop their talents more freely. Pop culture has been one of their preferred outlets. In addition, the dramatic advances in information technology further enhanced Japan's technological superiority, and they helped create new forms of culture and artistic expression, such as anime and video games. This set of developments has facilitated the transmission of Japanese ideas in the form of pop culture.

As for the reception stage, one of the reasons why Japanese anime appeals to young people around the world today may be that the end of the Cold War has liberated human beings from ideological confrontation, creating an environment where they can freely pursue diverse cultures. Many people in the world now prefer contemporary expressions in art and culture instead of the missionary preaching of ideals. This is a situation apparently favorable to Japan, which is not good at projecting ideals. Moreover, the global proliferation of a mass consumption economy combined with a growing middle class has given an edge to the global spread of Japan's popular culture, which has been supported for literally centuries by a general public with a high level of interest in and appreciation for various forms of artistic expression. (For example, the *ukiyo-e* [woodblock prints] of the Edo era were widely appreciated by the ordinary people of the time.) The pop culture now being exported from Japan has already acquired a competitive edge by passing a severe test in the domestic market.

The most important factor on the receiving side probably has to do with the psychology of contemporary human beings. While enjoying the freedom and material prosperity that are the fruits of modern rationalism, people feel perplexed at the growing divide between rich and poor, cutthroat market competition, environmental destruction, and identity crises, as well as the social unrest and terrorism that have arisen partly because of their inability to resolve these issues. For those who have some doubts about modern life but cannot articulate them, the messages from Japanese anime emphasizing human complexity and the importance of coexistence with nature may appear to offer some hints for problem-solving options superior to reliance on the simple dichotomy of rewarding good and punishing evil.

Susan Napier has written, "There is perhaps one more, arguably postmodern, 'anxiety' that could be added to the world of anime, however." Anime films "offer up worlds that exist as warnings or alternatives to the conformity of contemporary society" (Napier 2001, pp. 236–37). In an interview, Miyazaki Hayao implied the depth of thought behind his anime by noting that the "entrance is wide with a low doorstill, but the exit is a little high." Speaking to Prime Minister Koizumi Jun'ichiro in 2004, a representative of the Iraqi karate world noted, "We always invite *sensei* [teachers] from Japan," so as not to lose the spirituality of Japanese martial arts (Kondo 2004). Whether it is anime or martial arts, what lies in the background of their popularity is apparently an unarticulated affinity to the traditional Japanese culture and philosophy that continue to survive in the midst of modernization.

In contrast to the Japanism of the past, which gave elitist European artists bogged down in conventional styles of expression a hint for a breakthrough but did not go much beyond exoticism, the "cool Japan" phenomenon presents, in the field of pop culture accessible to a much wider audience, Japanese ideas that are not necessarily amenable to clear linguistic expression, thus generating interaction among youth around the world and giving comfort to an anxious public. Here, unlike in Hollywood movies, such ideas do not assert (project) scientific, clear-cut solutions for problems based on the dichotomy of good and evil. Nor do they preach ideals as in Hollywood films concerning "individualism, capitalism, liberalism, and democracy" (Fraser 2004). They instead portray humans as complex creatures, implying (presenting) a message that there is no such ideal type in reality. There is no "imposition," and the interpretation of what is implied is left to the viewers.[6] What Nakano Yoshiko says in this volume (Chapter 7) about the "approachable modernity" that young people in Asia find in Japanese pop culture may reflect this fact. This is why and how ordinary people around the world have come to find Japanese pop culture attractive and are ready to accept it.

So what position do these ideas hold in Japan's public diplomacy? In August 2004, as part of its organizational reform, Japan's Ministry of Foreign Affairs created the Public Diplomacy Department (with this writer appointed its first director general). Its purpose is to build a system in which Japan's soft power is maximized. It was not so easy, however, to set the guidelines for what the new organizational unit should achieve. In particular, securing necessary resources to overcome Japan's culture-based weakness in aggressively projecting values was anything but easy. Even concerning the presentation of values through culture and art—areas of Japanese competence—debates about how the government can and should take advantage of Japan's soft power have continued endlessly within the ministry and at the Japan Foundation, which is Japan's main apparatus of cultural exchanges similar to the British Council.

The following are examples of concrete projects to implement policies to achieve the objective of the reform already initiated by the ministry. First, the Council for the Promotion of Cultural Diplomacy, composed of seventeen diverse experts, was established under Prime Minister Koizumi. The proposal that this council submitted on July 11, 2005, defined harmony, compassion, and coexistence, among others, as important values for Japan—in other words, as resources of soft power. It is noteworthy that this proposal for the first time explicitly identified Japanese pop culture as a "gateway" to Japanese culture in general. It then pointed out the importance of inviting many intellectually and artistically talented young people to Japan from around the world as a means of transmission. It also argued that the Japanese value system could contribute to world peace by serving as a bridge between diverse cultures and values (Council for the Promotion of Cultural Diplomacy 2005; Aoki, Kondo, and Wang 2005; Kondo 2005).

Second, the ministry established an annual conference, modeled on Britain's Public Diplomacy Strategy Board, for the sharing of views and experiences among participants invited from all walks of life concerning the attractions of Japanese culture and effective ways of disseminating information about those attractions, as well as for exchanges of comments and suggestions. Third, "World Civilization Forum 2005" was held on July 22, 2005. Under the chairmanship of Professor Amartya Sen, a Nobel laureate in economics, the high-level panelists in various fields from fourteen countries around the world discussed the ideal shape of human civilization in the twenty-first century, especially how to eliminate conflicts between religions and cultures, and ensure that true justice prevails in the world (NIRA 2005; A. Sen 2006). This represents the first implementation of the recommendation made to Prime Minister Koizumi in allowing the Japanese value system that emphasizes harmony and coexistence over self-assertion to serve as a bridge linking different values.

While these certainly represent the adoption of a more proactive stance toward wielding soft power by the Foreign Ministry than ever before, the ministry is clearly trying to limit itself to what it can and should do in full recognition of the nature of soft power. In the belief that public diplomacy must be centered on the cooperative interaction of individuals, it has tried to facilitate the formation of networks for them, but unlike its counterparts in China and South Korea, it has turned down requests for direct government support of cultural creation, as typified by the anime industry.

Given the nature of Japan's soft power and its recently set public diplomacy guidelines, this writer does not agree with Douglas McGray's assessment that, as a cultural superpower now equipped with the new media of cartoons and anime, "it is hard to imagine that Japan will be content to remain with so much medium and so little message" (McGray 2002). This precisely reflects a conventional American mind-set, assuming that projection is the natural mode of transmission; it is not the Japanese approach. Japanese-style public diplomacy may appear weak, but it is far from being an inadequate policy by any means. Indeed, a recent BBC survey indicates that Japanese-style modest public diplomacy has been producing a steady flow of successful results (BBC World Service 2006).[7] This is also a prerequisite for Japanese pop culture to remain "cool."

Soft Power and Public Diplomacy Policies

If the government wants to wield soft power in public diplomacy, it should refrain from directly controlling the stages involving personal subjectivity, such as the transmission of soft power's resources and acceptance by the recipient. What it must do instead is to concentrate its efforts on building an environment where ideas and culture are freely created by the private sector and where the market test of interaction between transmitters and receivers is easily conducted. By connecting people and organizations in various fields and levels engaged in transmitting its soft power and by offering places for their interpersonal and cross-cultural exchanges, the government should pursue the goal of enhancing the overall effects of its soft power through cooperative interaction and mutual stimulation. The role of the public diplomacy unit of the Foreign Ministry is to be the hub of this network.

While facilitating the forming of networks and the sharing of ideas, the government does not intervene in the decisions made about what constitute the resources of soft power, what are the most effective methods of transmission, and what means are effective for which counterparts. Moreover, neither the government nor any individual or organization controls the entire process. What participants draw from the interaction within the networks, what decisions they make, and how they translate these decisions into action are all up to them. This is the natural consequence of understanding that the operation of soft power is centered on the interaction among the participants of a network. The role of the government as a facilitator and network hub may appear to be one of limited influence, but still it is an extremely important role within the newly emerging structure of international relations involving a variety of actors connected with one another horizontally.[8]

When directly transmitting messages to gain support for its policies, the government must be sensitive to the responses of the recipients, being fully aware of the risks arising from the dearth of opportunities for cooperative interaction. It also needs to make all possible efforts to overcome cultural constraints that limit its ability to wield soft power by paying constant attention to choosing appropriate methods of transmission with great flexibility. Still, the government is prone to make mistakes.

The first sort of mistake occurs when the government confronts initial failures in measures that it has taken. It is easy for those in government to think that since their country is endowed with good soft power resources, any failure to get others to accept these resources must be due to inadequate transmission. This fuels the argument that the budget for public diplomacy should be increased. This pressure has indeed increased in Washington since anti-American sentiment surfaced in the Middle East soon after the outbreak of the war in Iraq. Certainly, in light of the trends of international relations in the twenty-first century, a significant increase in the budget for public diplomacy is a prime task. However, unlike in the case of hard power, the reason why other countries have not accepted the messages of soft power is not limited to the inadequate volume of those messages. Given the significant importance of the interaction between transmission and reception in the work of soft power, increasing the transmission of messages with low acceptance levels alone will not improve the results. If anything, it is liable to produce adverse effects (Hoffman 2002). The budgetary increases should not be directed simply toward a quantitative expansion of existing programs. They must be allocated for the qualitative improvement of analytical skills, interagency coordination, and communication skills required for more effective transmission of the country's soft power resources to ensure more favorable reception by the targeted countries.

Second, when the government transmits messages, it tends to be preoccupied with their immediate impact on the target, disregarding how they may be received elsewhere over the long term. Government messages generally have clear objectives that yield short-term results to meet the short-term cycles of elections and announcements of poll results. Consequently, they tend to present direct, often dichotomized messages, such as "we are in a conflict between good and evil" (Albright 2006; Fullilove 2006), that are targeted at specific constituencies and have not gone through the time-consuming process of market testing. Therefore, when other audiences receive such messages, antipathy may be easily aroused, possibly leading to a weakening of the country's soft power. The manipulation of external information also flows back to the home country (Armstead 2004). When transmitting government messages, therefore, multifaceted considerations are necessary to complement the lack of market testing.

Third, there is always a temptation for the practitioners of public diplomacy to take highly visible measures and oversell their impact in order to justify the practitioners' work and their calls for increased appropriations. They must recognize that there is evidence that governments can succeed when low-visibility strategies are pursued (Manheim 1994, p. 121) and that, although policy evaluation and feedback to the policy planners is undoubtedly important, quantitative exaggeration of the measures taken often raises skepticism and even becomes counterproductive in many ways (Tuch 1993, pp. 113–20). Public diplomacy should stay subtle. The inherent dilemma of public diplomacy is that any attempt to sell it publicly will reduce its impact.

Conclusion

The oft-seen failure of governments to take advantage of their countries' soft power may be attributed to insufficient awareness of the importance of this sort of power and to the confusion caused by their inability to get a proper handle on the qualitative differences between hard power and soft power and between public diplomacy and propaganda. This chapter attempts to present a better understanding of such characteristics of soft power as the *individual subjectivity* and *cultural constraints* that distinguish it from hard power, and the *cooperative interaction* between transmitter and receiver that differentiates public diplomacy from propaganda. Each government needs to establish its own effective public diplomacy strategies, in full recognition of its cultural characteristics, and in close collaboration with markets, which do most of the work. It has to free itself intellectually from the legacy of the Cold War, a period in which even government-driven propaganda for democracy was effective thanks to the weakness of the competition it faced, namely, the dishonest and clumsy propaganda deployed by the Soviet Union (Riordan 2003, p. 121).

While governments have to leave much of the working of soft power to markets, honest and systematic in-depth policy evaluation based on accumulated experience and supported by continuous surveys of targeted countries might provide policy makers with some tools to overcome, at least partially, the thick wall of subjectivity by revealing behavioral patterns in these countries. This could eventually equip policy makers with some ability to predict the outcomes of policy inputs directed to that particular audience.

In this respect, it is encouraging to see new approaches emerging, such as "behavioral economics," and "economics and psychology," based on the awareness that although human behavior is not perfectly rational or driven purely by self-interest, as assumed by traditional social science, the deviation from rationality follows a certain set of rules (Thaler 1994). This academic trend, together with the advance of complexity theory, network theory, and cognitive science, promises to eventually unravel the issues of subjectivity and culture more scientifically and develop into policy theory as well (Fisher 1972). Until then, we have no choice but to continue to use trial and error, coordinating our efforts closely with the work of markets.

Notes

1. Grand tea master Sen Souoku said that Japanese culture is a "*sassuru* [perceiving] culture" (S. Sen 2006). This illustrates the distinctive nature of traditional Japanese culture, in which the transmission of a cultural message waits for the recipient to "perceive" it, and the transmitter only gives hints to help him or her to do so.

2. Andrew Kohut and Bruce Stokes presented an interesting analysis based on polls, drawing the conclusion that it is American leaders' rhetoric, rather than public sentiment, that promotes aggressive export of American ideals (Kohut and Stokes 2006).

3. Jane Yamazaki has attempted to analyze the circumstances that caused the victim countries not to accept Japan's apologies after the war (Yamazaki 2006).

4. In the fall of 2004, the leader of a group of ten high school teachers from Indonesian *pesantren* (Islamic boarding schools) who were visiting Japan said at the end of the tour, "I want to thank the Japanese government. I was moved to find that the teachings of Islam, such as respect for others and reverence for nature, are even more deeply rooted in Japan than in Indonesia." Japanese listeners were in turn moved by this statement, which deepened their understanding of Islam. This episode demonstrates the powerful impact exchange programs can have on both participants and hosts even in a short period of time.

5. Sociologist Kenneth Boulding divided power into the three categories of destructive, productive, and integrative power; among these, it is clear that "integrative power" corresponds to soft power. It is important to recognize that by referring to "the capacity to bind people together" or to "build up communication networks," he implied that there is also a concept of "cooperative interaction" in his integrative power (Boulding 1990, pp. 25, 110).

6. Refer to the "perceiving" nature of Japanese culture mentioned in note 1.

7. As announced on February 3, 2006, the BBC World Service Global Poll, a survey conducted in thirty-three countries, showed that among nine major countries and regions, Japan is the country most widely viewed as having a positive influence. (Europe as a whole got the most positive ratings.)

8. Concerning twenty-first-century public diplomacy taking the form of a network, see Hocking 2005, pp. 35–39, and Leonard and Alakeson 2000.

References

Albright, Madeleine. 2006. "Good vs. Evil Does Not Work as Foreign Policy." *Financial Times,* March 24.

Aoki, Tamotsu, Seiichi Kondo, and Min Wang. 2005. "Cultural Exchange: A National Priority." *Japan Echo* 32 (6): 31–35.

Armstead, Leigh. 2004. *Information Operation: Warfare and the Hard Reality of Soft Power.* Washington, DC: Brasseys.

BBC World Service. 2006. "Global Public Opinion." February 3. http://www.worldpublicopinion.org/pipa/articles/home_related/168.php?nid=&id=&put=168&lb=hmpg (accessed June 12, 2006).

Boulding, Kenneth E. 1990. *Three Faces of Power.* Newbury Park, London: Sage Publications.

Council on Foreign Relations. 2003. *Finding America's Voice: A Strategy for Reinventing U.S. Public Diplomacy.* New York: Council on Foreign Relations.

Council for the Promotion of Cultural Diplomacy. 2005. "Establishing Japan as a 'Peaceful Nation of Cultural Exchange.'" http://www.kantei.go.jp/foreign/policy/bunka/050711bunka_e.html (accessed June 12, 2006).

Fisher, Glen H. 1972. *Public Diplomacy and the Behavioral Sciences.* Bloomington: Indiana University Press.

Fraser, Matthew. 2004. *Weapons of Mass Destruction: Soft Power and American Empire.* New York: Thomas Dunne Books, St. Martin's Press.

Fukuyama, Francis. 2006. "After Neoconservatism." *New York Times Magazine,* February 19.

Fullilove, Michael. 2006. "When Reality No Longer Matches Rhetoric." *Financial Times,* June 6.

Hocking, Brian. 2005. "Rethinking the 'New' Public Diplomacy." In *The New Public Diplomacy: Soft Power in International Relations.* Ed. Jan Melissen. New York: Palgrave Macmillan: 28–46.

Hoffman, David. 2002. "Beyond Public Diplomacy." *Foreign Affairs* (May–June): 83–95.

Hughes, Karen. 2005. "The Mission of Public Diplomacy." Testimony at confirmation hearing before the Senate Foreign Relations Committee. July 22. http://www.state.gov/r/us/2005/49967.htm (accessed June 17, 2006).

Kohut, Andrew, and Bruce Stokes. 2006. *America Against the World: How We Are Different and Why We Are Disliked.* New York: Times Books.

Kondo, Seiichi. 1997. *Yugamerareru Nihon imeji: Washinton no pasepushon gemu* (The distorted image of Japan: The perception game inside the Beltway). Tokyo: Simul Press.

———. 1998. "The Japan-U.S. Auto Talks: A Case Study of Public Relations." *Japan Review of International Affairs* 12 (2): 127–42.

———. 2004. "A New Direction for Japanese Diplomacy." *Japan Echo* 31 (6): 31–34.

———. 2005. "A Major Stride for Japan's Cultural Diplomacy." *Japan Echo* 32 (6). http://www.japanecho.co.jp/sum/2005/320609.html (accessed December 15, 2007).

Lennon, Alexander T.J., ed. 2003. *The Battle for Hearts and Minds: Using Soft Power to Undermine Terrorist Networks.* Cambridge, MA: MIT Press.

Leonard, Mark, and Vidhya Alakeson. 2000. *Going Public: Diplomacy for the Information Society.* London: Foreign Policy Centre.

Leonard, Mark, and Conrad Smewing. 2003. *Public Diplomacy and the Middle East.* London: Foreign Policy Centre.

Manheim, Jarol B. 1994. *Strategic Public Diplomacy & American Foreign Policy: The Evaluation of Influence.* New York: Oxford University Press.

McGray, Douglas. 2002. "Japan's Gross National Cool." *Foreign Policy* 130 (May–June): 44–54.

Melissen, Jan. 2005. "The New Public Diplomacy: Between Theory and Practice." In *The New Public Diplomacy: Soft Power in International Relations.* Ed. Jan Melissen. New York: Palgrave Macmillan.

Napier, Susan J. 2001. *Anime from Akira to Princess Mononoke.* New York: Palgrave Macmillan

Newson, David. 1988. *Diplomacy and the American Democracy.* Bloomington: Indiana University Press.

Nye, Joseph S., Jr. 2004. *Soft Power: The Means to Success in World Politics.* New York: Public Affairs.

National Institute for Research Advancement (NIRA). 2005. *World Civilization Forum 2005 Report: Toward a New Paradigm for the World: How to Bring Young People Together to Overcome Differences in the World*. Tokyo: NIRA.

Pei, Minxin. 2003. "The Paradoxes of American Nationalism." *Foreign Policy* (May–June): 30–37.

Riordan, Shaun. 2003. *The New Diplomacy*. Cambridge: Polity.

Ross, Christopher. 2003. "Public Diplomacy Comes of Age." In *The Battle for Hearts and Minds: Using Soft Power to Undermine Terrorist Networks*. Ed. Alexander T.J. Lennon. Cambridge, MA: MIT Press.

Rothkopf, David. 1997. "In Praise of Cultural Imperialism?" *Foreign Policy* (Summer): 38–53.

Rugh, William A. 2006. *American Encounters with Arabs: The "Soft Power" of U.S. Public Diplomacy in the Middle East*. Westport, CT: Praeger Security International.

Sen, Amartya. 2006. *Identity and Violence: The Illusion of Destiny*. New York: W.W. Norton.

Sen, Souoku. 2006. "Dento to Bi-ishiki wa eien nari" (Tradition and aesthetic feelings live forever). *Chuo Koron* (February): 120–34.

Takeda, Shigeo. 2004. *Gemu riron wo yomitoku* (Reinterpreting game theory). Tokyo: Chikuma Shinsho.

Thaler, Richard H. 1994. *Quasi Rational Economics*. New York: Russell Sage Foundation.

Tuch, Hans N. 1993. *Communicating with the World: U.S. Public Diplomacy Overseas*. New York: St. Martin's Press.

Yamazaki, Jane W. 2006. *Japanese Apologies for World War II: A Rhetorical Study*. London: Routledge.

12

Official Soft Power in Practice

U.S. Public Diplomacy in Japan

William G. Crowell

Characteristic of the notion of "soft power" is that it can be practiced by nearly any person or institution at any point where states or peoples intersect. In discussing the topic, therefore, one must specify what type or element of soft power is meant. With respect to relations between states, the most salient form in which governments apply soft power is through public diplomacy.[1]

Practiced informally by the United States since its birth, public diplomacy as an integral component of American diplomatic practice really began with World War I. From the beginning, American public diplomacy was a combination of informa-tion activities advocating U.S. government policy, cultural and educational activities promoting better understanding of American society and culture, and personal and professional ties with foreign elites. The combination, while superficially reasonable, was not always compatible. Too often, resources for cultural activities were co-opted for informational activities that artists, educators, and even cultural officers sometimes considered akin to propaganda. This internal tension has characterized American public diplomacy to the present (Arndt 2005; Cummings 2003; Malone 1988).

During the Cold War, soft power in its broadest sense was considered a potent weapon against communism and the Soviet Empire. Secretary of State John Foster Dulles famously said that communism would be undermined by means of the gradual influence of Western ideas and culture—"peaceful evolution"—rather than by violent invasion. By "peaceful evolution," Dulles meant the elements considered to constitute soft power—trade, ideas, culture, people-to-people contact. He believed that over time these would subvert the communist system, a threat immediately recognized by com-munist leaders such as Mao Zedong, who feared and sought to thwart it.[2]

In a more positive incarnation during the Cold War, soft power aimed at rebuild-ing the devastated societies of Western Europe and Japan, and it was applied in many forms to develop and sustain support for Western alliances. Countering Soviet propaganda provided such strong justification for American cultural and information programs that when the Cold War ended, some thought the need for these programs had ceased. Combined with a congressional desire to cut spending and pressure to reorganize government, this led to merging the U.S. Information Agency (USIA) into the Department of State (DOS) on October 1, 1999. The possible ramifications of this move became painfully clear following the 9/11 terrorist attacks two years later, and policy makers, think tanks, and others since have scrambled to find an answer to the question of the day—"Why don't they understand us?"—and to repair America's public diplomacy apparatus.[3]

In this context, it is instructive to examine those places where U.S. public diplomacy has been effective. Nowhere have such efforts been more consistently successful than in Japan. There are many reasons for this, not all of which can be controlled or influenced by the United States. While the subject of public diplomacy in the U.S.-Japanese relationship is a topic worthy of study in itself, it can also provide object lessons for considering new directions for U.S. efforts elsewhere.

U.S. Public Diplomacy Goals for Japan

The primary functions of any U.S. embassy are to represent the United States to the host country, to gather information and report to Washington policy makers, and to promote the United States and its policies to the host country. By definition, public diplomacy is one of an embassy's principal missions and engages not only the Public Affairs Section (PAS) but others as well. To achieve maximum effectiveness in fulfilling this mission, the embassy sets both long-term and short-term targets, which in turn determine public diplomacy goals.

From the first, the overarching goal of U.S. public diplomacy in Japan has been cementing close relations and underscoring shared values. This goal has remained the rationale for public diplomacy activities, even as short-term specific goals have shifted. Since the beginning of the Cold War, it has been clearly understood, if not always articulated, that the *raison d'être* of embassy public diplomacy is to foster support for the security alliance. In the current international climate, the United States looks to Japan "to continue forging a leading role in regional and global affairs based on our common interests, our common values, and our close defense and diplomatic cooperation" (White House 2002).

Based on this premise, the U.S. mission in Japan, through its annual Mission Performance Plan (MPP), has specified four general themes for emphasis: counter-terrorism, regional stability, weapons of mass destruction, and economic prosperity.[4] Each subsumes a series of particular concerns; for example, counterterrorism includes immigration, relevant training for third countries, ship container security, and countering the movement of money destined for terrorist organizations. Economic prosperity might encompass opening Japanese markets to American goods, reforming the banking sector, corporate governance, and trade issues.

Because pursuit of these issues with the Japanese involves influencing opinion, public diplomacy—conducted primarily by PAS—is key to addressing them with the government of Japan, the Japanese news media, the intelligentsia, and the public. Naturally, PAS's ability to do so is very much determined by the resources at its disposal.

Resources

In evaluating the resources an embassy has at its disposal for its public diplomacy efforts, one must consider both the mission's total resources and as well as PAS's own personnel, funds, and infrastructure. Currently the U.S. Embassy in Tokyo employs approximately 250 Americans and 375 foreign service nationals as employees.[5] Aside from PAS, public diplomacy concerns mainly the ambassador and the political and economic sections, and to a lesser extent, the commercial and agricultural sections. Nearly everyone in the embassy, however, becomes involved at some point. This can result in additional burdens for PAS, but it also expands the resources on which it can draw.

The resources that PAS/Tokyo specifically controls for conducting public diplomacy comprise ninety American and Japanese employees and a budget (FY2006) of $8,153,635.[6] Staff are spread among Tokyo elements (Information, Culture, Information Resource Center, Tokyo American Center) and branch operations in the consular cities—Sapporo, Nagoya, Osaka, Fukuoka, and Naha. Of the eighteen Americans, all but one—the head of Press Translation and Media Analysis—are Foreign Service personnel (fifteen officers, one secretary, one specialist). All officer positions are language designated, meaning incumbents should have successfully tested at the required level of host-country language proficiency. Despite the costs in time and money, DOS considers it essential to train officers to a level of professional competency.[7]

Despite consolidation, the PAS budget has remained separate from the DOS embassy budget,[8] and the public affairs officer determines its allocation. While the nearly $8 million FY2006 budget may seem substantial, approximately two-thirds goes to fixed costs, such as foreign service nationals' salaries. This leaves just under $2.7 million for programs divided among Tokyo elements and the constituent public affairs sections. In FY2004, $1.7 million[9] was spent on program activities by Tokyo elements and $570,400 by the consulates. In FY2005, however, the PAS/Japan budget was cut 5 percent (about a 20 percent cut in nonsalary money) to meet public diplomacy needs elsewhere.

Aside from money allocated to PAS/Japan to support the embassy's public affairs activities, there are two other major expenditures of U.S. government money (excluding U.S. military public affairs) contributing to American public diplomacy in Japan. The first is in the U.S. contribution to the Japan–United States Educational Commission (JUSEC). In FY2006, direct and indirect contributions from the American side totaled $1,935,200.[10] In recent years both sides have felt pressure to cut their allocations; the higher contribution from the government of Japan—$3,101,010.20 in FY2006[11] has probably helped to sustain the U.S. government contribution. The other major U.S. government expenditure is for the Japan–United States Friendship Commission (JUSFC). JUSFC is supported by a trust fund established using the proceeds generated by the return to Japan of certain U.S. facilities in Okinawa. Income from the fund is available "for the promotion of scholarly, cultural and public affairs activities between the two countries." As of the end of FY2006, the trust fund stood at $39,520,101.

The commission had spent nearly $1.7 million from the proceeds of the trust fund on programs and had administrative expenses (rent, salaries, etc.) of $703,814.

Programs and Activities

The U.S. public diplomacy program in Japan is among the most extensive and complex the U.S. government conducts worldwide.[12] Its programs, structure, and goals do not differ significantly from those of other major U.S. embassy programs. Differences are found largely in the country-specific themes (major themes tend to be the same worldwide), the training required of officers assigned to a "hard language" post, and accommodations made to the local communications environment. The materials, equipment, speakers, and support supplied from Washington are the same as would be found in any comparable post.

A convenient approach to understanding the activities of the U.S. mission in Japan is Joseph Nye's three dimensions of public diplomacy: daily communications, strategic communication, and development of lasting relationships (Nye 2004, p. 107ff). Although conceptually the differences among these may seem obvious, in practice the boundaries between dimensions are not always clear, and activities may overlap.

Daily Communications

The greater part of PAS/Tokyo's resources is devoted to daily communications, and the Information Division conducts the preponderance of this work. The Information Division daily produces several fliers for distribution to Japanese media, other missions in Tokyo, and government of Japan offices. These are also available electronically. Branch public affairs sections at the consulates distribute these materials to local and regional media as well. Distributed materials include electronic journals and other occasional publications supplied from Washington, containing major policy statements and speeches, and *Rapid Responses,* which provide in-depth policy statements, analyses, and fact sheets. These are usually drawn from materials supplied electronically from Washington for reproduction and dissemination by the embassy. The post also produces a quarterly Japanese-language electronic magazine, *American View. Press Releases* furnish locally generated materials, such as speeches delivered by the ambassador and other U.S. government officials. *Notices to the Media* are sent to local news media to advise them of press conferences, briefings, and events. Further daily contact is maintained through the embassy's Web site, which contains important texts and information in English and Japanese.

Also important are the Information Resource Centers at the embassy at each American Center. These have replaced the familiar libraries of earlier years and concentrate on providing sophisticated reference services using print and electronic resources. Primarily directed at opinion leaders, including officials, journalists, academics, business leaders, and public intellectuals, American Center Resource Services also field queries from the general public. The reference service responds to over 10,000 queries annually from all sectors. The Information Resource Center also conducts outreach and marketing through courtesy calls and on the embassy Web site. Recently, it has instituted monthly seminars for students in a tentative reversal of a short-sighted policy of the last years of USIA to no longer to target students. Finally, daily communication is maintained through the personal contacts that embassy and consulate officers, as well as foreign service nationals, have with opinion leaders.

Strategic Communications

According to Nye, in this dimension a set of simple themes is developed and symbolic events and communications to advance government policy are planned to occur over the course of a year (Nye 2004, pp. 108–9). This pretty much describes what occurs in American embassies worldwide. Each year the Tokyo embassy prepares an MPP setting forth a set of broad themes addressing the most important bilateral issues. Under these themes, the embassy develops a further set of specific actions and goals to be pursued by each embassy section. For PAS, this means developing public diplomacy activities in support of MPP goals. Beyond these policy-driven themes, PAS plans programming around standing themes of American society, politics, history, and culture as part of its overall mission to promote mutual understanding, although "Mutual Understanding" is no longer a primary theme of the MPP. Finally, the MPP includes benchmarks by which the mission is expected to evaluate its work at the end of the year.

As one would expect, the mission themes guide the daily communications through the selection of policy documents and background materials for distribution and in the organization of press conferences, though these may also be determined by events unforeseen when the MPP was written. These themes also guide the annual planning of the Cultural Section's speaker program in considering possible events and recruiting academics, government officials, writers, and artists to be speakers. A plan for the coming year detailing themes and topics and setting forth when speakers on particular topics will be needed is submitted to Washington. Depending on the topic, the Washington program office then recruits academics, specialists, writers, and government officials as speakers. Speakers may be brought to Japan in person to speak at the American Centers, think tanks, universities, or business organizations. When that is not possible, as when a speaker is needed on short notice to respond to an unforeseen development, digital videoconferences may be arranged with invited Japanese.

The selection of speakers often can be sensitive and seems to have become particularly so since USIA was absorbed by DOS. While in the past the general operating principle of most USIA officers was to show the spectrum of American opinion in order to provide context and gain credibility for official policy messages, the DOS's political leadership has sometimes sought to narrow that spectrum to refract only the hues that put administration policy in the best light. During the Reagan administration there were accusations of a "blacklist" to exclude speakers, and at the end of 2005 there were press allegations of a "litmus test" being applied to ensure that only supporters of the administration's Iraq policy were being sent abroad (Strobel and Landay 2005).

But most public diplomacy officers understand that a speaker program is strongest when it avoids giving the impression of presenting only true believers.

PAS may also recruit speakers locally from among visiting academics, local American business leaders, or embassy officers. Embassy officers can be particularly effective, since they usually speak Japanese and know the issues well. Moreover, audiences often wish to hear official thinking on a given issue and to know that their views are being expressed directly to a representative of the U.S. government.

Mission themes are also used as criteria for determining the selection of individuals to be invited to the United States under the auspices of the International Visitor Leadership (IV) Program. Likewise, the content of materials distributed to selected individuals by the American Center Resource Services in their outreach activities is also guided by these themes. By coordinating activities around selected themes, PAS hopes to reach an audience that has a potential "multiplier effect" through retransmitting and explaining the message to a broader audience.

Development of Lasting Relationships

Nye has written that as the United States tries to meet the public diplomacy challenges that face it in the Middle East, most important will be the development of a long-term strategy of cultural and educational exchanges leading to a richer and more open civil society. Moreover, he noted, often the "most effective spokespersons for the United States are not Americans but indigenous surrogates who understand America's virtues as well as our faults" (Nye 2004, p. 12). While one could offer numerous examples to support Nye's point, none is more compelling than Japan. At the end of World War II, the cultural gap and the level of misunderstanding between Americans and Japanese was perhaps as great as any that exists today. While the two countries still disagree on many points of policy and experience serious trade frictions, the relationship has developed into what Ambassador Mike Mansfield often referred to as the "most important bilateral relationship in the world, bar none." That achievement is in no small measure due to the "official soft power" exercised by both sides.

Embassy public diplomacy activities aimed at fostering long-term relationships are conducted primarily by the Cultural Section. These include grants to nonprofit organizations, educational institutions, and cultural entities to support relevant projects. Some of these are one-time activities, such as a cultural presentation or a conference. In other cases grants will be made in consecutive years to a single organization to support ongoing activities. In FY2004, twelve grants totaling $460,941 were given to support three music performances; an art exhibit; two youth exchanges; and travel for a half dozen study groups variously comprising local and national legislators, local government officials, journalists, and think tank members who variously traveled to the United States, Korea, and Okinawa to be briefed on security affairs, economic issues, and local government operations.

One of the best-known U.S. government public diplomacy programs is the International Visitor Leadership Program (known until 2004 as the International Visitor or IV

Program), with roots stretching back at least to 1940. The program worldwide invites upward of 4,500 individuals to the United States to meet and confer with their professional counterparts and to experience the United States firsthand. Of these, in FY2006 fifty individuals came from Japan. Another eighteen "voluntary visitors"—persons who met the criteria for the International Visitor Leadership program but are traveling for their own purposes—were given short-term programs while in the United States.

The question of the dangers posed by cultural gaps and resulting misunderstandings was among the factors that motivated Senator J. William Fulbright to create the program of educational exchanges that bears his name.[13] The Fulbright Program for Japan began in 1952 and in its early years was funded entirely by the U.S. government. Under its auspices, Japanese were sent to the United States to study for graduate and undergraduate degrees. Then, at the end of 1979, a binational commission—the Japan–United States Educational Commission—was created, and the principle of funding by both sides was established. JUSEC's board comprises ten members, five from each side, and operates independently, though there are two members from the embassy and two from the government of Japan (one from the Ministry of Education, Culture, Science and Technology and one from the Ministry of Foreign Affairs). In FY2006 JUSEC made awards to forty-seven Japanese and fifty-four Americans. An active alumni group has developed and has been very successful in raising funds to support the program. Japanese alumni comprise prominent educators, artists, jurists, scientists, journalists and government leaders; their number includes Nobel laureates and recipients of other honors. Indicative of the program's prestige was the participation of Their Imperial Highnesses, the emperor and empress, and the crown prince and princess in the fiftieth anniversary celebration in 2002.

Another important aspect of JUSEC's work supported by Washington is the educational information services provided for Japanese who wish to study in the United States. In 2005–6, JUSEC's Educational Information Services fielded an estimated 613,000 queries. According to the Institute for International Education (IIE), in 2004–5 there were 38,712 Japanese students in the United States, the fourth-largest group after Indians, Chinese, and Koreans. Still, this represents a decrease of 8.3 percent over the previous year, which had seen a slight increase following annual declines in the wake of 9/11.[14] There were 4,100 U.S. students in Japan, a 10 percent increase over 2003–4 (IIE 2006). While most Japanese students pay their own way, they are potentially a significant source for Nye's "indigenous surrogates." The extent to which they might come to fill that role, however, depends on a multiplicity of variables, including language ability, field of study, personal interest, and opportunity. In any event, the widely held and optimistic view that when "foreign students undertake studies in the United States, they return to their home countries immersed in American values, attitudes, and modes of thinking" (Fraser 2003) needs to be examined carefully.

A third important contributor to official U.S. soft power is the Japan–United States Friendship Commission (JUSFC). Congress established the commission as an independent federal agency in 1975. Income from the trust fund administered by JUSFC is used for the promotion of scholarly, cultural, and public affairs activities between the two countries. The commission's decisions are made by its board of eighteen members, which is divided between U.S. private and public sector representatives, two of whom are DOS assistant secretaries (JUSFC 2006; Auslin forthcoming). The embassy exercises no oversight over commission programs but can voice its concerns about commission programs or priorities through the DOS representatives on the commission board. On an informal level, there is close consultation between the commission and the embassy on programs. JUSFC is also the U.S. secretariat for CULCON (U.S.-Japan Conference on Cultural and Educational Interchange), as is the Japan Foundation for Japan. CULCON is a twenty-four-member board comprising three government officials and nine private citizens from each side. Its purpose is to advise the two governments on ways to improve educational and cultural relations. As the source of U.S. CULCON funding, DOS oversees its annual budget and plays a significant role in shaping CULCON policies and programs (JUSFC 2006).

Often the most formidable public diplomacy resource an embassy has is its chief of mission. In the words of a ranking embassy officer, "the ambassador is the most important element to creating an effective public diplomacy program." The Tokyo embassy has been well served by a series of ambassadors considered elder statesmen, including Mike Mansfield, Michael Armacost, Walter Mondale, Thomas Foley, and Howard Baker. Their stature resonated well in Japan, and all had ties with important Japanese well before they were appointed ambassador. Their prominence and the respect accorded them made it possible, when necessary, to address the Japanese people directly through the media and be heard. Moreover, because of their experience with political campaigning and press coverage, they tended to be little bothered by poor or sensationalist reporting and less likely to overreact and inadvertently lend credence to the reports. On cultural matters, ambassadors' spouses have sometimes been the embassy's most important representatives. They have worked closely with the CAO (cultural affairs officer) to organize programs at the ambassador's residence and elsewhere. A striking example was Joan Mondale, a practicing potter and arts activist. She spoke throughout Japan on the importance of public art and initiated channels that still exist. Similarly, Bonnie Armacost, a trained musician, worked closely with the CAO on cultural programming. But even spouses who are not themselves artists have been effective representatives of aspects of the United States beyond security and trade, and they have been instrumental in getting the ambassador involved in cultural and educational events.

Obstacles and Challenges

Japan would seem to be a comparatively fertile environment for American public diplomacy. The populace is highly educated, the news media are well developed, and the United States sparks considerable interest. Embassy and consulate officers have easy access to opinion leaders—editors, academics, government officials, and public intellectuals—and their participation and endorsement are often sought for Japanese cultural activities. Yet, obstacles and challenges do exist, some thrown up by the Japanese communications environment and others self-inflicted.

Many of the elements making Japan a good environment for public diplomacy can become obstacles to having one's message heard. Even when it is heard, there is no certainty a message will be heard accurately. The media-rich environment offers many sources of information, and conflicting messages abound. Though news media can access a wide range of sources of information about the United States, they tend to accept their own sources over any other. Many have their own U.S.-based bureaus and correspondents. There is no shortage of interpreters of American actions and pronouncements, some with long U.S. experience and a sophisticated understanding of events, others much less capable but influential nonetheless. Many media figures embrace a set of enduring assumptions about the bilateral relationship that are difficult for an embassy public diplomacy operation to overcome.

The ability of a U.S. government message to be heard is hampered, too, by the particular tradecraft and institutions of Japanese journalists. The greatest challenge is posed by the *kisha kurabu* (reporters clubs) that are attached to all major (and many minor) government offices, organizations, and corporations (Freeman 2000). Superficially analogous to the "press corps" found at the White House, State Department, or Capitol Hill, the *kisha* clubs differ in significant ways. Most important is that while in the United States the relationship between the press corps and the entity it covers is basically adversarial, that of a *kisha* club to its host entity is usually cozy and symbiotic. Consequently, reporting from *kisha* club reporters closely follows the particular spin of their host, and reports by different club reporters tend toward sameness. Because the clubs are "closed shops," outside reporters cannot gain access to the information provided to club reporters. Club reporters do not seek comments from other parties, including the embassy, when the story involves a bilateral issue, so the embassy often finds itself having to try to turn a story that has already hit the press.

Another obstacle is the Japanese language. Although English literacy in Japan is growing and there is keen interest in things American, most Japanese unsurprisingly prefer to obtain their information in their own language. American policy statements, background information, and speeches and statements must be translated, a costly and time-consuming process. Additionally, because the most effective means of conveying a message remains personal contact, officers must have extensive and costly language training.

Other challenges derive from frictions arising from the significant U.S. military presence in Japan. Military public affairs and community relations operations make a sustained effort to maintain good relations with the local population, but incidents involving individual servicemen—no matter how minor—can swiftly turn into national front-page news and overshadow important bilateral issues. For Japanese politicians who have no other issue to get behind, criticizing the bases and calling for reduction of their impact seem an easy vote magnet.

On issues pertaining to the security alliance and the U.S. bases, the embassy's public affairs activities must be closely coordinated with the Ministry of Foreign Affairs and Japan Self-Defense Agency. Whereas the American approach usually tends to favor openness and transparency, embassy officers sometimes find that their Japanese counterparts are sensitive to domestic political considerations. Even when a public affairs strategy could show the U.S. military taking positive steps on a difficult matter such as the environmental impact of the bases, Japanese officials may see it as just another opportunity for base opponents to remind voters of the problems the bases cause.

Additional challenges to the conduct of U.S. public diplomacy have appeared in the wake of the 9/11 terrorist attacks. While most Japanese were sympathetic to the United States and there was an outpouring of support symbolized by a huge mound of flowers placed in front of the embassy by individual Japanese, many were also heard to comment that the United States had brought the attack on itself by its actions. The United States no longer seemed as strong or secure as it once was. Immediately following the assault on New York's World Trade Center, Japanese corporations advised their employees to avoid American airlines, though there was no evidence that U.S. flights were more vulnerable than any others. Tightened U.S. visa restrictions resulted in frustrating delays, and heightened embassy security fueled the image of an America besieged. Already considered by many to be a violent and chaotic society, the United States became a less attractive destination for travel or university study.

A final challenge has been the high cost of doing business in Japan. The dollar cost of foreign service nationals' salaries, for example, has more than doubled in the past two decades, while budgets have remained flat or even declined. As resources have been shifted to other priorities or regions such as the Middle East, those available to support public diplomacy in Japan have diminished. The most visible evidence of this has been a reduction of American Centers around the country. At the peak, there were twenty-three mostly freestanding American Centers with libraries open to the public and programs to inform the local residents (the focus was on the "successor generations," students, and opinion leaders) about American policies, culture, and society. Currently there are just six centers, four of which are located inside consular facilities, where access is strictly controlled. The exceptions—in Fukuoka and Tokyo—are located in tall office buildings, where their presence is obscured.

Aside from the challenges of the Japanese communications environment, there are other obstacles that might be described as "self-inflicted." These derive largely from the structure of the public diplomacy apparatus and the bureaucratic behavior of those who work within it. At the root of these problems is the notion that because cultural and informational (policy advocacy) activities ultimately aim at the same goal—the acceptance or at least understanding of U.S. policies—the two functions can be combined. This has long been the subject of debate.

When USIA was created in 1953, many of the cultural activities were retained in the DOS's Bureau of Cultural Affairs at the behest of Senator J. William Fulbright, who feared that his eponymous exchange program would be tainted by "propaganda" (Arndt 2005, pp. 262, 272). While the functions were separated in Washington, they became joined overseas, where USIA officers administered cultural activities. Many found this practice unsatisfactory and advocated variously that both functions be combined in an independent agency (i.e., USIA) or in DOS, or that the two functions be separated completely.

The question was taken up in 1973 by a panel chaired by Frank Stanton, former chairman of CBS. In a report issued in 1975, the Panel on International Information, Education and Cultural Relations concluded that information and cultural and educational programs should be under DOS. But, since educational and cultural programs provided "general" knowledge about the United States (as opposed to policy), they should be in an autonomous cultural affairs agency whose director reported directly to the secretary of state. Such an arrangement, the panel thought, would provide the programs with sufficient distance from daily policy concerns while avoiding the disadvantages of placing them in an independent entity (Malone 1987). Although there was widespread recognition of the wisdom of the Stanton recommendations, there was also resistance. The question was settled by the Carter administration, which combined both functions in a single agency, the U.S. International Communications Agency (USICA), which replaced USIA. The USIA name was restored in 1982; in October 1999, the agency was absorbed by DOS and put under a newly created undersecretary for public diplomacy and public affairs. The Stanton panel had ultimately gotten half of what it recommended—but not the better half.

These developments were not simply a matter of manipulating flowcharts. The result has been subordination of educational and cultural activities to policy advocacy and loss of the separation—in Washington and in the field—thought necessary to avoid the taint of propaganda. It has also given rise to a view that funds intended for educational and cultural activities are fungible and can be shifted to policy advocacy. As budgets have tightened, there has been an inclination to cut educational and cultural activities in favor of information activities.[15]

Subtler than reprogramming budgets has been the use of educational and cultural programs for policy advocacy. One Tokyo CAO was criticized in his annual performance evaluation for devoting too much of his budget to cultural activities, and a newly arrived deputy director of the Tokyo American Center was told by the public affairs officer that the center was to be the embassy's "propaganda shop." Not only have speaker programs increasingly focused on policy issues, but pressure has also mounted to recruit speakers known to support administration policies. While some might think this only logical, such an approach vitiates the effort to demonstrate that American foreign policy is arrived at through "a rational debate" (in the words of one CAO). More seriously, it has begun driving away audience members, who have told officers and foreign service nationals that they no longer find American Center programs interesting.

Combining educational and cultural functions with information also means that they are administered by public diplomacy generalist officers rather than officers specialized in culture or education. Since the merger of USIA into DOS, foreign service officers from the political, economic, and administrative "cones" can—and do—bid on public diplomacy positions. While they may be adequate to the task, the result is a bit like using one's shoe to drive a nail: it may get the job done and perhaps not leave a heel mark on the wall, but it is not the most effective tool. More seriously, this development reflects a misapprehension that almost anyone can do public diplomacy work, unlike the economic and political cones, which are thought to require special training. Finally, assignments are sometimes made with an eye to individuals' managerial strengths rather than to their qualifications to represent and project American culture to the Japanese.

It should be noted that some public diplomacy generalists do possess rich backgrounds and deep commitment to culture and education and have earned the respect of Japanese artists and educators. They have demonstrated energy and creativity in addressing the challenges facing a CAO. A salient example was Interlink, a program initiated in 1985 to promote collaboration between cutting-edge Japanese and American musicians. Through the efforts of the CAO, more than half the funding was raised from non–U.S. government sources, and Japanese participants did much of the work. A decade later, however, the public affairs officer ordered the then CAO to end the program so the resources could be directed to more policy-oriented activities. But such officers are increasingly rare, and there is a danger that CAO slots will be occupied by officers who, though otherwise talented, have little experience in educational and cultural affairs. Such officers will be unable to achieve fully the goals of promoting appreciation of American culture and society. In the short term, this may seem unimportant, but as U.S. leaders are beginning to appreciate, the long-term ramifications can be critical.

Impact and Assessment

Perhaps the most difficult facet of public diplomacy is assessing its effectiveness. Many forms of hard power lend themselves to quantitative evaluation, for instance, numbers of bridges destroyed, enemy soldiers killed, trade dollars lost through sanctions. But as former USIA director Edward R. Murrow remarked, "No cash register rings when a man changes his mind" (Malone 1988). Yet assessment is necessary to justify expenditures of taxpayers' money and to direct program planning and resource allocation. While one can count "inputs"—press conferences held, policy statements distributed, speeches given, exchange visitors sent, and information requests answered—measuring how a mind has been changed or a person's understanding has been deepened is more difficult. The impact of some activities may not be immediate; the debriefing of an exchange visitor done upon return may yield impressions different from those held a year or even a decade later. Focus groups and polling can assess attitudes in a general way, but understanding how those attitudes were influenced by specific public diplomacy activities is much harder. Ultimately, much of the information will remain anecdotal.[16] Still, as with any activity funded by the American taxpayer, a good-faith effort at assessment is expected.

PAS/Tokyo tries to measure the embassy's public diplomacy effectiveness in several ways. The Information Division enumerates press events, recording the principal (i.e., who spoke or was interviewed), type of event, and media outlets reached. The Cultural Division's Program Development Office prepares reports on speaker programs that include program summaries, audience, and a judgment of program effectiveness. The Information Resource Centers maintain statistics of users at each center, volume and themes of queries, and outreach activities. For International Visitor Leadership Programs, the visitor's U.S. escort shares a written report with the embassy, and the nominating officer is expected to debrief the visitor. Most of this reporting focuses on embassy "inputs." Outcome is more difficult to assess, much less quantify. To some extent, the effect of press events can be gauged from resulting media coverage or editorials. PAS's Press Translation and Media Analysis unit does track national and regional media closely and report on such coverage. But for speaker programs, cultural functions, or exchange programs, aside from participant comments, one must rely on the officer's subjective judgment. The effectiveness of such reporting depends on the objectivity and forthrightness of the report's author. Too often, however, making one's program appear successful may seem more important than critical assessment, and concern about Freedom of Information Act requests from speakers seeking evaluations of their programs can discourage candor.

One approach to the general problem is through public opinion polling and focus groups. PAS regularly commissions such studies for its own use, and it carefully tracks Japanese polls. While polls cannot evaluate program effectiveness, they do offer generally reliable indications of public perceptions of the United States and the bilateral relationship that can be useful in assessing program effectiveness. The generally favorable view of the United States reflected in such studies suggests that despite occasional hiccups and disagreements, the relationship is strong, and that perhaps the embassy's public diplomacy efforts have yielded positive results.[17]

Conclusions and Lessons

After September 11, 2001, Americans were baffled that anyone could hate them so, a perplexity compounded by polls in the Middle East showing minimal support for U.S. actions in Afghanistan. The situation has grown worse with the debacle in Iraq. One consequence has been a renewed interest in public diplomacy. In this context, it seems natural to ask whether there are lessons are to be learned from the U.S. experience with Japan. That experience is not so irrelevant as it might seem. After all, the U.S.-Japanese relationship has evolved from being violently adversarial and having few "shared values" to a strategic and economic partnership. This development is in large measure the fruit of soft power. The lessons that might be learned from this experience include the following.

1. Cultural and educational programs are not intended as a response to an immediate crisis. Needed is a long-term vision and an understanding that the payoff for educational and cultural programs should be a reservoir of goodwill and understanding that will come into play when a crisis does occur.[18] Because this long-term approach is ultimately incompatible with a short-term focus on policy advocacy, the two should be separated. Cultural and educational programs perhaps should be removed from the DOS entirely and away from policy considerations of the moment.

2. Thoughtful consideration is needed of what should constitute public diplomacy with a society or culture that not only has little in common with the United States but also is frankly hostile to the very values it represents. The shared-values approach will not work. It took deep commitment on both sides (Japanese more than American) to overcome a wide cultural gulf between the United States and Japan. In the absence of even minimal respect for American values, public diplomacy will require subtlety, patience, and humility.

With the bilateral relationship so strong and multifaceted, one might reasonably ask whether a large U.S. public diplomacy effort toward Japan is still needed. In answering this question, one must bear in mind that though there exist soft power relations of many sorts between the two countries, they are not always interchangeable. One of the dangers of the "soft power" concept is that it is rather nebulous and may mislead policy makers into concluding that because private sector educational and cultural or trade relations are flourishing, there is no need for robust government programs. But private and public interests do not always coincide, and private efforts may not reach crucial segments of the society or may even impart an undesired message.

Given the importance of enduring relationships to successful public diplomacy, before reducing resources for Japan, U.S. policy makers ought to consider where Japan and the bilateral relationship are likely to be fifty or more years hence. It may well be that the next half-century will see Japan desiring to maintain itself as a regional influence and identifying ever more closely with East Asia at the expense of the United States. The continued rise of China as an economic and military power may force greater accommodation between the two countries. Increasing confidence and comfort in Japan's own role as a military power may bring a desire among Japanese policy makers and others to be less dependent on the United States. Such a development could find popular reinforcement from a growing sense of a need for national pride fed by anti-Americanism of the sort described by Watanabe Yasushi elsewhere in this volume. While it seems improbable that Japan would once again become a military adversary of the United States, it could cease to be the "reliable" ally it now is. If the U.S. government does not work to maintain the reservoir of goodwill, Americans may once again find themselves wondering, "Why don't they understand us?"

Notes

I wish to express my appreciation to the Public Affairs Section, U.S. Embassy/Tokyo, to JUSEC, and to JUSFC for their assistance. I also wish to thank several former colleagues and friends, including Robin Berrington, David Cordell, Dr. Eric Gangloff, Mary Kirk, Chris Livaccari, Ray Scofield, Dale Sturdavant, and Arthur Zegelbone. I am also grateful to the other participants in the seminars and to the staff of CGP and SSRC for their trenchant comments. Responsibility for the views expressed herein and for errors, however, is entirely my own.

1. "Public diplomacy" has referred to governmental and nongovernmental activities of many stripes. The term is used here in a narrow sense to denote specifically those cultural and information activities conducted by the U.S. Department of State to promote understanding of American society and culture and acceptance of U.S. policies.

2. See Brady 2005. The end of the Cold War notwithstanding, fear of peaceful evolution in communist states has not dissipated. Compare COPVN 2004.

3. Most striking was HR 3969, Freedom Promotion Act of 2002. Proposed by Congressman Henry Hyde, this bill would have directed the secretary of state to make public diplomacy an integral part of foreign policy formation and execution. (That it was thought necessary to write this into law perhaps suggests the source of the United States' image problems.) For other initiatives, see "Public and Cultural Diplomacy Timeline" (Center for Arts and Culture 2004; cf. Advisory Committee on Cultural Diplomacy 2005; Bayles 2005; Johnson and Dale 2003). The ongoing discussion can be readily followed on the University of Southern California's Center for Public Diplomacy Web site: http://uscpublicdiplomacy.com/index.php.

4. Prior to 2002 the MPP included upwards of twenty such issues, including mutual understanding, which comprised such topics as U.S. society, American studies, and the arts. To streamline the MPP, DOS limited the themes to four. "Mutual Understanding" was dropped as a goal and its component activities subsumed under the other themes, becoming in effect *means* to achieving those goals.

5. FSNs are locally hired nationals who work in support or staff positions. Because American ex-pats are increasingly hired for these positions, they have recently been designated "locally employed staff" (LES). This bit of bureaucratese and its insensitive acronym have not been appreciated by either local staff or many of their American supervisors, who continue to use "FSN."

6. This excludes salaries of American Foreign Service Officers, which are paid from the DOS budget in Washington.

7. For an officer without Japanese, language and area studies require nearly two years of full-time study in the United States and Japan. Besides the cost of instruction, the officer continues to receive full salary and benefits, and DOS covers housing, dependent education, and language training for the officer's spouse, if she or he desires it.

8. At the time of consolidation, Congress was concerned lest a funds-starved State Department redirect the monies received from the USIA budget to other activities, and it "firewalled" many of those funds. Although there has been pressure to combine budgets, for the foreseeable future it appears that the firewall will remain.

9. This excludes $327,000 for International Visitor grants paid from a Washington allotment.

10. This is down from $2,502,462 in FY2004. FY2006 direct allocation was $1.8 million, which was up from the previous year because of a one-time embassy contribution of ¥50,320,600. The indirect allocation of $120,000 paid for stateside administrative costs, enrichment activities for grantees, and other costs.

11. Based on exchange rate of ¥110 to US$1. The government of Japan allocation was ¥350,000,000, down from ¥362,659,000 in FY2004.

12. Comparative public diplomacy budget figures for FY2003 are as follows: Japan, $8,863,000; Germany, $7,226,448; India, $4,386,512; France, $3,482,950; China, $1,826,042; United Kingdom, $1,472,000 (UK figures are for FY2002).

13. Although he had earlier considered the idea of an educational exchange program, Senator Fulbright said the bombings of Hiroshima and Nagasaki focused his thoughts. With such weapons at his disposal he felt that world leaders could not afford to miscalculate and that ignorance in high places posed a danger (Woods 1995, p. 129).

14. This stunning decline appears related more to economic and demographic developments within Japan than to anything in the bilateral relationship. See the comments in the "Japan Country Fact Sheet," Institute of International Education, http://opendoors.iienetwork.org/?p=113181 (accessed 11/30/07).

15. Early in the Reagan administration, when USIA director Charles Z. Wick wanted to use exchange monies to support plans for a satellite television network, Congress passed a "charter" to protect exchange funding. There were even suggestions that the exchange programs be relocated to the Smithsonian Institution (Arndt 2005, p. 528; Malone 1988, pp. 124–25).

16. Two U.S. government studies bemoan that most reporting now focuses on anecdotal evidence or on "inputs." The Djerejian report recommends measuring "progress toward the more fundamental objective of achieving changes in understanding and attitudes about the United States" (Djerejian 2003, p. 66; GAO 2003). This will require substantially increased funding and manpower, however, and in some countries may simply not be possible because of cultural sensitivities and suspicion. The experience of the Pew Project for the People and the Press in assessing foreign attitudes toward the United States could be instructive here.

17. Polling done for PAS over the past two decades indicates that more than 50 percent and sometimes high as 80 percent of the Japanese people polled view the United States favorably. Since 1996, more than half have considered relations between the United States and Japan to be good.

18. "Goodwill and understanding" is not intended here as the amorphous concept referred to derisively as "warm and fuzzy" by policy advocacy types who considered themselves to be more "realistic." Rather, it should be understood in the way businesses consider "goodwill" to be an intangible asset important to their success and that has led a corporation like Altria, parent company of the tobacco manufacturer Philip Morris, to grant upward of $210 million to the arts since 1958.

References

Advisory Committee on Cultural Diplomacy. 2005. "Cultural Diplomacy: The Linchpin of Public Diplomacy." http://www.state.gov/r/adcompd/rls/54256.htm (accessed October 5, 2005).

Arndt, Richard. 2005. *The First Resort of Kings: American Cultural Diplomacy in the Twentieth Century*. Washington, DC: Potomac.

Auslin, Michael. Forthcoming. *Pacific Cosmopolitans: The Cultural Encounter Between Japan and the United States*. Cambridge, MA: Harvard University Press.

Bayles, Martha. 2005. "Goodwill Hunting." *Wilson Quarterly* 29 (3): 46–56.

Brady, Anne-Marie. 2005. "From Opening Minds to Regimenting Minds: A Comparison of Propaganda Policy in Gorbachev's Soviet Union and Jiang Zemin's China." http://www.cishsydney2005.org/images/Anne-MarieBradyIC7v2.doc (accessed December 7, 2005).

Center for Arts and Culture. 2004. "Cultural Diplomacy: Recommendations and Research." http://www.culturalpolicy.org/pdf/CulturalDiplomacy.pdf (accessed November 4, 2005).

COPVN. 2004. "Media Unmask Peaceful Evolution Scheme." Interview with Vu Duy Thong, Head, Media Service Under the Party Central Commission on Culture and Ideology, Communist Party of Vietnam, August 27. http://www.cpv.org.vn/details.asp?topic=29&subtopic=118&id=BT2780465045 (accessed February 15, 2005).

Cummings, Milton C. 2003. "Cultural Diplomacy and the United States Government: A Survey." Center for Arts and Culture. http://www.culturalpolicy.org/pdf/MCCpaper.pdf (accessed December 22, 2005).

Djerejian, Edward P. 2003. "Changing Minds, Winning Peace: A New Strategic Direction for U.S. Public Policy in the Arab and Muslim Worlds. Report of the Advisory Group on Public Diplomacy for the Arab and Muslim World." http://www.state.gov/documents/organization/24882.pdf (accessed December 22, 2005).

Fraser, Matthew. 2003. *Weapons of Mass Distraction: Soft Power and American Empire*. New York: St. Martin's Press.

Freeman, Laurie Anne. 2000. *Closing the Shop: Information Cartels and Japan's Mass Media*. Princeton, NJ: Princeton University Press.

Government Accounting Office (GAO). 2003. "U.S. Public Diplomacy: State Department Expands Efforts but Faces Significant Challenges. Report to the Committee on International Relations." House of Representatives. September. http://www.gao.gov/new.items/d03951.pdf (accessed December 22, 2005).

Institute for International Education (IIE). 2006. *Open Doors 2006*. http://opendoors.iienetwork.org (accessed June 30, 2007).

Johnson, Stephen, and Helle Dale. 2003. "How to Reinvigorate U.S. Public Diplomacy." *Backgrounder* 1645. http://www.heritage.org/Research/PublicDiplomacy/bg1645.cfm (accessed December 1, 2007).

Japan–United States Friendship Commission (JUSFC). 2006. *JUSFC Biennial Report 2005–2006*. http://www.jusfc.gov (accessed June 29, 2007).

Malone, Gifford D. 1987. "Public Diplomacy: Organizing for the Future." In *Rhetoric and Public Diplomacy: The Stanton Report Revisited*. Ed. Kenneth W. Thompson, 1–25. Lanham, MD: University Press of America.

———. 1988. *Political Advocacy and Cultural Communication: Organizing the Nation's Public Diplomacy*. Lanham, MD: University Press of America.

Nye, Joseph S., Jr. 2004. *Soft Power: The Means to Success in World Politics*. New York: Public Affairs.

Strobel, Warren P., and Jonathon S. Landay. 2005. "U.S. Said to Use a Litmus Test to Block American Speakers Iraq Policy Critics Considered Targets." *Boston Globe,* December 4.

Tenney, Francis B. 1995. *The Japan United States Friendship Commission: A History of the Commission Commemorating the 20th Anniversary, 1975–1995.* www.jusfc.gov/pdf/historyofthecommission.pdf (accessed December 1, 2007).

Thompson, Kenneth W. 1987. *Rhetoric and Public Diplomacy: The Stanton Report Revisited.* Lanham, MD: University Press of America.

The White House. 2002. *National Security Strategy of the United States of America.* http://www.whitehouse.gov/nsc/nss.pdf (accessed February 7, 2003).

Woods, Randall B. 1995. *Fulbright: A Biography.* Cambridge: Cambridge University Press.

13

Japan Does Soft Power

Strategy and Effectiveness of Its Public Diplomacy in the United States

Agawa Naoyuki

Dave Barry, a nationally well-known humorist based in Miami, Florida, visited Japan and subsequently published a book titled *David Barry Does Japan* in the early 1990s (Barry 1992). Barry, in his uniquely hilarious way, observed some aspects of Japanese society and culture and found them to be quite different from the society and culture of the United States. The book was effective in introducing Japan to average Americans who had little or no knowledge of the island country in a pre-Ichiro, pre-anime era.

Since then, Japan's pop culture and baseball players, among other things, have become staple commodities in almost every American household. Japan is definitely cool now. How did it happen? Has Japan's soft power been exercised effectively? Did the government of Japan play a role through its public diplomacy? Perhaps we should invite Dave Barry back to Tokyo and ask him to write another book about Japan.

This chapter examines the use and effectiveness of Japan's soft power. It initially analyzes the way in which the Japanese government uses soft power through its public diplomacy. It describes the objectives, actors, and budget of Japan's public diplomacy, and compares them with those of other countries.

This chapter then evaluates the effect of Japan's soft power on the relationship between Japan and the United States. It assesses the changes in the perceptions of Japan in the United States over the past fifteen years and especially after September 2001, the post-9/11 period. It uses the results of polls as well as anecdotal evidence for this purpose.

Based upon the foregoing assessment, the chapter evaluates the effectiveness of Japan's use of soft power in achieving its foreign policy objectives toward the United States.

Japan's Public Diplomacy

Objectives

Japan's strategic objective is to secure peace and prosperity for its people. This goal has not changed since ancient times. However, Japan adopted a new way of achieving it after World War II. Prime Minister Koizumi Junichiro stated in his speech in Jakarta,

Indonesia, on April 22, 2005, that Japan's determination, declared in Bandung fifty years before, "to develop itself as a peaceful nation . . . remains steadfast to this day" (Koizumi 2005). More recently, Foreign Minister Aso Taro expressed the same view at the Center for Strategic and International Studies in Washington, DC, on May 3, 2006, when he stated that "devastated by long years of war, the Japanese people . . . resolved that Japan would never again embark on military aggression" and that "instead the Japanese people advanced a consistent policy of peace and happiness through economic prosperity and democracy" (Aso 2006b). Japan conducts its foreign policy in this spirit. Public diplomacy is a vital element in it.

A primary means of securing peace and prosperity for Japan over the past sixty years has been Japan's alliance with the United States. Accordingly, maintaining and strengthening this alliance is a major objective of Japan's foreign policy. Japan's public diplomacy in the United States naturally focuses on creating an environment conducive to that endeavor. The premise is that the more favorable the American people's view of Japan is, the more support the alliance will receive from them. In Chapter 12 in this volume, William G. Crowell states that the *raison d'être* of the United States Embassy's public diplomacy in Japan is the same; to foster support for the security alliance.

Actors

Japan's public diplomacy is by no means conducted exclusively by the government of Japan, let alone the Ministry of Foreign Affairs (MOFA).[1] Private corporations, universities and other educational institutions, think tanks, and nonprofit organizations all play an important role in this area of public diplomacy. Government agencies other than MOFA, particularly the Ministry of Science and Education and its Agency for Cultural Affairs, are active in conducting international cultural and exchange programs.[2] Nevertheless, MOFA is still the principal strategic planner, actor, and promoter of Japan's public diplomacy.

Ministry of Foreign Affairs

The Public Diplomacy Department belonging to the Foreign Minister's Secretariat of MOFA is principally responsible for MOFA's public diplomacy.[3] Each of Japan's 189 embassies and consulate offices around the globe also conducts public diplomacy within its jurisdiction. For that purpose, MOFA dispatches officers to these embassies and consulate offices to take charge of press and cultural matters.

At some of Japan's major embassies and consulate offices, such as that in Washington, DC, and New York, MOFA has also established and runs separate Japan Information and Culture Centers (JICCs). Officers and members of each JICC are almost exclusively engaged in information services and cultural programs. At smaller embassies and consulate offices, however, there often is only one officer responsible for public diplomacy. He or she is likely to have other duties as well.

The annual budget for the Public Diplomacy Department for fiscal year 2005 was approximately US$243 million (MOFA 2006).[4] This figure has been steadily decreasing at least since 2001, when it was approximately US$286 million (MOFA 2006). It does not, however, include the amount used for certain exchange and educational programs, including some official development assistance programs handled by the Economic Cooperation Bureau of MOFA.

Japan Foundation

One feature of Japan's public diplomacy is that the Japan Foundation, formerly a subsidiary of MOFA and since October 1, 2003, an independent administrative agency, plays a major role in Japan's public diplomacy. In fact, close to 50 percent of the annual budget for the Public Diplomacy Department is used as a direct grant to the Japan Foundation. For fiscal year 2005, the Japan Foundation received approximately US$117 million from MOFA (MOFA 2006). This amount accounts for roughly 80 percent of the Japan Foundation's total budget. Most of the remaining 20 percent is derived from donations by private individuals, corporations, and foundations, and interest income earned on endowment capital (Japan Foundation 2005, p. 52). It is more or less accurate to characterize the Japan Foundation as an implementing arm of MOFA's public diplomacy, although the Japan Foundation solicits advice from independent, third-party committees on many of its programs, particularly those in the United States.

As such, the Japan Foundation focuses on three kinds of activities: cultural and art exchanges, Japanese-language programs, and Japan studies and intellectual exchanges (Japan Foundation 2005, p. 2). To engage in these activities worldwide, the Japan Foundation has four offices in Japan as well as nineteen offices in eighteen other countries. In particular, it operates the Japan Culture Houses and Centers in eleven countries in such cities as Rome, Paris, Beijing, and Sao Paulo (Japan Foundation 2005, p. 61).

In theory, under the current arrangements, MOFA sets the policies and direction of Japan's public diplomacy, and the Japan Foundation implements these policies in various countries. However, in reality, things do not always work that way. For example, the Japan Foundation often asks embassies and consulate offices located in cities without the Japan Foundation's facilities to implement its art and cultural programs. Washington, DC, is an example of this mode of operation. MOFA's JICCs, attached to a few Japanese embassies and consulate offices on the one hand and the Japan Foundation's Japan Cultural Houses and Centers on the other hand, have similar missions and functions.

Also, the Japan Foundation sometimes seems to plan and implement its own programs quite independent from and without coordination with MOFA. This occasionally creates tension and policy inconsistency between the two.

Comparisons with Other Countries

It is difficult to compare the scale and quality of Japan's public diplomacy with that of other major countries. Each country has a different governmental structure, tradition, and style of handling public diplomacy. Accordingly, merely comparing the amount of the published budgets ostensibly allocated to public diplomacy in each country would run the risk of comparing apples to oranges.

However, some raw data are available. Based on these figures, it seems relatively clear that Japan's budget for public diplomacy is smaller than that of countries of comparable size.

Statistical Data

For instance, the United States allocated a total of approximately US$606 million to public diplomacy and cultural and educational programs in 2003 (MOFA 2006).[5] The United States has been increasing its budget for public diplomacy since 2002. This compares with Japan's 2003 budget for public diplomacy of US$255 million (MOFA 2006). If, however, one takes into consideration the fact that the United States is more than twice as big as Japan in terms of gross domestic product and population, Japan's budget for public diplomacy may not look that small compared to that of the United States.

More striking is a contrast between Japan's budget for public diplomacy and the public diplomacy budgets of some European countries. For instance, the United Kingdom spent approximately US$2,667 million for public diplomacy in 2003, more than ten times the amount Japan spent.[6] France spent US$1,546 million,[7] and Germany US$640 million[8] for public diplomacy in 2003, both significantly more than Japan. Only Italy's budget for public diplomacy is slightly smaller than Japan's at US$211 million.[9] Italy's figure is followed by Canada's US$70 million[10] and Australia's US$44 million.[11] It seems that major Western democracies tend to spend proportionately much more money on public diplomacy than either the United States or Japan (MOFA 2006).

Incidentally, the Japan Foundation itself is also much smaller than comparable national agencies engaged exclusively in public diplomacy in terms of budget, number of overseas offices, and number of employees. The annual budget for the British Council of the United Kingdom was US$820 million in 2003, which is more than five times larger than that of the Japan Foundation. Similarly, the 2003 annual budget for the Goethe Institute of Germany was approximately US$250 million, roughly 1.7 times as big as that of the Japan Foundation (*Gaiko Forum* 2005).

In 2003, the British Council had 282 offices abroad and the Goethe Institute had 128, while in 2000, L'Alliance Français, a loose federation of French language and cultural associations worldwide headquartered in Paris, had 1,135, some 200 to 300 of which receive subsidies from the French government (MOFA 2006). The Japan Foundation has nineteen (*Gaiko Forum* 2005). Also in 2003, the British Council employed about 5,300 people worldwide, while the Goethe Institute employed 3,100 (*Gaiko Forum* 2005, p. 65). The Japan Foundation employed 348 (*Gaiko Forum* 2005).

Reasons for Japan's Smaller Budget

Why is Japan's budget for public diplomacy smaller than those of other countries of comparable size and character? A few factors may explain the difference.

Jurisdictional Differences. First, there are some jurisdictional differences. European agencies in charge of public diplomacy undertake a broader range of activities than MOFA or the Japan Foundation. For instance, the British Council and the French Foreign Ministry are in charge of technical assistance in the area of development cooperation; in Japan this responsibility is undertaken primarily by the Japan International Cooperation Agency (JICA), an independent administrative agency specializing in official development assistance. The British Council and the French Foreign Ministry also handle academic exchange programs; in Japan they are undertaken by institutions affiliated with the Ministry of Science and Education.

Also, the French Foreign Ministry is in charge of the primary and secondary education of their citizens residing abroad. In Japan, the Ministry of Science and Education is mainly responsible for primary and secondary education of Japanese citizens residing abroad. Thus European governments' budgets for public diplomacy tend to look larger than that of Japan's (MOFA 2006).

Language Programs. Second, European countries spend much larger sums of money and energy on language education than Japan does. As already noted, the total budget of the Goethe Institute is about 1.7 times as large as that of the Japan Foundation (*Gaiko Forum* 2005). On an operational cost basis, the Goethe Institute spends approximately 40 percent of its budget on language education (Goethe Institute 2005); the Japan Foundation spends only 29 percent of its budget on language education (Japan Foundation 2005).

Furthermore, as also noted, the British Council, the Goethe Institute, and L'Alliance Français all have many more offices and employ more personnel abroad than the Japan Foundation. This is precisely because it is mainly through these offices that they conduct their language programs abroad. These offices are more or less capable of sustaining their own operations through language course and examination fees paid by students.

The same cannot be said of the Japan Foundation, which conducts its Japanese-language programs with subsidies from the government. In view of the increased demand for Japanese-language courses across the globe, MOFA is now contemplating the expansion of the Japan Foundation's language programs and making them financially more self-sustaining along the British, German, and French models (Okada 2006; Aso 2006a).[12]

Reluctant Public Diplomacy. Third, Japan seems to have been somewhat hesitant to conduct public diplomacy through government channels. Japan's cultural diplomacy started out as government propaganda activities toward China in the early twentieth century. In fact, MOFA's cultural section was part of the Asian Bureau until they were separated in the 1930s. This may partly explain the slow and timid beginning of Japan's public diplomacy after World War II. This may also explain the eventual establishment of the Japan Foundation as a separate arm of Japan's cultural diplomacy, a history that in many ways is similar to that behind the establishment of the Goethe Institute in postwar Germany (MOFA 2006).

Related to this historical factor is Japan's traditionally elite-oriented public diplomacy. MOFA has concentrated on cultural programs at its embassies and consulates abroad and on inviting political, academic, and cultural elites to Japan. These programs naturally tend to be somewhat exclusive, of relatively small scale, and limited in impact. There has been little emphasis on reaching out to the general public.

Japan's traditionally elite-oriented approach may also explain the relatively minor involvement by and coordination with nongovernmental organizations (NGOs) in the area of public diplomacy. In contrast, NGOs play a particularly important role in U.S. public diplomacy. The International Visitor Leadership Program, sponsored by the U.S. Department of State, is in actuality implemented largely by local not-for-profit organizations across the country.

However, in the era of globalization, democratization, and instant communication, the general public exercises much more influence than before on the direction of foreign policy. Also, Japan's pop culture is increasingly popular worldwide, particularly among the world's youth; it has become a potent tool of Japan's public diplomacy. Accordingly, Japan is now beginning to focus more on the general public of each country and region of the world as the target of its public diplomacy, promoting and exporting pop culture, language, and various Japanese brands (Okada 2006; Aso 2006a).

More Economic than Cultural. Fourth and last, the postwar Japanese government has placed more emphasis on economic cooperation than cultural diplomacy as a means of improving Japan's relationship with and image in other countries, particularly developing nations. Japan's priority regarding nations in the developing world was put on helping them to overcome the daunting poverty issue, not on sharing culture and art with them. In 1984–86, Japan extended a grant to Egypt to build an opera house in Cairo; this generated an enormous amount of goodwill toward Japan among the Egyptian people. The government was roundly criticized domestically, however, for undertaking an economically useless project (MOFA 2006).

Recently, though, this perception has begun to change. Economic assistance and grants to developing countries are expected to shrink in amount as the grantee nations one by one reach a higher level of economic development. As a result, Japan's diplomacy toward the nations of the developing world may contain less economic and more cultural elements in the future.

Cost of Public Diplomacy Toward the United States

There is no figure with respect to the amount of money MOFA spends on public diplomacy toward the United States each fiscal year. However, the Japan Foundation consistently spent approximately 10 percent of its annual budget for activities in the United States from 2000 through 2004 (Japan Foundation 2005, p. 64). Thus, the United States ranks number one among countries in which the Japan Foundation conducts various cultural, educational, and exchange programs.

In addition, the Japan Foundation Center for Global Partnership (CGP) and its funds account for approximately half of the Japan Foundation's programs in the United States (Japan Foundation 2005; CGP 2005). CGP was founded as a division of the Japan Foundation in April 1991 under a strong initiative by the late foreign minister Abe Shintaro with a separate and independent endowment for its activities. This was done with the purpose of promoting a closer and tighter relationship between Japan and the United States. Abe and others took this action in appreciation of the critical importance of the bilateral relationship going forward into the twenty-first century. At the time of the CGP's founding, the two countries were going through some difficulties associated with the first Gulf War and various economic and trade frictions (CGP 2005).

Relative Weight of Public Diplomacy

It is difficult to determine the relative weight given to public diplomacy in the overall structure and activities of Japan's foreign policy. For instance, the proposed budget of MOFA for 2006 for official development assistance was approximately US$4,045 million, while US$269 million was to be allocated for public diplomacy (MOFA 2006). As stated above, the size and scale of public diplomacy in Japan's foreign policy would look very different if all or part of the official development assistance budget were counted as a component of public diplomacy.

There is one difficulty in assessing the relative weight of Japan's public diplomacy. As noted above, many other government agencies and private entities are engaged in public diplomacy but exercise little coordination with one another. Some agencies and entities do not even perceive their overseas information and cultural programs as part of public diplomacy.

The recently convened Council on the Promotion of Cultural Diplomacy was probably the first instance in which the prime minister's office, with assistance from MOFA and the Agency of Cultural Affairs, tried to coordinate policies and themes for Japan's public diplomacy and find facts about each agency's public diplomacy programs. Foreign Minister Aso also encouraged private initiatives as well as public-private partnerships in the area of public diplomacy, particularly in pop culture and Japanese-language programs (Aso 2006a). Accordingly, public diplomacy seems to be gaining momentum and becoming an important and vital component of Japan's foreign policy.

Public Diplomacy Is Important at the Embassy in Washington, DC

One Growth Area

Similarly, public diplomacy is considered important at the Embassy of Japan in Washington, DC. The Press and Culture Section in charge of public diplomacy is one of the five major sections of the embassy covering respective policy fields. It is the only section that has a separate operational arm, the JICC.

Ambassador Kato Ryozo and other key members of the embassy support the embassy's efforts in conducting various cultural, educational, and academic programs as well as exchanges to enhance Japan's images in the United States. Members of political, defense, economic, and other sections of the embassy facilitate public diplomacy by providing speakers, participants, material, and information at various forums.

I was under the impression during my term at the embassy that the significance of public diplomacy was growing. This phenomenon seems to be linked to the realization in recent years that it pays to promote a public image of Japan and its culture in the United States. Public diplomacy certainly is one area where many new initiatives are possible and being undertaken. As Ambassador Kato has stated, public diplomacy is one growth area of Japan's diplomacy (Kato 2003).

Challenges and Limitations

Public diplomacy at the embassy, however, is not without problems and issues. It has limited resources, both financial and human. Members of the Press and Culture Section are typically not professionals in cultural programs and exchanges. Some are language specialists who happen to land at the section for a few years. Some are more talented in the field of press relations. Personnel are rotated in every few years to yet another field or country after accumulating know-how in conducting public diplomacy in the United States.

In fact, with due respect to Joseph Nye's theory of soft power, few members, if any, of the Press and Culture Section stop and think on a daily basis about the significance of one's own work in the area of public diplomacy in achieving Japan's foreign policy goals. Year-round, embassy members' endeavors are more mundane.

Soft Power at Work

Japan Is Cool

In his book *Soft Power: The Means to Success in World Politics,* Nye pointed out that despite the slowdown in Japan's economy in the 1990s, Japan actually increased its cultural influence during that period and into the 2000s. Citing McGray (2002), Nye pointed to an increase in "Japan's global cultural influence," seen in the spread of pop culture, including *Pokémon* cartoons, video games, and animation, in addition to traditional arts, designs, and cuisine (Nye 2004, p. 86).

I also witnessed many instances of Japan's soft power at work in the United States during my term at the embassy. First and foremost, the so-called Japan-cool phenomenon has factored even more heavily in American society than described in McGray's article.

In addition to the examples given by Nye, Japan's soft power ranges from movies, *manga* (comic books), costume plays, and the use of Japanese vegetables and fruits such as *shiitake* and *soba* in the American diet, to seemingly non-Japan-related fields of art such as jazz, modern and classical ballet, and Japanese players in major league baseball, most notably Ichiro and Matsui. The Japanese female duet Puffy, which became popular in the United States through their singing as well as an anime series featuring them, is the latest example.

What is perhaps unique about this Japan-cool phenomenon is its universality. For more than 150 years, certain Japanophiles have been attracted to the exotic nature of things Japanese, admiring artistic works ranging from Hokusai's woodblock prints to Chikamatsu's tragedies in Bunraku. Today, however, American people, particularly younger ones, seem to be attracted by things Japanese not because they are of Japanese origin, but simply because they are cool. Toyota or Honda cars attract American consumers not because they are Japanese (actually, they are mostly made in the United States), but because they are of high quality. Sushi is served at Japanese restaurants as well as at French cafes in Manhattan and the law school cafeteria at the University of Virginia. The movie *Shall We Dance* was a big hit not because it was about the midlife crisis of a Japanese wage earner, but more likely because it was a generic tale of a midlife crisis of a Joe or a Bill in any American city.

Never Has It Been This Good

Aside from the Japan-cool phenomenon, it is often said that Japan's relationship with the United States has never been as good as it is now. Japan is a very important ally and friend of the United States. That is what many people within and outside the Bush administration stated during my term at the embassy. One heard the same view outside the Beltway as well.

Poll Results

I often encountered this view perhaps because of my position and role at the embassy. However, some poll results and anecdotal evidence seem to support this impression as well. For instance, the Gallup poll conducted in February 2004 found that Japan ranks fourth among countries the American people view favorably: 75 percent of the respondents chose "very" or "mostly" favorable to categorize their views on Japan. Only Australia, Canada, and Great Britain rank higher than Japan (Gallup Organization 2007).

Similarly, the Yomiuri-Gallup joint poll conducted in November 2004 found that roughly 68 percent of American respondents trust Japan (*Yomiuri Shimbun* 2004). The Gallup poll conducted in February 2005 on behalf of MOFA, the results of which were released in August 2005, also shows that 72 percent of the general public and 90 percent of the intellectuals in the United States trust Japan (MOFA 2005).[13] These are remarkably high figures.

Perhaps more significant is the upward trend in favorable views on Japan held by the American people over the past fifteen years. According to the February 2006 Gallup poll, between November 1991 and November 1995 favorable views on Japan were constantly below 50 percent except in February 1994 (54 percent), hitting their lowest (46 percent) in June 1994 and November 1995. By comparison, since May 1999, the figure has constantly remained higher than 70 percent, peaking at 79 percent in February 2002 (Gallup Organization 2007). Clearly, the American people's perception of Japan has significantly improved over the past fifteen years.

Incidentally, contrary to the somewhat generally held impression, this tendency toward more favorable views of Japan is not limited to the American people. A BBC World Service survey conducted from October 2005 through January 2006 found that in thirty-one of the thirty-three countries polled, the majority or plurality said that Japan's influence in the world is mainly positive. This is the highest rating among the nine countries and regions whose influence was assessed. Perhaps not surprisingly, China and South Korea did not think Japan's influence in the world was positive (World Public Opinion 2006).

Positive Views on Japan Rising

Although there is relatively little statistical evidence to support it, I feel, based on my conversations with Americans of all walks of life, that their views on Japan have noticeably improved during my term at the embassy. Before I arrived at the embassy in September 2002, many people had warned me that Japan had disappeared from the American radar screen. Two and a half years later, Japan was the topic of the town in Washington, DC.

It is noteworthy that Congressman Tom Lantos (D-CA), who conducted a hearing on alleged unfair labor practices of the U.S. subsidiaries of Japanese corporations in 1991, proposed and succeeded in passing a resolution (H. Con. Res. 418) in the House of Representatives in July 2004 commemorating the 150 years of excellent relations between Japan and the United States. Lantos allegedly decided to propose this resolution upon reading a full-page advertisement placed by the Japanese government in the *Washington Post* in March 2004 chronicling 150 years of the bilateral relationship.

Public Diplomacy by the Japanese Government

The Japanese government has little ability on its own to generate this Japan-cool phenomenon or generally favorable views toward Japan. However, the government believes there are things that it can do to promote and strengthen Japan's soft power and, furthermore, to translate it into soft power with political value and foreign policy implications.

JET Program

For instance, the Japanese national and local governments have been funding and running the Japan Exchange and Teaching (JET) Program since 1987. As Nye mentioned in *Soft Power,* this program brings thousands of young Americans, among others, to

Japan to teach English in public schools (Nye 2004, p. 110). Many former participants in this program have pursued Japan-related careers after returning to the United States, while others have gone into fields unrelated to Japan. Most of the returnees, regardless of which career path they take, remain close friends of Japan—a huge asset to Japan's relationship with the United States.

The number of applicants for the JET Program in the United States has been steadily increasing over the past four years. More than a thousand young men and women head for Japan annually from the United States, with the total number of JET alumni in the country now standing at 20,000 (MOFA 2006).

The embassy is the center of the JET Program in the United States, with two resident JET coordinators. Together with consulate officers in several cities in the United States, it annually publicizes the program, recruits and interviews applicants, and selects, educates, and sends off to Japan the newly chosen JET Program members. I am of the view, based on my experiences at the embassy, that the JET Program is one of the most, if not the most, successful exchange programs that the Japanese government conducts as part of its public diplomacy.

Japan Bowl and Other Programs

The Japanese government through the embassy also sponsors or supports similar exchange and educational programs. The Japan Bowl, a speech contest for American high school students studying Japanese; the Mansfield Fellowship Program, through which midlevel government officials of various agencies of the U.S. government spend a year or two at their counterpart Japanese government agencies; and the Japan Fulbright Memorial Fund Program, through which selected American schoolteachers visit Japan for three weeks and visit Japanese schools, are but a few of such programs.

Furthermore, the Abe Fellowship Program, which awards grants to scholars, journalists, and other professionals for their study of various aspects of U.S.-Japanese relations or global issues that have implications for the bilateral relationship, is CGP's primary project (CGP 2005). CGP was also a cosponsor, with the Social Science Research Council, of the seminars that are the foundation of this project on soft power.

The Japan Foundation announced at Ambassador Kato's official residence in Washington, DC, on November 10, 2004, that it would fund US$685,000 to pay for 50 percent of the initial cost necessary to establish the Japanese advanced placement (AP) program. This program will enable high school students to earn college credits by studying Japanese and achieving a certain level of fluency. Ambassador Kato and Dr. Gaston Caperton, president of the College Board, which runs the AP program, were present at the occasion (College Board 2004).

Personal Soft Power

One aspect of Japan's soft power that Nye failed to mention in discussing Japan's public diplomacy is the personal relationship and trust that politicians, diplomats, members of Japan's armed forces, and other members of the Japanese government establish with their counterparts and the general public in other countries, including the United States.

The Koizumi-Bush Relationship

Most notably, former Prime Minister Koizumi established a close and warm personal relationship with President George W. Bush during his tenure. Unlike past Japanese prime ministers, Koizumi apparently did most of the talking while Bush did most of the listening when they met.

Many have wondered how Koizumi succeeded in establishing this special relationship with Bush while most of his predecessors failed to do so with their counterparts. No doubt Koizumi's outgoing personality and his frankness earned the trust of the president. Koizumi's ability to speak English is a factor as well, but it is not the decisive one, for a few past prime ministers spoke better English than he.

It is noted that Koizumi is a Japanese of the postwar generation less burdened and less inhibited by the memories of war and occupation by the United States. After all, he was the one who kept visiting the Yasukuni Shrine throughout his premiership despite strong protests from neighboring countries and many in the United States.

Ironically, Koizumi's iconoclastic and less memory-bound attitude may have made him much easier to communicate and work with for Bush, who also seems little bound by prejudice and the memories of the war. Their relationship contrasts sharply with the very cordial, but reserved relationship fifteen years ago between President George H.W. Bush, a World War II veteran whose airplane was shot down by the Japanese over Chichijima Island, and Prime Minister Miyazawa, who as a young Japanese bureaucrat immediately after the war had the difficult and delicate task of dealing with the mighty American occupation authorities.

Abe Shinzo, who is of an even newer, more assertive generation, succeeded to Koizumi as Japan's prime minister, but he had to resign before establishing a truly natural and personal relationship with President George W. Bush. It therefore still remains to be seen whether the Elvis-singing, baseball-throwing Koizumi was a one-and-only phenomenon. In any event, a close personal relationship between the leaders of the two countries is, indeed, a form of soft power.

Ambassadors and Diplomats

Similarly, Ambassador Kato has been an effective envoy to Washington, DC, having earned the trust of the U.S. government at the highest level. In particular, his love of baseball, coupled with his encyclopedic knowledge of major league baseball history and statistics, has struck a chord with the American people and greatly helped him perform his duty in the United States.

Japan Self-Defense Force's Soft Power Projection

In addition, the Japan Self-Defense Force (JSDF) troops stationed in Samawa, Iraq, conducted public diplomacy as a part of their operation: They have earned the trust of many of the local Iraqi people by showing to them their diligence, discipline, readiness, and high morale as well as their goodwill, humility, and friendliness. Although the deployment of JSDF to Iraq itself was perceived to be a quintessential exercise of hard power, the nonmilitary nature of the operation coupled with these virtues resulted in a strong showing of Japan's soft power. That, in turn, has helped them earn an excellent reputation among the armed services of the United States and other countries.

I believe that troops engaged in various military operations increasingly need to use soft power to be effective in accomplishing their respective missions, particularly in a postcombat stabilization phase of a military campaign. This is true particularly with respect to overseas operations by JSDF. Because Article 9 of the Japanese Constitution prohibits the threat or use of force except in strict self-defense, members of the JSDF have to accomplish their missions by somehow persuading the people in their operational areas to take certain actions rather than forcing them to do so. This is precisely what Nye defines as soft power.[14]

Effectiveness of Japan's Soft Power in the United States

How much of this excellent bilateral relationship and favorable view of Japan can be credited to the exercise of Japan's soft power and, in particular, to its public diplomacy?

As Nye pointed out, with soft power one gets desired outcomes without resorting to tangible threats or payoffs because soft power rests on the ability to shape the preferences of others (2004, p.5). At the same time, precisely for that reason, soft power is less tangible and harder to measure or quantify than hard power. The same is true with Japan's soft power. Nevertheless, some tentative observations may be presented here regarding the effectiveness of Japan's soft power.

Soft Power Helps Achieve Japan's Foreign Policy Goals

First, soft power does help to achieve Japan's foreign policy goals. The Japanese government consciously employs soft power in order to achieve its foreign policy objectives worldwide and toward the United States.

This is due partly to historical forces. Because Japan renounced the threat or use of force (an important element of hard power) as a means of resolving international disputes in its constitution, adopted in 1946, the government has had to resort more to soft power in pursuing its foreign policy goals over the past sixty years. This tradition continues.

Hard Power Enhances Soft Power

Second, hard power sometimes enhances soft power. The recent surge in favorable views held by Americans toward Japan and the prevalence of the Japan-cool phenomenon seem to coincide with the exercise of Japan's hard power, namely, deployment of the JSDF in the Indian Ocean (as part of Operation Enduring Freedom) and Iraq (as part of Operation Iraqi Freedom).

It is probably not a coincidence that favorable views toward Japan peaked in February 2002, according to the February 2006 Gallup poll, cited above, right after Japan deployed a JSDF fleet consisting of an oil tanker and a few destroyers to the Indian Ocean and the Arabian Sea to supply fuel to the coalition navies' vessels engaged in Operation Enduring Freedom. In fact, the "very" favorable views on Japan continued to climb steadily: from 17 percent in February 2002, to 18 percent in February 2003, and to 19 percent in February 2004 (Gallup Organization 2007).

Prime Minister Koizumi's support for President Bush in the Iraq war and the subsequent deployment of the JSDF troops to Iraq have helped boost these results even when the war in Iraq is not necessarily popular either inside or outside the United States. Many Americans witnessed Japan's involvement in Operation Enduring Freedom and Operation Iraqi Freedom. As a result they seem to have felt that Japan shared not only interests but also values with the United States.

In this sense, Japan is transforming hard power into soft power. Japan's political values and foreign policy decisions, two other sources of soft power according to Nye (2004, p. 11), together with limited use of military power, strengthened its soft power vis-à-vis the United States. Nye himself pointed out that hard and soft power sometimes reinforce each other (2004, p. 25). The case of the deployment of the JSDF troops in Iraq is particularly noteworthy because, as stated above, troops, an instrument of hard power, are prohibited from exercising that very hard power in operations and instead are required to assert their soft power. I believe that the soft aspect of military power should be further explored.

Incidentally, the favorable views toward Japan dropped from 60 percent in March 1991 to 48 percent in November 1991 (Gallup Organization 2007). This can be explained only by Japan's reluctance to participate in any meaningful way in the first Gulf War in the first quarter of 1991, during and after which Japan was roundly criticized for its "checkbook diplomacy." One may conclude that reluctance in the use of hard power sometimes reduces the effectiveness of soft power.

Too Much Hard Power Weakens Soft Power

Third, the perceived possession of too much hard power sometimes reduces the effectiveness of soft power. Although Japan holds relatively modest military power, it was perceived in the 1980s and even during the first half of the 1990s to be invincible in its economic might. In fact, the least favorable opinion about Japan in the recent past was a 46 percent rating registered in June 1994 and November 1995 (Gallup Organization

2007). Tension between the two countries was particularly high for approximately two years following the breakdown of the talks in February 1994 between Prime Minister Hosokawa and President Clinton over the resolution of certain economic and trade issues between Japan and the United States.

Ironically, perhaps partly because Japan today is no longer perceived to be an economic threat to the United States, views toward Japan seem to have improved in the 2000s. More important, both the Japanese government and Japanese industries have put a lot of effort into making bilateral economic relations more palatable to the American public.

Japanese direct investment in the United States, the promotion of Americans to top management positions in Japanese corporations' U.S. subsidiaries, enhanced community and consumer relations, increasing local content in their products, and active participation in charity and volunteer activities have all helped Japanese businesses to become accepted as part of the American community. Japanese businesses active in the United States have thus wisely exercised their soft power. One may conclude that soft power can indeed smooth the rough edges of hard power.

More Aggressive and Wiser Use of Soft Power

Fourth, and finally, Japan can and should use its soft power more aggressively and wisely. Although there have been significant improvements in the American people's views toward Japan, there are still areas of misunderstanding and misperception that need correction.

Nye pointed to some limitations on Japan's soft power. Most notably, he maintained that the residual suspicion that lingers in China and Korea sets limits on Japan's soft power (2004, p. 87). He argued that the Japanese government's unwillingness to deal frankly with its record of foreign aggression in the 1930s is a limit on its soft power (2004, p. 88). I somewhat disagree with this assessment. Nevertheless, the perception is there, as seen in the recently renewed controversy over the issue of "comfort women." The Japanese government needs to continue to tackle this sensitive issue with skill, frankness, and facts through its public diplomacy.

How Much Public Diplomacy Should the Government Do?

In this connection, it is difficult to determine the optimum level of the Japanese government's involvement and efforts in public diplomacy in maximizing Japan's national interest. To begin with, we do not know and cannot know for sure how a particular educational, cultural, or exchange program conducted by the Japanese government results in a favorable view toward Japan in a specific way.

It is my experience that the impact and effectiveness of each program or event that one undertakes at the embassy are extremely hard to determine. Success or failure is often measured in terms of the number of programs one plans and implements a year or the size of the audience that a particular event draws. If so, the level of activities in public diplomacy is inevitably determined not by the desired level of investment, but by the availability of funds and human resources. Neither is abundant at the embassy or elsewhere within the government.

Some may conclude that the Japanese government is doing a relatively good job in an effective use of soft power, considering the comparatively small budget allocated to public diplomacy. Others may point out that the Japanese government has relatively little to do with the effectiveness of Japan's soft power and that the great impact of Japan's soft power worldwide is based largely on Japan's innate cultural, artistic, scientific, and technological strength nurtured over the years. One may never know the answer.

The Government Does Play an Important Role in Public Diplomacy

I believe, however, that the government does play an important role in public diplomacy. Ultimately, it is not the size of the budget or programs that matters. Rather, the most important elements are the vision and theme that the government, working with private sector players, can establish in order to implement more effective use of soft power.

Conclusion

Richard Armitage, undersecretary of state during the first term of the George W. Bush administration, stated at the ceremony on March 31, 2004, commemorating the 150th anniversary of the conclusion of the Treaty of Kanagawa that the U.S.-Japanese bilateral relationship had come a long way in 150 years and that now the two countries work closely together in almost every corner of the world. He poetically remarked that their joint endeavors to deal with problems worldwide ranged "from a tiny tear drop in Sri Lanka to reconstruction in Samawa" (Armitage 2004). To this may be added the joint humanitarian efforts between Japan and the United States, together with Australia and India, toward the victims of the tsunami disaster of December 2004 in countries around the Indian Ocean.

Indeed, Japan and the United States have come a long way. And it is "little short of a miracle," as the former U.S. ambassador to Japan, Howard Baker, often remarked, that the two countries "became friends, let alone allies, in such a brief time since the end of that great Pacific conflict" (Embassy of the United States 2005).

Because the two countries benefit greatly from this close bilateral relationship and because together they have a lot to offer to the rest of the world, their joint task is to maintain and further improve this special relationship. Soft power can play an important role in that endeavor.

Although one can endlessly ponder the meaning of soft power from an academic point of view, for those of us who practiced and continue to practice public diplomacy in Washington, DC, soft power is essentially the constant efforts to bridge the gap between the United States and Japan through lectures, exhibits, performances, conferences, cultural exchanges, and press relations in order to set up the optimal environment in which the two countries can cooperate with each other. It is a continuing dialogue, a never-ending task that lacks any immediate, discernible, or tangible results.

In a larger sense, what one gains through these efforts to engage in public diplomacy through the effective use of soft power is an accumulation of shared experience. Shared experience will result in trust. Trust in turn leads to the realization and reconfirmation that despite significant cultural differences, Americans and Japanese have much in common.

Diplomacy believes in the possibility of resolving differences and confrontations without resorting to violence. Public diplomacy perhaps believes in the possibility of sharing virtue and humanity. Japan shall continue to use its soft power in seeking that ultimate goal, in the United States and elsewhere.

Notes

1. The term "public diplomacy" has no fixed usage in Japan. It is sometimes referred to as "public diplomacy" in Japanese alphabets. At other times it is translated as "*bunka gaiko,*" or "cultural diplomacy." In December 2004, Prime Minister Koizumi appointed seventeen noted citizens to form a discussion group, the Council on the Promotion of Cultural Diplomacy, to deliberate upon the promotion of cultural diplomacy (Council on the Promotion of Cultural Diplomacy 2005). The council met seven times and presented its final report, entitled *Establishing Japan as a "Peaceful Nation of Cultural Exchange,"* to the prime minister in July 2005. This seems to be the first endeavor to define and set the direction of Japan's cultural diplomacy and hence public diplomacy.

2. *Follow-up Measures by Relevant Government Ministries and Agencies Concerning the Final Report of the Council on the Promotion of Cultural Diplomacy* (Office of Prime Minister of Japan and His Cabinet 2005) indicates that, in addition to MOFA and the Agency for Cultural Affairs, such ministries and agencies as the Cabinet Office; Ministry of Internal Affairs and Communication; Ministry of Economy, Trade and Industry; and Ministry of Agriculture, Forestry and Fishery all conduct programs in the area of public diplomacy.

3. The official name in Japanese of this department is the Public Relations and Cultural Exchange Department. Matters related to press relations are handled separately by the Office of the Press Secretary, also within the Foreign Minister's Secretariat.

4. The equivalent of ¥2,845 million at the exchange rate of ¥117/$1. This yen/dollar rate is used hereafter regardless of the fiscal year.

5. This figure includes the budget for public diplomacy as part of the diplomatic and consulate programs as well as the budget for educational and cultural exchanges. For comparison purposes, figures for FY2003, the year in which data is available for all the countries whose public diplomacy budgets are reviewed, are used in this chapter. These and other data on budgets for public diplomacy are derived from an unpublished internal chart prepared in June 2005 by the Public Diplomacy Department of MOFA, entitled *Budgets of Major Countries for International Cultural Exchanges,* made available to the author.

6. The equivalent of €1,651 million, converted into Japanese yen at the ¥189/£1 exchange rate and further converted into U.S. dollars at the ¥117/$1 rate. It includes budgets for the British Council, BBC World Service, and BBC Morning Service.

7. The equivalent of €1,350 million, converted into Japanese yen at the ¥134/€1 exchange rate and further converted into U.S. dollars at the ¥117/$1 rate. It includes figures for all governmental agencies. Of this figure, €1,108 million is for France's overseas cultural programs.

8. The equivalent of €559 million, converted into Japanese yen and then into U.S. dollars

at the rates shown in note 7. This amount is for Germany's overseas cultural and educational programs.

9. The equivalent of €184 million, converted into Japanese yen and then into U.S. dollars at the rates shown in note 7. This amount is the budget for cultural exchanges and promotion, including activities at Italian Cultural Houses abroad.

10. The equivalent of C$103 million, converted into Japanese yen at the exchange rate of ¥79/C$1, and further converted into U.S. dollars at the ¥117/$1 rate. This amount is the budget for public diplomacy of the Ministry of Foreign Affairs and Trade of Canada.

11. The equivalent of A$65 million, converted into Japanese yen at the exchange rate of ¥79/A$1 and further converted into U.S. dollars at the ¥117/$1 rate.

12. Okada (2006) pointed out that the number of those who study the Japanese language abroad increased more than threefold, from 730,000 in 1988 to 2,360,000 in 2003.

13. The same Gallup-MOFA poll conducted in February 2007 on behalf of MOFA (MOFA 2007) shows that 74 percent of the general public and 91 percent of intellectuals in the United States trust Japan, the highest percentage points in the poll's history.

14. It is noteworthy that the JSDF troops stationed in Iraq donated soccer balls to children in Samawa and attached to each of their water trucks a sticker of a popular Japanese animation movie figure, Captain Tsubasa. See Ebata 2005.

References

Armitage, Richard. 2004. Statement at the Ceremony Commemorating the 150th Anniversary of Japan-U.S. Relationship. Washington, DC. http://www.state.gov/s/d/former/armitage/remarks/30975.htm (accessed July 29, 2007).

Aso, Taro. 2006a. *A New Look at Cultural Diplomacy: A Call to Japan's Cultural Practitioners: Speech by Minister for Foreign Affairs Taro Aso at Digital Hollywood University.* April. http://www.mofa.go.jp/announce/fm/aso/speech0604-2.html (accessed June 6, 2006).

———. 2006b. *"Working Together for a Stable and Prosperous East Asia": Lessons of the Past, a Vision for the Freedom to Dream.* May. Washington, DC. http://www.mofa.go.jp/announce/fm/aso/address0605.html (accessed May 21, 2006).

Barry, Dave. 1992. *Dave Barry Does Japan.* New York: Ballantine Books.

Center for Global Partnership (CGP). 2005. *The 2004 Annual Report.* Tokyo: Center for Global Partnership.

College Board. 2004. "Japanese Officials and the College Board Announce an Advanced Placement Program Course in Japanese Language and Culture." Press release, November 10. http://www.collegeboard.com/press/article/0,3183,39697,00.html (accessed June 5, 2004).

Council on the Promotion of Cultural Diplomacy. 2005. *Establishing Japan as a "Peaceful Nation of Cultural Exchange."* Tokyo: Office of Prime Minister of Japan and His Cabinet. A provisional translation of the report is available at http:kantei.go.jp/foreign/policy/bunka/050711bunka_e.html (accessed December 10, 2007).

Ebata, Yasuyuki. 2005. *Report from MOFA's Samawa Liaison Office, Operation Captain Tsubasa: Water Tankers Delivers Dreams and Hope.* Samawa. http://www.mofa.go.jp/mofaj/area/iraq/renraku_j_0412a.html (accessed July 29, 2007).

Embassy of the United States. 2005. *Transcript, Ambassador Baker Speaks at LDP 50th Anniversary Forum.* Tokyo. http://japan.usembassy.gov/e/p/tp-20050125-62.html (accessed June 4, 2006).

Gallup Organization. 2007. *Perceptions of Foreign Countries.* http://www.gallup.com/poll/content/print.aspx?ci=1624 (accessed December 10, 2007).

Gaiko Forum. 2005. "Comparison of the Japan Foundation with Similar Cultural Exchange Institutions of A Few Foreign Countries." *Gaiko Forum* (December).

Goethe Institute. 2005. *The 2004 Annual Report.* http://www.goethe.de/mmo/priv/912306-STANDARD.pdf (accessed June 4, 2006).

Japan Foundation. 2005. *The 2004 Annual Report*. Tokyo: Japan Foundation.

Kato, Ryozo. 2003. Statement at the Conference of Cultural Officers Stationed in the United States. Washington, DC.

Koizumi, Junichiro. 2005. *Speech by H.E. Mr. Junichiro Koizumi, Prime Minister of Japan*. Jakarta. April. http://www.mofa.go.jp/region/asia-paci/meet0504/speech.html (accessed May 21, 2006).

McGray, Douglas. 2002. "Japan's Gross National Cool." *Foreign Policy* 130 (May–June): 44–54.

Ministry of Foreign Affairs. 2005. *A Summary of Polls Conducted in the United States Toward Japan*. http://www.mofa.go.jp/mofaj/area/usa/yoron05/gaiyo.html (accessed June 4, 2006).

———. 2006. Various published and unpublished information, charts and documents provided by the Public Diplomacy Department of MOFA to the author including: *Budgets of Major Countries for International Cultural Exchanges* (2005); *Breakdown of the Proposed 2006 Budgets for the Public Diplomacy Department* (2006); *Follow-up Measures by Relevant Government Ministries and Agencies concerning the Final Report of the Council on the Promotion of Cultural Diplomacy;* and *Summary of Important Budget Items: Diplomacy with the Support of People*. I am deeply indebted to my former colleagues at MOFA who generously extended their assistance to me in the course of preparing this chapter.

———. 2007. *A Summary of Polls Conducted in the United States Toward Japan*. http://www.mofa.go.jp/mofaj/area/usa/yoron07/index.html (accessed July 29, 2007).

Nye, Joseph S., Jr. 2004. *Soft Power: The Means to Success in World Politics*. New York: Public Affairs.

Office of Prime Minister of Japan and His Cabinet. 2005. *Follow-up Measures by Relevant Government Ministries and Agencies Concerning the Final Report of the Council on the Promotion of Cultural Diplomacy*. Tokyo: Office of Prime Minister of Japan and His Cabinet.

Okada, Maki. 2006. "Public Diplomacy in the Era of Democracy and Globalization." *Gaiko Forum* (May).

World Public Opinion. 2006. "Global Poll Finds Iran Viewed Negatively." http://www.world-publicopinion.org/pipa/articles/home_page/168.php?nid=&id=&pnt=168&lb=hmpg1 (accessed May 21, 2006).

Yomiuri Shimbun. 2004. "Summary of the Yomiuri-Gallup Joint Poll." Morning Edition, December 16.

V

Civil Society

14

Mr. Madison in the Twenty-first Century

Global Diffusion of the People's "Right to Know"

Lawrence Repeta

On December 19, 2005, Azerbaijan joined more than sixty nations that have adopted freedom of information laws granting individuals a statutory right to demand information from government. A few days earlier, a group of "economists, social workers, activists of grassroots level organizations and media practitioners" met in Dhaka, Bangladesh, to discuss the need for a similar law in their country.[1] Thus the worldwide movement for a people's right to know about the operations of government penetrates distant corners of the world.

When the United States adopted its Freedom of Information Act in 1966, there was no such law anywhere outside of northern Europe. When the Berlin Wall came down in 1989, fewer than fifteen countries had adopted such laws. At the time the Azerbaijani Parliament acted, there were more than sixty. The spread of laws enforcing a "public right to know" by providing public access to government files is so prevalent that democracy activists have labeled the freedom of information law a "threshold requirement" of democratic government (Blanton 2002).

This chapter examines freedom of information laws as a soft power resource and the dynamics of their growth and influence.

Freedom of Information and the American Goal of Democracy Promotion

American government leaders frequently trumpet the message that promoting democracy is a primary objective of American foreign policy. The State Department has explained that

> supporting democracy not only promotes such fundamental American values as religious freedom and worker rights, but also helps create a more secure, stable, and prosperous global arena in which the United States can advance its national interests. In addition, democracy is the one national interest that helps to secure all the others. Democratically governed nations are more likely to secure the peace, deter aggression, expand open markets, promote economic development, protect American citizens, combat international terrorism and crime, uphold human and worker rights, avoid humanitarian crises and refugee flows, improve the global environment, and protect human health. (U.S. Department of State nd)

Few Americans would disagree with this statement; they disagree only in the selection of means to achieve it. Should the primary means be force or persuasion?

At hearings held to confirm the appointment of Condoleezza Rice as secretary of state, U.S. senator Lamar Alexander (R-TN) phrased the issue this way: "My own view of that is that there is more than one way to spread freedom around the world. One way is to change a regime and try to make a country more like ours. Another way might be to celebrate our own values and strengthen ourselves and be a good example."[2] With these words, it almost appears that Senator Alexander was parroting Joseph Nye's (2004) own formulation of soft power.

Since the end of the Cold War, the world has seen a remarkable development in democracy promotion—by persuasion rather than force—through the spread of freedom of information laws. A freedom of information law provides legal protection for the right to know by empowering citizens to directly demand access to government files. Under the terms of a typical freedom of information law, information requesters need not rely on the intervention of legislators or other influential figures or pay bribes to officials who directly control the information they seek; ordinarily, they need not even explain their reasons for seeking the information. Freedom of information laws provide legally enforceable rights to anyone who seeks information from government and thus serve as tools to promote citizen knowledge and participation in public policy making and as bulwarks against corruption.

The notion that citizens hold such a right to know has been a prominent thread in American political philosophy since the founding of the nation. It has been expressed by drafters of the U.S. Constitution in the eighteenth century, by activists who led the campaign to establish a freedom of information law in the 1950s, by several recent presidents, and by government officials charged with overseeing application of the U.S. Freedom of Information Act and training and advising officials throughout the U.S. government. During the past decade and a half, this core democratic value has set a good example emulated by dozens of countries around the world aspiring to create more open and democratic governments. This is soft power at work.

The Right to Know as an American Value

Genesis of the U.S. Freedom of Information Act: The Role of the Press

The U.S. Freedom of Information Act was signed into law by President Lyndon Baines Johnson on July 4, 1966. The presidential statement issued that day explains the significance of the new law:

> This legislation springs from one of our most essential principles. A democracy works best when the people have all the information that the security of the nation permits. No one should be able to pull curtains of secrecy around decisions which can be revealed without injury to the public interest. . . . I signed this measure with a deep sense of pride that the United States is an open society in which the people's right to know is cherished and guarded. (White House 1966)

This achievement was preceded by nearly two decades of lobbying by articulate citizens motivated by fear of excessive secrecy in the executive branch of the U.S. government. The need for government secrecy is greatest in times of war, when military forces are in action and human lives and perhaps the survival of the nation may be at stake. During World War II, the greatest secret of all was the Manhattan Project, America's development of the atomic bomb. Although it involved the participation of thousands of workers at more than thirty sites around the country, and required a massive expenditure of funds (approximately $20 billion in present value) and six years to complete, the project was successfully kept secret from the American people and the U.S. Congress. The secrecy program was so successful that not only was the public unaware of the Manhattan Project, but President Harry Truman himself did not learn of it until the day after the death of Roosevelt, his first full day on the job as president of the United States (Andrew 1995, pp. 149–50).[3] (The Soviet Union, however, had already obtained detailed information through a network of well-placed informants.)

Although the war ended in 1945, the desire of government officials to exercise broad secrecy powers lived on. As described by Herbert Foerstel, "In the years immediately following World War II, the American people anticipated the lifting of wartime secrecy and censorship, but the hopes of both the public and the press were quickly dashed" (Foerstel 1999, p. 14). World War II was followed by the Cold War, global in scope and highly ideological in character. This was a war between communism and capitalism, and though not a single shot was fired on American soil, the nation would be gripped in anticommunist hysteria led by demagogues such as Senator Joseph McCarthy and others who saw a golden opportunity to build political fortunes by portraying themselves as patriots and their opponents as untrustworthy because they were "weak on communism."[4] Congress complied with demands for a new secrecy structure in this period by passing such laws as the Atomic Energy Act of 1946 and the National Security Act of 1947, and Cold War presidents issued new orders establishing the modern system of information classification.[5] Secrecy not only remained a key feature of governance, but became deeply institutionalized.

The search for a counterweight to this new secrecy regime was led by a small number of activist leaders of the American news media. Kent Cooper, who spent forty-five years with the Associated Press and retired as its executive director in 1950, is generally credited with coining the phrase "the right to know." Cooper became one of the first of many leaders of the American Society of Newspaper Editors who called for a law protecting this right. As summarized by Foerstel, "Many of Cooper's colleagues joined the fight against government secrecy. Throughout the 1950s, the American Society of Newspaper Editors (ASNE) and its Freedom of Information (FOI) committee, under the direction of a series of dedicated committee chairmen, led the charge for the public's right to know" (Foerstel 1999, p. 16).[6]

The Freedom of Information Committee achieved a major breakthrough when it retained Harold Cross, a famed media lawyer and counsel to the *New York Herald Tribune*, to prepare a report on federal, state, and municipal information policies and practices. The result would be published in book form in 1953 under the title *The People's Right to Know.* Advocates for a citizen's right to know to serve as a check on excessive government secrecy now had a carefully researched, comprehensive study of the issue.[7]

Cross argued that a right to know is inherent in the U.S. Constitution and that newspapers in particular enjoy a legal right to inspect government records. For the government to deny such access without a specific grant of authority by Congress, he argued, was an unconstitutional restriction on the freedom of the press as enshrined in the First Amendment and prevented news reporters from serving the people's constitutional right to know. Cross eloquently summarized the issue as follows: "The public business is the public's business. The people have the right to know. Freedom of information about public records is their just heritage. Citizens must have the legal right to investigate and examine the conduct of their affairs" (quoted in Foerstel 1999, p. 18).

Genesis of the U.S. Freedom of Information Act: The Role of Congress

The appearance of Cross's book coincided with the heyday of McCarthyism, a period that featured a campaign of demagoguery led by U.S. Senator Joseph McCarthy, the Un-American Activities Committee of the U.S. House of Representatives, Richard M. Nixon (elected vice president in 1952), and other politicians who terrified the American people with exaggerated claims of a communist threat to the nation. A Republican sweep of the 1952 national elections placed McCarthy and his supporters at the peak of their power to influence legislation and public opinion. They promoted public hysteria with shocking accusations of large-scale infiltration by communist agents of U.S. government agencies, Hollywood movie studios, and other influential institutions in American society. These charges were almost entirely untrue. McCarthy himself would ultimately be exposed as a liar and would be formally denounced by a resolution of the U.S. Senate in 1954, but not before the careers of many innocent people were destroyed.

One key element of the frenetic anticommunist campaign was the creation of "loyalty review boards" charged with investigating government employees accused of undefined charges of "disloyalty" to the United States. The evidence for such charges was usually kept secret, so accused individuals had little opportunity to defend themselves. As a result, thousands of government employees placed under investigation in the late 1940s and early 1950s either resigned "voluntarily" or were discharged (Stone 2004, Chap. 5, esp. pp. 341–52).

The excesses of the loyalty boards would lead to the appearance of a new champion for a citizen's right to know. This new leader was a congressman from California, first elected in 1952, named John E. Moss. Deeply disturbed by the wild accusations and threats against government employees, Moss wanted to learn the basis for these actions. According to one account, "he had sought information from the Eisenhower Administration's Civil Service Commission to verify its claim that 2,800 federal employees had been fired for 'security reasons'; he wanted to know whether these reasons were based on allegations of disloyalty or espionage or on other matters that could also be grounds for discharge—like a misstatement on a job application. The commission refused to release the information, and Moss found that he had no means to compel its release" (Moynihan 1998, p. 172). News reporters were not the only victims of excessive government secrecy; even members of Congress had difficulty getting information. Creating a means to compel government disclosure became Moss's most important mission as a legislator.

The Democrats gained control of the U.S. House of Representatives two years later, and Moss was appointed to head a new Special Subcommittee on Government Information to investigate suppression of information by the government. In his letter establishing this subcommittee, the committee chairman wrote, "Charges have been made that government agencies have denied or withheld pertinent and timely information from those who are entitled to receive it. . . . An informed public makes the difference between democratic government and mob rule. If the pertinent and necessary information on government operations is denied the public, the result is a weakening of the democratic process and the ultimate atrophy of our form of government" (Foerstel 1999, p. 22).

Freedom of Information and the Constitution of the United States

Descendants of the McCarthy-era FOI Committee presently celebrate the birthday of James Madison as Freedom of Information Day.[8] Madison is their hero because his prolific writings laid the foundation for a right to know. He clearly explained that such a right is inherent in a representative democracy, where sovereignty resides not with a monarch, but with the people themselves. Madison captured the idea with great flair in his oft-quoted declaration delivered before a fledgling Congress in 1794: "If we advert to the nature of republican government . . . we shall find that the censorial power is in the people over the government, and not in the government over the people."[9] In order to exercise this "censorial power" in an intelligent manner, the people need information (Splichal 2000, pp. 5–6). Madison encapsulated this idea in the words "Knowledge will forever govern ignorance. A people who mean to be their own governors must arm themselves with the power that knowledge gives."[10]

But Madison and the other framers did not hit upon the idea of a freedom of information law. Instead, they relied on the power of the press to deliver information to the people. They had firsthand experience of the great power of an unfettered press both to spread information and to mobilize citizens to action. Thomas Paine's incendiary 1776 pamphlet *Common Sense* remains one of the great bestsellers in American history. This call to action and countless others that appeared in colonial pamphlets and broadsheets built broad support for a war of independence. Thomas Jefferson, draftsman of the Declaration of Independence, once explained the role of the press thus: "The formidable censor of the public functionaries, by arraigning them at the tribunal of public opinion, produces reform peaceably, which must otherwise be done by revolution" (Splichal 2000, p. 6).

Although the words "right to know" do not appear in the U.S. Constitution (or in other writings of the founders), advocates and influential twentieth-century scholars such as Alexander Meiklejohn and Thomas Emerson declared that a right to hear is inherent in the right to speak; therefore, constitutional protections for freedom of speech and of the press must include a right to receive information. This constitutional foundation was cited by Congressman Moss himself on the day he introduced his freedom of information bill to the House of Representatives when he said, "Inherent in the right of free speech and of free press is the right to know. It is our solemn responsibility as inheritors of the cause to do all in our power to strengthen those rights—to give them meaning" (Congressional Record 1966).

The American news media secured robust constitutional protection through a series of Supreme Court decisions both before and after World War II. The Court repeatedly cited the writings of Madison and other founders and stressed the right of free speech as the means to guarantee all other rights in a democratic society, and the constitutional role of a free press as a provider of information to a self-governing people. For example, in the *Grosjean* case, decided nearly two decades before Harold Cross wrote his influential book, the Court had already declared that the purpose of the constitutional guarantee of a free press is to preserve "a vital source of public information."[11] When the nation confronted the problem of Cold War secrecy, the American press had already acquired the power and prestige to lead a new movement for openness in government.

The Global Freedom of Information Movement

Democracy and Transparency

In February 2005, President Vicente Fox of Mexico opened the proceedings of the third annual International Conference of Information Commissioners with a speech praising the virtues of openness in government. Fox, Mexico's first president from outside the dominant political party that ruled Mexico for an unbroken string of seventy-one years, proclaimed,

> Democracy and transparency always go hand in hand. There is no real democracy without permanent citizen participation. A true government cannot exist if citizens do not count on ample information and the necessary mechanisms to watch over authorities' good performance.
>
> In democracy, transparency and accountability constitute an obligation for all public servants. (Fox 2005)

Mexico's freedom of information law came into force in 2002 and has been praised by experts as one of the world's most progressive.[12] The enthusiasm of the Mexican government for its new transparency regime made Cancún a natural site for a conference on open government. Similar to the freedom of information laws of many countries, Mexican law created the position of information commissioner, an officer with responsibility to oversee the operation of the nation's freedom of information law. Typically, these officers develop administrative rules, train other government officials, make periodic reports of results achieved to senior officials and the national legislature, and, of greatest importance, hear complaints from citizens denied access to government information. Some information commissioners even have the power to overturn nondisclosure decisions by government agencies. The success of a freedom of information system may depend heavily on the authority of the information commissioner. More than four hundred persons from around the world attended the three-day Cancún conference, which featured presentations by speakers from more than two dozen countries. The International Conference of Information Commissioners itself issued a "Declaration of Cooperation" that said, "Participation in the knowledge of public entities is a legal right of the information society. Without discrimination, any person must be allowed access to the documents of public agencies. A transparent public administration, open to citizen participation in its decisions, is a prerequisite of a modern democratic society" (International Conference of Information Commissioners 2005). The declaration was signed by forty-three information commissioners from seventeen different countries. Only a few years before, few of these countries had either freedom of information laws or information commissioners.

The world experienced a sudden explosion of interest in freedom of information laws in the 1990s. According to Thomas Blanton, during this "decade of openness," "26 countries—from Japan to Bulgaria, Ireland to South Africa and Thailand to Great Britain—enacted formal statutes guaranteeing their citizens' right of access to government information" (Blanton 2002, p. 50). The trend has continued since. As noted above, Mexico joined the group in 2002 and Azerbaijan in 2005. Other recent members of this club include India and Argentina (2002) and Turkey (2003).

Why do people in so many countries find the freedom of information law attractive? In countries that introduced democratic governments in the 1990s, freedom of information could be viewed as an adjunct to a democratic constitution. Thus, most former Warsaw Pact countries now have freedom of information laws in force, and some have included a right to know in the constitution itself. Hungary was first, passing a freedom of information law in 1992. Blanton explained that "the Hungarian law was, in part, the new regime's revenge against its communist predecessors, opening their files and making them accountable for previous misdeeds" (Blanton 2002, p. 53).

Freedom of information is especially attractive to reformers in countries that face serious bribery and corruption problems.[13] By requiring transparency and thus creating a risk of exposure, freedom of information laws are commonly seen as an antidote. A highly publicized scandal sometimes serves as the catalyst for a successful freedom of information movement.

In his comprehensive survey of worldwide freedom of information laws, David Banisar explained their attractiveness by recasting Madison's thoughts in twenty-first-century language: "Access to government records and information is an essential requirement for modern government. Access facilitates public knowledge and discussion. It provides an important guard against abuses, mismanagement and corruption. It can also be beneficial to governments themselves—openness and transparency in the decision making process can assist in developing citizen trust in government actions and maintaining civil and democratic society" (Banisar 2004, p. 2).

Japan's Transparency Story

Thirty years before the Cancún event, a handful of elite Japanese scholars and activists had already discovered the American freedom of information model and fallen under its sway. At least since Professor Okudaira Yasuhiro published a Japanese translation in 1972, the U.S. Freedom of Information Act has been a continuing source of inspiration to Japan's democracy activists.[14] In 1975, the consumer activist Nomura Katsuko published a Japanese translation of a guide to the U.S. FOIA written by the staff of Freedom of Information Clearinghouse, a nonprofit advocacy group launched by Ralph Nader in the early 1970s. As the decade of the 1970s drew to a close, a progressive governor of Kanagawa Prefecture formed a team to study the feasibility of an open records system to apply to prefectural files. As a key element in the project, the prefecture funded tours to the United States and Sweden by academic experts charged with examining the systems in those countries for reference in drafting Kanagawa's own rules (Repeta 2003). The Kanagawa project coincided with parallel work in other local governments in urban population centers such as Saitama, Osaka, and Tokyo. By the end of the 1980s, most Japanese prefectures and cities had adopted ordinances empowering residents to demand access to local government files (Repeta 1999).

Despite continued opposition by Japan's insular national government, a small but effective network of scholars and activists continued to advocate for a national law throughout the 1980s and 1990s. The opportunity for a breakthrough appeared with the fall of the Miyazawa administration due to a no-confidence vote in the Diet in 1992, followed by the first non–Liberal Democratic Party administration since 1955. Under the authority of a cabinet led by the socialist prime minister Murayama Tomiichi, a committee was appointed to draft a proposed freedom of information law for Japan in 1995. The timing was right. When the committee delivered its report the following year, it was swept into a much broader movement for administrative reform, leading to passage of a national freedom of information law in 1999. This law came into effect in 2001.

The Japanese law is far from perfect. With elastic categories of exempt information, high user fees, and broad government discretion to delay disclosure in sensitive cases, Japan's law generally provides a poor model for other countries aspiring to build open governments. However, the law does express the straightforward mission of ensuring "that the government is accountable to the people," and some Japanese courts and administrative review panels have interpreted the law in an expansive manner. In the first two to three years following implementation, the news media focused national attention on Japan's new experiment in transparency. Reporters used the law to file thousands of requests, leading to frequent news stories based on newly uncovered documents. Without question, a seed was planted.

So far, however, the Japanese government has not perceived its information disclosure system to be a soft power resource. For example, no Japanese representative has appeared at the gatherings of information commissioners described above. There does not appear to be any governmental effort to inform foreign observers of Japan's achievements in freedom of information. This is unfortunate. Overall, Japan has a good story to tell. One of the most innovative features of Japan's system is the appointment of nongovernmental commissioners to administrative panels that hear appeals of nondisclosure decisions. As a low-cost and relatively objective means of processing such appeals, this model may be a good fit for many countries.

The Role of Nonstate Actors

Nye noted that "the information age has been marked by an increasingly important role of nonstate actors on the international stage." He wrote that nongovernmental organizations (NGOs) "develop new norms directly by pressing governments and business leaders to change policies and indirectly by altering public perceptions of what governments and firms should be doing" (Nye 2004, p. 90). This is a precise description of the role played by NGOs in spreading freedom of information laws around the world.

Publication of Thomas Blanton's article "The World's Right to Know" in *Foreign Policy* in the summer of 2002 coincided with the launch of freedominfo.org, "a virtual network of transparency activists." The Web site is managed by the National Security Archive under Blanton's direction and was funded primarily by a grant from the Open Society Institute. It serves as a clearinghouse of information regarding global developments in government transparency. The Web site carries individual country reports, recent developments from around the world, and links to other transparency groups. One feature, a compendium of news reports featuring FOI disclosures published during the preceding year, provides a quick reference to noteworthy cases. Samples from the 2005 edition include disclosure of Canadian government documents revealing that immigration officials had succumbed to influence from criminal gangs, a South African court order to disclose documents reporting irregularities in the weapons trade, the release of a report condemning food safety practices at the posh London department store Harrods, and more.[16]

The launch of freedominfo.org on July 4, 2002, was followed on September 28 by a newly declared International Right to Know Day and birth of the Freedom of Information Advocates Network, a virtual network which presently counts over 100 NGOs from more than forty countries as members. Its purpose is to facilitate the exchange of information between NGOs working to promote the adoption and effective implementation of freedom of information laws and to provide a forum for collaboration and development of ideas and strategies.[15] Members celebrate International Right to Know Day with conferences, awards ceremonies, and other events that aim to raise public awareness of the right to request and receive information.

The Freedom of Information Advocates Network and other such efforts are examples of the international NGO movement described in Chapter 15 of this volume, by Katsuji Imata and Kaori Kuroda. Compared to the highly publicized efforts of international NGOs in such areas as poverty reduction, treatment of infectious diseases, environmental protection, and other issues of broad popular interest, the open government movement is small and little known. But the movement employs the same dynamic, with members seeking active cross-border participation to build momentum. (Japanese participation in the international freedom of information campaign is minimal. Obvious reasons include lack of funding, the language barrier, and low public appreciation of the value of government transparency.)

Journalists and public-spirited citizens who seek more honest and accountable forms of government can be found in every country of the world. During the 1980s and 1990s, otherwise unrelated individuals and citizen groups in Eastern Europe, India, Mexico and elsewhere found the right to know to be an ideal tool to promote democracy and good government. The new international network of transparency NGOs supports them by providing model laws to study, success stories to emulate, and well-honed responses to the standard objections made by government officials, who invariably resist the introduction of a system that reduces their arbitrary power.

Any description of the global FOI movement must make special reference to the contribution of Article 19, an international NGO founded in 1987 "which defends and promotes freedom of expression and freedom of information all over the world."[17] Article 19 has played a central role in propagating information disclosure laws, collaborating with democracy proponents in the former Warsaw Pact countries of Eastern Europe to promote the right to know since the 1990s. Article 19 campaigns feature linkage with local grassroots organizations capable of understanding the freedom of information message and advocating with local governments. Legal experts and organizers from Article 19 and its allies travel to target countries to conduct workshops on-site in order to drive home basic concepts, explain the details of freedom of information laws, and discuss the infrastructure needed to make such laws work.

As the freedom of information movement was succeeding in Eastern Europe, Article 19 expanded its campaigns to South Asia, Latin America, Southeast Asia, and Central Asia. It achieved a significant breakthrough in June 1999 with publication of "Public's Right to Know—Principles on Freedom of Information Legislation," drafted by Toby Mendel, head of the organization's law program, followed by publication of a Model Law on Freedom of Information two years later.[18] These documents provide a comprehensive blueprint for citizens in any country who seek to promote transparency in government.

The National Security Archive has also played a critical role in the global campaign, serving both as a model of a nongovernmental research organization devoted to the use of freedom of information laws and other tools to obtain government information, as well as a source of expertise in planning and organizing international events and campaigns. The Hungarian-born philanthropist George Soros and the NGOs and foundations he launched and continues to support have also played essential roles, especially in organizing and funding NGOs and transparency projects. Soros established the Open Society Institute as a means to realize his vision of "open societies" around the world. Establishing a right to access information in government files is a key element of the open society concept. Soros was active in promoting democracy development in Eastern Europe for many years before the historic events of 1989. With the new openness, Soros expanded his activities in Central and Eastern Europe and around the world, and in 2002 established the Justice Initiative, based in New York, which among its other activities promotes freedom of information at international and regional forums and in more than two dozen countries, with increasing attention devoted to Africa and Asia.[19] Countless individuals and citizen organizations around the world, some with the support of sophisticated international NGOs and philanthropists, and others acting on their own, have played important roles in the campaign both in their own countries and across borders.

A potentially powerful permutation of the global transparency movement arose in 2004 when Article 19, freedominfo.org, and other transparency NGOs joined forces with Bank Information Center, the Bretton Woods Project, and other NGOs that specialize in monitoring and advocating reform at multilateral financial institutions, such as the World Bank, Asian Development Bank, and others. Together this NGO coalition formed a new program called the Global Transparency Initiative.[20] Because multilateral financial institutions are not subject to national laws of member countries, they cannot be bound by traditional freedom of information laws. The founders of Global Transparency Initiative adopted a strategy of lobbying multilateral financial institutions to adopt transparency regimes or at least expand the range of documents made available for public inspection. Accused of a "democracy deficit" by high-profile critics, some multilateral financial institutions have been willing to adopt reforms, if only as a means to improve their public images.

The Role of the U.S. Government

Banisar explained that "most FOI laws around the world are broadly similar. In part, this is because a few countries' laws, mostly those adopted early on, have been used as models. The U.S. FOIA has probably been the most influential law. Canada's and Australia's national, provincial and state laws have been prominent with countries based on the common law tradition" (Banisar 2004, p. 4).

The U.S. FOIA and commonwealth laws have provided models for others to follow, featuring broad rights of information access, with defined categories of information exempt from disclosure. Many parties have joined in promoting this model. The discussion above suggests that the "demand-pull" from activists and officials in countries seeking advice and information has been a powerful force. We must also recognize that the "supply push" delivered by officials of the United States and other early-adapter governments has been important. The American effort has featured a partnership between the State Department and other agencies charged with public diplomacy, on one hand, and the undisputed center of freedom of information expertise in the U.S. government, a little-known office of the Department of Justice called the Office of Information and Privacy (OIP), on the other.

OIP was created in 1981 and was led by the same pair of codirectors for nearly a quarter century. (Each recently announced his retirement.) Its regular activities include publication of a newsletter and authoritative guidebook to the U.S. FOIA used in all government offices and by lawyers around the United States, consultations with federal agencies regarding specific FOIA requests, and service as counsel on behalf of the U.S. government in selected cases.

Although its core mission is purely domestic, OIP has evolved into a powerful engine of public diplomacy. For example, in 2003 OIP directors and staff provided briefings and FOIA materials

> to representatives of the nations of Japan, Peru, Canada, Brazil, Germany, Hong Kong, Bosnia-Herzegovina, South Korea, Thailand, Poland, Israel, China, and Australia. It also provided such briefings to the Comptroller of the Mexican Senate, Members of the Parliament of Uganda, Members of the Parliament of Indonesia, and a Mexican Transparency Commissioner. At the request of the China Law Center of Yale Law School and in coordination with the Department of State, OIP's deputy director traveled to Shanghai, China in order to engage in several days of discussions of openness-in-government principles with both national and provincial officials, including the substantive review of draft legislation, in preparation of the "open government information" law scheduled to be adopted there in mid-2004. (Office of Information and Privacy 2003, sec. f)

Such OIP diplomacy has a long history. By its own count, OIP has met with representatives of more than eighty countries since the office was founded. As noted above, such encounters are not restricted to meetings in Washington, but include trips abroad. As in the case of the China visit, OIP diplomacy is inevitably in greatest demand when countries are seriously considering initial legislation creating a freedom of information law.

Freedom of Information Is but One Feature of Democratic Government

One must be careful not to confuse aspirations with achievements. Although many countries have adopted freedom of information laws based on the U.S. and commonwealth models, the mere adoption of a freedom of information law does not convert an otherwise repressive government into a shining example of democracy. In his landmark study, *Blacked Out—Government Secrecy in the Information Age,* Alasdair Roberts compared the movement of the 1980s, when "affluent, anglophone, stable, parliamentary democracies" including Australia, New Zealand, and Canada adopted FOI laws, with the 1990s, when FOI laws arrived in the world of "soft states" "struggling with poverty, political disenfranchisement and widespread corruption." Among the necessary conditions for a successful freedom of information system, he listed "a decent system of recordkeeping and a reasonably professional civil service" along with adequate resources to administer the law. In cases where such systems are lacking and government service is characterized by widespread corruption, he posed the question whether we should view the adoption of an FOI system as a genuine reform or merely as an act taken for the sake of appearances (Roberts 2006, esp. pp. 107–23).

No information disclosure law is absolute. Even the most sophisticated systems in the wealthiest countries with rich democratic traditions always establish a list of categories of information exempt from disclosure. Typical categories include information concerning national security, the privacy of individuals, ongoing criminal investigations, and trade secrets or other confidential business information. Requesters and government officials frequently disagree on whether such exceptions apply in a particular case. Unbiased third-party review is critical to resolve such disputes. Undoubtedly, the most important factor in the success of a freedom of information law, aside from the wording of the statute itself, is the independence and power of courts or other third-party review organs to require recalcitrant governments to disclose information that power holders would rather keep confidential. In countries where courts are unable to effectively enforce commercial agreements or bring criminals to justice, it is unlikely that they will succeed in enforcing the terms of a "pie-in-the-sky" openness law.

A recent Article 19 report noted "the oft repeated assertion by those involved in promoting FOI, that the adoption of a FOIA is merely the beginning of a process to guarantee the public's right to know" (Article 19 2002, p. 5). In order to succeed, freedom of information systems need the kind of infrastructure described by Roberts and courts with the independence and authority to enforce them. Above all, the process must be driven by individual citizens and groups able to identify information of significance, to challenge government denials when necessary, and to put information to good use once they have it in hand.

The Future of the Global FOI Movement

There is no guarantee that even a well-crafted freedom of information law will work. And political tides can suddenly turn against transparency. Continued effort by the news media, citizen organizations, and sympathetic government officials is required for the global movement to continue its march forward. What will be the source of future leadership?

Recent developments display the international character of leadership in the global movement. The U.S. role is not as prominent as it once was. For example, the International Conference of Information Commissioners is probably the first global government-to-government coordinating body at work on information disclosure policy. The first four annual gatherings have been held in Capetown, Berlin, Cancún, and Manchester. The Cancún "Declaration of Cooperation" was signed by commissioners from governments in seventeen countries, but the list of signatories does not include anyone representing the U.S. government.[21] The information commissioner concept itself owes its inspiration to the "ombudsman" office common in parliamentary democracies; there is no such office in the U.S. federal government. (OIP is not neutral, as the information commissioners are intended to be; it represents the U.S. government in FOI disputes.) The Article 19 "Model Law" was drafted not by an American lawyer but by a Canadian, and it explicitly provides for an information commissioner, a feature common to Canadian national and provincial systems. Recent years have also witnessed significant new transparency programs originating outside the United States that did not involve significant American participation.[22]

Perhaps the most significant factor affecting the future American role in the global FOI movement is the U.S. government's own information policies. Since taking office in 2001, the Bush administration has displayed severe hostility toward the public right to know, blocking public access to government information through a multitude of policies and measures.[23] Although the antidisclosure policy of the Bush administration was well established before September 11, 2001, it was accelerated and expanded in the crisis atmosphere that followed. This does not bode well for American influence in the area. It remains to be seen whether future American governments will reverse or significantly change this approach.

As noted at the outset, although nearly all Americans agree that promoting democracy should be a central goal of U.S. policy, there is disagreement over means. The idea of a citizen's right to know represents just one thread in American political philosophy. It conflicts with an even more powerful modern bias toward the use of military force to solve international disputes. In the most prominent recent example of this bias, President George W. Bush paradoxically chose war as the means to promote democracy in the Middle East.

Military operations require secrecy and thus conflict with a citizen's right to know. Military leaders can use the threat of attack to justify wide-ranging secrecy in government operations. Even in times of peace, it is difficult for the world's greatest and most aggressive military power to serve as an example to other nations seeking transparency in government. Maintaining the reputation of "an open society in which the people's right to know is cherished and guarded" is far more difficult when the world is awash in images of American brutality such as the high-tech bombing of homes and the inhumane treatment of prisoners, and when the American president asserts that any street corner within the United States or without is a potential battle zone in a "war on terror."

In much the same manner that government officials created the modern system of national security secrecy in the early years of the Cold War, the Bush administration has radically changed American standards of openness and secrecy. Although the modern concept of a right to know was carefully cultured in the United States, one is left to wonder whether the United States will retain a central role in the global movement and whether non-Americans will continue to recognize the United States as a credible advocate of government transparency.

Notes

1. Syed Ishtiaque Reza, "People's Right to Know." *Financial Express,* December 15, 2005.

2. Paul Richter and Richard B. Schmitt, "Rice Wins Backing for Senate Confirmation." *Washington Post,* January 19, 2005.

3. The basic facts of the Manhattan Project were unknown to the American public until

reported in *Life* magazine in a pair of articles that appeared in 1949 and 1950 (Moynihan 1998, pp. 140–42).

4. Under the direction of J. Edgar Hoover, the FBI compiled a list of nearly a half million Americans they considered threats to national security and placed countless individuals under surveillance. The House Un-American Activities Committee interrogated hundreds of suspected communists including famous actors and other figures, leading to a Hollywood blacklist, deportation of innocent individuals, and other abuses of civil liberties. Senator McCarthy delivered the infamous speech in which he falsely declared that he had a list of more than 200 communists employed by the State Department with the knowledge of the secretary of state in February 1950 (Lief and Caldwell 2004, pp. 110–14).

5. Thomas Blanton has summarized the key forces during this period that led to the modern system of national security secrecy in the United States as follows: "the initially voluntary restrictions created by the Manhattan Project scientists on nuclear weapons information as early as 1940, the total mobilization of U.S. society during WW II, and the institutionalization of these procedures in peacetime by the Cold War apparat, especially the National Security Act of 1947" (Blanton 2003).

6. The Freedom of Information Committee was led during these years by Basil L. Walters of Knight Ridder, James S. Pope of the *Louisville Courier-Journal* and James Russell Wiggins of the *Washington Post* (Foerstel 1999, p. 16).

7. In the words of one scholar, Cross's book "became the bible of the FOI movement, the scholarly foundation for every major piece of federal legislation in the field, and a scrupulously researched but passionately written sourcebook for advocates of freedom of access at local, state and national levels" (Kennedy 1996).

8. Among many celebrations of national Freedom of Information Day around the United States, perhaps the most prominent is held in Washington, DC under the sponsorship of the First Amendment Center, an affiliate of The Freedom Forum, a nonpartisan foundation dedicated to promoting freedom of speech. For details concerning this Freedom of Information Day event, see http://www.firstamendmentcenter.org/press/information/topic.aspx?topic=FOI_Day (accessed on December 5, 2007).

9. 4 *Annals of Congress* 934 (1794), cited in Splichal 2000, p. 2.

10. James Madison, letter to W.T. Barry, August 4, 1822; pertinent portion reprinted in *The Complete Madison* 337, ed. Saul Padover (1953), cited in Splichal 2000, p. 6.

11. *Grosjean v. American Press Association,* 297 U.S. 233 (1936).

12. "Among all these countries, including the United States, Mexico stands out as a leader," said Alasdair Roberts, a public administration professor at Syracuse University whose book, *Blacked Out: Government Secrecy in the Information Age,* is to be released next month. "It's not just that Mexico adopted a law. Mexico invested in oversight and enforcement capacity. They invested in technology capacity to collect and track requests," Roberts said. "Fox made it clear that he was taking this seriously." The IFAI has created a unique system for filing freedom-of-information requests. Requests can be filed anonymously through the IFAI's Web site, www.ifai.org.mx/english_version, eliminating fears among a still wary public that there will be reprisals for challenging the government. The IFAI commission, which meets in open session every Wednesday, acts as a clearinghouse for requests and, in sensitive cases, as an intermediary between petitioners and government agencies to determine what information should be released. S. Lynne Walker, "For Mexico, Open Records Unlock Doors," Copley News Service, November 20, 2005.

13. Transparency is universally recognized as an effective antidote to corruption. The founders of the most prominent international NGO engaged in anti-corruption efforts even designated their organization "Transparency International." For details, see http://www.transparency.org (accessed on December 5, 2007).

14. Okudaira's translation was published in the June 1972 edition of *Horitsu Jiho,* one of Japan's most prominent legal journals. The overall theme of the volume was the "People's Right to Know."

15. The Internet address of the Freedom of Information Advocates Network provides details of its activities. See http://www.foiadvocates.net (accessed on December 5, 2007).

16. Reports on International Right to Know Day are published on two Internet Web sites. See http://www.freedominfo.org/features/20060928.htm and http://www.foiadvocates.net/rkd07.php (both accessed on December 5, 2007).

17. Article 9 takes its name from Article 19 of the Universal Declaration of Human Rights, which states, "Everyone has the right to freedom of opinion and expression; the right includes freedom to hold opinions without interference and to seek, receive and impart information and ideas through any media regardless of frontiers." The Article 19 Internet address is at http://www.article19.org (accessed on December 5, 2007).

18. Texts of these and other documents are available at http://www.article19.org/publications/law/standard-setting.html (accessed on December 5, 2007).

19. The freedom of information activities of the Open Society Institute Justice Initiative Internet are described at http://www.justiceinitiative.org/activities/foifoe/foi (accessed December 5, 2007).

20. The activities of the Global Transparency Initiative are described at http://www.ifitransparency.org (accessed on December 5, 2007).

21. The signatories do include information officers from the states of New York and Connecticut (International Conference of Information Commissioners 2005).

22. See, for example, the information disclosure provisions of the Aarhus "Convention on Access to Information, Public Participation in Decisionmaking, and Access to Information in Environmental Matters." The text of the convention is available on the Web site of the United Nations Economic Commission for Europe. See http://www.unece.org/env/pp/ (accessed December 5, 2007).

23. With one major exception, this new secrecy policy has been implemented mainly through actions by government agencies without any change in law. For example, many agencies have removed materials from public Web sites. They have also adopted a range of new information categories, such as "sensitive but unclassified," which cannot override the freedom of information law itself, but do alter administrative practice in order to restrict access. The most significant change in law itself is the law creating the Department of Homeland Security, which also created a new category of information labeled "critical infrastructure information," which can place a broad range of information beyond public access. Much of this information was readily available to information requesters before these measures took effect. News organizations and public interest groups have published countless criticisms of the Bush secrecy policy. A convenient compendium of many such reports is presented in Laura Gordon-Murnane, "Shhh!!: Keeping Current on Government Secrecy," *Searcher* 14, 1 (2006), http://www.infotoday.com/searcher/jan06/Gordon-Murnane.shtml (accessed June 18, 2007).

References

Andrew, Christopher. 1995. *For the President's Eyes Only.* New York: Harper Perennial.

Article 19. 2002. "Promoting Practical Access to Democracy: A Survey of Freedom of Information in Central and Eastern Europe." http://www.article19.org/pdfs/publications/freedom-of-information-survey-of-central-ande.pdf (accessed June 28, 2007).

Banisar, David. 2004. "The Freedominfo.org Global Survey, Freedom of Information and Access to Government Record Laws Around the World (May 2004)," http://www.freedominfo.org (accessed February 6, 2006).

Blanton, Thomas. 2002. "The World's Right to Know." *Foreign Policy* (July–Aug) http://www.freedominfo.org/documents/rtk-english.pdf (accessed June 28, 2007).

———. 2003. "National Security and Open Government in the United States: Beyond the Balancing Test." In *National Security and Open Government: Striking the Right Balance.*

Ed. Campbell Public Affairs Institute. Syracuse, NY: Campbell Public Affairs Institute, Syracuse University, 31–71.

Congressional Record. 1966. "Clarifying and Protecting the Right of the Public to Information, Statement of the Honorable John E. Moss," 13642, June 20, 1966. http://www.johnemossfoundation.org/foi/cr_JEM.htm (accessed June 18, 2007).

Foerstel, Herbert. 1999. *Freedom of Information and the Right to Know.* Westport, CT: Greenwood Press.

Fox, Vicente Quesada. 2005. "Inaugural Comments upon Opening of the Third International Conference of Information Commissioners." Cancun, Mexico, February 21, 2005.

International Conference of Information Commissioners. 2005. "Declaration of Cooperation." Cancun, Mexico, February 21–23, 2005.

Kennedy, George. 1996. "How Americans Got Their Right to Know." http://www.johnemossfoundation.org/foi/kennedy.htm (accessed June 18, 2007).

Lief, Michael S., and H. Mitchell Caldwell. 2004. *And the Walls Came Tumbling Down.* New York: Scribner.

Moynihan, Daniel Patrick. 1998. *Secrecy.* New Haven, CT: Yale University Press.

Nye, Joseph S., Jr. 2004. *Soft Power: The Means to Success in World Politics.* New York: Public Affairs.

Office of Information and Privacy. U.S. Department of Justice. 2003. Annual FOIA Litigation and Compliance Report, "Description of DOJ Efforts to Encourage Compliance with the Act," http://www.usdoj.gov/oip/03rep.htm (accessed December 10, 2007).

Repeta, Lawrence. 1999. *Local Government Disclosure Systems in Japan.* Seattle: National Bureau of Asian Research.

———. 2003. "The Birth of the Freedom of Information Act in Japan: Kanagawa 1982," Working Paper 03.03. MIT Japan Program. http://www.freedominfo.org/features/20030908.htm (accessed June 18, 2007).

Roberts, Alasdair. 2006. *Blacked Out: Government Secrecy in the Information Age.* New York: Cambridge University Press.

Splichal, Sigman L. 2000. "The Right to Know." In *Access Denied: Freedom of Information in the Information Age.* Ed. Charles N. Davis and Sigman L. Splichal. Ames: Iowa State University Press, 3–22.

Stone, Geoffrey R. 2004. *Perilous Times: Free Speech in Wartime.* New York: W.W. Norton.

U.S. Department of State. ND. "Democracy." http://www.state.gov/g/drl/democ/ (accessed June 18, 2007).

White House. 1966. Statement by the President upon Signing S. 1160 (July 4, 1966). http://www.johnemossfoundation.org/foi/LBJ.htm (accessed June 18, 2007).

15

Soft Power of NGOs

Growing Influence Beyond National Boundaries

Imata Katsuji and Kuroda Kaori

The power that nongovernmental organizations (NGOs) possess on the global scene is becoming more noticeable with each passing year. In many realms—including fields as diverse as humanitarian assistance, development assistance for poverty reduction, peace and security, human rights, the environment, national and international governance and accountability, and corporate social responsibility—NGOs collectively have become a powerhouse, utilizing expert knowledge, analytical skills, financial muscle, media savvy, and public education capacities.

This power can be viewed as a type of soft power, and our role in this chapter is to explore the soft power of NGOs with particular reference to Japanese NGOs. But first, in order to place NGOs within the framework of the soft power argument, we need to clarify the definition of soft power as it applies to non-state actors.

Second, we turn our attention to NGOs and their role in the post–Cold War era. Here, we will limit our scope of analysis to so-called international NGOs that are actively engaged not only in provision of international development aid and humanitarian assistance but also in influencing public policy in this "global governance" age.

In the third part of the chapter, we specifically turn our attention to Japanese NGOs and discuss their soft power within the analytical framework that we lay out in the preceding sections.

Soft Power and Non-state Actors

International relations theorist Joseph Nye, who introduced the concept, acknowledged that soft power does not belong only to states. He defined soft power as "attractive power" (Nye 2004, p. 6) and noted that the concept is applicable even to personal relationships: "If I am persuaded to go along with your purposes without any explicit threat or exchange taking place—in short, if my behavior is determined by an observable but intangible attraction—soft power is at work" (Nye 2004, p. 7). Yet, in describing various dimensions of soft power, Nye focuses on the types of power that belong to the state—military and economic power (hard power) on the one hand and culture, political values, and foreign policies (soft power) on the other. It is the state that coerces or co-opts, and in the latter case, the state makes use of its soft power as an effective tool for public diplomacy. In this particular context, the concept of soft power assumes that its holder is expected to make *strategic use* of such power for *a particular interest.* In other words, soft power is *a means* to achieve some *goal* of its holder.

How, then, can the concept be applicable to non-state actors as the active entity that exerts soft power? Nye described non-state actors as forces that are becoming more and more powerful in the global information age, thus wielding soft power to an extent that cannot be ignored. This includes NGOs and their global campaigns as well as intergovernmental organizations such as the United Nations and the World Trade Organization. Nevertheless, it is not so straightforward to think of these entities as having soft power, because these non-state actors do not have the same characteristics as states with respect to the formulation of the soft power argument

The most salient difference is that while nation-states possess soft power in addition to their military and economic power (indeed, soft power has been defined in contrast to the hard power that states also possess), non-state actors usually do not possess these other "hard" types of power. Also, while non-state actors might deploy the power of attraction (i.e., soft power) for a particular strategic interest, deployment of such power usually entails some kind of interaction (collaboration, conflict, etc.) with the state's interest, which adds a layer of complexity to the soft power of non-state actors and its implications.

Thus, in examining the soft power of non-state actors, one has to take into account this additional dimension and describe its relationship to the state. When we single out the soft power of NGOs, their relationship to the state becomes one of the central themes. Certain NGOs pursue organizational missions that are compatible with the foreign policies of the state where they are based, while other NGOs and civil society organizations may be consistently critical of the activities of the state in a given field. Furthermore, a large number of international NGOs have gone beyond national boundaries in their attempts to influence an increasingly globalized decision-making system, which brings them to a level where they are bound to compete with various states in the realization of particular policy outcomes.

An interesting feature of the soft power of non-state actors takes shape when they take a critical stance toward the state. From the state's point of view, to have a domestic non-state actor as a vocal critic gives rise to the possibility of tension and conflict. For all the obvious reasons, the state may want to suppress such activity. Nevertheless, if it tolerates such activities by non-state actors, a state can often end up increasing, rather than decreasing, its own attractiveness, as a state can be respected for having allowed non-state actors under its sphere of influence to behave in such a way. In our view, the soft power of the United States, for example, is inseparable from its protection of speech and freedom of expression as laid out in the First Amendment to the Constitution, which protects voices that criticize and sometimes condemn the state's actions. Simply put, "America" as a theoretical construct is popular and attractive in part because it allows a diversity of opinions, including those that are highly critical of its own state.

When we say that the soft power of non-state actors, especially that of NGOs, is becoming more and more manifest today, we are referring to their expressive and communicative power. At the same time, if their actions emanate from a particular state, we view their soft power as contributing to the soft power of that state as well. Nye called this "meta–soft power"; as summarized by Watanabe Yasushi, it is "the state's capacity and introspective ability to criticize itself, saying that this most fundamentally defines a country's attractiveness, legitimacy, and reliability."[1]

We see a good part of American soft power arising out of this "meta–soft power." Howard Zinn and Anthony Arnove's *Voices of a People's History of the United States* (2004) is a case in point; while this well-known volume is quite critical of the American state and describes people who have vocally opposed various aspects of America's political and social system, the book helps boost readers' image of the country rather than tarnish it. The history of the United States is tainted with various incidents of oppression, discrimination, and disenfranchisement that were sanctioned by the system, but the fact that there were people who fought against such a system—and the fact that these very people have become heroes in contemporary eyes—is what makes this book attractive. The book is of course about people, but it is also about the system (i.e., the state) that allowed them to speak out, if not necessarily when they most needed to be heard.

Incorporating this aspect of soft power—"meta–soft power"—will enrich the discussion of soft power, especially that of non-state actors. A narrower version of soft power is where the holder (whether a state or non-state actor) deploys it in order to advance a specific strategic interest. However, the soft power of non-state actors is often *expressive* in nature; that is, the holder of the power (the non-state actor) uses its soft power not for any strategic intent of the state but for something independent of the state's intent. This distinction is useful for our discussion of NGOs and their soft power.

International NGOs, Civil Society, and Soft Power

> Though poorly understood and imperfectly applied in practice, concepts like the "new diplomacy," "soft power," and "complex multilateralism" place civil society at the center of international policy debates and global problem-solving (Edwards 2001, p. 1).

International NGOs and Soft Power

The post–Cold War era witnessed an upsurge in the number and vitality of civil society organizations in most parts of the world (Salamon and Anheier 1997; Lewis 1999). The expansion of civil society was so rapid and so global that Lester Salamon (1993) described it as an "associational revolution." In the 1990s, a set of global issues emerged; some of these issues were new, while some had been submerged during the Cold War period. Globalization, which has contributed much to the world economy, has had tremendous—and largely negative—impacts on the world's poor. Other criti-

Table 15.1

Global Size of the Leading International NGO Networks

Network	Annual Budget (FY)
CARE	$550 million (2000)
Médecins Sans Frontiéres	$304 million (1999)
Oxfam	$504 million (1999)
Plan International	$311 million (2002)
Red Cross (International Federation of Red Cross and Red Crescent Societies)	$230 million (2001)
Save the Children	$368 million (1999)
World Vision	$600 million (1999)
WWF/World Wide Fund for Nature	$350 million (not known)

Source: Clark 2003b, pp. 133–36.

cal issues include the global environment, sustainable development, HIV/AIDS and other infectious diseases, good governance, corporate social responsibility, women's empowerment, human rights, and labor issues.

Civil society has become a prominent force in dealing with these emerging and pressing needs. The provision of international development assistance and humanitarian aid is certainly one of the areas where NGOs have come to play an increasingly important role from the 1990s onward. Some NGOs increasingly stood out from among the numerous organizations, becoming formidably powerful on the global scene; brand names such as Oxfam, CARE, and Save the Children have seeped into our everyday life to a degree comparable with corporate brands such as Toyota or Microsoft. These "super-NGOs," as they are sometimes called, now have annual budgets of several hundred million dollars and thus are comparable in budgetary size to some UN agencies, such as the United Nations High Commissioner for Refugees.[2] Table 15.1 shows the annual budget of eight large international NGO networks.

As aptly described in the book *Going Global* (Lindenberg and Bryant 2001), these multinational NGOs have gained brand recognition, financial strength, expertise in the field, and human resources that make them significant players on the global scene, not only in delivering services for humanitarian assistance and development, but also in presenting policy views and frameworks influencing aid, trade, and debt.

As they become powerful players on the global scene, the relationship of such NGOs to the state has become a topic of interest. It is useful for our purposes here to examine the lineage of these large NGOs. Primarily discussing the state of humanitarian NGOs, Abby Stoddard (2003, pp. 27–28) traced the tradition of large NGOs to three origins: religious, Dunantists, and Wilsonians.

The religious tradition's basic tenet is compassion and service, and although it does not aim to proselytize in a direct way, it has missionary work as its antecedent. Catholic Relief Services and World Vision are some present-day examples of NGOs that fall into this tradition. The second group, the Dunantists, is a group that can trace its origins to the vision of Henri Dunant, who started the Red Cross movement in the 1860s. Although the Red Cross itself is not usually considered an NGO, its humanitarian principles have been widely shared by the NGO community. Today, Save the Children, Oxfam, and Médecins Sans Frontiéres (also known as Doctors Without Borders) are considered as falling into this category.

Of particular interest to us is the third group, known as the Wilsonians—named after American president Woodrow Wilson. It is argued that most U.S. NGOs fall into this tradition. Unlike their European counterparts—especially those of the Dunantist tradition—where we can find at the roots of those NGOs political and intellectual opposition to government actions, Wilsonians see "a basic compatibility between humanitarian aims and U.S. foreign policy" (Stoddard 2003, p. 27).

An organization that is introduced as a "quintessential" member of the Wilsonian tradition is CARE, which has its origin in the aftermath of World War II, when it started as Cooperative for American Remittances to Europe, delivering food parcels (CARE packages) under the Marshall Plan for reconstruction of war-ravaged European nations. Outside the United States, the Dutch government and its NGOs embody a Wilsonian tradition of basic cooperation between government and NGOs in humanitarian action.

It is in this particular tradition, the Wilsonians, where NGOs can possibly be viewed as an extension of the state's interests. NGOs are called "partners" of states in humanitarian action and development. Indeed, it is probably true to say that the U.S. government has been making use of U.S. NGOs for strategic purposes. The scale of this cooperation is very large; the U.S. government provided $2.8 billion to NGOs in 2003 (Office of Private and Voluntary Cooperation 2004). This is more than fifty times the scale of official development assistance channeled to NGOs in Japan, which amounted to some ¥5.5 billion, or US$46 million, in 2002 (Ministry of Foreign Affairs 2002a).

It is also our general impression that U.S. NGOs do not have as many reservations as NGOs in Japan and elsewhere about having strong ties and affinity with their government. This is not to say that there are not battles and struggles between the government and NGOs—there are,[3] but it is still true to say that there is a proximity of attitude and philosophy among those engaged in international development work in the United States, regardless of whether they are working for the government or NGOs.

It is important to note, however, that the specific relationship between the government and particular NGOs can vary from close partnership to strong opposition—it usually falls somewhere in between—and thus it is not the case that U.S. NGOs are always the embodiment of the Wilsonian tradition.[4] After the Bush administration took office in 2000, there were voices within the U.S. NGO community that expressed tension and strains in their dealings with the government.

On the contrary, after the Labor Party took office in 1997 and the government of the United Kingdom created a ministry solely responsible for development matters (the Department for International Development, or DFID), there seemed to be a trend of growing partnership between the UK government and its NGOs. For example, a funding program for UK NGOs managed by DFID, called the Partnership Programme Agreement, is a large-scale (from about US$1 million to tens of million dollars per year) partnership agreement that entails little scrutiny regarding the use of the funds. It is more like a core support grant provided to leading UK NGOs, such as Oxfam, Save the Children, and Action Aid, based on the premise that these NGOs and the government share a key strategic interest in development. Regardless of how it is viewed by the NGOs, it has become a powerful tool to promote DFID's interests.

From the narrower view of soft power, NGOs can indeed be a state's great instruments. A program such as the Partnership Programme Agreement is testimony to how the state can wisely make use of the power and potential of NGOs while at the same time extending its own interests. A caveat here, however, is that British NGOs seem to be buying into this partnership only because they see the state, represented here by DFID, as sharing their fundamental priorities regarding global poverty reduction and the promotion of human rights. When DFID was created, development interests—interest in global poverty alleviation—were separated from diplomatic interests. NGOs may feel that such a close partnership with the government exists because this differentiation is clear both in principle and in practice.

In the 1980s and 1990s, most donors viewed NGOs as "implementing partners" (the term still used by UN agencies) in a relationship in which donors were the ones who made decisions as to what needed to be done while NGOs were the state's "agents" in providing services. The situation has changed since then. When an NGO's annual budget is larger than that of the United Nations High Commissioner for Refugees, and when the NGO's primary support comes from the public and not from institutional donors, it has broad ramifications for the state-NGO relationship. NGOs can still be viewed as agents for carrying a state's soft power, but viewing them in such a manner might obscure the very point that makes them NGOs—that they are independent, autonomous bodies with a mission to make a difference in the world, irrespective of any state's interests and power.

Moreover, we need to take notice of the fact that NGOs and their activities are less and less bound by national boundaries. The term "global citizen" sounds naive—yet it is their aspiration to embody a sense of global citizenship and responsibility that makes the work of these NGOs highly attractive to many. When feeling attracted to Save the Children, for example, we do not need to know whether it is a UK-based or U.S.-based NGO, although if we take a careful look, there are definitely different state-NGO relations at play surrounding each organization. An important aspect of the soft power of NGOs is that it goes beyond particular nation-states.

Global Campaigns: Information Technology and Civic Action

In recent years, civil society movements beyond national boundaries have come to prominence for their role in global problem solving. These movements are often initiated and led by policy-influencing NGOs or civil society organizations (CSOs) that have a mission to deal with global issues that challenge humanity. Usually, the term

"CSOs" includes not only NGOs that work on international development, human rights, and the environment, but also national, regional, local, and community-based groups that work on issues facing youth, women, and persons with disabilities, as well as trade unions, consumers' organizations, faith-based and interfaith groups, and certain professional associations (Clark 2003a, p. 1). Some significant examples include the campaign to increase access to drugs to treat HIV/AIDS, the Jubilee 2000 campaign focusing on debt relief for the poorest countries, and the Nobel Peace Prize–winning NGO network the International Campaign to Ban Landmines (ICBL).

The most recent 2005 global campaign for poverty elimination, called the Global Call to Action Against Poverty (GCAP), is a loosely affiliated network of more than 100 national campaigns.[5] It also links with other networks, including the Jubilee movement, as well as other campaigns that work for economic and social justice. One of the salient features of this campaign is its approach of bringing together a loose alliance of disparate actors around the shared goal of ending poverty: campaign participants include existing coalitions, community groups, trade unions, individuals, religious and faith-based groups, campaigners, as well as a large number of individuals, mainly young people, who have been connected by the Internet. The Japanese national coalition supporting this campaign, "Hottokenai Sekai no Mazushisa," or "Don't Let It Be—World Poverty," is featured in the next section of this chapter.

Nye pointed out that the information age opened up new opportunities for loosely structured network organizations having limited human and financial resources (Nye 2004, p. 90). Individuals are also empowered by information technology that gives them instant access to information. Indeed, the Internet—Web sites and blogs—has become a primary communications tool used by many recently formed global networks. The Free Burma Coalition, launched in 1995, is an online community of Burmese exiles and supporting activists in some twenty-eight countries; it broke new ground by being the first international civil society campaign mediated entirely through the Internet. ICBL is also a cybercampaign—it serves as an Internet-mediated umbrella of several hundred groups concerned with armaments and with humanitarian and human rights issues (Clark 2003b, pp. 152–55). GCAP has estimated that the individual participants in its campaign encompass more than 120 million people from more than 100 countries worldwide.

Another recent example in Japan is a loose antiwar network called World Peace Now,[6] which emerged and mobilized tens of thousands of young people before the Iraq War broke out in 2003. It is worth noting that core members of this network were not all active members of any existing organizations. They were highly motivated individuals who marched in the streets due to personal convictions, rather than due to a sense of loyalty to any particular group. In addition to the above-mentioned structured movements, people concerned with other global issues such as global warming, fair trade, and ethical sourcing are on the increase. One example is the LOHAS (Lifestyles of Health and Sustainability) movement, which has captured the hearts of many young, "socially minded" people.

When such individuals are able to form a loose grouping or network to exercise power to motivate a significant number of people and to influence policy making, something influential is definitely at work. Here, we are no longer talking about NGOs. Rather, we are witnessing socially conscious individuals that join in various global or local movements—or "networks"—and these individuals are from a variety of backgrounds.

Needless to say, as global problem solving is increasingly affected by these agglomerations of "people power," the issues of legitimacy, accountability, and representation come into play. After all, these people are unelected and often unaccountable "transnational civil society actors" (Florini 2001). What gives them legitimate voices within the globalized decision-making system? Indeed, civil society has ostensibly become a powerful global force, but this legitimacy argument is far from settled yet.

As a phenomenon related to soft power, these looser civil society "networks" provide an important case that needs to be examined. Their soft power is not under the control of a particular state, nor does it belong even to a particular set of organized groups—for example, NGOs. When we find such a loose amalgamation of interests and a spontaneous or even "leaderless" network, it is not easy to discern whose interest is at play, or for what purpose. What we can say for sure is only that this is certainly a type of soft power that is being generated and that is leaving tangible effects.

Japanese NGOs and Soft Power

Japanese NGOs: Size and Scope

As in most parts of the world, the Japanese nonprofit sector has grown significantly and has heightened its visibility over the past ten to fifteen years. The number of Japanese international NGOs (J-NGOs) increased to more than 400 in the late 1990s (Yamauchi 1999). J-NGOs are a diverse group of organizations, ranging from a handful of large, professional, and formal organizations to many small, grassroots-oriented, and informal groups whose operation depends largely on unpaid staff or volunteers. Note here, though, that *the largest* J-NGOs (see Table 15.2) usually have a budget of approximately ¥1 billion or less (some tens of millions of U.S. dollars), whereas the "super-NGOs" described above often have a budget of several hundreds of millions of U.S. dollars—a difference in size of at least one to ten.

The fields in which J-NGOs work are sometimes divided into the four general categories of development, the environment, human rights, and peace (JANIC 2004). The location of their work is heavily concentrated in Asia. Activities undertaken by J-NGOs mainly include service provision to people in poor countries, including mid- to long-term development activities and emergency relief. Notably, J-NGOs and their networks have increasingly begun to be fairly active in policy work, advocacy, and campaigning (Kuroda and Imata 2003). However, their influence over foreign assistance policy reform or formation is still limited. This is mainly because J-NGOs are not yet considered by the government to be a legitimate policy partner, and hence funds and support from both institutions and the general public for such activities are

Table 15.2

Ten Largest NGOs in Japan by Budget Size

Organization	Annual Budget (FY)
Nihon UNICEF Association	$119.0 million (2002)
Plan Japan (Nihon Foster Plan)	$27.6 million (2002)
World Vision Japan	$14.7 million (2002)
Japan International Food for the Hungry	$9.3 million (2001)
Médecins Sans Frontiéres, Japon	$9.3 million (2002)
OISCA	$8.1 million (2002)
JOICFP	$8.0 million (2002)
WWF Japan	$7.5 million (2002)
Shanti Volunteer Association	$6.1 million (2001)
Peace Winds Japan	$6.1 million (2002)

Source: Kansai Kokusai Koryu Dantai Kyogikai 2003.
Note: Annual budgets are calculated with the conversion rate of $1 = ¥120.

very limited, which discourages J-NGOs from building the capacity required to fulfill a stronger policy-related role.

The relationship between J-NGOs and the government has changed profoundly over the recent decade as the Japanese government has come to consider NGOs potential partners for implementing Japan's official development assistance (ODA). Since the Ministry of Foreign Affairs (MOFA) launched its NGO support system in 1989, other agencies, including the Japan International Cooperation Agency (JICA), have expanded support for NGOs. There has also been a strengthening of NGO-government dialogues concerning ODA projects and policies, as well as government support for building NGO capacities. However, the portion of the ODA budget channeled to NGOs still remains small at less than 1 percent (Ministry of Foreign Affairs 2002b), which is significantly smaller than the approximately 30 percent prevailing in the United States, 9 percent in Canada, and 6 percent in Germany (Mekata 2004). It is often argued that the Japanese government lacks the political will to strategically and effectively use J-NGOs for its state interests. This may be so partly because J-NGOs overall remain small in comparison with the NGOs based in other industrialized countries. However, it may also be due to a failure on the part of the government to see the soft power that can be exerted by J-NGOs in influencing foreign relations.

J-NGOs have come to play a certain significant role as service providers in development assistance and humanitarian relief. At the community level, many J-NGOs have established positive relationships with individuals and organizations in the local communities in which they operate. However, the overall profile of J-NGOs remains low, especially in countries in Africa and Central Asia, where not many J-NGOs are present. Moreover, they have not changed their traditional work style, which is focused at the community or village level. In fact, unlike many Western NGOs, J-NGOs are not yet effectively connected to the recently established global networks of CSOs that are engaging groups from different backgrounds and communities.

J-NGOs and International Networks

Since the 1990s, J-NGOs have participated in international networks within civil society, particularly those created on the occasion of a series of UN conferences held to address key social issues around the globe. However, it is a fairly recent phenomenon for J-NGOs to have strategically become involved in international society to achieve their missions. The creation of the Japan Campaign to Ban Landmines (JCBL) in 1997 as a part of the global network of the ICBL is one of the first prominent examples where J-NGOs participated in global campaigns.

This network was launched after attempts over several years by various NGOs that had advocated the need for strengthening this movement in Japan, which had failed to generate public pressure to support their goals. While consciously working with the ICBL, the JCBL appealed to the general public through the mass media and pressured the government to take concrete action, which in the end led to the Japanese government ratifying the Ottawa Treaty to ban landmines. Although it is argued that the government's decision was made in response to pressure from transnational civil society and other international sources rather than from domestic actors, it is fair to say that the JCBL and other J-NGOs played a crucial role in subsequently mobilizing and educating the general public about the issue of landmines (Kuroda 2003). In addition, the role of J-NGOs in the campaign became known globally by researchers and civil society practitioners, which has given the rest of the world an impression of a new face of Japanese organizations not seen before.

Similarly, Jubilee 2000 Japan was launched in 1998 to join the global Jubilee 2000 campaign. The Jubilee campaign worldwide was considered a successful global campaign. It certainly had an impact on the decision by the Group of Eight (G8) countries to announce a US$100 billion debt-cancellation package for the poorest countries at the G8 Summit in Cologne, Germany, in 1999 and the G8's further commitment to 100 percent cancellation of country-to-country debts at the end of that year. Like other Jubilee campaigns, the Japan campaign also was a broad-based civil society coalition that included international NGOs, trade unions, religious groups, other civil society organizations, and researchers.

There have been a few other cases where J-NGOs linked up with bilateral or multinational networks of NGOs. One example was a U.S.-Japanese NGO framework for dealing with global issues facing humanity. A number of NGOs joined a public-private partnership created through a government-to-government initiative, the U.S.-Japan Common Agenda, to deal with global issues including education, health, the environment, and humanitarian assistance in 2000.[7] As a result of this initiative, several U.S.-Japanese partnerships materialized on the ground, including a global partnership between the U.S. NGO Mercy Corps and the Japanese NGO Peace Winds Japan, through which both cooperated to provide humanitarian assistance to victims of earthquakes in Iran, India, and Afghanistan,[8] as well as Hurricane Katrina in the United States.

Nevertheless, compared to the active participation by NGOs in other industrialized countries, the involvement of J-NGOs in global networks remains limited. Similarly, the participation of J-NGOs in recent global campaigns tends to have been mainly on the part of those organizations that are affiliated with their own global networks, such as World Vision Japan and CARE Japan, or by those rare organizations that benefit from individuals having advanced skills in communicating in English or that have access to some form of external communication support (Kuroda and Imata 2003).

The Japan Platform

In recent years, J-NGOs have actively been engaged in disaster relief and humanitarian assistance in emergency situations, such as natural disasters and postconflict reconstruction. Although individual NGOs had been engaged in these areas for a fairly long time, the Japan Platform is a notable case of scaling up Japanese involvement in postconflict situations and disaster relief. It was founded in August 2000 as a trisectoral partnership bringing together government, NGOs, and business. The initial intent was to strengthen the ability of J-NGOs to provide emergency relief in response to natural disasters and refugee situations more effectively and more quickly. The Japan Platform was designed to realize a joint effort for all three parties involved: it enabled NGOs to provide swift and effective relief on the ground; the government, represented by MOFA, was able to use this mechanism to create a public-private partnership in emergency situations and promote the national interest; and leading corporations could provide financial and nonfinancial contributions to communities in need via NGOs, as a part of their corporate citizenship activities. The Japan Platform is governed by individuals representing NGOs, MOFA, some leading corporations, foundations, and the media. In FY2002, MOFA provided grants of ¥697 million (about US$5.8 million) to the Japan Platform, which worked as a conduit to operational J-NGOs that constituted members of its NGO unit. The Japan Platform has helped its member NGOs grow in providing humanitarian assistance through a number of on-the-ground experiences. Some have been critical of the Japan Platform, however, and assumed that it exists only to implement projects for the government and thus the NGOs involved in the platform have lost its NGO ethos and dynamism.

Thus far, member organizations of the Japan Platform have delivered assistance in response to natural disasters in Mongolia, Iran, and India, and to the postconflict situation in Afghanistan, Liberia, Sudan, Iraq, Indonesia, and Pakistan.[9] Thanks to its close relations with MOFA, the endeavors of the platform have certainly added value to Japanese public diplomacy. The Japan Platform is often called upon by a subcommittee on international NGOs within the ruling Liberal Democratic Party to discuss issues relating to emergency relief and humanitarian assistance in various affected parts of the world. It seems that parliamentarians boast of the Japan Platform as a symbol of Japan's contribution to the world. The Japan Platform has even created the Japan Platform Students, which is a loose network of students who sympathize with the Japan Platform and its goals. Because of a good deal of media coverage and an expansion of its supporters through its student network, the Japan Platform has gained a high profile in Japanese society as well as within Japan's diplomatic circles.

This certainly is a case of soft power being utilized by Japanese NGOs. Here, the Japanese government played a crucial (if not central) role in creating the Japan Platform and in making it a beacon of Japan's soft power on the global scene. It made use of the motivation and commitment of J-NGOs and the interest of the general public in promoting Japan's national interest and in raising the profile of Japan's role in global emergency response and humanitarian affairs.

NGO-Led Campaign Against Poverty

As briefly mentioned above, the Global Call to Action against Poverty is a global alliance of organizations, networks, and national campaigns committed to eradicating extreme poverty. The GCAP network worked together in 2005 to take action across the world to pressure world leaders to tackle the causes of poverty, and to meet and exceed their own promises regarding supporting achievement of the Millennium Development Goals.[10] This 2005 campaign specifically asked world leaders to work on trade justice, debt cancellation, and a major increase in the quantity and quality of aid. The campaign grew to include more than 100 countries in which national coalitions were established. A Japanese national campaign was officially launched in late May of 2005. This campaign, named "Hottokenai Sekai no Mazushisa" (Don't Let It Be—World Poverty) was in 2005 run by a steering committee composed of representatives from Japanese NGOs and other groups, and was supported by a coalition of approximately sixty Japanese nonprofit groups (such as international development NGOs, women's groups, peace and human rights groups, consumer cooperatives, etc.), by the White Band Project, which is led by a commercial public relations company, and by supporting companies, activists, and student and volunteer groups.[11]

The GCAP agreed to promote the "white band" (on wrists, arms, necks, buildings, etc.) as the symbol to unite all the activities that were led by national coalitions. Throughout the world, GCAP coalitions campaigned around key events in 2005 with White Band Days, which immediately preceded the G8 Summit in Gleneagles, Scotland, in July; the UN World Summit in New York in September; and the WTO Ministerial Conference in Hong Kong in December. The white band demonstrated solidarity among campaigners in their global fight against poverty. Many national campaigns manufactured white bands for sale or free distribution in order to send the message: "End poverty now."

The Japanese campaign was quite successful in selling white bands. In the latter half of 2005, it had sold more than 4.5 million bands. It also made the term "poverty" an everyday word. This white band movement expanded rapidly and involved numerous young people, many of whom voluntarily initiated events and seminars to disseminate the campaign message on and around the three White Band Days. The worldwide antipoverty movement pressed the Japanese government to improve and increase overseas aid so that Japan's international policies would truly begin to work for people living in poverty. GCAP is said to have influenced the announcement and commitment made by Prime Minister Junichiro Koizumi at the G8 Summit to increase the volume of ODA by US$10 billion over the next five years.

There are some implications of this nationwide movement, although a full examination of this ongoing campaign will require more time. First, the network went significantly beyond the type of NGO/CSO coalition witnessed in the case of the Jubilee 2000 campaign, as it appealed to a much wider segment of society through mass media and new media (mainly the Internet) and involved celebrities wearing the white bands. As a result, this campaign mobilized the public to a degree that no other NGO-led campaign in Japan ever has. It spread so rapidly, however, that as a result, the core message of policy demands was often left behind.

Second, because of the sales of white bands, this campaign took on a new aspect as an advocacy campaign—a unique marriage of commercialism and a political campaign. This feature became controversial, as the usage of the proceeds from the sales of white bands was said to go to advocacy work, instead of going directly to "charity" activities. More problematically, this advocacy work was not well defined or specified at the sale of the band, which confused many buyers of the product.

Third, the Japanese campaign became known to the rest of the world through the GCAP as a Japanese civil society movement. Indeed, some of the events throughout the nation on the second and third White Band Days were reported on by domestic and international media outlets, and photos from the events were carried on the GCAP Web site.

This campaign provides an example of soft power led by Japanese NGOs. The state's involvement in this campaign has been minimal, and the campaign was not at all led by the interests of the Japanese government. Still, it became quite high profile in the world and as a result might have helped heighten the image of Japan abroad. In this example, the soft power of a Japanese civil society movement not only transcended national boundaries but also engaged a large network of people, associations, and CSOs much broader than established NGOs. Often, established NGOs tend to become conservative (organizationally, if not politically) and less active politically as they mature and become professionalized. This is generally the case in many countries, and Japan is no exception. Integral to the Hottokenai movement was broad-based people's participation, which allowed for innovative linkages and approaches to engage members of society. We would be remiss in discussing the soft power of civil society if we paid attention to only the established NGO community. The relationship between NGOs and wider segments of civil society needs to be further examined.

Conclusion

As this chapter has shown, NGOs and civic action in dealing with global issues have gained considerable strength over the past couple of decades. As for the relevance of NGOs to the soft power argument, with particular reference to Japanese NGOs, we may note the following:

First, NGOs effectively exert soft power in various forms. As in the case of U.S. NGOs in the Wilsonian tradition, UK NGOs joining in Partnership Programme

Agreements with the UK government, and member NGOs of the Japan Platform, when there is a match and affinity between the agenda of a state and the interests of NGOs, NGOs can be deemed to be an effective "agent" of the state's soft power. Of course, NGOs are by design and definition independent bodies, and would not completely become agents of the state. When there is a shared interest, however, state-NGO partnerships can arise and can become a strong force of soft power, as we are witnessing with UK NGOs and DFID joining up; although they have different views on certain issues such as trade, they have jointly lobbied the European Union, international organizations, and other G8 governments in the area of debt relief for the poorest nations and an increase in the volume of aid.

Second, the soft power of non-state actors, especially that of NGOs, shows a unique aspect where such power is outside the scope of state influence. Here, this soft power manifests two distinct features. One is that it naturally tends to transcend national boundaries and begins to reveal "global" characteristics based on universal values. The other is that the "actor" that carries such soft power is becoming more and more removed from particular groups—oftentimes established NGOs—and is transformed via an array of informal networks or coalitions.

Third, the roles and strength of NGOs have a lot to do with soft power. If the roles and strengths of NGOs are fairly limited, NGOs' soft power is rather weak. As described in this chapter, Japanese NGOs may carry soft power in the fields of development and humanitarian assistance, but to a fairly limited extent. The government's attitudes toward NGOs, public trust, and NGO capacities are all intertwined. Indeed, the issue of trust in NGOs on the part of the general public is significant. Only 30.5 percent of the respondents to an opinion survey conducted by the Cabinet Office in Japan in August 2004 said they "trust nonprofit organizations." In the United Kingdom, according to a survey on public attitudes on development conducted as part of the National Statistics Omnibus Survey 2001, 61 percent of respondents acknowledged the contribution to international development made by international NGOs, a higher percentage than acknowledged the contribution of the United Nations (38 percent), industrial nations' governments (20 percent), or the IMF and the World Bank (18 percent).

Finally, although Japan may not yet provide fertile ground for nurturing the soft power of NGOs, the recent experience with the Hottokenai campaign shows a glimpse of what is possible. Again, the key will be the involvement of wide segments of society. Thus, the challenge for J-NGOs is how to engage with the larger public and become an effective catalyst for the promotion of a type of soft power that goes beyond the interests of the state.

Notes

The authors would like to thank Mr. Richard Forrest for editing assistance provided for this chapter.

1. Watanabe Yasushi, "Revisiting Soft Power," Japan Foundation Center for Global Partnership, http://www.cgp.org/index.php?option=article&task=default&articleid=342 (accessed November 24, 2006).

2. As of 2003, the combined annual budget for all the organizations affiliated with World Vision was about $1.1 billion, which exceeded the annual budget of the United Nations High Commissioner for Refugees, which was about $1 billion (including headquarters and all field operations). This is more than fifty times the scale of official development assistance channeled to NGOs in Japan, which amounted to some ¥5.5 billion, or $46 million, in 2002 (Ministry of Foreign Affairs 2002a).

3. One of the authors, Imata Katsuji, has outlined the relationship between the U.S. government and NGOs in Mekata ed. 2004, Chap. 2.

4. Of course, we must note here that it is impossible and somewhat absurd to treat NGOs in a given country as having a single unified voice or a homogenous attitude toward their own government. Rather, their diversity in political views, as well as their type of work and sector of expertise, is at the heart of their value and nature as NGOs.

5. http://www.whiteband.org (accessed November 24, 2006).

6. http://www.worldpeacenow.jp/ (accessed November 24, 2006).

7. This program was promoted by the authors' organization, CSO Network Japan, and its U.S. counterpart, the U.S.-Japan Public Private Partnership, from 1999 to 2003.

8. Relief Web, http://www.reliefweb.int/rw/RWB.NSF/db900SID/SODA-66652W?OpenDocument (accessed November 24, 2006).

9. http://www.japanplatform.org (accessed November 24, 2006).

10. The Millennium Development Goals are eight goals that range from halving extreme poverty to halting the spread of HIV/AIDS and providing universal primary education, all by the target date of 2015, and that form a blueprint agreed to by all the UN signatories and all the world's leading development institutions at the UN Millennium Summit in 2000.

11. http://www.hottokenai.jp (accessed November 24, 2006). The author's organization, CSO Network Japan, was instrumental in forming this coalition and running the campaign by participating in the Steering Committee as well as by providing the secretariat function.

References

Clark, John, ed. 2003a. *Globalizing Civic Engagement: Civil Society and Transnational Action.* London: Earthscan Publications.

———. 2003b. *Worlds Apart: Civil Society and the Battle for Ethical Globalization.* London: Earthscan Publications.

Edwards, Michael. 2001. "Introduction." In *Global Citizen Action.* Ed. Michael Edwards and John Gaventa, 1–14. Boulder, CO: Lynne Rienner Publishers.

Florini, Ann M. 2001. "Transnational Civil Society." In *Global Citizen Action.* Ed. Michael Edwards and John Gaventa, 29–40. Boulder, CO: Lynne Rienner Publishers.

Japan NGO Center for International Co-operation (JANIC). 2004. *Kokusai kyoryoku direkutori 2004* (2004 Directory of Japanese NGOs concerned with international co-operation). Tokyo: JANIC.

Kansai Kokusai Koryu Dantai Kyogikai. 2003. *NPO Journal* Vol. 3 (October 2003).

Kuroda Kaori. 2003. "Japan-Based Non-governmental Organizations in Pursuit of Human Security." *Japan Forum* 15 (2).

Kuroda Kaori, and Imata Katsuji. 2003. "Evolution of 'Legitimacy' Discussion of International Development NGOs and Its Absence in Japan." Paper presented to ARNOVA Annual Conference, Denver, CO, November 20–22.

Lewis, David, ed. 1999. *International Perspectives on Voluntary Action: Reshaping the Third Sector.* London: Earthscan Publications.

Lindenberg, Mark, and Coralie Bryant. 2001. *Going Global: Transforming Relief and Development NGOs.* Bloomfield, CO: Kumarian Press.

Mekata Motoko, ed. 2004. *NGO sekutaa ni kansuru 6 kakoku hikaku chosa: MDBs tono renkei ni mukete* (Comparative study of the NGO sector in six countries: In pursuit of partnership with MDBs). Tokyo: Research Institute of Economy, Trade and Industry (in Japanese).

Ministry of Foreign Affairs. 2002a. *Heisei 14 nendo NGO shien yosan gaisan yokyu no gaiyo* (Outline of estimated annual budget to support NGOs requested of the treasury by ministries and government department in FY2002). Tokyo (in Japanese).

———. 2002b. *Nihon NGO shien musho shikin kyoryoku* (Grants support for NGOs in Japan). Tokyo: Non-Governmental Organization Assistance Division (in Japanese).

Nye, Joseph S., Jr. 2004. *Soft Power: The Means to Success in World Politics.* New York: Public Affairs.

Office of Private and Voluntary Cooperation. 2004. *Report of American Voluntary Agencies Engaged in Overseas Relief and Development Registered with the U.S. Agency for International Development (VolAg Report).* Washington, DC: Bureau for Humanitarian Response, U.S. Agency for International Development.

Salamon, Lester. 1993. *The Global Associational Revolution: The Rise of the Third Sector on the World Scene.* Baltimore, MD: Johns Hopkins University Center for Civil Society Studies.

Salamon, Lester, and Helmut K. Anheier. 1997. *Defining the Nonprofit Sector.* Manchester, England: Manchester University Press.

Stoddard, Abby. 2003. "Humanitarian NGOs: Challenges and Trends." In *HPG Report 14 (Humanitarian Action and the "Global War on Terror": A Review of Trends and Issues).* Ed. Joanna Macrae and Dele Harmer. London: Overseas Development Institute, pp. 25–36.

Yamauchi Naoto, ed. 1999. *NPO deta bukku* (Nonprofit organizations data book). Tokyo: Yuhikaku (in Japanese).

Zinn, Howard, and Anthony Arnove. 2004. *Voices of a People's History of the United States.* New York: Seven Stories Press.

About the Editors and Contributors

Agawa Naoyuki is a professor and the dean of the School of Policy Management at Keio University. He earned a BSFS degree (1977) and a JD degree (1984) from Georgetown University. Agawa teaches American constitutional history and Japanese-U.S. relations at Keio. He has also practiced international trade and banking law with U.S. and Japanese law firms and taught at the University of Virginia Law School as visiting professor. He served as Minister for Public Affairs at the Embassy of Japan in Washington, DC, between 2002 and 2005. He was the recipient of the Yomiuri-Yoshino Sakuzo Award in 2005 for his book on American constitutional history. Agawa held an Abe Fellowship at the University of Virginia Law School for the 1995–96 academic year.

Anne Allison is Robert O. Keohane Professor and chair of cultural anthropology at Duke University. An anthropologist who specializes in contemporary Japan, she is the author of three books: *Nightwork: Sexuality, Pleasure, and Corporate Masculinity in a Tokyo Hostess Club* (1994), *Permitted and Prohibited Desires: Mothers, Comics, and Censorship in Japan* (1996), and *Millennial Monsters: Japanese Toys and the Global Imagination* (2006).

Philip G. Altbach is Monan Professor of Higher Education and director of the Center for International Higher Education at Boston College. He has been a fellow of the Japan Society for the Promotion of Science, and was the 2005–6 Distinguished Scholar Leader of the Fulbright New Century Scholars Program. Currently directing the program, he most recently coedited *Worldclass Worldwide: Research Universities in Asia and Latin America* (2007).

William G. Crowell is a retired senior foreign service officer. He held various postings in Japan, China, Iceland, Mali, and Washington, specializing in academic and cultural exchanges and presswork. He earned a doctorate in Chinese history from the University of Washington and has written on the history of early imperial and medieval China. He currently lives in Eugene, Oregon, where he teaches and writes.

Matthew Fraser is a senior research fellow at the INSEAD business school in Fontainebleau, France. He was a professor of communications at Ryerson

University in Toronto from 1997 to 2006. After graduate studies at the London School of Economics, Oxford University, and Université de Paris I (Panthéon-Sorbonne), he earned a doctorate in political science at the Institut d'Etudes Politiques de Paris. From 1998 to 2003 he wrote a regular column on the media industries for the *National Post*, where he was appointed editor in chief in 2003. His latest book, *Weapons of Mass Distraction: Soft Power and American Empire*, was published in 2005.

Horie Miki is associate professor in the Education Center for International Students at Nagoya University, where she teaches a graduate course on international education and undergraduate courses on intercultural relations. Her main research interest is policy studies on the internationalization of higher education. Horie also advises Japanese students on study abroad opportunities and works with international students. She received a PhD in educational policy and administration from the University of Minnesota in 2003.

Imata Katsuji is currently codirector of CSO Network Japan and is seconded to CIVICUS: World Alliance for Citizen Participation in South Africa as its Deputy Secretary General-Programmes. He has fifteen years of experience in program and organizational management of nonprofit organizations. His work encompasses facilitating a global civil society campaign, doing research on international NGOs, and conducting workshops on nonprofit management. He has an MA in public policy from the University of California at Berkeley, an MA in interdisciplinary studies in social science from the University of Tokyo, and a BA from International Christian University in Tokyo.

Kondo Seiichi is ambassador to the United Nations Educational, Scientific and Cultural Organization (UNESCO). He graduated from the University of Tokyo and read philosophy, politics and economics (PPE) at St. Catherine's College, Oxford. Kondo has been a career diplomat since 1972. Having served in Manila, Washington, and Paris, he was appointed deputy secretary-general of the Organization for Economic Cooperation and Development in 1999, director-general for public diplomacy, Ministry of Foreign Affairs, in 2003, and ambassador for international trade and economy in 2005.

Kuroda Kaori has been codirector of CSO Network Japan since April 2004. She was on a Japan Foundation Center for Global Partnership NPO Fellowship with Social Accountability International in New York in 2006. Prior to her current position, she worked for the Asia Foundation Japan office as senior program officer and then assistant representative. Before moving to the nonprofit sector, she worked at Mitsubishi Heavy Industries in Tokyo and the Center on Japanese Economy and Business at the Columbia University School of Business in New York. She received a master's degree from the Harvard Graduate School of Education in 1991.

As executive director of the Tokyo Foundation's Scholarship Division since 1997, **Ellen Mashiko** is responsible for fellowship and professional development training programs, including two unique endowment programs involving seventy-seven universities and consortia in forty-eight countries. Prior to joining the foundation she held positions at the University of Hawaii, Japan-U.S. Educational Commission, and Waseda University. Her professional interests focus on the sustainable development and transnationalization of higher education.

David L. McConnell is professor of anthropology at the College of Wooster in Wooster, Ohio. His book, *Importing Diversity: Inside Japan's JET Program* (2000), explores the cultural form and meaning of internationalization in Japan and received the 2001 Masayoshi Ohira Prize. McConnell was a Fulbright scholar at Kyoto University from 1988 to 1990 and received his PhD from Stanford University in 1991. He spent the following year at Harvard University as an advanced research fellow at the Program on U.S.-Japan Relations and as an affiliated scholar at the Center for Science and International Affairs at the John F. Kennedy School of Government.

Nakano Yoshiko is assistant professor in the Department of Japanese Studies at the University of Hong Kong, where she teaches intercultural communication and media. She received her PhD in sociolinguistics from Georgetown University, and has worked as a researcher for TV documentary programs on international conflicts. She moved to Hong Kong in 1997 and coedited the volume *Reporting Hong Kong: Foreign Media and the Handover* (1999). Her most recent work, *Onajikama no meshi* (coauthored with Dixon H.W. Wong, 2005), examines how Japanese electric rice cookers went local and global with the help of Chinese intermediaries. She was an Abe Fellow in 2000–2001 and an Asia Leadership Fellow in 2003.

Joseph S. Nye, Jr., is Distinguished Service Professor and former dean of the Kennedy School of Government at Harvard University. He earned a PhD in political science from Harvard. In 1994–95 he served as assistant secretary of defense for International Security Affairs. Nye is the author of numerous books and more than 150 articles published in professional and policy journals. In 2004 he published *Soft Power: The Means to Success in World Politics.* He is a fellow of the American Academy of Arts and Sciences and of the American Academy of Diplomacy. He is an honorary fellow of Exeter College, Oxford. He is the recipient of Princeton University's Woodrow Wilson Award, and the Charles Merriam Award from the American Political Science Association.

Patti McGill Peterson is currently senior associate at the Institute for Higher Education Policy. She was executive director of the Council for International Exchange of Scholars and vice president of the Institute of International Education from 1997 to 2007. She is president emerita of Wells College and St. Lawrence University, where she held presidencies from 1980 to 1996. She served as chair of the U.S.-Canada Commission for Educational Exchange and the American Council on Education's Commission on Academic Leadership, and was president of the Association of Colleges and Universities of the State of New York. Peterson speaks and publishes on the subjects of U.S. and international higher education and public policy as it relates to educational and third-sector organizations.

Lawrence Repeta is a professor at Omiya Law School in Japan, where he teaches courses in U.S. law and codirects a legal clinic on freedom of information. In 2006, he published *Yami wo Utsu: Secrecy and the Future of America,* a study of American open government activists. He is a founding director of Information Clearinghouse Japan, an NGO devoted to promoting transparency in government (www.clearinghouse.org). During the 2003–4 academic year, he conducted research in freedom of information law as an Abe Fellow at the National Security Archive in Washington, D.C. He is a member of the Washington State Bar Association.

Sayuri Guthrie-Shimizu is associate professor of history at Michigan State University. She received her PhD in American history from Cornell University. She is the author of *Creating People of Plenty: The United States and Japan's Economic Alternatives, 1950–1960* (2001) and numerous articles on U.S.-Asian relations, and a coauthor of *Nichibei kankeishi* (2001). She is currently working on a transnational historical study of baseball's diffusion to the American West, Pacific Islands (Guam and Hawaii), Japan, and Asia under Japanese colonial rule in the late nineteenth and early twentieth centuries. She received an Abe Fellowship (2003–4) for her international ocean resource conservation research.

Sugiura Tsutomu is adviser to the Marubeni Research Institute and was its director for five years beginning in 2001. He is also a special subcommittee member for Tokyo Council for the Arts. He was the first director of cultural activities for the Maison de la Culture du Japon à Paris for two years (1997–99). After graduation from the University of Tokyo, he built his career through Marubeni's research and art divisions.

Watanabe Yasushi is a professor of cultural policy at Keio University. He earned a PhD in social anthropology from Harvard University. He teaches American studies, cultural policy, and human security. His books include *After America: Trajectories of the Bostonians and the Politics of Culture* (2004), which won a Suntory Prize for Social Sciences and Humanities and a Hiroshi Shimizu Award of the Japanese Association for American Studies, and *The American Family: Across the Class Divide* (2005). During the 2003–4 academic year he was a recipient of an Abe Fellowship, which he held at the Weatherhead Center for International Affairs at Harvard University. In 2005, he was awarded a JSPS (Japan Society for the Promotion of Science) Prize and a Japan Academy Medal for his research.

Yonezawa Akiyoshi is an associate professor at the Center for the Advancement of Higher Education (CANE) at Tohoku University and is engaged mainly in comparative studies of higher education. Prior to that, he worked at the National Institution for Academic Degrees and University Evaluation (NIAD-UE), the Research Institute for Higher Education at Hiroshima University, the Organization for Economic Cooperation and Development, and the University of Tokyo as an expert on sociology in higher education. He has been a visiting scholar at Oxford University and Xiamen University in China.

Index

Abe Fellowship Program, 234
Abe Isoo, 159
Abel, Richard, 175
Abe Shintaro, 230
Abe Shinzo, 14, 56, 235
Addicted to War (Andreas), 11
Afghanistan war, 10, 219
African Institute for Capacity Development
   (AICAD), 59
Agawa Naoyuki, xix, xx, xxix, xxv, 11, 19,
   224-240
Ajami, Fouad, 16
Akihito, Crown Prince, 165
Aladdin, 181
Albright, Madeleine, 172, 203
Alexander, Lamar, 246
Alhurra, 184, 186
Al Jazeera, 184
Alliance Français, L,' 228
Allison, Anne, xi, xxi, xxvii, 99-110, 112, 134, 197
Altbach, Philip G., xxvi, xxvii, 37-53, 39, 44,
   78, 87
Althusser, Louis, xxii
American Academy of Diplomacy, 37
American Council on Education, 50
American Society of Newspaper Editors
   (ASNE), 247
Andreas, Joel, 11
Andrew, Christopher, 247
Anheier, Helmut K., 264
Anime (Japanese animation)
  in China, 112, 113-115
  marketing of, 149
  traditional roots of, 148
  in United States, 101, 102, 108, 109
  world popularity of, 133, 133*t*, 134, 135–136*t*,
    147, 199-200
Anti-Americanism
  in Japan, xxiv, xxvii, 3, 5-16
  in Muslim world, 181, 185, 195, 196, 202
Anti-Americanism (Revel), 11
Anti-Japanese movies, Hollywood, 175, 176, 180

Anti-Japanese sentiment, in China, 111, 113,
   115, 119-120
Aoki Tamotsu, 22, 201
Appadurai, Arjun, xxi
Arab-language satellite networks, 184-185
Armacost, Bonnie, 214
Armacost, Michael, 214
Armitage, Richard, 239
Armstead, Leigh, 203
Arndt, Richard, 207, 216
Arnove, Anthony, 264
"Arsenal of Democracy," 178
Article 19, 254, 255, 257, 260n17
Asahi Shinbun, 10, 63, 119-120, 125n3
Asakawa Kan-ichi, 6
ASEAN (Association of Southeast Asian
   Nations), 59
Asian studies programs, 68
Aso Taro, 111, 121, 124, 149, 225, 228, 230
Association of International Educators, 41
Association of JET (AJET), 23
Astro Boy, 100, 114
Atarashii Rekishi Kyokasho o Tsukuru Kai, 12
Attention economy, 129
Aum Shinrikyo, 15
Auslin, Michael, 214
Australia
  educational exchange in, 4, 45
  public diplomacy of, 227
  transnational higher education of, 48
Avatar, 109
Azerbaijan, 245, 251

Bailey, Gauvin Alexander, 38
Baker, Howard, xxv, 214, 239
Baker, James, 7
Baldwin, David, x
Balio, Tino, 176
Banisar, David, 251-252
Barber, Benjamin, 173
Barry, Dave, 224
Barthes, Roland, 102, 138